The Chinese State in the Era of Economic Reform

The Road to Crisis

Edited by
Gordon White

*Professorial Fellow,
Institute of Development Studies, University of Sussex*

M. E. Sharpe, Inc.
Armonk, New York

Published in the United States in 1991 by M. E. Sharpe, Inc.
80 Business Park Drive, Armonk, New York 10504

Published in Great Britain by Macmillan Academic and Professional Ltd.

Printed in Hong Kong

Library of Congress Cataloging-in-Publication Data
The Chinese state in the era of economic reform: the road to crisis /
[Gordon White, editor].
p.   cm. — (Asia and the Pacific)
Includes bibliographical references and index.
ISBN 0-87332-853-1
1. China — Economic policy — 1976 - 2. China — Politics and
government — 1976
I. White, Gordon. 1942 –   II. Series: Asia and
the Pacific (Armonk, N.Y.)
HC427.92.C4673   1991
338.951'009'048 — dc20

90-29275
CIP

To the memory of John Gardner (1939–88),
a respected colleague and valued friend.

Contents

John Gardner, 1939–88

Few of us are provided with Chinese names that reflect our personality. John Gardner was an exception, given the name Gao Jiang ('High River') by a group of PRC students at Manchester University in the late 1970s. They chose the name not for phonetic reasons but because, to them, it captured John's natural bustling energy and forceful personality. How right they were and how sad that John's untimely death on 16 May 1988 has deprived us of a unique teacher, scholar and friend.

Teaching contemporary Chinese politics to undergraduates in the mid-1960s was not easy. There were barely a dozen student texts in print, most of them based on the relatively orderly days of the 1950s and early 1960s. As the Cultural Revolution with its burgeoning non-official press got underway, so an immense burden was placed upon any teacher. Those of us who took the first undergraduate course which John taught after his appointment at Manchester in 1966 learned quickly that we had a winner. Here was a teacher who not only filled the gaps in our texts and blended in readings of the Red Guard press, but one who convinced us that the study of China was *interesting* and worthy of effort. In short, John was an inspirational teacher and Manchester undergraduates and graduate students from elsewhere who followed in his professional footsteps owe him an irredeemable debt for enthusing us and for providing a fine pedagogical model to follow.

John's research interests were broadly based. An abiding interest, stemming from his graduate student days at the School of Oriental and African Studies at London University in the 1960s, was the politics of mass mobilisation in the PRC. Over twenty years have passed since the publication of his study of the Wufan campaign in Shanghai, but it remains a classic for its meticulous attention to primary sources and rigour of analysis. The same may be said of the steady stream of papers which John published on his second main interest: the politics of education in the PRC. An early piece analysed the ways in which education policy had reflected and contributed to the elite debates of the pre-Cultural Revolution period; subsequent articles grappled with the tortuous course and costs of the so-called 'Revolution in Education'. If they have a single characteristic, it is that, unlike some, John was never afraid to subject his sources to the most critical analysis – not for him the idiocies of rehashed 'two-line struggle' articles which plagued so much 'scholarly' writing during the Cultural Revolution decade.

Nor, for that matter, did John neglect the fundamental principle that whether for undergraduates or specialists, writing on contemporary China should be (as he would put it) 'a good read'. He loathed self-indulgent displays of obscure footnotes and other silly academic paraphernalia, feeling that interest could and should be captured without such devices which frequently distracted the reader without just cause. In this, John was a most helpful co-author and fellow researcher. When one was blinkered or bogged down, John could be relied upon to offer unfailing help on matters of style and content. His ability to recognise fundamentals and to write and teach with precision and directness stood John in good stead when, after the Cultural Revolution, British firms were anxious for information on the China market. John never claimed to be an economist, but the contextual papers which he produced from the late 1970s onwards contained some of his most perceptive anlyses of contemporary developments and it is unfortunate that they could not reach a wider audience which they deserved.

Other things will also never be. For some years John had been collecting material inside and outside China for a book on China's police system. His earlier work on Shanghai in the 1950s (on which he was a mine of information) had established an enduring interest in the coercive side of things in China and the ideas which he had developed pointed to the prospect of an historic study which would have been of seminal importance to our understanding of compliance in China. During our last conversation, John also spoke at length about drawing back from the empirical to write a systems study of PRC government and he would have been very well-equipped to do so.

The early 1970s were years when it was virtually impossible to visit China for research. The Chinese powers-that-be had either taken unwarranted exception to the work of some individuals or had decided, defensively, that it was 'too complicated' to allow sinologists into China. John was one of a tiny group of optimists who believed that one need not sell one's integrity in order to obtain a visa and was instrumental in bringing about a visit to China in April 1976 of fifteen young British sinologists. Out of that visit came the shared conviction that British sinologists, whatever their primary discipline, had much to learn from each other and had suffered professionally from there being no forum where such exchanges could take place. The result was the formation of the British Association of Chinese Studies (BACS) later in 1976. John would not claim sole credit for the establishment of this Association but it is undeniable that John's period as BACS President (1979–80) coincided with full recognition of the Association as the voice of our profession in the corridors of power (and research grants).

As a friend and companion, John was without peer. Whether freezing to death in a Chinese dormitory or chewing the cud in more amenable surroundings, there was much to be gained from John's lively and infectious sense of the ridiculous. He cared intensely about his students and even more so about the welfare of his friends. I and others know few who could be so generous with their time and sympathy when it was called for.

John had many extra-curricular interests, and many things – too many to recall here – gave him pleasure or made him laugh. He thrived on the rollicking good fun of the Flashman novels, but was equally happy reading of the elegance of the old Italian court. He was glad to stage self-mocking recitals of the pop songs of his youth or to retire quietly to the tranquillity of a formal garden or a simple bow of cut flowers – the memories of a complete man are legion. But John's deepest concern of all – for his beloved children – was permanent in its strength. To Paul and Sara, in sad recognition of a fine man, we send our deepest sympathy.

DAVID CHAMBERS

Notes on the Contributors

Robert Benewick is Reader in Politics, University of Sussex. Recent publications include *Reforming the Revolution: China in Transition*, (with Paul Wingrove) and *The Crowd in Contemporary Britain* (with George Gaskell).

Marc Blecher is Professor of Government and Chair of Third World Studies at Oberlin College, and Visiting Professor of Political Science at the University of Chicago. His latest books are *China: Politics, Economics and Society: Innovation and Iconoclasm in a Revolutionary Socialist Country* (1985) and *The Tethered Deer and the Hard-Work Market: The Political Economy of Shulu County in Maoist and Post-Maoist China* (forthcoming).

Donald C. Clarke is Assistant Professor of Law at the University of Washington School of Law, Seattle. He formerly taught Chinese and Japanese law at the School of Oriental and African Studies, University of London. He has published in the *China Quarterly*, the *Harvard Law Review* and *Law in Japan*.

Elisabeth J. Croll is a Research Fellow in the Department of Sociology and Anthropology at the School of Oriental and African Studies, University of London. She has undertaken regular investigation on village and family institutions in China and her books include *Feminism and Socialism in China*, *The Politics of Marriage in Contemporary China*, *Chinese Women since Mao* and *Food Supply in China and the Nutritional Status of Children*.

David A. Dyker is Senior Lecturer in Economics in the School of European Studies, Sussex University. His publications include *The Process of Investment in the Soviet Union* and *The Future of the Soviet Economic Planning System*.

Jude Howell has recently completed a DPhil on China's Open Door Policy at the Institute of Development Studies. She has taught in Chongqing and Shanghai for two years and spent a further year in Xiamen Special Economic Zone and Chengdu conducting research on the Open Door Policy.

Daniel Kelliher is Assistant Professor of Political Science and East Asian Studies at the University of Minnesota. He is now finishing a book on conflict between state and peasant in China, based on research he carried out while living in Hubei province.

Barry Naughton, an economist, is Assistant Professor at the Graduate School of International Relations and Pacific Studies (IR/PS), University of California, San Diego. His current research on the Chinese economy includes industrial and financial reforms, macroeconomic policy, and industrial policy and the pattern of development since 1949.

Tony Saich is an Associate Professor at the Sinologisch Instituut, Leiden and a Senior Research Fellow at the International Institute of Social History, Amsterdam. His recent publications include *China's Science Policy in the 80s* and *The Origins of the First United Front in China: The Role of Sneevliet (Alias Maring)*. Currently he is producing a documentary history of the CCP before 1949 together with members of the Fairbank Center, Harvard.

Eberhard Sandschneider is presently working as an assistant professor at the Research Unit on Chinese and East Asian Politics, the Saar University, Saarbrücken, West Germany. Among his recent publications are *Militär und Politik in der Volksrepublik China, 1969–1985*, and several articles on Chinese politics and developmental issues in Taiwan and South Korea.

Gordon White is a political scientist working on the political economy of socialist patterns of development, with particular reference to China. His books include *Micropolitics in Contemporary China* (with Marc Blecher), *Party and Professional: the Political Role of Teachers in Contemporary China* and *Developmental Studies in East Asia* (ed. 1988)

Christine Wong teaches economics at the University of California, Santa Cruz. She has just completed a book on rural industrialisation in China during the Cultural Revolution decade and is working on a study of the role of local governments in reforms in Chinese industry. Her recent publications include *New Perspectives on the Cultural Revolution* (co-edited, 1990) and articles in recent issues of *Modern China* and the *Journal of Comparative Economics*.

Zhu Ling is Associate Professor and Deputy Director of the Research Department of Political Economy at the Insititute of Economics, Chinese Academy of Social Science, Beijing. Her recent publications include *Rural Reform and Peasant Income in China*, *Resource Allocation in Chinese Village Communities*, and *The urban bias involved in operating mechanisms of monetary institutions*.

The Road to Crisis: The Chinese State in the Era of Economic Reform

Gordon White

After the Beijing massacre of 4 June 1989, the Chinese state faces a political crisis of a scale and depth unprecedented since the Communist Party came to power in 1949. Though the Communist regime has faced both economic crisis (notably the aftermath of the Great Leap Forward) and political instability (notably during the Hundred Flowers Movement and the Cultural Revolution), it has managed previously to meet the challenge and take action to restore some degree of political 'normality', and refurbish the party's injured prestige. In the late 1980s, however, the Party faces a dual crisis: an economic impasse which has developed as the reform programme ran into increasing difficulties from 1985 onwards, and a political crisis, reflected and intensified by the indiscriminate state violence in Beijing on June 4. This leaves a regime led by ancient revolutionaries without ideological clothes, its legitimacy shredded and lacking a credible programme for solving the nation's deep economic problems. It is indeed paradoxical that a market-orientated economic reform programme – which was adopted in part to recoup the prestige and legitimacy of the Communist Party-state that had been badly shaken by the Cultural Revolution – should culminate in a set of events further intensifying the crisis of the Chinese state. How could it be that the reforming regime of Deng Xiaoping – which had achieved much in raising popular living standards, energising the economy, allowing greater cultural and intellectual freedom, opening doors to the external world and even achieving marginally greater political freedom and opportunities – had committed an act of state violence unprecedented in the history of the People's Republic. Why have Chinese politics been catapulted back into earlier eras of the Cultural Revolution and Anti-Rightist Movement of 1957, which one had assumed to be things of the past?

This volume, which was set in train before the June 1989 events, is intended to explore the impact of the economic reform programme on the

Chinese state. We are using the term 'state' in a broad sense to denote a complex organisational system comprising three sets of basic institutions, at central level and below: political (notably the Communist Party and the system of people's representative congresses), administrative (governments at each level and their subordinate bureaucratic agencies) and coercive (the People's Liberation Army).

The book's contributors were initially asked to address three sets of questions: (i) To what extent has the *economic role* of the Chinese state been changed by the reform programme of the past decade? The economic reformers have envisaged a leaner, less obtrusive developmental state,[1] one which is more selective in its interventions; which relies less on the directive controls of traditional central planning and secures its socio-economic objectives by more indirect, 'parametric' methods of planning and regulation; which is less centralised, devolving power to local governments and non-state agencies – notably economic units such as companies and enterprises; which, while abandoning many of its previous functions, takes on new ones (such as macro-economic regulation, social welfare, financial auditing, legal regulation); and which becomes more 'bureaucratic' in Weberian terms, with more streamlined institutions and more professionalised administrators. To what extent have these reformist ambitions been realised? Has the traditional Stalinist model of state planning and management been supplanted by a new form of market-facilitating state presiding over a 'socialist commodity economy'? (ii) To what extent can or should *economic reform be accompanied by political reform*, that is, changes in the institutional structures of power and public life? What are the projects for political reform, both official and unofficial, which have emerged over the past decade and what has been their net impact, if any? To what extent can the existing ideological framework of Marxist-Leninist orthodoxy generate practical alternatives for the organisation of political life? What are the social and political forces which favour or oppose political changes? What specific forms would political innovation take and how feasible would these be in the context of a Leninist mono-party state? (iii) How are *economic reform and political reform related*? Is the former a stimulant to or constraint on the latter? How do we evaluate two apparently contrasting arguments: first, that political reform must await the completion of a successful economic reform programme, since the potentially disruptive nature of the latter requires a strong state to manage the process; second, that after a certain point economic reforms will stall unless the political environment becomes more flexible and competitive. Are not certain minimum political changes necessary to ensure the successful operation of a 'socialist commodity economy' (for example, an effective system of contract law and some institutional means to accommodate competing socio-economic interests)? To the extent that economic reforms are successful and change thereby the balance of power between state and society, does this not undermine the power of the Leninist party-state and create the structural conditions for a more 'pluralistic' political system? If so, what form would this have taken?

This is a broad and ambitious agenda of questions and we cannot claim to have fully addressed and answered all of them. Moreover, our inquiry opened up even broader issues: for example, concerning the impact of the 'open door policy' on the Chinese state and the impact of economic reforms on Chinese social structure. The purpose of this brief introductory essay is not to attempt a comprehensive review of these complex issues, but to draw out some of the main conclusions of our collective endeavour with regard to our major theme – the changing nature of the Chinese state and its relations with society and economy during the decade of economic reform from 1979 to 1989.

1 ECONOMIC REFORM: THE PURPOSE AND NATURE OF THE TASK

The programme of economic reform which was inaugurated by the Third Plenum of the Party's Central Committee in December 1978, had its origins in the political misfortunes of the Cultural Revolution decade (1966–76) and the perceived problematic performance of the Chinese economy during the 1960s and 1970s. On the economic side, the reformers sought to readjust certain strategic macro-economic imbalances in the economy (from heavy towards light industry, industry towards agriculture, investment towards consumption, state towards collective and private business), raise efficiency in the use of labour, land and capital through the introduction of market mechanisms which devolved economic decisions from state officials to enterprise managers, and reap the benefits of the international division of labour by expanding foreign trade and encouraging foreign investment. In short, as it emerged in the 1980s, this was a programme of potentially radical economic de-Stalinisation.

But the political motivations underlying the reforms were as important as the economic, if not more so, in giving impetus to the new policies. At the international level, Chinese leaders were increasingly aware that China was being outperformed by its neighbours and rivals in East and Southeast Asia, most irksomely by its political alter ego, the Guomindang (Kuomintang) regime in Taiwan. Internally, the credibility of the Communist regime had been seriously shaken by the ideological confusion, political infighting and social disorder of the Cultural Revolution, and there was increasing frustration and discontent among the general population over restrictions on their economic and social life as well as the sluggish or non-existent progress in raising popular living standards. From the very start of the economic reform programme, it was seen to be a way of solving these fundamental political problems: of restoring China's rightful status as a world power and reconstructing the battered legitimacy of the regime by providing the dramatic improvements in popular welfare which Chinese socialism had promised but, as of the late 1970s, had not delivered.

This fundamental *volte face* posed serious political risks for the Chinese regime, as it would for any Leninist system embarking on the storm-tossed voyage to 'market socialism'. They were heading for *terra incognita* and had no precise map to guide them; that is why any notion of a new development 'strategy' is misleading – and why in his approach to economic reform, Deng Xiaoping is more like Livingstone than Napoleon. Not only were the problems of managing an increasingly market-orientated economy potentially intractable and destabilising, but the economic reforms could well generate pressures for political reforms which would challenge the ideological assumptions and political structure of orthodox state socialism. As of 1978, however, China's reformist leaders clearly thought the potential political and economic benefits outweighed potential costs. The task ahead was a difficult one, however, and would require a skilled, determined and united leadership to see it through.

The story of the post-Mao reform era takes us in effect from crisis to crisis – the former arising from the Cultural Revolution decade (1966–76) and the latter (in April–June 1989) from the economic reforms. To understand this process, we need to know with more precision how the economic reform programme has affected the Chinese state, and Chinese politics more generally over the past decade. We can divide our inquiry into three broad areas, each of which is explored in some detail by the contributors to this volume: first, the economic role of the state and state-economy relations; second, the politico-administrative nature of state institutions themselves and the political 'rules of the game' more generally; third, relations between state and society. At the beginning of the reform period, China's leaders had contrasting attitudes to these three areas. On the first, they were unanimous in their desire to reduce the state's direct intervention in economic affairs and produce a more dynamic, competitive and autonomous economic system. On the second issue, however, the desire for and political impetus towards political reforms was much weaker. The approach adopted was of marginal reforms within the continuing Leninist framework of Deng Xiaoping's 'Four Basic Principles' (the socialist road, the dictatorship of the proletariat, the leadership of the Communist Party, and Marxism-Leninism-Mao Zedong Thought). Though opinions among the leadership have varied, there has been an underlying consensus that economic reform takes precedence over political reform in both timing and degree. On the third issue, that of social changes arising from the reforms and their potential political implications, at least until fairly recently there appears to have been little awareness or anticipation.

If we examine actual changes or continuities in these three areas over a decade of reform (1979–89), we will be in a better position to make sense of the politics of the reform process which culminated in the tragedy of June 1989.[2]

2 RELATIONS BETWEEN STATE AND ECONOMY: THE POLITICAL ECONOMY OF REFORM

Since the main thrust of the reforms was to engineer an economic break-through by transforming relations between state and economy, it is appropriate that we begin by assessing whether this structural aim has been achieved. I will begin by stating a general conclusion that, while the economic reformers have been successful in enlivening and diversifying the Chinese economy and granting greater autonomy to enterprises and individuals, they have failed to achieve a decisive breakthrough to a new form of developmental state and the desired new relationship between state and economy. At the same time, as part of a more general process of political decay, the central government in particular has gradually lost its power to control and regulate economic events.

Success in emancipating and diversifying economic activity has been striking though this has varied over time and sector. If one were to view the reforms from the perspective of late 1984 they would have been seen as a striking success, particularly in their effects on real standards of living in both urban and rural areas. From 1985 onwards, certain basic problems, which had already been visible, intensified and became more intractable: infrastructural constraints in basic industries, transportation and commu-nications; technological backwardness; resource constraints, particularly a dwindling area of arable land and a deterioration in the quality of land due to lack of investment and inadequate maintenance of agricultural infrastructure; diseconomies of (small) scale in agriculture; the failure to achieve a decisive step forward in the urban industrial reforms in terms of structural change or improvements in productivity; increasingly serious macro-economic imbalances visible in growing inflation, over-investment, escalating wage hikes and deficits in both state finances and foreign trade: increasing foreign indebtedness and a breakdown of the controversial 'single-child family policy' introduced to rein back population growth. Anyone visiting China in late 1988 or early 1989 could not fail to be aware of the scope and intensity of this evolving economic crisis and the social discontent to which it was giving rise – indeed, it provides the backdrop for the tragic Beijing drama of mid-1989 and much of the fuel for the political passions and antagonisms generated then.

If the economic impact of the reforms has varied over time, it has also varied across policy area or economic sector. The resounding success, at least until 1985, was in agriculture where the collective mode of production was dismantled and replaced by an increasingly commercially-oriented household economy. Production, productivity and incomes climbed, encouraged by more favourable price policies and a more flexible procurement system. Another area of success was the policy of opening to the international economy which brought benefits in terms of foreign investment, technology transfer, increased employment and expertise levels and more dynamic economic activity generally, particularly in areas favoured by geography or policy (particularly the coastal provinces of the south-east). By contrast, however, reforms in the state urban/industrial sector, not launched in earnest until 1984, were much less successful. There were some areas of limited improvement: the urban economy became more dynamic and diverse as the collective and private sectors expanded, particularly in commerce and services, and state enterprises themselves enjoyed greater freedom in marketing and supply, finance and labour management. The economic impact of these changes, however, was ambiguous to say the least, particularly given the failure to grasp the nettles of reforming the price structure, the ownership system and relations of production within the enterprise. Moreover, the previous bureaucratic structure of economic planning and management, though modified to some extent, still remained basically intact.

Bearing these chronological and sectoral variations in mind, what broad trends can we detect over the reform decade in the economic role of the state and state-economy relations? First, certain economic powers have been devolved to enterprises, households and individuals. In the country-side, the peasant household supplanted the production team as the basic unit of agricultural production through a *de facto* privatisation of agriculture. In both rural and urban areas, a second economy flourished in industry, commerce and transportation, composed of collective industries, economic 'associations' in the countryside, rural specialised households and private petty capitalist and individual businesses. A 'third economy' operated within the state sector itself as state enterprises increasingly produced and traded outside the plan. New forms of ownership emerged (most notable was the Stone Computer Company in Beijing) and various types of joint Chinese-foreign or wholly foreign enterprises operated under a relatively loose framework of controls. In the financial sphere, as Barry Naughton graphically demonstrates, increasing amounts of financial resources were held in the hands of non-state enterprises and households and in the form of 'retained profits' in state enterprises. Concurrently, the proportion of total investment made directly out of the central state budget declined substantially, as Naughton also demonstrates.

Second, there has been a major shift of economic power from central to local governments at provincial level and below, partly the result of conscious policy and partly as one aspect of a more general dispersion of economic power within the state machine.[3] The latter involves not merely redistribution of power vertically between levels of government but also horizontally between individual government departments at a given level, each of which have been keen to generate 'extra-budgetary revenue' for their own purposes in the 'entrepreneurial' ways described in my own and Marc Blecher's contributions to this volume. Decentralisation of economic power and resources to local governments had been a recurrent feature of the Maoist period, a process analysed by Christine Wong in her article here. This phenomenon of economic localisation has intensified during the post-Mao reforms and can be seen across the board: examples in this book are in the open policy on foreign trade and investment (Howell) and in the domestic investment and banking system (Naughton). But local decentralisation also affects economic planning and management more generally, taxation, price controls and the allocation of material supplies to industry. This process has been accentuated by specific central policy initiatives, for example, by granting greater financial autonomy to the localities through revised revenue sharing arrangements and moves to strengthen the role of the larger cities as agents of economic coordination. Moreover, changes in the structure of the economy – the move from heavy to light industry, large-scale to small-scale enterprises, state to collective and private enterprises – have also served to strengthen local governments which are mainly responsible for the latter categories. By 1989, the power of the central government was visibly dwindling and the Chinese economy was beginning to look more like a patchwork of 'independent kingdoms' (some called them 'economic fiefdoms') than an integrated national economy.

This dual dispersion of economic power has seriously reduced the capacity of the central government to implement policy, regardless of whether this is in a 'reformist' or 'conservative' direction. This constraint is a dual one: it is not merely a matter of not being able to secure administrative compliance down the long chain of bureaucratic command, but also of garnering the financial resources necessary to underpin central policies. Part of the loss of control involves the inability to extract government revenue from an increasingly complex and recalcitrant economic system – the Chinese state has found itself facing a fiscal crisis, dwindling sources of revenue being counterposed against escalating demands on the treasury, the latter arising from increasingly vocal demands for extra resources from sectoral interests (education is a good example) and a heavy burden of consumer subsidies to cushion urban populations from the rise in agricultural procurement prices and inflationary pressures generally.

Yet how does one square this pervasive loss of political control over economic affairs to local governments, government departments, enterprises, households and individuals with my initial argument that there has been no decisive change in the basic system of economic planning and control. Three processes lie behind the answer. First, while the traditional state planning system may remain basically intact, its scope of operation has decreased and the autonomy of its subordinate enterprises has increased. While state enterprise still remains partly subservient to the plan and its bureaucratic executors, their ability to set the terms of their own, extra-plan production and exchange has increased significantly. Second, structural diversification and commercialisation of the economy have expanded it beyond the bounds of the old state sector, creating an ever widening 'second economy' which is resistant to state control. For example, an economist from the State Planning Commission complained in September 1989 that 'the government now has under its control only 60 per cent of national construction, mostly basic industries, while the other 40 per cent, mostly processing industries, are running wild in the hands of collectives and private business people'.[4] Third, much of the economic power accruing to local governments may continue to be exercised in traditional directive ways, despite policies to the contrary emanating from Beijing.

One should not, however, exaggerate, this pessimistic argument about the lack of change in the institutional character of the Chinese state and the behaviour of its officials in the realm of economics. As we shall see in the next section, there has been some degree of organisational innovation and diversification which reflects an attempt to redesign state institutions to cope with the new demands of a market economy and prefigures the emergence of what Howell calls the 'market-facilitating state'. Progress, however, has been uneven and the result has been at best a hybrid 'half-way house' wherein the new and the old developmental states intertwine, often in economically unproductive ways.

However, these countervailing tendencies to the centre's gradual loss of control have been uneven and weak. Commonsense suggests that it is difficult to implement a radical (or even a moderate) reform programme within a basically unreformed institutional structure and a cadre of officials whose behaviour has either not changed or has changed in directions inimical to reform goals. While much of the basis for the increasing loss of government control over the reform process reflects the success of reform policies, the relative lack of institutional change and adaptation puts the central leadership in a serious dilemma which reflects an unresolved tension between the need to decentralise economic power on the one hand and to construct a new framework of economic regulation on the other. This complex combination of institutional immobilism and economic decentralisation and diversification has led to a loss of central initiative and control which has bedevilled attempts to set up a comprehensive and effective framework of macro-economic regulation in accordance with the reformist principle of 'guidance' rather than 'directive' planning.

3 STATE INSTITUTIONS AND THE POLITICAL SYSTEM: PLUS ÇA CHANGE . . .?

(a) State Economic Institutions

In this section, I shall focus on the impact of the decade of economic reform on the organisational character and behaviour of state institutions, concentrating on administrative and political agencies – Sandschneider's case-study provides a detailed analysis of the main coercive institution, the People's Liberation Army. We have already alluded to important trends in those sectors of the government administration concerned with economic planning and management. Let us now look at these developments with more precision, under the two headings of institutional adaptation and institutional diversification.

Institutional adaptation
If we focus on those state institutions directly affected by changes in the economic system, the picture is not one of institutional immobility or passivity. There has been considerable reorientation both of relations between state organs and of specific state institutions, some along 'progressive' lines consonant with the desired institutional logic of economic reform, others

designed rather to defend institutions against, or profit from, the reforms
in ways which ill accord with the new canons of institutional behaviour.

First, there has been considerable *reallocation of functions between
institutions*, some sectors losing, some gaining, others merely changing
their powers and responsibilities. The major trend is the reallocation of
institutional functions from traditional directive/managerial to regulative
agencies. This is particularly visible in the area of finance where there have
been two significant transfers of institutional power: first, responsibility
for investment finance has been shifted from the state budgetary system
(implemented through the network of finance bureaux) to the banking system; second, there has been an (only partly) successful attempt to transfer
the responsibility for state claims on the net revenue of state enterprises
from the relevant economic branch departments (with funds extracted
through profit remittances) to fiscal agencies (with funds recovered by
taxation). These changes have created two important new challenges for an
emerging new form of developmental state – those of designing and operating systems for regulating an increasingly complex system of financial
institutions (Naughton shows how difficult this process has been) and of
monitoring, and extracting resources from, an increasingly complex system
of economic actors (for example, official complaints about widespread tax
evasion have been common in recent years).

Second, we are able to detect the *adaptation of existing state institutions*
to the new economic environment. 'Adaptation' is of course a vague term
and, from a reformist point of view, some forms of adaptation have been
positive, others ambiguous or counter-productive. On the positive side, for
example, Howell demonstrates in the case of the open policy how a wide
range of institutions have adapted to accommodate the presence of foreign
capital: state banks have operated in a more decentralised way and have
expanded certain of their functions (such as foreign exchange regulation);
state financial bureaux have expanded their activity to include the regulation of foreign and joint ventures; labour organs have adapted to the special
circumstances of Special Economic Zones where industrial relations are
significantly different from the rest of China. At the local level, White
describes how certain urban agencies have expanded to meet the need to
regulate a diversifying economy: for example, the role of industrial and
commercial agencies has increased to accommodate the expansion of urban
collective and private industrial, commercial and service sectors.

In contrast to the above 'positive' forms of adaptation, other state
agencies have responded in ways which, while creative, are not in tune
with the spirit of the reforms and may even serve to block or divert them.
Here we enter the kaleidoscopic realm of 'state entrepreneurship', dealt

with by Blecher and White, but surely requiring more study. While the phenomenon is complex, we can discern two basic types in our case studies: first, there is conservative entrepreneurship, as in the case of the Shanghai Textile Bureau discussed in my article, where a 'creative' institutional innovation – in this case the establishment of a Financial Allocation Centre – served basically to recoup certain financial powers which the bureau was losing as a result of reforms in industrial administration. Second, there is the phenomenon of reactive entrepreneurship described in detail by Blecher in the case of Guanghan County in Sichuan province, where state agencies, surrounded by enterprises and individuals taking advantage of the new economic environment to enrich themselves and urged by the political leadership to behave in a more dynamic and less bureaucratic fashion, decide to take 'a piece of the action' by 'going into business' themselves. This may take a variety of forms: first, a state economic agency may undertake to organise the enterprises under its authority in efforts to meet external competition or find new markets; second, alternatively, the agency may set up new companies to exploit potentially profitable ventures either independently or in partnership with other state or non-state actors – this contributes to a proliferation of 'quasi-state' agencies which has been a general feature of the reform era and to which we return below; third, while the preceding are both forms of institutional behaviour, there is a 'corrupt' version whereby individual officials use their powers and connections to engage in economic activities in order to feather their own nests. A myriad of examples of the latter two phenomena in all their Byzantine complexity was revealed in the 1989 campaign to review new companies and curtail those established 'illegally' (for example, see the fascinating case of Li Rui, a veteran Party official in Shandong province who was brought to justice in September 1989 for illegally establishing a network of companies).[5]

Though these two forms of state entrepreneurship – the conservative and reactive – are very different, the economic consequences of both types may be problematic from a reform perspective. Obviously so in the conservative case but also in reactive cases because, first, the motivations for institutional creativity may be bureaucratic or political rather than purely economic, and, second, even when an endeavour is motivated by the profit motive, the resulting ventures may not involve competitive behaviour (since the participants are mobilising resources through bureaucratic privileges and institutional connections rather than market means) nor that essential component of entrepreneurial behaviour, risk, since such ventures can often be rescued by bureaucratic means if they get into trouble. Regardless of its specific form and consequences, however, state entrepreneurship is a phenomenon of central relevance to the theme of this volume since it represents a complex and sometimes bizarre fusion of bureaucratic and market behaviour, and reinforces an emerging picture of a state which is indeed changing in response to the economic reforms but not necessarily in the 'right' (i.e., reform) direction.

Institutional proliferation and diversification
This process is an important component of the Chinese state's organisational response to the economic reforms. In addition to the new enterprises arising from state entrepreneurship discussed above, we can discern two other forms of institutional proliferation: (i) the creation of new state agencies at various levels to undertake regulative functions required by a changing economic environment. Examples are rife in many fields but we can point to certain types: for example, new institutions whose function it is to *co-ordinate* across increasingly complex areas of governmental responsibility and economic activity (for example, planning committees in urban district governments, or the State Council Leading Group for Foreign Investment established in August 1986 to co-ordinate across an increasingly complex network of institutions dealing with foreign investment); or agencies established to carry out specific *new functions* emerging from the process of economic reform (such as the burgeoning network of auditing bureaux required to supervise government and enterprise budgets, the expansion of the legal system to provide courts specialising in economic disputes, and the plethora of institutions required to regulate the Special Economic Zones); (ii) the mushrooming of intermediate or 'quasi-state' institutions, most often in the form of companies or corporations, designed to act as an intermediary between enterprises and state agencies proper, or to assist or extend the work of the latter (prominent examples are the Labour Service Companies attached to local labour bureaux and other state units which are designed to generate employment, reallocate labour and regulate industrial relations, or various kinds of financial agencies empowered to handle foreign and local capital, or import-export companies established under the aegis of the Ministry of Foreign Economic Relations and Trade). These organisations are important in that they inhabit a new hybrid institutional world which is neither fully state nor enterprise but a fusion of both. Some of these 'quasi-state' institutions – such as, for example, the China International Trust and Investment Corporation and its local affiliates – are now major actors on the Chinese economic scene.

To summarise, this section on institutional responses in the state economic sector has buttressed our emerging finding that successful adaptation to the needs of a market-orientated economy does not mean 'less' state but rather different types of state institution and activity which may ultimately result in a larger and more complex system of state institutions. In the current Chinese case, however, poised as it is between institutional immobilism and adaptation, the new institutional system, rather than displacing the old, interpenetrates or overlays it to create a dualistic state. This section also reminds us that the responses of state institutions to the economic reforms cannot be reduced to bureaucratic immobility and opposition, but have involved a great deal of creative adaptation with a variety of institutional motives and economic consequences. The information on institutional proliferation also reminds us that the Chinese state is becoming more complex, with the consequence that the politics of the economic policy process in any specific sector is itself also becoming more complex. This is a factor which may make the overall task of political leadership and macro-economic co-ordination more difficult, further reinforcing our earlier concern about an increasing trend towards unmanageability of the economic reform process.

(b) State Political Institutions

It is obvious that we should begin here with an analysis of the Chinese Communist Party which is the political nervous system of the Chinese state system and Chinese society generally. As we have already remarked, the Dengist leadership has from the outset put economic reform far ahead of political reform; in fact, the reform project involved the creation of a market economy while retaining a basically Leninist political system. This seems contradictory yet not impossible given the fact, for example, that Taiwan has had something similar until very recently.[6]

But even relatively conservative leaders such as Deng Xiaoping recognised that there needed to be *some* change in the Party's role to accommodate the more complex and dynamic economic environment which would be created by the economic reforms. This conception of political change involved an attempt to bring about greater clarity in the Party's role in relation to other institutions (most notably the government bureaucracy, an emerging legal system and state enterprises), specifically involving the need to focus on the Party's political role while disengaging from the pervasive administrative responsibilities it had accumulated over thirty years of power. The result, it was hoped, would be a stronger, 'leaner' party, disencumbered from detail and better able to exercise its leadership over Chinese society and economy.

In spite of this early recognition (visible in a key speech by Deng Xiaoping in 1980), the issue of political reform has been the subject of heated debate within the CCP leadership, and did not come squarely onto the reform agenda until 1986, as Saich points out. While officially-sanctioned reforms to the Party were wider-ranging – including the desire to foster more internal democracy, recruit more educated and reform-minded people as Party members and promote younger and more professional members to leadership posts – the key reforms which affected the structural role of the Party in state and society were two: the attempt to separate the Party from the government administration and reduce the role of the Party committee in state enterprises and other basic-level units. Saich discusses these reforms in detail and his findings support a general conclusion that little has in fact changed. To the extent that marginal changes had taken place in the position and functions of the Party, moreover, they have been frozen or reversed in the aftermath of the June 1989 massacre.

Other areas of political reform have not fared any better, as evidenced by Robert Benewick's analysis of the fate of proposals to strengthen the role of the state's representative institutions (the system of people's congresses) and basic-level 'self-governing' organisations such as urban residents' committees and rural villagers' committees as part of a broader process of political 'institutionalisation'. He concludes that, despite an urgent need to strengthen the role of these institutions as agencies which can accommodate the new groups and pressures arising from rapid socio-economic change, progress has been halting and uneven and has lagged far behind the pace of economic reform. Similarly, movement towards strengthening the role of an independent legal system has also been relatively marginal, as Donald Clarke points out in his piece.

Rather than extend the litany of failures in political and institutional reform, it is more productive to enquire why so little has changed. Certain key explanatory factors suggest themselves. First, at the *ideological* level, both the first and the second generations of CCP leaders, who have been responsible for steering the post-Mao reforms – the 'old Guard' of revolutionaries symbolised by Deng Xiaoping, who were shaped by the politics of revolutionary and anti-imperialist struggles, and their successors, represented by Li Peng and Zhao Ziyang, who came to political maturity in a context of post-revolutionary politics and economics on the Stalinist model – in varying degrees still adhere to a traditional version of Marxist-Leninist politics, the framework of which is defined by Deng's Four Basic Principles. Even if they had been open to alternatives, with the exception of the aborted Czech reforms of 1968 no other political model has been available to them, at least until the mid to late 1980s with the rise of Gorbachev and the startlingly rapid changes in Poland and Hungary. At the level of *power structure*, the Communist Party has enjoyed a position of unrivalled institutionalised political dominance which bestows a range of social, economic and political benefits on its officials and members which they have no pressing reason to place in jeopardy through political reform. At the *policy* level, there are concerns (not without foundation) on the part of the leadership that, since the process of economic liberalisation is politically tortuous and potentially destabilising, there is an overriding need to maintain a 'strong state' and a single source of strategic political decision.

However, though purposive political reform has been relatively minimal, in reality there has been a good deal of political change, not merely in the form of the pervasive loss of political control discussed earlier, but an over-all decline in the authority of the state socialist regime. At the *ideological* level, both the damning attacks on the 'ultra-leftism' of Mao Zedong and his followers on the one hand and the manifest incompatibility between the official ideology of 'Marxism-Leninism-Mao Zedong Thought' and the emergent principles and reality of market socialism on the other hand have led to a decline in the political efficacy of the official ideology as a constitutional and motivational force. At the level of *power structure*, the position of the Party has been eroded by the partial redistribution of economic power resulting from the reforms and increasing corruption among the ranks of Party officials. At the *policy* level, the credibility of the Party as a force for national leadership has been undermined by the intensifying problems arising from reform policies over the past few years.

This alarming and accelerating contradiction between the lack of politi-cal reform and a gradual decline in the regime's power and authority, found vivid expression in the events of April-June 1989. The Chinese leadership, unlike their Polish and Hungarian counterparts, resorted to repression and reverted to an earlier generation of leaders and an earlier pattern of politics which served to intensify the contradiction still further.

4   STATE AND SOCIETY: THE POLITICAL SOCIOLOGY OF REFORM

Though it is hard to study the phenomenon with any precision given the current lack of fieldwork opportunities in China, the era of economic reform has given rise to significant changes in Chinese social structure and state-society relations. Chinese society has become more complex in terms of both structure and attitudes: at the macro-level both cities and countryside have experienced greater social differentiation under the impact of economic changes and, in the cities at least, there has been a rapid spread of heterodox ideas particularly as a result of the policy of opening to the West; at the micro-level, as Croll points out, there have been important changes in the organisation of families and households in the rural areas. Chinese society has also become more fluid and dynamic with greater horizontal mobility within the countryside, between countryside and cities and between regions, significant upward mobility (in economic terms at least) and a widespread process of 'delocalisation' as the boundaries of previously cellular communities have broken down or become more porous.

Structural change has also been reflected in the emergence of new groups or strata under the impact of the reforms: in the countryside as Kelliher argues, 'new rich peasant' individuals or households which have made money quickly through specialised agricultural production or diversification into local trade and transportation; in the cities, private business people generally and a small number of successful entrepreneurs who have amassed small fortunes through initiative or good connections and, harder to discern, a growing number of entrepreneurial managers in state enterprises well attuned to the logic of a more competitive economy. In both rural and urban areas, moreover, there are increasing numbers of itinerant unskilled and skilled labour operating away from home on a contract or otherwise temporary basis. The 'floating population' in the cities has increased and was clearly an important element in the widespread urban unrest of 1989.

While empirical studies differ on whether Chinese society is more unequal than before the reforms, this issue is perhaps less relevant than the observed facts that many Chinese *perceive* various inequalities arising from the reforms and that these perceptions have given rise to social hostilities and conflict. In some cases, these perceptions reflect the rise of the rapidly rich who are resented by their less fortunate or enterprising neighbours; in other cases, they represent the differential impact of the reforms on existing social categories (for example, intellectuals are economically vulnerable since their salaries are fixed and they have little scope to earn bonuses on the job unlike state workers who are able to pressure enterprise managers into providing bonuses in cash and kind; or urbanites who are suffering the effects of food-price inflation and resent the fact that certain elements of the peasantry are better off than themselves). These tensions have of course been intensified during the period of high inflation which developed in the late 1980s.

Along with this process of social differentiation has come a redistribution of social power – away from the state and its ancillary agencies and towards individuals, households and groups. Particularly dramatic has been the shift in the balance of power between the state and the rural household after the introduction of the 'responsibility system' and the *de facto* privatisation of agriculture. Economic decentralisation and diversi- fication has meant a dispersion of resources, and control over resources, to enterprises (public, co-operative or private), households and individuals which has opened up the potential for a new social sphere which is at least partially autonomous in relation to the state. Throughout the 1980s, there were signs that this social space was being occupied by new organisations organised 'from below', a process which one could characterise as the formation of a new 'civil society' (this was particularly apparent in the business sphere with new organisations of small private business and entrepreneurs' associations) but it was also visible among the formerly docile 'mass organisations' (hitherto controlled along Leninist lines) which began to twitch, like Frankenstein monsters, with unaccustomed political life (the Women's Association and the trade unions, for example).

Unsurprisingly, these trends have been of major significance for rela- tions between state and society. Increasing social complexity and fluidity, combined with the redistribution of socio-economic power, have made problems of social control and management of social tension more difficult. Nowhere is this more apparent than in the one area where the state has sought a major extension of its power over society since 1979 – population policy. As Croll demonstrates, the concerted effort by Party and state to impose a single-child family policy has been thwarted by the newly-won economic power of peasant households and their consequent ability to resist state pressure and avoid or adjust to the material penalties designed to punish disobedience.

The state has responded to the social impact of the reforms by attempting to encourage the growth of, and develop political collaboration with, the new 'progressive' strata which have come to prominence in the reforms. This is particularly visible in the countryside where the regime has fostered the emergence of a new elite of entrepreneurs and specialised producers which Kelliher sees as tantamount to the adoption of a new 'class line' in the countryside (in contrast to the previous Maoist line of 'relying on the poor and lower-middle peasants'). Likewise in the urban sector, reform policies have sought to reinforce the power of managers in relation to their workforces and encourage the activity of entrepreneurs. At the national level, central policy has sought to reward the richer and more fortunately situated eastern provinces to the detriment of the poorer provinces of the interior. This strategy of 'betting on the best' may be politically problematic since it earns the hostility of those not so well-favoured without at the same time necessarily acquiring the gratitude and support of the beneficiaries.

It would seem that, as of 1989, the Chinese State has failed both to comprehend and come to terms with this new social situation. The expansion of a partially autonomous 'social space' and the concomitant emergence of 'civil society' found dramatic expression in the popular upsurge of April–June 1989 when autonomous organisations of workers and intellectuals sprang up like bamboos after the rain and the burgeoning urban private sector flexed its political muscles. Some degree of political and institutional reform would seem to be necessary to create channels of institutionalised interaction between state and society, in particular to accommodate the rise of the organisations of civil society.

CONCLUSION

In the aftermath of the June 1989 massacre, it is easy to be pessimistic about the prospects for future political reform. However, it is important to identify what would be the conditions which could underpin effective political reform so as to mitigate some of the intensifying political problems we have identified. One important factor is *political leadership* – since China's leaders, both 'conservative' and 'reformist', are locked into the past, there is a need for a third generation more attuned to the realities of the 1980s (both at home and in the other state socialist countries in Eastern Europe) and more willing to sponsor political and institutional as well as economic reform. It is particularly crucial for such a leadership, which many believe to be waiting in the wings, to project a new vision of Chinese socialism – one which can define and implement programmes of social and political as well as economic reform and unite these into a conception of the whole. Without this, the ideological and political space created by the decline of traditional Marxist-Leninism will be filled with heterodox ideas which may displace socialism completely as a practical and desirable future for China and leave the CCP stranded as an historical irrelevance. Such a leadership would also need to develop a new political style of compromise and consultation rather than command. The implementation of an alternative vision would require them to consult and co-opt widely – by mobilising the reform constituency within the Party, particularly those Party intellectuals with ideas for constructive change, by setting up the institutionalised means whereby social interests outside the Party – hitherto ignored or repressed – can find some way of making their voices heard and of exerting some influence on decision-making processes, and by responding in some degree to the demands for some form of 'democratisation' of political institutions. Without these innovations, it is difficult to see how the CCP could retain the political authority and control necessary to manage a sustained process of radical economic reform. Without them, continued efforts at purely economic reform would result in a depressing cycle of relaxation, discontent, protest and repression with escalating costs in terms of further loss of the regime's ideological authority and political credibility, as well as the costs borne by the population in terms of loss of life and freedom.

Such innovations would not necessarily involve rapid 'democratisation' in the short or medium term along Polish or Hungarian lines. Indeed, given the specific characteristics of present-day China – as a very poor country with an overwhelmingly peasant population which still requires major interventions from a dynamic developmental state capable of taking difficult strategic decisions, as a nation with a long tradition of authoritarian rule and a concomitant political culture which cannot be rapidly transformed, and as an enormous, increasingly complex and diverse society which requires a stable political centre to maintain national unity – it is not clear that any form of rapid democratisation is either feasible or desirable. Though political and institutional reform is clearly needed in the near future, the Chinese political system would still remain authoritarian and under the aegis of the CCP. Even the proponents of radical reform have recognised the continued need for a 'strong state' and during 1986 to 1989 some were proposing a theory of 'new authoritarianism' along the lines of the successful modernising regimes of South Korea and Taiwan.[7] Though the massacre of June 4 has temporarily stilled this debate about alternative political futures, it remains an urgent necessity. While in the short term, the political response to the urban uprising of April-June 1989 has been regressive, those events demonstrated the urgent need for political and institutional change and in the longer term may provide a powerful political impetus for the emergence of a new generation of leaders with a mandate for deeper-going reform.

NOTES

1. For further analysis of the notion of the 'developmental state' in the East Asian context, see my (ed.) *Developmental States in East Asia* (London, Macmillan, 1988); for a discussion of different forms of developmental state, see my 'Developmental States and Socialist Industrialisation in the Third World', *Journal of Development Studies*, vol. 21, no. 1 (1984), pp. 97–120.
2. For preliminary analysis of the June 4 massacre, see Amnesty International, *People's Republic of China: Preliminary Findings on Killings of*

Unarmed Civilians, Arbitrary Arrests and Summary Executions since 3 June 1989 (London, August 14 1989); Michael Fathers and Andrew Higgins, *Tiananmen: The Rape of Peking*, (*The Independent*, London, 1989).

3. For sophisticated analyses of central-local relations both before and during the reform decade, see Christine P. W. Wong, 'The problematic role of the local sector in post-Mao reforms', paper for a conference on 'China in a New Era: Continuity and Change', Manila, 1987; and Jonathan Unger, 'The struggle to dictate China's administration: the conflict of branches vs. areas vs. reform', mimeo, Contemporary China Centre, Australian National University, Canberra, 1987.

4. 'Economist examines problems of 'grim' economic situation', *Xinhua* [New China News Agency], in English, 6 Sept. 1989, in *BBC, Summary of World Broadcasts: Fareast* [swb] 0556 (8 Sept. 1989)

5. 'Veteran cadres expelled from Party, companies dissolved', *Xinhua*, in Chinese, 11 Sept. 1989, in swb 0561, 14 Sept. 1989.

6. For an analysis of the Taiwan case, see Robert Wade, 'State intervention and 'outward-looking' development: neo-classical theory and Taiwanese practice', in White, ed., *Developmental States in East Asia*, 1988, pp. 30–67, and A. Amsden, 'Taiwan's economic history: a case of Etatisme and a challenge to dependency theory', *Modern China*, 5: 3, 1979, pp. 341–80.

7. For more contributions to this debate, see Du Ruji, 'Reflections on new authoritarianism', *Zhengzhixue Yanjiu* [Political Studies Research], 3:1989, pp. 21–25; Rong Jian, 'Is new authoritarianism feasible in China?', *Shijie Jingji Daobao* [World Economic Herald], Shanghai, 16 Jan. 1989; Hao Wang, 'A theory of transitional democratic authoritarianism', *Political Studies Research*, 3:1989, pp. 16–20.

Part 1
The Economic Role
of the State

1 Central Planning and Local Participation under Mao: the Development of Country-Run Fertiliser Plants

Christine P. W. Wong

Seeking an appropriate role for the state in managing the development process has been a persistent problem throughout the history of the People's Republic of China. From the mid-1950s to the late 1970s, this history was dominated by a recurring cycle of centralisation-decentralisation. Dissatisfied with the Soviet model and its attendant bureaucratisation and stratification, Mao launched his assault on the central planning apparatus by drastically curtailing its allocative role, first with the Great Leap Forward campaign, and later with the Cultural Revolution. Rather than transferring resource allocation to the market, however, Mao had turned it over substantially to the lower level administrative units of provinces, cities, prefectures, counties and rural collectives, and called on them to develop their economies on the basis of 'self-reliance'.[1] It is by now well-known that this strategy of administrative decentralisation was largely unsuccessful. While injecting some flexibility into the system and allowing some local economies to flourish, local management of resources introduced many new rigidities as well. By the late 1970s, the fragmentation and compartmentalisation of resources under the control of regional and functional authorities was widely perceived as a key source of inefficiency in the Chinese economy.[2] Furthermore, recurrent macroeconomic problems engendered considerable policy instability, with high tides of decentralisation invariably followed by periods of recentralisation. In the words of one Chinese economist, the problem was that 'centralisation (led) to rigidity, rigidity (led) to complaints, complaints (led) to decentralisation, decentralisation (led) to disorder, and disorder (led) back to centralisation' (Jiang Yiwei 1980, p. 55).

23

This paper re-examines the Maoist strategy of administrative decentralisation during the Cultural Revolution period. This re-examination is timely for two reasons. First, in the post-Mao period, a great deal of new information has become available about the Cultural Revolution that enables us finally to piece together the main outline of the 'Maoist development strategy' and to reconcile a great deal of conflicting information about how that strategy was implemented. Second, there is an urgency to learning about the problems of decentralisation during the Maoist period since China seems once again on the verge of relapsing into the cycle of centralisation-decentralisation. After a decade of near-continuous decentralisation, the post-Mao reform program has stalled. Amidst worsening inflation, signs of creeping recentralisation were evident by late 1988 – rationing had been re-introduced for some key consumer goods including pork, and administrative allocation was resumed over a growing portion of producers' goods.[3] Once again, it is the government's inability to maintain macroeconomic balance that has created a crisis and forced reconsideration of its role in economic management. In the wake of the June 1989 massacre and the expected economic downturn, it is more likely than ever that a retrenchment from market-oriented reforms and a swing back toward centralisation will soon occur.

This paper advances a new argument about the Maoist strategy of decentralisation. While much was said by Mao about tapping local initiative, 'not draining the pond to catch the fish', about the wisdom of 'the mass line', and so on, his main objective was to harness these forces to promote national goals, which were defined by the Party/state/himself. In this light, the strategy of administrative decentralisation is seen primarily as an attempt to improve implementation of central policies, rather than a devolution of real decision-making authority to lower level units. By properly imbuing them with an appreciation of 'the whole country as a chessboard', local officials would be expected to carry out resource allocation in faithful conformity with policies formulated by the centre. In this way, Maoist decentralisation was meant to effect what Michael Ellman called 'indirect centralisation', with decisions made by local officials, but which were 'exactly those that would have been made if the central authorities had made them' (Ellman, 1979, p. 33).

This argument is constructed through a detailed examination of one component of the rural industrialisation programme, the development of small-scale chemical fertiliser plants. Rural industrialisation was a central pillar of Mao's development strategy, to which substantial resources were devoted during the Cultural Revolution period. In many respects, the rural industrialisation programme provides perfect illustration of how Maoist decentralisation was supposed to work. Because of its critical role in the Agricultural Mechanisation Programme, overall objectives and guidelines for the rural industrialisation programme were formulated by the Party/state, which also provided seed money and technical aid to initiate development. Once underway, however, responsibilities for planning, finance, and day-to-day management of the programme were turned over to local governments. To enable them to take on these growing tasks, many resources were transferred to local control, and generous incentives were offered, along with moral exhortations, to induce compliance with goals of the national programme.

In quantitative terms, the results were impressive. Under the call to build 'Dazhai-type counties' that combined agricultural and industrial production, three-quarters of the 2000–odd counties in the country had built a small fertiliser plant by the end of the Cultural Revolution. Virtually all of them had at least one cement plant and a farm machinery plant. 95 per cent of the communes and 60 per cent of the production brigades had set up workshops to repair and manufacture farm tools and simple machinery. By 1979 there were nearly 800,000 industrial enterprises, plus almost 90,000 small hydroelectric stations, scattered in villages and small towns, employing some 24 million workers and producing over 15 per cent of the gross value of industrial output. Altogether, rural industry supplied the bulk of modern inputs to agriculture, producing all farm tools and nearly all of the small and medium farm machinery, more than half of the chemical fertilisers, two-thirds of the cement, and 45 per cent of coal output (see Table 1.1). In their predominantly 'aid-agriculture' orientation, these enterprises conformed remarkably to the strategy of 'walking on two legs', freeing the modern sector to concentrate on its own reproduction.

In economic terms, the programme was disastrous, which also makes it typical of Maoist programmes. Due to a variety of technical and supply problems, capacity utilisation rates were extremely low across-the-board in rural industry. In spite of a plethora of subsidies, rural enterprises ran losses totalling more than 2 billion yuan in 1978, accounting for more than half of all the losses of state-owned industry. Their inefficiency imposed high costs on agriculture as well: fertilisers produced by the small plants cost 2–3 times the world market price in terms of fertiliser-grain price ratios, and their quality was so poor that they were commonly blamed for the declining yield-responses in Chinese agriculture. The farm machinery turned out by small plants was often of shoddy quality, contributing to extremely low rates of utilisation.

By tracing the implementation of the programme to build small fertiliser plants, I will show that in spite of repeated calls for local self-reliance, the

TABLE 1.1   *Contribution of output from rural industry,*
1978/79

	Number of plants	Estimated total output
		(million metric tons)
I. The Five Small Industries		
Farm machinery (1979)	County level: 1000+ manufacturing plants 2,400 repair and manufacturing plants	
	Commune level: 45,000 repair and assembly plants	
	Brigade level: 450,000 repair and assembly stations	
Nitrogenous fertiliser (1979)	1,539	7.28
Phosphorous fertiliser (1979)	Over 1,000	over 5
Cement (1979)	3,400+	49.1
Iron and Steel (1978)	501	11** (iron) 6** (steel)
Hydroelectricity (1979)	Nearly 90,000	11.6 billion kwh
Coal (1978)	20,000+	276
II. Commune and Brigade Industries (1979)	751,000	
III. Rural Industry	780,000	

SOURCE: Wong, *Maoism and Development*, manuscript, Chapter 4.

TABLE 1.1 *(Continued)*

% Total for industry	Output value	As % all Industry	Employment
	(billions yuan)		(millions)
	30.4*	6.6	5.0*
All hand tools virtually all machinery of more than 20hp	7.9	1.5	(county level and above)
54	6.5*		0.75
80–90	0.7*		
67	2.7*		
22.5 (iron)	1.1* (iron)		
13.1 (steel)	2.2* (steel)		
24 (hydro-electric	1.0*		
45	8.3*		
	39.7	8.7	18.73
	70.1*	15.3	23.7*

* Estimated
** Capacity

central state was involved in virtually every aspect of the programme, from research and development to finance, providing equipment and technical aid, to providing current supplies of coal and electricity, and a plethora of production and distribution subsidies. At the same time, very generous incentives were offered to induce local support for the programme. These incentives turned over to local control virtually all allocative decisions in the small plants, even while the plants continued to be included directly and indirectly in state material and financial plans. This led increasingly to a separation of control from responsibilities and created an incentive structure that was all in favour of local expansion. Through this examination of the development of fertiliser plants, I will assign the major portion of blame for both the industry's problems and for the growing problems of macroeconomic control on the unsuccessful resolution of the tension between state control and local participation.

RURAL INDUSTRIALISATION POLICIES

Achieving agricultural mechanisation was assigned high priority during the Cultural Revolution period. A programme proposed by Mao and adopted by the First National Conference on Farm Mechanisation held in July 1966 in Hubei, called for the mechanisation of ploughing, irrigation and drainage, processing of agricultural produce, transportation, as well as the increased use of chemical fertilisers.[4] These mechanisation targets translated into rough production targets to be achieved in industry through the third, fourth and fifth five year plans (1966–1980). For example, the plan estimated that by 1980, industry would need to have produced some 800,000 large and medium tractors, 1.5 million small hand-held tractors, and 82 million horsepower of irrigation and drainage equipment. Given Mao's preference for decentralisation and a 'walking on two legs' strategy in technology choice, the Hubei conference called for the development of local industry to meet these needs. The key industries to be developed at the local level included not only farm machinery and chemical fertilisers, but also iron and steel and nonferrous metals, to provide the needed inputs for farm machinery production. Under the separate but related policy that later came to be called the 'industrial province' policy, provinces were assigned the primary role for planning and co-ordinating development of local industries. The county was chosen as the key level for building the 'five small industries' of chemical fertiliser, farm machinery, iron and steel, cement, and electricity, the package of rural industries that were to 'form a local industrial system to serve agriculture'.

To provide seed funding, a special allocation of 8 billion yuan was made during the fourth five year plan period, to be used specifically for building key projects in the 'five small industries' (Fang, 1984, p. 467). In addition, it was decided in 1970 (partially retroactively) that funding under the budgetary item of 'aid to people's communes' should also be used for rural industrialisation. During 1966–1978, much of the over 7 billion yuan allocated under this category went to setting up farm machinery repair and manufacturing stations at the commune and brigade levels (Interview in Beijing, May 1982, and Ministry of Agriculture, 1979; 51–3). Though these sums were small compared to total investment in industry during these periods, in many localities they provided seed money to initiate rural industrialisation.

Another important component of state aid was the technology and equipment provided by central ministries. For the 'five small industries', a good deal of research and development was undertaken by central research institutes throughout the 1950s and 1960s, aimed at developing small-scale technology and perfecting prototype plants and equipment. In the chemical fertiliser industry, prototype small plants were first built during the Great Leap Forward, with blueprints provided by the Ministry of Chemical Industries. Even though these proved problematic and were mostly closed down after the GLF, the Ministry continued its research efforts and was instrumental in pushing through technical improvements that spawned a new generation of small fertiliser plants during the Cultural Revolution period.[5] Similarly, in the farm machinery industry, the First Ministry of Machine-building played an active role in developing prototype models of machinery for domestic production (Interviews in Guangdong and Beijing, 1982).

Even with the substantial material and technical support, however, under the policy of decentralisation all was routed through local governments. A trial *baogan* system was proposed in 1970, whereby provinces took responsibility for the unified allocation of investment funds, equipment, and construction materials for the five small industries (Deng Liqun, Ma Hong and Wu Heng, 1984; 142). Although it is not known whether this system was fully implemented, such subcontracting arrangements characterised much of the interaction among administrative levels during the Cultural Revolution period, whereby each level was assigned specific responsibilities, along with the resources needed to carry them out. Through this combination of turning over resources to local management, setting up turnkey plants at the local level with seed money and technical aid, and strengthening local machine-building industries, the strategy was to help localities to gradually acquire the technical and productive capabilities for building, managing, and supplying local industries to meet local needs. Next we turn to the fertiliser industry to see how this strategy went awry.

THE POLICY ENVIRONMENT FOR SMALL FERTILISER PLANTS

As with all rural industries, anecdotal reports from the Cultural Revolution period tended to emphasise the self-reliant aspects of local fertiliser plants. Because of their small scale and lower technical requirements, these enterprises could be financed from local savings, using local materials and labour to produce for a local market. Though they were often set up with some 'seed money' from the state and technical aid, once in operation these enterprises were locally managed and self-sustaining, requiring little supervision or coordination from above. For example, one report told of how the Changshou County Chemical Fertiliser Plant (in Jiangsu province) was financed. Peasants were overjoyed when they heard in 1966 that plans were underway in the county to build a small fertiliser plant. To contribute toward investment, production teams vied with each other in withdrawing their collective accumulation funds from the bank. Since total investment costs for the plant (with annual capacity of 5000 tons of ammonia) worked out to only a little more than 2 yuan per *mou* for the county's farmland, the burden was well within local financial capability. After giving due consideration to the needs of agricultural production, the county revolutionary committee decided to borrow 3.09 million yuan from one-third of the county's communes and production teams. The rest of the investment, another 1.25 million yuan, was raised by the county financial departments. Since going onstream in May 1970, the plant supplied 80 jin of fertiliser per year to each *mou* of farmland, surpassing the target set in the Agricultural Mechanisation Programme. Furthermore, when the plant turned a profit, loans from production teams were repaid with interest (Shen Xingda and Chen Zhaoxin 1976, pp. 10–13 and interview with a plant official, June 1982).

In reality, the development of small fertiliser plants was a key project during the Cultural Revolution, and the extent of state involvement in the industry was much greater than previously believed. In the fertiliser industry, provinces were assigned the overall responsibilities for allocating funds, equipment, coal supplies and technical personnel for the fertiliser plants. Rather than acting simply as agents in distributing block transfers of resources allocated under state plans, this arrangement often required provinces to take on substantial planning initiative in developing supplementary local supplies, since state allocations were deliberately kept below the actual needs of the fertiliser plants. In addition, provinces often provided a variety of financial subsidies, including production subsidies to the plants themselves, as well as price subsidies paid to the suppliers and distributors of their inputs and outputs. Counties were responsible for the day-to-day operation of the plants. In this task, they made production plans, recruited workers, coordinated supplies and deliveries, and allocated the finished products from the plants. Initially, the Ministry of Chemical Industries had played an active role in approving projects, and small plants were often built under provincial supervision and management. In the early 1970s, there was a further decentralisation of resources and responsibilities, when counties assumed greater autonomy over investment as well (fieldwork information, June–July 1982).

Given the substantial mixing of resources and sharing of responsibilities under the arrangement of 'subcontracting by administrative level', it is often difficult to decipher either the exact origin of resources provided or the locus of decision-making. Fortunately, for the purpose of evaluating the Maoist decentralisation strategy, it is sufficient to ascertain whether resources were *local*, stemming from the county or collective, or *state*, coming from the central government, its ministries, and provincial departments. In this section, I will attempt to make this distinction for some key aspects of investment decisions.

FINANCING INVESTMENT

Anecdotal reports such as the one from Changshou County implied that much of the investment funding for small fertiliser plants was raised locally, outside of the state sector. However, this is not borne out by aggregate statistics, which show that state budgetary allocations for investment and technical renovations for small fertiliser plants totalled over 8 billion yuan during 1958–80. (These are estimates made by the Ministry of Chemical Industries and reported in Li Wenji 1981, p. 4). If these estimates are correct, and if the ratio of investment to fixed capital formation was about two-thirds, then state funds directly financed about two-thirds of total investment in the industry.[6]

These budgetary allocations were supplemented by a mixture of borrowed funds and 'internal resources' of the county and its enterprises. As the example from Changshou showed earlier, agricultural collectives were also expected to contribute by lending portions of their public accumulation funds (and labour). While borrowing from collective accumulation funds clearly tapped a source of savings outside the state sector, the use of 'local' funds of governmental units and enterprises is much more ambiguous. In the consolidated budgetary accounts in China, virtually all state revenues are collected by local governments, and it is often difficult to distinguish 'local' funds from those destined to be remitted upward through the hierarchy. In the Changshou case, the 1.25 million yuan that was raised by county financial departments may well have come from state budgetary revenues. During the Cultural Revolution period, much of what was called 'local, self-raised funds' were actually funds directly and indirectly transferred out of the state budget, mainly by tapping enterprise depreciation funds, diverting enterprise profits, and exempting enterprises from tax payments.[7] Since these three sources involve funds that were either transferred from, or destined for, the state budget, I will consider them state funds for the purpose of this accounting.

'Replacement and renovation' funds are set aside by enterprises and entered as current production costs for replacing worn-out capital. As part of the fiscal decentralisation policy that sought to place more resources under local management, beginning in 1967 local enterprises were allowed to retain these depreciation and major repairs allowances. With the decentralisation of all nonmilitary enterprises to local control in the early 1970s, local governments gained control over the bulk of 'replacement and renovation' funds. With these funds growing to several billion yuan by the mid-1970s, they had become a large and stable source of revenue for local governments, the bulk of which was diverted to investment in new enterprises. As indicated by the Ministry of Chemical Industries estimate cited above, these depreciation allowances were pooled with budgetary allocations to finance the bulk of investment in small fertiliser plants.

Another important source of 'local' funds was the diversion of enterprise profits, which took various forms; by including investment expenditures in current production costs, by allocating 'assignments' to state enterprises to provide equipment, funds and technical aid to setting up new enterprises; and by 'borrowing' funds, equipment and personnel across enterprises. All of these involved transferring investment costs to the state budget through depleting profits or creating losses, under practices that were condoned and even encouraged by the various levels of government. Under the system of remitting most or all industrial profits and losses to the state budget, neither local governments nor enterprises had any interest in profitability *per se*. In addition, local governments were given the authority to grant temporary tax relief to local enterprises in financial difficulty, which provided an opportunity to divert tax revenues to local use.[8]

The relevance of these irregular financing practices is reflected in the typical development path followed by small fertiliser plants, almost all of which began with design capacities of 3000 or 5000 tons of ammonia per year. Once their initial technical problems were solved, many plants embarked on expanding their capacity by adding a second or even third set of equipment. For example, the Xinhui County Fertiliser Plant (Guangdong) went onstream in 1972 with a design capacity of 5000 tons. By 1974 it began the second phase of construction, when a second set of equipment was added to double the plant's capacity. In a visit to the plant in 1982, I was told that most of the 7 million yuan investment for the second phase was 'raised' by the plant itself, with only a minor portion from state funds. The manager explained that 'most of the (investment) costs was included under production costs, which accounted for our huge losses during the mid-70s'. Similarly, the neighbouring Kaiping Plant attributed their high costs during the early 1970s to the expansion project that went onstream in 1975, explaining that 'we had a lot of basic capital construction expenses during those years' (fieldwork information, June–July, 1982). Since the portion of investment financed by the diversion of profits (and losses) cannot be estimated, we can assume that it is not included in the figure of 8 billion yuan cited by the Ministry of Chemical Industries. When all these supplementary sources of finance are included, the true share of state funds in total investment in small fertiliser plants was greater than two-thirds.

FINANCING OPERATING COSTS

An important consideration in applying the policy of local self-reliance to rural industrialisation was that these plants should be self-supporting. To this end, the structure of prices was set to allow a plant performing at an average level to generate revenues in excess of costs. In 1958, handbooks on small fertiliser plants had projected costs of ammonium bicarbonate to be around 100 yuan/ton (see, for examples, Ministry of Chemical Industries 1958: 6; and Xie Zheng 1958: 1). With wholesale prices set at 150–190 yuan/ton, small plants should have been very profitable. Some were. For example, the 10 plants in suburban Shanghai reported that once they overcame initial technical problems, beginning in 1963 they operated profitably even though prices were lowered 5 times between 1963 and 1966, so that the wholesale price in 1966 was only half what it had been in 1961 (*Shanghai Jingji* 1981, p. 249). In 1975, the Lin County Fertiliser Plant was reportedly earning a 33 per cent annual rate of return to investment on a wholesale price of 180 yuan/ton (ARSID 1975, p. 99,

TABLE 1.2 *Machine-building capabilities by province*

Province	Number of fertiliser Plants 1/	1975 Gross of industrial output 2/	Acquisition date	Comment
Jiangsu	77	26.59	1958	Province made its first set of equipment in 1958. By 1970, it was more than self-sufficient in the manufacture of fertiliser equipment, making more than 20 sets/yr.
Hebei	120	24.87	1958*	NA
Shandong	135	20.99	1966	Province had made over 100 sets by 1973.
Guangdong	86	20.28	pre-1966	In 1966, province made 10 sets of equipment for plants with annual output capacities of 3,000 tons of ammonia, and 4 sets of equipment with annual output capacities of 5,000 tons of ammonia.
Sichuan	100	17.47	pre-1970	In 1971, over 350 factories were organised to build a total of 43 sets of equipment for small fertiliser plants.
Henan	148	11.96	1968	By May, 1972, 50 small fertiliser plants had been built with locally made sets of equipment. Basically self-sufficient.
Hubei	43	10.10	pre-1971	Province's 100+ country-level machinery plants co-operate in making complete sets of equipment.
Zhejiang	53	8.42	pre-1970	NA
Hunan	91	8.40	1970	Province had made 80–90 sets by November 1975. 23 sets made in 1970 alone.
Gansu	20	7.73	NA	Lanzhou Chemical Company had helped build or expand 12 plants during 1970–72.
Anhui	73	7.33	1971	In 1971–72, equipment of various kinds has been produced to equip plants in 28 counties.
Shanxi	84	6.78	NA	NA
Guangxi	73	4.93	1970	Wuzhou City Boiler Works produced 15 complete sets of equipment for fertiliser plants.
Fujian	37	4.63	pre-1971	NA

SOURCE: Wong, *Maoism and Development*, manuscript, Chapter 4 (which also cites specific sources for each province).

Table IV-6). As recently as 1980, spokesmen for the Ministry of Chemical Industries claimed that at current prices, a plant producing 40,000 tons of ammonium bicarbonate could generate profits of 2–3.6 million yuan per year (Li Qingchun and Sun Weiming, 1982, p. 101). Instead, technical and supply problems in the industry, along with falsified accounting, pushed actual costs to much higher levels, averaging 250 yuan/ton in 1976, before the inclusion of subsidies.[9]

Because of the much higher-than-expected costs, production subsidies began to be introduced in the early 1970s to help sustain production in small fertiliser plants. These subsidies were authorised by the central government and set by authorities in each province (Fang, 1984, p. 467). In Guangdong Province, they appeared to have been set on a firm-by-firm basis, ranging from 10 to 40–50 yuan per ton of fertiliser output. In Xinhui County, for example, these subsidies began in 1972 at 40 yuan per ton. In 1978 they were reduced to 20 yuan, and in 1979 to only 10 yuan. In neighbouring Kaiping County, the fertiliser plant received subsidies only during 1974–77, when they were 20 yuan/ton (Fieldwork, 1982).[10] If we assume subsidies of 15–20 yuan/ton were applied to all of the estimated 200 million tons of ammonium bicarbonate produced during 1966–80,[11] we can estimate that direct subsidies totalled 3–4 billion yuan.

As beneficiaries of the effort to hold down costs in the 'aid-agriculture' industries, fertiliser plants also enjoyed reduced prices for their inputs, the most important of which are electricity and coal. Applying an estimated subsidy of 3 fen/kwh and an average use of 1841 kwh/ton of ammonia output (derived from the 1976–80 average), an indirect subsidy of 12.3 yuan/ton output and a total of 2.5 billion yuan is derived for the industry's electricity-use for the period.[12] The subsidy embedded in coal supplies for fertiliser production is more difficult to estimate, since coal prices were allowed to vary to some extent across localities to reflect different cost conditions, so that fertiliser plants faced very different prices for this input. Nevertheless, a conservative estimate of 2.1 yuan per ton fertiliser output, or a total of 460 million yuan, can be derived from average losses in coal mining operations, which are used as proxies for the gap between the real resource cost of mining coal and the supply price.[13]

Finally, in spite of these subsidies, cumulative losses for the industry totalled over Y4.5 billion during the 15 years from 1966 to 1980 (Li Wenji 1983, p. 45), which were more or less routinely absorbed by the budget at the various administrative levels. These cumulative losses constituted the largest item of indirect subsidy to the small fertiliser plants, although a substantial part may have gone to financing investment. Adding together

TABLE 1.3 *Provincial distribution of fertiliser plants*

Provinces	Remaining number of plants	Closures	Highest number reported	1977
Anhui	73		73	
Beijing	8	−3	11	
Fujian	36	−1	37	37
Gansu	6	−14	20	
Guangdong	57	−29	86	80
Guangxi	55	−18	73	73
Guizhou	10		10	
Hebei	120		120	
Heilongjiang	20	−29	49	
Henan	148		148	
Hubei	43		43	
Hunan	91		91	88
Jiangsu	73	−4	77	
Jiangxi	35		35	
Jilin	21	−1	22	
Liaoning	46		46	
Nei Menggu	13	−6	19	12
Ningxia	17		17	
Qinghai	5		5	
Shaanxi	30	−3	33	
Shandong	128	−7	135	
Shanghai	10	−1	11	11
Shanxi	84		84	
Sichuan	100		100	100
Tianjin	1		1	
Xinjiang	7		7	7
Xizang	1		1	
Yunnan	22	−26	48	
Zhejiang	53		53	
Column Sum	1313	−142	1435	
Actual Total			1539	

SOURCE: Wong, *Maoism and Development*, manuscript, Chapter 4.
Where numbers are not available for the benchmarked years, the highest previous reported number issued. Beijing, Shanghai, Tianjin, Tibet, Qinghai are taken out as outliers.

TABLE 1.3 *(continued)*

1976	1975	1974	1973	1972	1971	1970	1965	
73						30		Anhui
	11							Beijing
32		29	27					Fujian
			15	9				Gansu
65	55	51	49	41			2	Guangdong
61	45	34	19		15			Guangxi
								Guizhou
119	100			45	45		1–2	Hebei
								Heilongjiang
146	121	86				16*	2	Henan
			43			10*	3	Hubei
87	86	84				2	1	Hunan
	77			72		57	12	Jiangsu
		20						Jiangxi
								Jilin
			46					Liaoning
	10						1	Nei Menggu
								Ningxia
							1	Qinghai
								Shaanxi
	114					55	7	Shandong
	114					11*	11	Shanghai
70						20	1	Shanxi
90	73	65		26		1	1	Sichuan
								Tianjin
								Xinjiang
	1	0	0	0	0	0	0	Xizang
			15					Yunnan
				31			5	Zhejiang
								Column Sum
								Actual Total

* 1969

the 'losses' of 4.5 billion yuan, production subsidies of Y3–4 billion, and the indirect subsidies of Y2.5 billion and Y460 million through the underpricing of electric power and coal supplies respectively, the total bill for fertiliser production came to an additional Y10.5–11.5 billion over reported costs. If spread uniformly over all output during the 1966–80 period, these subsidies would have added 230–250 yuan/ton to the cost of ammonia, or 50–55 yuan/ton to the cost of ammonium bicarbonate (equal to an additional 20–25 per cent). Even though most of these subsidies and losses were paid out of county and provincial budgets, under the highly centralised fiscal system in use during the Cultural Revolution period, they were eventually passed along to the state budget.

THE PROVISION OF PRODUCTION EQUIPMENT

As described earlier, the Ministry of Chemical Industries had played a key role in the research and development of small-scale fertiliser plants. Once the technology was developed and prototype plants were designed, however, the task of making production equipment for small plants was gradually turned over to provincial coordination, with provinces encouraged to strive for self-reliance and self-sufficiency in equipping the plants. To this end, much technical assistance was provided in helping provinces to acquire the machine-building capability. Central design and research institutes provided the blueprints and training, along with the key machine tools. Because the manufacture of the high pressure compressors and other equipment needed in fertiliser production require large-scale, complex machine tools, these machine-building plants were often elaborately equipped. For example, a 1975 delegation of visitors found the Xinxiang Prefectural Chemical Equipment and Accessory Plant (in Henan Province) to be equipped with sophisticated machinery imported from Japan, Italy, Korea, and the Soviet Union, along with equipment made in China's leading industrial centres including Beijing, Tianjin, Wuhan and Changchun (ARSID, p. 98).

Table 1.2 presents a summary of provincial reports on their ability to produce fertiliser equipment. Since machine-building is a skill-intensive industry that is highly dependent on an available pool of trained and experienced workers, the level of sophistication of machine-building enterprises tends to be correlated with the level of industrial development in the region. It is therefore not surprising that the industrially most developed provinces had acquired the equipment manufacturing capability at the earliest date: Jiangsu, Hebei, Shandong and Guangdong were the top four provinces in gross value of industrial output (excluding the three large municipalities of Beijing, Shanghai, Tianjin and the Northeast provinces). What is salient is that this capability spread quickly to other provinces with distinctly lower levels of industrial development, testifying to the commitment of state resources to effect this outcome. In 1975, a spokesman in the Ministry of Chemical Industries confirmed that about half of the provinces were able to produce whole sets of equipment.[14]

In some provinces, locally made equipment quickly supplanted state-allocated equipment. Comparing Tables 1.2 and 1.3 , we find the number of fertiliser plants in Hunan and Shandong provinces to correspond closely to the reported numbers of sets of equipment made. In Henan province, by 1974 about 60 of the existing 86 plants were reportedly using equipment produced and installed by factories in the province (Henan Provincial Service, 20 October 1974, BBC W799/A/22). Similarly, in Guangdong Province, while early plants were mostly equipped with machinery from Shanghai, plants built in the mid-late 1970s were almost entirely equipped with machinery made within the province (fieldwork information, 1982). Nevertheless, state-owned plants continued to produce a significant portion of production equipment. For example, during 1971–73, machine-building plants in Shanghai reportedly produced 300 sets of equipment, which accounted for about 60 per cent of all plants added during the period (see Table 1.1) (NCNA January 11, 1974, in SCMP 5539: 52–3). In addition to the Shanghai plants, large-scale chemical plants in Nanjing, Lanzhou and Henan were also reportedly making fertiliser equipment for state allocation.

DYSFUNCTIONAL OUTCOMES

What we can deduce from the examination of the policy environment for small fertiliser plants is as follows: firstly, the costs of financing investment and operating losses were borne mostly by the state; secondly, the responsibilities for supplying equipment and current inputs remained substantially with the state; thirdly, however, the advantages of the fertiliser plants as symbols of modernity and progress, the jobs created, and the fertilisers produced all accrued to the counties. This lopsided incentive structure allowed localities to socialise the (financial) losses while privatising the gains. Not surprisingly, county governments had little incentive to prevent inappropriate projects or to run the enterprises efficiently.

Both technically and financially, small fertiliser plants were in the late 1970s performing at a level that was far below not only levels expected

TABLE 1.4 *Fertiliser Plant Indexes*

	Number of Plants at Peak	No. of Counties/ Towns	Peak Index	1977	1977 Index
Anhui	73	78	0.94	73	0.94
Fujian	37	65	0.57	37	0.57
Gansu	20	78	0.26	20	0.26
Guangdong	86	107	0.80	80	0.75
Guangxi	73	86	0.85	73	0.85
Guizhou	10	83	0.12	10	0.12
Hebei	120	148	0.81	120	0.81
Heilongjiang	44	85	0.52	49	0.58
Henan	148	124	1.19	148	1.19
Hubei	43	79	0.54	43	0.54
Hunan	91	97	0.94	88	0.91
Jiangsu	77	75	1.03	77	1.03
Jiangxi	35	88	0.40	35	0.40
Jilin	22	58	0.38	22	0.38
Liaoning	46	64	0.72	46	0.72
Nei Menggu	19	49	0.34	33	0.34
Ningxia	135	115	1.17	135	1.17
Shaanxi	33	98	0.34	33	0.34
Shandong	135	115	1.17	135	1.17
Shanxi	84	108	0.78	81	0.75
Sichuan	100	193	0.52	100	0.52
Xinjiang	7	84	0.08	7	0.08
Yunnan	48	125	0.38	52	0.76
Zhejiang	53	68	0.78	52	0.76
Column Sum				1398	
Reported National Total				1450	0.75
Average			0.642		
Minimum			0.083		
Maximum			1.194		

SOURCE, Wong, *Maoism and Development*, manuscript, Chapter 4.
Where numbers are not available for the benchmarked years, the highest previous reported number is used. Beijing, Shanghai, Tianjin, Tibet, Qinghai are taken out as outliers.

TABLE 1.4 (*continued*)

1973	1973 Index	1970	1970 Index	1965	1965 Index	
51	0.65	30	0.38			Anhui
29	0.45					Fujian
15	0.19					Gansu
49	0.46	2	0.02	2	0.02	Guangdong
19	0.22					Guangxi
						Guizhou
45	0.30	2	0.01	2	0.01	Hebei
36	0.42					Heilongjiang
16	0.13	16	0.13	2	0.02	Henan
43	0.54	10	0.13	3	0.04	Hubei
2	0.02	2	0.02	1	0.01	Hunan
72	0.96	57	0.76	12	0.16	Jiangsu
						Jiangxi
						Jilin
46	0.72					Liaoning
1	0.02	1	0.02	1	0.02	Nei Menggu
						Ningxia
						Shaanxi
101	0.88	55	0.48	7	0.06	Shandong
45	0.42	20	0.19	1	0.01	Shanxi
26	0.13	1	0.01	1	0.01	Sichuan
						Xinjiang
15	0.12	7	0.06			Yunnan
31	0.46	5	0.07	5	0.07	Zhejiang
		208		37		Column sum
		455		87		Reported national total
	0.394		0.175		0.022	Average
	0.020		0.005		0.000	Minimum
	0.960		0.760		0.160	Maximum

in the technical blueprints, but also below average performance of the mid-late 1960s. Part of the problem was that expansion of any programme from a small, experimental base to a massive programme of national scope inevitably runs into bottlenecks in supply, problems of labour recruitment, dilution of technical supervision and support, and so on. These problems were greatly exacerbated by the rapid pace of construction, which far outstripped the economy's capability to keep up with the growing demand for inputs. The Ministry of Chemical Industries had originally planned to add 20–40 small fertiliser plants per year during the Third and Fourth Five Year Plans. This was quickly exceeded with the start of the Cultural Revolution, when the pace accelerated and averaged over 120 plants per year during the 1970–78 period. At the peak during 1970–73, 147, 174, 191, and 141 plants were built. This rapid pace of plant construction severely strained the economy's capability to supply coal, equipment and technical personnel. The resultant decline in the quality of coal supplies, capital goods and labour all contributed to the many technical problems faced by the industry. During 1970–76, technical and supply problems combined to produce very low rates of capacity utilisation, which hovered between 50–70 per cent, contributing to the high costs (Wong [manuscript] chapter 4).

These problems were also exacerbated by the locational pattern of development, which seemed to stress regional equalisation over economic considerations. The location of fertiliser plants near coal resources and markets is crucial to their economic viability, since the diseconomies of their small size have to be offset by the savings in transport costs. Because fertiliser production involves bulky inputs of coal, with a weight ratio of input to output that is close to one, the transport-saving advantage of locating near users can be realised only if inputs are also locally available.

However, two broad features of the locational pattern suggest that the distribution of coal resources was not the most important factor in project selection. First, there was an unmistakable trend toward regional equalisation. Table 1.4 shows the ratio of fertiliser plants to the number of counties or towns converging toward 1 in most provinces. By the end of the period, in 1978, 16 of the 26 provinces and regions had more than 0.5 plants per county or town, and 12 of them had 'basically' reached the goal of building small fertiliser plants, with a plant index of 0.7 or more, including many provinces that had few coal resources. Indeed, a later assessment by the Ministry of Chemical Industries concluded that conditions did not exist for supporting production in small fertiliser plants in the two 'Guang's' (Guangdong, Guangxi), the two 'Hu's' (Hunan, Hubei), Jiangxi and Fujian

(Li Wenji, 1983, p. 44). Nonetheless, all but Jiangxi had plant indexes exceeding 0.5: 0.57 in Fujian, 0.8 in Guangdong, 0.85 in Guangxi, 0.54 in Hubei, 0.94 in Hunan. Even in Jiangxi, there were more than 35 plants (Table 1.4).

The second feature is that a province's machine-building capability seemed to be an important factor in determining the number of plants built. For the coal-poor provinces such as Guangdong, Guangxi, and Hunan, it seemed to be the dominant factor that overrode other considerations in plant construction. In comparing Tables 1.2 and 1.3, the equalisation of plants across provinces seemed to follow roughly the spread of the capability to make production equipment. Since machine-building capability is uncorrelated to the availability of coal, this feature also indicates that coal was not the key determinant of plant location.

CONCLUSION

The problems of the chemical fertiliser industry provide stark illustration of Maoist policies gone awry. On the one hand, the industry suffered from many inefficiencies associated with central planning, where local officials have little incentive to economise on the use of state resources. This is seen in the problematic locational pattern of fertiliser plants, where local participation failed to prevent the selection of inappropriate plant sites. Instead, from the county's perspective, the fertiliser plants had come to be seen as 'entitlements' – with policies that gave all the benefits of local production to the localities while freeing them from bearing the costs of failure, all the incentives were in favour of building more plants, whose location was of concern only in defining claims to state resources.

The inefficiencies of overcentralisation are even more clearly illustrated by the pattern of coal supplies for small fertiliser plants. In 1979, it was found that nationwide, only one-quarter of all small fertiliser plants were using 'local' coal as feedstock, and less than half were using coal from within the province. The situation was only slightly better for fuel coal, with 25.6 per cent using local coal for fuel and 54.5 per cent using coal from within the province (Li Wenji, 1983, p. 57). Paradoxically, while this is important evidence pointing to the failure of small fertiliser plants to realise transport savings, it actually contains little information about the location of plants relative to coal resources.

As long as small fertiliser plants were entitled to coal allocations from higher levels, local officials had little incentive to find local supplies for them. This was especially true in the coal-scarce southern provinces,

TABLE 1.5 *Interprovincial Transfers of Coal*
(thousands tons)

Provinces	In-shipments	Out-shipments	Net transfers
Anhui	3290	5970	2680
Beijing	12760	2650	−10110
Fujian	2350	0	−2350
Gansu	4180	700	−3480
Guangdong	4910	0	−4910
Guangxi	2040	0	−2040
Guizhou	0	2580	2580
Hebei	0	12120	2490
Heilongjiang	9200	6010	
Henan	3850	15400	11550
Hubei	10740	0	−10740
Hunan	3100	140	−2960
Jiangsu	11180	2640	−8540
Jiangxi	1660	770	−890
Jilin	5850	620	−5230
Liaoning	21220	950	−20270
Nei Menggu	4520	6120	1600
Ningxia	210	5250	5040
Qinghai	1130	0	−1130
Shaanxi	1760	4280	2520
Shandong	5440	5860	420
Shanghai	15180	0	−15180
Shanxi	0	74260	74260
Sichuan	1290	0	−1290
Tianjin	9640	0	−9640
Xinjiang	0	1660	1660
Xizang	na	na	0
Yunnan	320	0	−320
Zhejiang	7300	0	−7300

SOURCE: *Chinese Coal Industry Yearbook* (1983) p. 75.

where the cost of extracting coal often exceeded the state allocation price. Furthermore, pervasive shortages through the Cultural Revolution period often raised the real value of coal far above state allocation prices.[15] In order to minimise costs or maximise local output and income, local coal would be husbanded for use in industries that were not entitled to state allocations. In Kaiping County, for example, the fertiliser plant used coal that originated in Anhui, Shanxi and Hunan and routed through the Canton coalyards, while the county's Jinji Coal Mine was supplying coal to the local cement plant (Interview information, May 1978).

Perhaps all that is conveyed by these aggregate figures on the origin of coal for small fertiliser plants is that, in 1979, approximately half the plants were located in provinces that were self-sufficient in coal supplies – hence half the small plants were using coal from 'within the province'. Indeed, Table 1.5 shows that in 1982, 11 of the 26 provinces were net exporters of coal, and these provinces accounted for 45 per cent of all plants (Table 1.3). If this interpretation is correct, then it seems the policy of incorporating supply for small fertiliser plants into state plans had produced an astonishingly dysfunctional and costly outcome.

As the same time, decentralisation had eroded central control over some crucial economic levers, most notably the overall pace of investment, as well as project selection. During the early part of the Cultural Revolution period, central ministries could assert control over the pace of development and the location of small fertiliser plants, through the allocation of investment funding and production equipment. By the early 1970s, this control was significantly eroded, when rural industries had reached a critical mass where they were generating substantial resources, both financial and material, that allowed local industrialisation to continue without state aid. The decentralisation of machine-building capability to provinces was a key contributor to this loss of state control, since local machine-building capability provided a source of capital goods outside of state channels, which completed the necessary ingredients for setting up production.

The problems of the rural industrialisation programme provide clear illustration of the contradictory impulses that motivated Maoist economic policies. Rural industrialisation was implemented under the principle of local self-reliance, where development was to be based largely on local resources and local initiative. Yet it was a programme rigidly controlled from the top, which determined the scope and objectives. The conflicting aims of local participation and central control interacted to produce a situation where control often became divorced from responsibility, with unforeseen and extremely undesirable outcomes. In the post-Mao reform period, many problems stem from the same source: how to turn over decision-making authority to lower level units and to induce them to behave in ways that conform to social objectives is a problem that remains to be solved.

ABBREVIATIONS

ARSID	American Rural Small-scale Industry Delegation
BBC	British Broadcasting Corporation, Summary of World Broadcasts: Far East
GYJJ	*Gongye Jingji* [Industrial Economics], (People's University, Beijing).
JJGL	*Jingji Guanli* [Economic Management], (Beijing).
NCNA	New China News Agency
SCMP	*Survey of China Mainland Press*, (Hong Kong, U.S. Consulate).

NOTES

1. This revised view argues that 'local self-reliance' was accomplished primarily by massive transfers of resources to local management, rather than through mobilisation of local resources. See Wong, 1990.
2. For examples of this view, see Ding Hua (1981), Liu Guoguang (1981), and Ma Hong and Sun Shangqing (1981). In the secondary literature, see Wong (1986b), Lyons (1987) and Tidrick and Chen (1987). This was commonly referred to as the problem of *tiaotiao kuaikuai*.
3. This included a variety of key producers' goods such as steel, lumber, coal and petroleum products. In contrast to earlier periods, nearly all of these administrative allocations were being made at the provincial level and below (interview information, Beijing, November 1988).
4. The 1966 plan was proposed by Mao and adopted by the First National Conference on Farm Mechanisation held in July 1966, in Hubei. It set ambitious targets for a 15-year period, to be achieved in three phases. During the first phase which was to take 5–7 years, mechanised ploughing would be expanded from about 15 per cent of farmland in 1965 to over 25 per cent, mechanised irrigation and drainage would be expanded from 32 per cent of farmland to over 50 per cent , and the application of chemical fertilisers would be raised from 13.5 to about 30 jin per mou. The processing of agricultural produce would be basically mechanised, and transport would be semi-mechanised. During the second phase, to be completed by 1975, one-half to two-thirds of all farmland would be mechanically ploughed, 60–65 per cent would

be mechanically irrigated and drained, chemical fertiliser use would reach 50 jin per mou, and processing and transport would be further mechanised. By 1980, at the end of the third phase, mechanisation should be basically completed (Fang Weizhong, 1984, pp. 412–3 and *Nongye Nianjian* 1980, p. 40).

5. For a detailed discussion of this development history, see Wong, 1986a: 1330–1.

6. At year end 1989, small plants had total fixed assets worth 8.8 million yuan (Li 1981, p. 4). Nationwide, the ratio of investment to capital formation was 70 per cent for the period 1950–79, with Y454 billion in added fixed assets from investments totalling Y652 billion. However, the ratio had declined spectacularly through the period, from 83.7 per cent during the FFYP to only 60 per cent during the third and fourth FYPS (Ma and Sun, 1981, p. 77).

7. For a detailed exploration of the financing of rural industry, see Wong, 1990.

8. Tax relief was often granted for income taxes on profits of collective enterprises, as well as turnover taxes (industrial-commercial taxes) for both state and collective enterprises. By exempting an enterprise from either income or turnover taxes, the local government reduces total cost and increases net profits, which can then be diverted in the usual fashion to investment or other uses.

9. This estimate is based on production cost data in Wong (manuscript), Chapter 4.

10. Subsidies were also reported in Henan's Nanyang Prefecture during 1971–81 (GYJJ 1982: 15, pp. 24–5), Jiangsu's Suzhou Prefecture, Shaanxi's Hanyang Prefecture, and Shandong province (Fieldwork, 1981–82, and the Chinese press, passim).

11. This is derived from the estimated cumulative output of 45.2 million tons of ammonia, Wong (1986a), Table 1.1.

12. This is a conservative estimate based on reported costs of around 5 fen/kwh for electricity used in fertiliser plants, compared with the normal state price of 8 fen for industrial use. Fieldwork information, 1981–82.

13. This is based on average losses of 1.8 yuan/ton in state-run mines and 4 yuan/ton in local mines (JJGL, 8: 1980), and assuming that fertiliser plants used equal portions of coal from each sector. An average coefficient of 3.27 tons of coal/ton ammonia for the 1976–80 period is used to estimate total coal use of nearly 160 million tons during 1966–80.

14. Interview with Tang Zhongnan, Minister of Chemical Industries, ARSID Notes, p. 40.

15. This was true whenever coal was a bottleneck that constrained local industrial growth, in which case the shadow price of coal would be equal to the marginal increase in industrial output made possible by an additional unit of coal.

48   *The Road to Crisis*

REFERENCES

Chen Dunyi and Hu Jishan (eds), 1983, *Zhongguo jingji dili* [China's Economic Geography], (Beijing, Zhongguo Zhanwang Chubanshe).

Deng Liqun, Ma Hong and Wu Heng (eds), 1984, *Dangdai Zhongguo de Jingji Tizhi Gaige* [Contemporary Chinese Economic System Reform] (Beijing, Chinese Academy of Social Sciences Press).

Ding Hua, 1981, 'A Basic Cause of Poor Results of Investment Lies in the Economic Management System – an Investigation of the Municipality of Huangshi', *Jingji Yanjiu* [Economic Research], 1981: 3.

Ellman, Michael, *Socialist Planning*, 1979 (London, Cambridge University Press).

Fang Weizhong, editor, 1984, *Zonghua Renmin Gongheguo Jingji Dashiji, 1949–1980* [Compendium of main economic events in the People's Republic of China, 1949–1980] (Beijing, Chinese Academy of Social Sciences Press).

Jiang Yiwei, 1980, 'The Theory of an Enterprise-based Economy', *Social Sciences in China*, I. 1.

Li Qingchun and Sun Weiming, 1982, 'Our Experience in Building Small and Medium-sized Plants in China', UNIDO, Seminar on Mini-Fertiliser Plants, Proceedings, Lahore, Pakistan, 15–20 November (668.62.S48s) pp. 87–107.

Li Wenji 1981, 'An Inquiry the Future Prospects of Our Country's Small-scale Nitrogenous Fertiliser Industry', a Masters Thesis at the Chinese Academy of Social Sciences, Beijing.

Li Wenji 1983, 'A Survey of the Small-scale Nitrogenous Fertiliser Industry in China', *Jingji Diaocha* (Economic Survey), 2, pp. 1–11; in JPRS-CEA-85–028, pp. 43–59.

Liu Guoguang (ed.), 1981, *Guomin jingji guanli tizhi gaige de ruogan lilun wenti* [Some theoretical issues in the reform of the national economic system], (Beijing, Chinese Academy of Social Sciences Press).

Lyons, Thomas P., 1985, 'China's Cellular Economy: a Test of the Fragmentation Hypothesis', *Journal of Comparative Economics*, 9, 2, (June) pp. 125–144.

Ma Hong and Sun Shangqing, Eds., 1981, *Zhongguo Jingji Jiegou Wenti Yanjiu* [Research on the problems of China's economic structure] (Beijing, Chinese Academy of Social Sciences Press).

Ministry of Agriculture, Policy Research Office, Ed., 1979, *Zhongguo Nongye Jiben Qingkuang*, [The Basic Situation of China's Agriculture] (Beijing, Agricultural Press).

Ministry of Chemical Industries, Industrial Design Department, Editors, 1958, *Gezhong Xiaoxing Huafeichang, Nongyaochang Dingxing Sheji Jieshao* [Introducing Selected Designs for Different Types of Chemical Fertiliser and Pesticide Plants] (Beijing, Chemical Industry Press).

Shanghai Jingji, [Shanghai's Economy], 1981 (Shanghai, People's Press).

Shen Xingda and Chen Zhaoxin, 1976, 'Small-scale Chemical Fertiliser Plants are Scattered throughout Our Rural Villages', *Jingji Daobao* [Economic Bulletin], Hong Kong, January 1.

Tam On-Kit, 1985, *China's Agricultural Modernization: the Socialist Mechanization Scheme* (London, Croom Helm Ltd).

Tidrick, Gene, and Chen Jiyuan, 1987, *China's Industrial Reform* (New York, Oxford University Press).

Wong, Christine P. W., *Maoism and Development: Rural Industrialization in the People's Republic of China*, manuscript.

Wong, Christine P. W., 1990, 'Maoism and Development: Local Self-reliance and the Financing of Rural Industrialization', in William Joseph, Christine Wong and David Zweig (eds), *New Perspectives on the Cultural Revolution* (Cambridge, Harvard University Press).

Wong, Christine P. W., 1986a, 'Intermediate Technology for Development: Small-scale Chemical Fertiliser Plants in China', *World Development*, October 1986a.

Wong, Christine P. W., 1986b, 'Ownership and Control in Chinese Industry: the Maoist Legacy and Prospects for the 1980s', in *Joint Economic Committee, U.S. Congress, China's Economy Looks Toward the Year 2000* (Washington, D.C., USGPO).

Xie Zheng, 1958, *Biandi Kaihuade Xiaoxing Danfeichang – Tansuan Qinganchang* [Small-scale Nitrogenous Fertiliser Plants are Sprouting Everywhere – Ammonium Bicarbonate Plants], Edited by the Anhui Provincial Association for the Popularization of Science and Technology (Beijing, Science Popularization Press).

Zhongguo Jingji Nianjian (ZGJJNJ) [Almanac of China's Economy] (Beijing: Economic Management Press), 1981, 1983.

2 Macroeconomic Management and System Reform in China

Barry Naughton

In a centrally planned economy, the dominant role of the state in the development process is clearly manifest in the nearly total state monopoly of investment. The state's taxation authority is harnessed to channel resources into new investment, and the mechanism of material balance planning is used to ensure that specific materials are directed to state priority projects. These priorities may include military objectives, but more generally the top priority is the rapid creation of a heavy industrial base through large-scale investment. However, as industrialisation proceeds, the objectives of the national leaders typically become more diversified and expand to include more than the single-minded pursuit of a heavy industrial base. Seeking improved efficiency and a greater diversity of output in order to meet a wider range of society's needs, such a leadership may contemplate a programme of economic reform. As part of this reform, the government seeks to improve the incentives of enterprises and households by giving them greater control over current income streams, a voice in investment decisions and some claim on the future product of those investment decisions. As a result, the state effectively abandons its monopoly over the investment process.

Yet while direct state control of investment is reduced, the desire of the state's leaders to direct and accelerate the industrialisation process remains at least as strong as before. As a result, those leaders face the difficult task of designing a system of indirect controls which can meet their objectives while simultaneously maintaining a stable macroeconomic environment conducive to economic reform. Since reforms typically involve major changes in the inter-sectoral distribution of income, balancing aggregate demands with the economy's potential supply can be extremely difficult. In China, the most important change in the inter-sectoral distribution of income has been that the share of disposable national income accruing to households has increased from 53 per cent to 65 per cent between 1978 and

50

1986, while income accruing to budgetary authorities has declined from 34 per cent to 23 per cent.[1] Thus, direct control of about one-eighth of national income has been taken away from the government and given to households. In this situation, the achievement of macroeconomic balance is in part a technical problem, demanding the creation of new instruments which will be effective in steering the economy under new conditions. It is also a political problem, for macro balance implies that the political system has managed to mediate effectively between competing claims on the total output of society during a period when those claims are changing dramatically. By controlling the budget deficit and the rate at which new bank credit is created, the state ultimately determines the rate at which economically effective claims on social output are allowed to expand – it controls the growth of aggregate demand. The political problem is thus whether the state can accommodate the vastly greater effective command over resources now exercised by households without creating macroeconomic imbalances. This requires either that the state's objectives be scaled back, or that new policies are created which allow the state to obtain its objectives indirectly. If it cannot somewhere reduce the claim on society's output to accommodate the increased demands of households, the result will be macroeconomic imbalance (inflation or intensified shortage), as total claims on society's output expand more rapidly than output itself. For the reform process to succeed in China, this transition process must be successfully managed.

This paper is divided into two major parts. First, I examine the broad changes in the roles, resources, and behaviour of major economic agents – government (predominantly central government), enterprises, and households. This begins with a primarily descriptive account, focusing on changes in saving and investment behaviour, and flows of saving between sectors. While the description is carried out in the economic vocabulary used in national income accounting, it should be borne in mind that underlying the changes so described are major changes in the disposition of control over output between different social groups. I then describe a dynamic process by which changes in macroeconomic balance affect the reform process. Since the changes under consideration are large, the transition towards a reformed economy is unlikely to be a smooth process. Instead, conflicts over resources and the direction of reform tend to create a cyclical pattern. In these cycles we can observe a double causality: reform causes changes in macroeconomic conditions and changes in macroeconomic conditions cause changes in reform strategies. This cyclical process can also be thought of as part of the long-term process of adjustment to the changing roles of different sectors in the economy.

The second part of the paper examines the question of whether, given the major changes described in the first part of the paper, the government possesses adequate instruments to maintain rough macroeconomic balance in the new economic environment. The Chinese government has attempted to move gradually from a reliance on its direct control over investment to manage the economy, to a reliance on indirect economic instruments, and in particular, monetary policy. While major successes have been recorded, as of 1988 the transition to a new set of macroeconomic instruments and policies has not been successfully made, and significant macroeconomic problems are surfacing in the Chinese economy. I briefly examine the causes of these problems, and the possibility that they can be overcome. The paper concludes with some observations about the changing role of the central government in the economy, and the prospects for future progress.

CHANGING BEHAVIOUR 1: SAVING AND INVESTMENT

Early in the reform process, Chinese economists proposed that the overall rate of investment in the economy should be reduced. Holding that excess rates of investment had unnecessarily depressed consumption and, by exceeding the economy's capacity, reduced overall efficiency, they called for a reduction in the pace of government mobilisation of investment resources. These economists argued that 'accumulation' – roughly equivalent to total investment – should be reduced to around 25 per cent of national income.[2] Actual accumulation rates had been consistently above 30 per cent during the 1970s, and had peaked at 36.5 per cent during the investment surge of 1978. While the political leadership never made a commitment to an accumulation rate as low as 25 per cent, it did accept the general principle of reducing that rate below 30 per cent, and the actual rate declined steadily to 28.3 per cent in 1981.[3] The decline in the weight of accumulation in the economy implied a reduction in the direct role of the central government, given the central role of the investment plan in government economic planning. Moreover, the reduction in government investment, by reducing total demand, permitted a 'slack' macroeconomic environment to emerge in 1981. As aggregate demand fell below aggregate supply, enterprises were forced to compete for customers, and this created many positive incentives for market-orientated behaviour by enterprises.[4]

However, accumulation as a percentage of national income began to increase again after 1981, and by 1985 reached 35.3 per cent, a level it has since maintained. Did this return to a high accumulation ratio – indeed close to that of 1978 – indicate that the intended restructuring of the economy miscarried and old relationships reasserted themselves? On

TABLE 2.1　*Net Saving*

Unit: Billion Current Yuan
Per cent of National Income

	Disposable National Income	Total Net Saving	Of which: Government	State Enterprises	Non-State Enterprises	Household
1978	331.5	110.1	66.4	22.2	16.3	5.3
	(100.0)	(33.2)	(20.0)	(6.7)	(4.9)	(1.6)
1979	370.9	115.7	51.2	32.3	18.7	13.5
		(31.2)	(13.8)	(8.7)	(5.0)	(3.6)
1980	406.1	122.5	49.4	31.1	16.0	26.0
		(30.2)	(12.2)	(7.7)	(3.9)	(6.4)
1981	434.6	124.6	46.6	38.1	13.3	26.6
		(28.7)	(10.7)	(8.8)	(3.1)	(6.1)
1982	471.4	132.1	43.1	39.9	15.9	33.2
		(28.0)	(9.1)	(8.5)	(3.4)	(7.0)
1983	526.9	155.3	50.5	37.7	18.2	48.9
		(29.5)	(9.6)	(7.2)	(3.5)	(9.3)
1984	628.5	198.1	65.5	30.9	22.9	78.8
		(31.5)	(10.4)	(4.9)	(3.6)	(12.5)
1985	764.8	230.1	90.8	36.4	28.6	74.3
		(30.1)	(11.8)	(4.8)	(3.7)	(9.7)
1986	875.8	281.8	82.8	45.7	47.8	105.5
		(32.2)	(9.5)	(5.2)	(5.5)	(12.0)

SOURCE: Macroeconomic Research Office, Economic System Reform Research Institute, 'The Macroeconomy in the Process of Reform: Distribution and Use of National Income', *Jingji Yanjiu*, 1987: 8, pp. 27–8.

the contrary. The rebound of investment occurred as shifts in economic relationships became more profound. As the direct role of the government declined, and the role of enterprises and households increased, those economic units dramatically increased first their saving, and subsequently their investment propensities. In an earlier paper, I examined the dramatic changes in financial saving propensities and inter-sectoral flows of investment through the medium of the consolidated balance sheet of the state banking system.[5] Recent work done in China allows us to add substantially to that picture by accounting systematically for national saving and investment.

Using standard national accounts (SNA), China's net domestic saving, as a proportion of disposable national income, declined from 33.2 per cent in 1978 to 28.0 per cent in 1982, before beginning to increase again. By 1986, total net saving had increased to 32.2 per cent of national income (see Table 1). This pattern of decline and subsequent rebound of saving (evident in the accumulation figures) is even more striking when net flows of foreign capital are included. The low point of national saving in 1982 corresponded with a period when China was accumulating foreign exchange reserves, so that there was a net outflow of capital during that period, whereas the increase of domestic saving between 1982 and 1985 corresponded with a renewed inflow of foreign capital. Thus, resources available for new net investment (expressed as a percentage of national income) declined from 33.6 per cent in 1978 all the way down to 25.6 per cent in 1982, before recovering to 35.1 per cent in 1986, actually above the immediately previous peak of 1978.

This pattern is composed of two separate trends. Saving of budgetary authorities and state enterprises has declined steadily as a proportion of national income since 1978, while saving of households and non-state enterprises has increased steadily (see Figure 2.1). The different pace of these offsetting trends (plus changes in net foreign capital inflows) created the pattern of decline and rebound in total saving and investment. The saving of budgetary authorities declined dramatically between 1978 and 1982, going from 20 per cent to 9 per cent of national income. During this initial period, the decline was only partially offset by an increase in household saving from 1.5 per cent to 7 per cent of national income, while enterprise saving held roughly constant as a proportion of income.[6] Indeed, some of the increase in household saving was actually direct compensation for the decline in saving of rural collectives, as households took over most of the responsibility for agricultural production. Since 1982, the behaviour of budgetary authorities has stabilised and saving of state enterprises has declined slightly. The increase in domestic saving since 1982 has come entirely from two sources: households (which have increased their saving to 12 per cent of national income in 1986), and non-state production units, primarily in rural areas, which have increased their saving from 3.4 per cent of national income in 1982 to 5.5 per cent in 1986, surpassing state enterprises for the first time. Thus, between 1978 and 1986, saving by the state economy (budgetary authorities and state enterprises) declined from 26.7 per cent of net national product to 14.7 per cent; while saving by the non-state economy (households and non-state enterprises, not including foreign capital) increased from 6.5 per cent of net national product to 17.5 per cent. Between 1984 and 1986, more saving was generated outside the state system than within it.

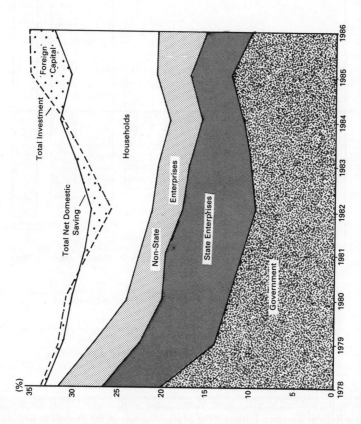

FIGURE 2.1   *Net saving by sector and total net investment (as percentage of disposable national income)*

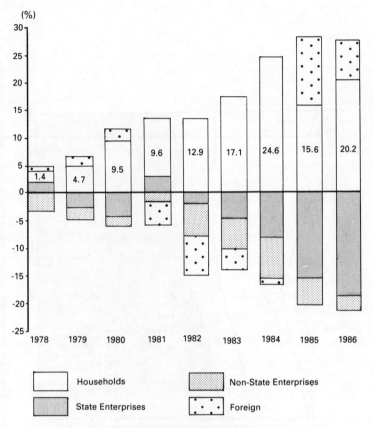

FIGURE 2.2   *Net sectoral surplus and deficit as a proportion*
of total investment (1978–86)

SOURCE: Reproduced directly from Macroeconomic Research Office, Economic System Reform Research Institue, 'The Macroeconomy in the Process of Reform: Distribution and Use of National Income', *Jingji Yanjiu*, 8, p. 22.

However, these changes in the sources of saving have not been fully matched by changes in control of investment. As a result, while previously most saving was converted to investment within the sector in which it was generated, inter-sectoral flows of saving have become increasingly important. Since these are credit flows, not uncompensated transfers, financial assets have become increasingly important in the economy. While previously all investment relied on internal financing, external financing has become increasingly significant. The graphic device originally developed by Goldsmith to illustrate the importance of cross-sectoral flows of saving can be used to show the change in the Chinese economy in this respect (see Figure 2.2).[8] However, in market economies, external financing includes equity and corporate bonds to varying degrees, while in China, virtually all external finance is provided through the state banking system. By far the most important form of financial intermediation is that provided when state banks collect household savings deposits and channel that surplus to the enterprise sector. About 40 per cent of household saving goes to construction of housing and other investments in rural areas, and 40–50 per cent goes into the bank, with the remainder funding co-operative and individual enterprises. Thus, the types of assets available to households are still very limited in practice, notwithstanding the novelty of a very small number of enterprise 'stock' issues and the availability of Treasury bonds. Moreover, interests rates on bank loans are still far from equating the supply and demand for funds (and could hardly be expected to do so in the presence of substantial price distortions), so the funds deposited with the state banking system are still allocated primarily by credit rationing. In practice, this means that a large majority of those funds are loaned to the state-owned economy, and their disposition is shaped to a large extent by the development priorities of central and local planners. Thus, there are important limitations to the development of financial intermediaries in the Chinese economy.

CHANGING BEHAVIOUR 2: THE DYNAMICS OF REFORM AND MACROECONOMICS

The changes in saving and investment behaviour described in the previous section require major adjustments in economic policy, as government investment and macroeconomic policies accommodate the changed sources and uses of national saving. These adjustments are one of the most important parts of the difficult transition process to an economically reformed system in any socialist country, and failure to solve them adequately has been an important cause of the limited success of reform in other socialist countries. The Chinese experience can be understood by comparing and contrasting it with a model of the socialist reform process developed by Nuti.[9]

In Nuti's view, 'accumulation bias' is a general characteristic of centralised economic systems. In his view, a successful economic reform process would necessarily consist of a democratisation of control over economic decision-making that would lead to a deceleration of accumulation. In that way, a slack macroeconomic environment would ultimately emerge that would allow markets to play an increasingly important role in a new, as yet undefined, form of socialist economy. Nuti points out, however, that previous socialist economic reform programmes have instead fallen into a vicious cycle around these issues. Economic reforms have typically been introduced during periods of deteriorating economic performance (disillusionment with the existing system is greatest at that time), and the first stages of economic reform have been accompanied by a limited decentralisation of control over resources without, however, a decisive reversal of 'accumulation bias'. Presumably this is because the central leadership is unwilling to abandon its direct control over investment resources, particularly if it fears that lower investment rates will lead to slower growth. Economic decentralisation combined with continued accumulation bias has led to an intensification of macroeconomic imbalance, which is reflected both in intensified shortages of goods within the planned sector, and inflationary pressures and/or shortages of consumer goods. As a result, central planners have been driven to intensify their control of the economy just as popular support for reforms is being eroded. Generally, these tendencies have brought the reform process to an end, and as early as the Czechoslovakian reform effort in 1959, we can observe a cyclical process of abortive economic reform.[10]

Many of the general features of this cyclical process are applicable to China, but in some ways the differences are even more striking. First, the commitment of the central government to reform in China has been exceptionally strong, and this has been accompanied by a willingness to reduce central government investment that has no parallel in other socialist countries.[11] Fixed investment financed directly through the government budget declined from 44 billion yuan in 1978 to 29 billion in 1981, before rising to 46 billion current yuan 1984, a level that has been maintained approximately constant since. As both the price level and total real investment have increased, the weight of budgetary in total fixed investment in the state-owned economy declined from 66 per cent to around 25 per cent by the mid-1980s.[12] Thus, changes in central government behaviour eased the reform process by reducing the competition for investment resources.

Second, and even more important, has been the rapid increase in household saving. Nuti's presumption that a democratisation of economic decision-making would necessarily lead to a reduction in economy-wide 'accumulation bias' has not been borne out in China. Instead, Chinese households increasingly resemble households in Japan and Taiwan that save large proportions of their incomes. It is as if there had been a suppressed demand for saving among Chinese households that emerged as soon as household behaviour adjusted to the increased security of financial saving, and to the vastly expanded opportunities for household investment and large-scale, or 'lumpy', consumption opportunities. While the increased demand for household investment (especially for rural housing and individual businesses) has increased the demand for investment goods, the increase in household saving has far exceeded the increase in investment demand. As a result, the net effect of changing household behaviour has been a very substantial increase in net saving (as shown by Figure 2.2), and a resulting amelioration of the macroeconomic pressures associated with reform.

Yet while changing behaviour at the government and household level has made it possible for the reform process to proceed, the progress of reform has not always been smooth, and there is a kind of cyclical reform process observable in China that bears many similarities to Nuti's formulation. In general, China's economy has continued to display many of the characteristics of a Kornai-style 'shortage economy'. Except for the brief episode of macroeconomic slack, caused by the drastic cutback of investment in 1981, there has been persistent upward pressure on prices, and persistent shortage of key commodities, particularly energy supplies. In part, this is because changes in enterprise behaviour (particularly state-owned enterprises) have not had the same beneficial effects as changes in the government and household sectors. As would be predicted in a Kornai-type economy in which enterprises are characterised by soft budget constraints, enterprise investment demand has expanded rapidly, and this has meant a persistent strain on aggregate supply. It is simply that the changes in government and household behaviour have prevented a drastic intensification of shortage from completely aborting the reform process. But this has still left the difficult policy task of mediating between the conflicting demands of further reform and rough macroeconomic balance.

As a result, the Chinese 'cyclical' process has taken on rather special characteristics, and there has been progress in reform alongside the periodic advances and retreats. In general, the Chinese reform process from 1979 through 1987 has been characterised by four successive macro/reform cycles, each of which can be generally characterised by a contractionary and expansionary phase. These phases have, in turn, a particular relation with the formulation and progression of economic reform. The cycle can be thought of as beginning with a contractionary phase, as planners attempt to respond to evidence of excess demand. Typically, Chinese policy-makers have attempted to respond to macroeconomic disequilibrium with two initiatives, one short-run and one long-run. In the short run, policy-makers reduce aggregate demand by reducing investment and/or consumption, and stress controlling the economy. At the same time, recognising that the problems in the economy are more fundamental than mere short-run disequilibrium, leaders determine to use the period of intensified control to draw up systematic reform measures. Thus, policy during these contractionary phases is characterised by a somewhat contradictory emphasis, including the need to immediately tighten control, and the necessity to lay the ground for major reforms in the future.

Typically, the short-run measures of macro control have had a rapid impact on the economy. The growth rate of production decelerates, and the problems that made contraction seem necessary (inflation, shortages, or trade deficits) quickly come to seem less pressing. In the meantime, economists and policy-makers working on reform design find their task is far from completion. Not only is the task of comprehensive reform design intrinsically difficult, but in addition, initial proposals often meet substantial political resistance (especially proposals for price reform). This is not surprising, for some of the largest beneficiaries of the early stages of reform have been enterprises and local governments that have gained control over substantial resources. Further systematic reforms often involve subjecting these early beneficiaries to a degree of market discipline and risk that they would just as soon avoid. Thus, while the need to impose macroeconomic discipline has apparently passed, there is no immediately available reform programme to serve as a blueprint for the next stage of economic change. In this situation, the political climate that allowed the central government to demand compliance with its contractionary policies changes rapidly. Political pressure for a renewal of expansionary policies builds, and these pressures are often cloaked in the rhetoric of reform ('enlivening the economy'). As a result, tentative plans for comprehensive reforms are pushed aside, and a hastily adopted decentralisation of finance and control over materials instead follows. This decentralisation may or may not involve significant redefinition of the rights and responsibilities of enterprises and other basic-level economic units. In either case, it leads quickly to an increase in investment and an acceleration in the growth rate. Initially, the acceleration of growth is proclaimed as a great success for the reform process, but ultimately the uncontrolled nature of the growth leads to the reemergence of excess demand, and the gradual increase in inflation, shortages of crucial goods (especially energy) and perhaps a large trade deficit. Eventually these problems cause the central government to reimpose contractionary policies, and begin again to design a more satisfactory overall reform strategy. Thus, one cycle is finished and the ground laid for the next cycle.[13]

Clearly this cyclical process bears important resemblances to the vicious cycle of abortive reform described by Nuti. The difference is that the reduction in budgetary investment and the increase in household saving permit decentralisation of resources to continue despite the cyclical process. Each cycle ends with a larger proportion of resources outside the direct control of central planners. Moreover, some of the cycles accomplish important institutional changes, giving enterprise greater and more clearly defined rights to autonomous operation. Simultaneously, there is a gradual process of developing the institutions and skills needed to direct an increasingly decentralised economy. Thus, while each cycle taken by itself presents a disappointing picture of frustrated expectations of reform, the process as a whole is one of substantial incremental change. But this change has been quite unbalanced: decentralisation has proceeded apace, while reform of the price and financial systems has lagged behind. Aspects of the reform process that require careful design (such as renewed definition of the meaning of 'state ownership') have remained eternally on the agenda, but never seem to get accomplished. The undesigned character of the Chinese reform has been widely recognised, not least by the Chinese themselves, who call it 'crossing the river by groping for stepping stones'. What is less widely appreciated is that this characteristic of the overall reform process is the result of repeated failures to agree on reform strategies that is in turn related to the cyclical process.

While a full review of the Chinese reform experience is beyond the scope of this paper, it is possible to briefly indicate the timing of the four cycles which have occurred through 1988.

Cycle 1: The reform process began in 1979, with a programme of 'readjustment' (i.e. contractionary policies) in April, combined with experimental reforms and the convening of groups to design a reform strategy in June and July.[14] By late 1979 and through 1980, improving economic conditions led to a rapid expansion of initially 'experimental' reforms (especially enterprise profit retention), while the initial reform design group, headed by Zhang Jingu, disappeared from view. Rapid growth of investment, and the emergence of significant inflation for the first time since 1962 ensued, and by December 1980, planners invoked a drastically intensified readjustment strategy for 1981. Thus ended the first cycle, but not before important permanent innovations in the role and autonomy of enterprises were adopted (4/79–2/81: 21 months).

Cycle 2: Although the next 'readjustment' was associated with an increasingly conservative ideological climate, intensive work was begun on a programme of price reform, then seen as a crucial component of comprehensive reform. By 1982, the outlines of a comprehensive price reform had been drawn up, but as economic conditions improved a further conservative initiative caused plans for price reform to be shelved.[15] Thus, further stages of economic reform took place without major revisions of state-set prices, and this period was characterised primarily by further decentralisation of financial resources without major restructuring of the system provisions involved[16] (2/81–7/83: 29 months).

Cycle 3: In mid year 1983, a renewed effort to bring rapidly expanding investment under control was made, in this case relying primarily on fiscal policy, including the promulgation of new central government taxes on enterprise resources, and administrative controls on investment. At the same time, the idea of a formal endorsement of the 'dual track' economic system began to gain currency among the economic advisers to Premier Zhao Ziyang. This idea enabled the Zhao-Hu leadership to proclaim their allegiance to the idea of a planned economy and weather the campaign against 'spiritual pollution', while still producing a semblance of movement in the area of economic reform. In this case, the idea became a reality during the explosive expansionary phase of late 1984, backed by the enterprise charter that officially permitted factories to buy and sell outside the plan at market prices. These measures, combined with a highly expansionary credit policy, created a period of explosive growth at the end of 1984 that brought a return to contractionary credit policies in the middle of the following year (7/83–7/85, 24 months).

Cycle 4: The contractionary policy was begun in mid-1985 and ratified by a Party plenum in October 1985. This plenum also stressed that in the short-run only modest reform measures could be contemplated, and called for preparatory work on major comprehensive reforms that could be implemented once macroeconomic balance was restored. Thus, 1986 was to be a year for restoring macroeconomic balance, while 1987 was to be the year of fundamental change in the economic system. By early 1986, contractionary macro policy was biting into economic growth rates, and industrial production actually declined slightly in the first two months of 1986. At the same time, a working group bringing together economists and politicians from several units, under the leadership of the Economic Reform Commission, was established to design comprehensive reform (The *fang' an ban'*). Once again, however, the early drafts of this comprehensive reform programme failed to elicit widespread agreement among influential policy-makers. Contractionary monetary policies were abandoned in April 1986, and industrial growth rates quickly recovered. By the fall of 1986, the plan for comprehensive reform was a dead letter, and the ideological turbulence at the end of the year brought a clear end to bold comprehensive reform measures. Since mid-1986, the Chinese economy has been growing very rapidly in an increasingly inflationary environment.

By September 1987, central planners were becoming increasingly nervous about the prospects of accelerating inflation in China. They thus began to call for the implementation of a contractionary macro policy beginning in the last quarter of 1987, which would have brought an end to the fourth cycle (7/85–9/87: 26 months). In fact, however, the implementation of the contractionary policy was abruptly abandoned in the early months of 1988, a development which may signal the beginning of a new phase of the Chinese reform process, discussed below.

These four cycles have in common a periodicity of about two years, as well as a general correlation between the emergence of new reform strategies and the trough of a macroeconomic cycle. However, each of the cycles has its own characteristics, and it would be a mistake to see them as the mechanical outcome of some inevitable process. Indeed, the development of 1988 may indicate that this peculiar Chinese reform dynamic has now run its course. Moreover, the cycles are not of equivalent important. Major reforms of industrial enterprises occurred during the expansionary phases of cycles 1 and 3, while cycles 2 and 4 witnessed some continuing decentralisation, but little institutional innovation.[17] However, the progressive decentralisation of control over resources in the Chinese economy has meant that the instruments used to reimpose macro control have tended to evolve away from administrative controls and toward fiscal and monetary policy. The first two cycles were terminated primarily by a direct reimposition of controls over investment, involving a reduction of central investment and an attempt to restrict decentralised investment. By the end of the third cycle, however, planners began to shift to a primary reliance on credit policy. Increasingly, planners have been attempting to use the banking system to impose control over the economy. This effort is the topic of the second part of this paper.

FIRST STEPS TOWARD A MACROECONOMIC POLICY: THE EXPERIENCE OF 1978–1987

In the preceding discussion of cyclical economic policy-making, the focus was on the interaction of macroeconomic policy and conditions and the design of an economic reform strategy. In the following sections, the discussion concentrates specifically on macroeconomic policy and the tools available for its implementation. The cyclical processes described above clearly imply a failure to develop and apply a consistent, reliable macroeconomic policy. Does this failure arise from the inadequacy of the control implements available to Chinese planners, or does it arise from the specific policy decisions made by the Chinese leadership? In order to answer this question, we must first briefly review the experience of the past eight years from the perspective of macroeconomic policy, with a special emphasis on the role of the banking system and monetary policy.

The banking system began to play a more important role in the Chinese economy almost immediately the reform process started in 1979. However, the role of the banking system in the early stages of reform was largely limited to the creation of a new system for financing fixed investment. Faced with difficult budgetary problems, and a situation in which the state investment plan was overcommitted to a variety of large, long-term projects, central planners turned to the banking system to give them additional flexibility in funding investment. In the early years 1979–80, virtually all the new bank credits went to create new capacity in light, consumer goods industries, generally in small or medium-sized projects. The expanded role of bank lending allowed planners to increase resources for light industry without going through the politically contentious process of redirecting budgetary investment away from existing projects: an entirely new funding mechanism was created. Bank lending, which funded only 1.6 per cent of state fixed investment in 1978, increased rapidly to 12 per cent of such investment in 1980. In this case, the small-scale, relatively dispersed and relatively profitable nature of much of this investment made it a particularly suitable object of bank financing.[18]

When macroeconomic problems emerged, however, the banking system was not sufficiently developed to serve as a major instrument of macroeconomic control. The brunt of the burden of adjusting to macroeconomic disequilibrium in 1981 fell on state budgetary investment, which was sharply reduced. In a sense, of course, this was using 'fiscal policy' to deal with macro problems, but more fundamentally it represented a recourse to the familiar direct control instruments of the administered economy. Besides reducing budgetary investment, planners promulgated administrative restrictions on fixed investments funded from other sources. Such restrictions of course included bank-financed investments, but bank lending actually increased in importance, funding 13.6 per cent of state fixed investment during 1981. In this case, bank-financed investments were simply considered as one among several categories within the general investment plan, and it was the adjustment of the plan itself that served as the primary mechanism for macroeconomic control. During the contractionary phase of 1983, planners began to view bank lending as a more flexible part of the investment plan, and they reduced credit for fixed investment so that it declined from 16.2 per cent of investment the previous year to 14.3 per cent. At the same time, planners implemented new taxes on enterprise financial resources, signalling the beginning of a slightly more sophisticated approach to macroeconomic control.

In both the preceding cases, however, bank lending for fixed investment was simply treated as one category of total fixed investment, regulated primarily by the central plan. There was no attempt to regulate the overall extension of credit in the economy via the banking system. Most bank credit finances the inventories used in the industrial and commercial systems, and there is little evidence of planners or bank officials trying to manipulate this aggregate to affect macroeconomic conditions at this time, though the situation had begun to change by late 1984. Ironically, one of the most important sources of the excessively expansionary policies followed at that time was a loss of control over bank lending. Essentially, credit quotas had always been set on different categories of bank lending, but in late 1984 credit quotas were either abolished, or more likely, were simply ignored in the heady, expansionist 'reform' atmosphere of the time. Under intense pressure from local leaders to expand credit for favoured investment projects, local bank branches vastly expanded lending. They may also have purposefully increased lending in order to position themselves for increases in lending quotas in future years. For whatever reasons, banks created new credit at a rapid pace in late 1984, flooding the economic system with liquidity. Overall loans increased rapidly, and the financing of fixed investment via bank lending jumped to 23 per cent in 1985.

As a result, during the course of 1985, China adopted an across-the-board contractionary monetary policy for the first time. In its initial stages, this policy simply served to sop up excess liquidity: enterprise bank balances were at record highs, and through most of 1985 the new contractionary policy had relatively little impact on production, because enterprises were simply drawing down excess bank balances. By the end of 1985, however, enterprises were beginning to be squeezed by a difficulty in obtaining access to bank credits. Difficulties in funding purchases of needed inputs surfaced, and industrial growth rates slowed drastically, becoming slightly negative in the first months of 1986. Certainly it had been demonstrated that monetary policy could have a major effect on the economy.

However, the central leadership began to be concerned about this effect: perhaps the contractionary policies were simply too costly? We must ask why contractionary policies were so strict at this time. There are important contributing reasons: first, the expansionary policies of late 1984 had really been much too excessive, and leaders were determined to correct the problems created at that time; second, planners (including bank officials) lacked reliable indicators of what an appropriate monetary policy should be in a situation where household and enterprise behaviour was changing rapidly. But the most fundamental reason was the inherent rigidity of the Chinese economic system itself. In the 1984/85 expansion, local political leaders had been able to compel local bank branches to expand lending beyond their quotas. The local bank branches knew that they could not be held accountable for violating their credit quotas so long as they had been under irresistible political pressure to do so. The distribution of political power in China meant that bank credit quotas were 'soft', just as enterprise budget constraints are commonly labelled 'soft'. This situation could be altered, to be sure, but it would be altered only by the adoption by the central political leadership of contractionary policies as a major point of the current political line. In a party plenum of October, 1985, 'contraction' was indeed adopted as official party policy. Only in this atmosphere could a contractionary monetary policy be carried out. In order to make credit quotas truly binding, it was necessary to elevate contractionary policy to the status of party policy: the contraction had to be 'strict', in order for it to have any effect at all.

Ultimately, however, the contraction was too 'strict' to be sustainable. During April, 1986, Premier Zhao Ziyang intervened to reverse the contractionary policy. Since he did not have the authority to reverse party policy, he adopted a circumlocution: the policy would continue to be contractionary, but would be modified to allow 'flexibility within contraction' (*jinzhong youhuo*): bank credits began to increase rapidly.[19] This episode throws a great deal of light on the workability of monetary policy in the Chinese economy. In principle, credit quotas are entirely capable of serving as an effective tool of macroeconomic management. Although credit quotas do not automatically discriminate between more and less profitable uses of bank funds in the way that higher interest rates do, they can effectively restrict aggregate demand. They are thus a slightly clumsy, but entirely workable, form of demand management. But this is the case only if credit quotas are 'hard', and must be respected by lower levels. However, such quotas are 'hard' only when the top political leadership actively stresses the importance of respecting those quotas (as was the case in late 1985 and early 1986).

Following the shift in policy of April 1986, bank credits expanded rapidly for the remainder of the year. Following the adoption of this expansionary policy, growth of currency in circulation and the overall economic growth rate both returned to quite high rates. Bank loans continued to fund 23–25 per cent of state fixed investment during 1986 and 1987. Less welcome was the fact that, beginning in January 1987, inflation also began to accelerate. The urban cost of living index was 5.1 per cent over its year-previous level in January 1987, but increased monthly to reach 8.2 per cent in August.[20] The growth of inflationary pressures and other evidence of an overheated economy led the leadership once again to consider contractionary policies, and in September they announced a policy of 'dual contraction', meaning both fiscal and monetary contraction. It was understood that this was to be a moderate contraction, but one that was to be implemented in a systematic and sustained fashion. We will discuss below the means through which such a policy was to be implemented. Even more important for the understanding of macroeconomic policy in China is the fact that the policy was never implemented in a sustained fashion. Some measures were taken during the last quarter of 1987, but during February 1988, references to the 'dual contraction' policy gradually disappeared from the press. By the end of the first quarter of 1988, it was clear that both total credit extended and currency in circulation had resumed the very high rates of growth that had been evident since April 1986. As in the 1985–86 episode, the central leadership had failed to stand behind a contractionary policy. By mid-1988, it is clear that an expansionary, even inflationary, macroeconomic environment has become the normal condition of the Chinese economy. This provides the basic context within which the changing role of the banking system needs to be understood.

RESHAPING THE BANKING SYSTEM

Beginning in 1983, the Chinese banking system began to be restructured into a system in which the People's Bank of China (PBC) would serve as a central bank, akin to the Federal Reserve Board in the United States, or more precisely, to the Bundesbank in the Federal Republic of Germany. The PBC would make loans to the specialised banks (including the Agriculture Bank and the newly established Industrial and Commercial Bank), which would use those funds, as well as deposits that they collected, to make loans. In turn, the specialised banks were required to maintain a certain proportion of their deposits in the PBC, effectively limiting the total quantity of loans they could make. PBC lending thus would determine the resources available to the specialised banks and the reserve requirements would determine the money multiplier which determines the size of the overall money stock. Up through the present, however, the PBC has been forced to continue to rely on overall credit quotas (now set separately for each bank) while the new system is gradually being worked out. The result is a fundamentally ambiguous system in which the banks operate with both reserve requirements and overall credit quotas. In a purely logical sense, only one of these constraints can effectively determine a given type of bank lending at any one time. Thus, if reserve requirements are really binding, credit quotas would be redundant, and vice versa. In the transition period, however, the dangers of further loss of control of bank lending are too great to allow an immediate transition to a dependence on reserve requirements, so credit quotas cannot be immediately abandoned. Unfortunately, this makes it difficult at times to analyse changes in monetary policy, since it is difficult to determine the proximate cause of changes in the money supply.

The dramatic changes in the banking system make management of that system through reserve requirements difficult during the transition period. For example, along with reserve requirements, an important change has been the institution of a system of inter-bank lending, with significant quantities of short-term funds flowing between the specialised banks. The result of this new opportunity has been an increase in incentives for the banks to minimise their deposits with the central bank (which earn a much lower rate of interest). Thus, while the formal reserve requirement was pegged at 10 per cent of deposits until late 1987, the specialised banks had been maintaining larger deposits in the central bank, with such excess reserves amounting to 11.56 per cent of deposits at the end of 1985. With the development of the inter-bank lending market, excess reserves have fallen steadily, and amounted to only 6.4 per cent of deposits in October, 1987. While indicating greater efficiency within the banking system, this drop in excess reserves has also contributed to the growth of the money supply by expanding the 'money multiplier'.[21] It is hard to know whether such changes are implicated in the rapid growth of lending during 1986 and 1987, but to the extent that the bank was relying on reserve requirements to govern the money supply, it would certainly be a factor. In any case, it serves as a reminder of the difficulties involved in learning to use the banking system as the primary instrument of monetary control.

The immediate problems with monetary policy, however, are more related to the autonomy of the banking system than to the technical problems of co-ordination within that system. Many lending decisions in China are made at the local level, and the provincial branches of the PBC play a crucial role in the overall determination of monetary policy. However, these provincial branches are strongly influenced by the wishes of party leaders and planners at the provincial level. This influence has many sources: occasionally it stems from the extra-legal authority enjoyed by local power-holders, and frequently from the authority over personnel decisions and infrastructure development that local leaders enjoy. Of even greater importance than these semi-coercive relations, however, is the simple fact that local banks are involved in a long-term collaboration with local planners, the ultimate intention of which is to accelerate economic development in that locality. Continued price distortions make it impossible for banks to base lend purely on profitability considerations, and they naturally look to local planning commissions for guidance on the priority sectors for development. It is thus inconceivable that local banks could be truly independent of local authorities under present conditions.[22] Local authorities naturally push for more lending, especially since the benefits of the loans accrue entirely to their locality, while the associated costs – excess demand and inflation – spill over to other localities.

In all countries, contractionary policies create political pressures on the national leadership. In most market economies, the central bank is given a certain amount of independence in order to insulate its decision-making from the influence of the political leadership. In China, however, the importance of local leaders in economic development implies that it is insufficient for the central government to simply accord the banking system independence. Instead, the central leadership must actively intervene to reinforce the macroeconomic policy being implemented through the banking system. Otherwise, local banks, being subject to the influence of provincial leaders, will be constantly tempted to exceed their lending limits, relying on the PBC to bail them out after the fact. This requires of the central leadership an active identification with contractionary policies, which naturally increases the political cost of such policies. In principle, this problem is the same regardless of whether bank policy is implemented through credit quotas or through reserve requirements. The potential merit of a reserve requirement system is that it holds the possibility of creating, in the long run, a set of objective rules that the central bank can insist on, giving it a warrant to refuse to retroactively endorse local branch behaviour that runs counter to a given monetary policy.

The adoption of contractionary policies in the fourth quarter of 1987 demonstrated at its outset an encouraging attempt to utilise the distribution of credit resources within the banking system to guide policy. Rather than simply reducing credit quotas, banking officials announced ten co-ordinated policy measures designed to reduce the overall growth of money and credit. Reserve requirements were raised from 10 per cent to 12 per cent, thus shrinking the money multiplier; the interest rate the PBC charges the specialised banks was raised to 7.2 per cent from a previous range of 4.68 per cent to 6.84 per cent; and 5 billion yuan in excess reserves maintained at the PBC by the Rural Credit Cooperatives were temporarily converted into required reserves. At the same time, some credit quotas were tightened, specifically through the requirement that lending to rural enterprises be frozen at the levels prevailing at the end of the third quarter

1987. Overall, the policy, as announced, displayed a new sophistication in the implementation of monetary policy.[23]

THE COSTS OF CONTRACTIONARY POLICIES

In spite of the promise and sophistication of the policies announced in the fourth quarter of 1987, they were soon abandoned by the central leadership. By its actions, the central leadership displayed its belief that the costs of contractionary policies outweighed the benefits. In part, this judgement is influenced by the necessity of active identification between the leadership and the macro policies being implemented, which automatically increases the political cost of contractionary policies. Moreover, the economic cost of contractionary policies is increased because interest rates play no role in their implementation. When interest rates fluctuate, the market automatically discriminates between producers on the basis of their ability to pay higher prices for capital, which ensures that within any given sector, less productive enterprises are most likely to reduce production.[24] In Chinese policy, some of the costs of contraction fall on highly productive enterprises, which would have been able to afford higher interests rates in a more marketised environment. The Chinese have attempted to mimic this effect by dividing all enterprises into three categories according to their 'credit worthiness', thereby insulating the best enterprises from the impact of contraction.[25] However, it is unlikely that such an administrative policy can substitute fully for flexible interest rates.

To understand the more general costs of contractionary policy, we must consider the potential differential impact on four main categories of lending. Each of these categories has an economic and political constituency that naturally resists restriction of its access to credit. The four categories are lending for fixed investment, agriculture, rural enterprises, and working capital for state industrial and commercial enterprises. These will be examined in turn.

We have noted above the dramatic changes in the funding of fixed investment in the state-run economy. By 1986, budgetary financing accounted for only 24 per cent, and bank loans for 23 per cent, of state fixed investment. (Enterprise retained funds accounted for 49 per cent, and foreign capital for 5 per cent). Yet the changes in the actual control of investment have been far less dramatic than these figures indicate. The central government began in 1983 to stress the continuing need to carry out investment in large-scale energy and transportation projects, unavoidably under the direction of the central government. This stress has continued, and in some respects intensified in subsequent years, with the result that by 1986, 44 per cent of state fixed investment spending went to central government projects. This was essentially the same proportion as in 1980–81, when budgetary finance played a much larger role.[26] These figures do not imply that all fixed investment bank lending goes to central government projects, since local government 'matching funds' are also drawn on for central government projects, especially electricity development. However, they do show that an ample supply of bank lending is essential for the government to complete its own priority investment programme, both because it provides substantial direct financing, and because it ameliorates the financial pressures on local governments that are squeezed between the need to contribute to central government projects, and their desire to pursue their own agendas. This relationship is crucial, because cutbacks in fixed investment lending would otherwise seem to be the least costly way to reduce aggregate demand. However, it would be difficult to do so without affecting the crucial central government sponsored program of energy and infrastructure development.

Agriculture and rural enterprises are both highly influenced by credit policy, since both have hard budget constraints. Agriculture, handicapped by the continuing influence of low-state-set prices, particularly for grain, is highly dependent on provision of subsidised credit for the purchase of agricultural inputs. As a result, the state makes an effort to shield agriculture from the impact of contractionary credit policies by setting separate quotas for agricultural lending. Nevertheless, such efforts are rarely entirely successful, particularly since the rural credit cooperatives provide about half of total agricultural credit, and these units have a direct interest in maintaining profitable lending policies. For example, in 1985, the imposition of a tight credit policy in the second quarter was one factor that caused a dramatic decline in demand for fertiliser, a decline that was in turn implicated in the poor showing of agriculture in that year. Similarly, demand for trucks, simple machinery, and some consumer durables is quite sensitive to credit availability.[27]

Rural enterprises are also overwhelmingly dependent on credit from the state banking system (including the rural credit cooperatives) for their start-up costs. A crude indication of this dependence can be drawn from Figure 2.3, which plots the increase in value added in township and village enterprises against the net increase in credit extended to those enterprises in each year. In most years, these figures are quite close: the rapid growth in this sector is closely related to growth of credit resources on which it can draw. Thus, there is no doubt that monetary policy is a powerful tool affecting the pace of growth of both agriculture and rural enterprises, and that monetary

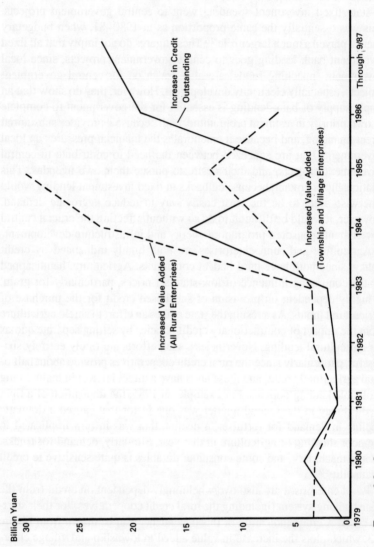

FIGURE 2.3 Increment to value added and credit extended to rural enterprises

policy can affect the pace at which these sectors draw resources into the production process. However, in this case, the very power of monetary policy imposes strict limits on the flexibility with which it can be deployed. These limits are due to the weakness of agriculture, on the one hand, and the strength of rural industrialisation, on the other. Clearly, agriculture cannot be made to bear the brunt of contractionary monetary policies, since the resultant decline in output would only exacerbate the more fundamental problems in the economy. Rural enterprises, on the other hand, have a crucial symbolic role as a symbol of the reform process. The dramatic deceleration of agricultural growth since 1984 has left rural industrialisation as the sole unambiguous success of the reform effort. As Deng Xiaoping has said, 'This has been our biggest success; moreover, it is one we by no means anticipated'.[28] As a result, the desire to rely on monetary policy to restrain inflationary pressures is hampered by the fear of throttling the one unambiguous success to which reformers can currently point.

This leaves the provision of working capital credit to state-run enterprises as the remaining focus of monetary policy. State enterprises are highly 'leveraged' – that is, they are highly dependent on bank credit for their working capital needs. This implies that they should be very responsive to changes in the availability of such credit, and this is in fact the case. However, the nature of their response creates substantial problems for policy makers. While highly dependent on bank credit for working capital, Chinese enterprises also retain substantial funds of their own. However, these funds are overwhelmingly used for one of two objectives: new fixed investment in the enterprise itself, and provision of bonuses and benefits to workers. Enterprises almost never use their own funds to finance working capital.

We may assume that enterprises have a direct interest in two immediate objectives. The first is to maximise the current benefits available to workers; the second is to maximise the future growth of the enterprise. The first objective can be thought of as the primary objective of the workers in the factory, while the second is the primary objective of the factory management. The objectives of the two groups coincide to the extent that the management must keep the workers happy in order to obtain increased output, and conversely the workers expect that growth of the factory will provide expanded future benefits to themselves and their offspring.[29] The two uses of enterprise retained funds correspond to these two enterprise objectives. By contrast, working capital (inventory accumulation) is basically a requirement of current production activity. Without major improvements in enterprise efficiency, a certain normal level of inventories are necessary to ensure regular production. In the short run, since efficiency increases are difficult to achieve, a reduction in bank credit requires enterprises to shift funds away from their investment and bonus funds in order to maintain current levels of production. However, enterprises resist this transfer of funds, and with good reason. Bank credits to fund inventories are relatively cheap, because real interest rates are low, and because these interest payments are included in production costs and can therefore be 'written off' from before-tax income. But if enterprise funds are used to finance inventories, those funds will in all likelihood be permanently lost to the enterprise: once they are tied up in financing inventories, the enterprise is unlikely to gain access to them again. As a result, the enterprise has an interest in defending its retained funds, while allowing production to suffer as a result of input shortages. The decline in production can be blamed on adverse national credit policy: that allows enterprises to maintain control over their existing retained funds, and even appeal for more lenient financial treatment since their difficulties are created by national policy, not by their own mistakes in production.

Of course, such behaviour reflects a relatively short time horizon. If enterprises face 'hard' budget constraints, and can draw retained funds only according to some fixed proportion to actual profitability, current difficulties in production will translate into future reductions in retained funds. But in order for enterprises to adopt a longer-run perspective, they must believe that their future retained funds will actually be affected by a slower growth (or decline) of output. For that to be the case, enterprises must believe (1) that future incentive rules cannot be manipulated to excuse them from the impact of production difficulties; and (2) that contractionary monetary policies must continue for a long enough period to make those production difficulties long-term. Neither of these conditions is likely to be fulfilled in China today. Past experience with incentive rules has shown that enterprises can blame difficulties caused by changed macro policies on 'external factors', and obtain more generous financial treatment as a result.[30] Moreover, the roughly two-year cycles in macro policy described above imply that contractionary policies typically only 'bite' for a few months: after this time, central planners tend to become alarmed at the reduction in industrial growth rates, and usually abandon contractionary policies. As a result, the implicit threat to enterprises – that they will lose future benefits if they do not compensate for reduced credit availability – simply lacks credibility. It is in the interests of enterprises to wait and see, keeping their own funds in reserve, and hoping they can ride out the short term disturbances to business as usual.

If contractionary monetary policy is to alleviate inflationary pressures, it must reduce aggregate demand more than it reduces supply. But if enterprises behave in the short-sighted way described in the preceding paragraph, the opposite will be the case in the short run. Demand for investment and consumption goods emanating from the enterprise will be unchanged even as production declines. According to some Chinese economists, this is precisely what happened in the early months of 1986. Even as industrial output declined, and a 'crisis' in availability of funds was widely proclaimed, total bonus payments continued to expand moderately.[31] If monetary policy is not credible in the long run, it cannot work in the short run. In the current situation, since contractionary policies have twice been abandoned in mid-course, establishing that credibility would be an extremely difficult task. Finally, for monetary policy to be effective, enterprise incentives must not be subject to renegotiation based on changes in monetary policy.

Thus, the Chinese leadership is unwilling or unable to impose the costs of contractionary policies on any of the four major categories of credit recipients. Because its unwillingness to apply credible contractionary policies is evident to state enterprises, they adopt strategies to evade the impact of short-run contractionary policies, thus ensuring that those policies will be relatively ineffective. The problems involved in Chinese macroeconomic policy are not due primarily to the inadequacies of the banking system, for that system can in fact be used to rapidly reduce aggregate demand. The fundamental problem is rather that the Chinese political system is unable to allocate the costs of contractionary policy in a way that the top leadership judges to be politically acceptable. It is true that the relative clumsiness of the credit rationing system increases the costs of contractionary policy, and thus aggravates the leadership's dilemma. But this is a contributing factor, rather than the fundamental cause of Chinese difficulties in macroeconomic policy formulation.

CONCLUSION

The inability of the Chinese government to formulate a credible macroeconomic policy has been increasingly evident over the past three years, and is directly reflected in the accelerating rate of inflation, displayed in Figure 2.4. Price rises were significant in 1980 and 1985, but in both those years were caused primarily by reforms in food prices, which were planned in advance and for which wages were raised in compensation. By contrast, beginning in 1986, price increases have tended to be across the board, with prices of manufactured goods rising nearly as rapidly as food prices (for instance, in 1987, 6.1 per cent vs. 10.1 per cent). In early 1988, inflation continued to accelerate. Moreover, because some prices remain fairly rigid, the emergence of generalised inflationary pressures causes a certain amount

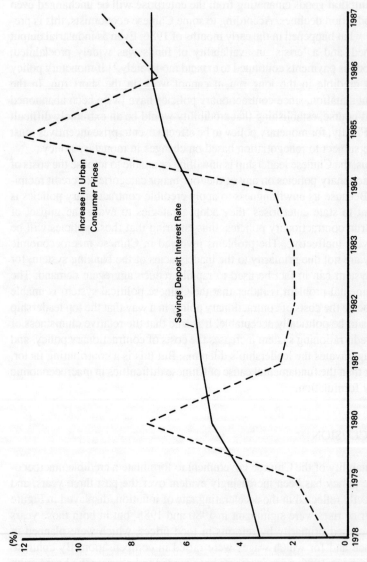

FIGURE 2.4 *Inflation and interest rates* (The price index is the comprehensive urban worker consumption price index; the interest rate is the annual average rate on one-year time deposits).

of 'anti-reform' of prices. For instance, while interest rates have generally risen, open inflation has risen more rapidly than the increase in interest rates, so that real interest rates have become slightly negative. This is shown in Figure 2.4, where the maintenance of inflation at or above the nominal interest rate (on one year savings deposits) through 1985–87 clearly shows the difficulties the Chinese have experienced. Similarly, housing rents have remained strictly controlled and have actually declined since 1983, so that this widely recognised price irrationality has become substantially worse in the past few years.[32] As a result of the price adjustments of 1980 and 1985, the differential between free-market and state commerce food prices had declined from 40 per cent to only 17 per cent by 1986, but since 1986 the differential has begun to increase again.[33] These problems should not be overemphasised: negative real interest rates are not limited to China, and some progress has clearly been made in rationalising and freeing prices. The point is rather that modest price revisions can no longer be relied on to reduce price irrationalities, and unless price reforms are actively accelerated, the situation may deteriorate.

The discussion in this paper leads inescapably to a few simple conclusions. Major changes in the inter-sectoral distribution of income have been accompanied by equally significant changes in the saving behaviour of different sectors, particularly the household sector. The Chinese have been extremely fortunate, in that the interaction of these changes has greatly ameliorated the macroeconomic strains created in the difficult process of transition to a reformed system. That has allowed reforms to progress and deepen, and has given the Chinese the opportunity to strengthen indirect instruments of macroeconomic control while avoiding catastrophic imbalances. But these changes have basically been fortuitous, and the Chinese government has not yet created a sustained, credible macroeconomic policy, in spite of the improved capabilities of the banking system. The macroeconomic problems that have emerged during the past two years present clear evidence of this.

The failure to develop a coherent macroeconomic policy reflects the partial and unbalanced character of the economic reforms that emerged during the 1980s. The continuing absence of systematic price reforms has meant that relative prices of energy and raw materials have remained low, and the central government has been compelled to take responsibility for the bulk of investment in these fields. Thus, while the central government no longer monopolises investment, it continues to directly manage a very large proportion of investment. Unlike the developmental states of the East Asian capitalist economies, which guide investment and provide selective direct investment in infrastructure and energy production, the Chinese state has maintained its role as the predominant manager of investment in the crucial heavy industrial sectors. However, having remanded much financial control to enterprises and local governments, the central state must now borrow from its citizens to carry out this investment policy, which puts substantial pressure on overall credit and macroeconomic balance. Thus, the redefinition of the Chinese developmental state has remained incomplete, in part because the diversification of objectives described in the first paragraph of this essay has remained incomplete.

The most pessimistic interpretation of the current situation would hold that China has now entered a stage in which the investment aspirations of the central government are in fundamental conflict with the decentralisation of resources implied by economic reform. If this were the case, the prospects for further reforms would be bleak indeed. However, such pessimism is not warranted, for the changes in behaviour at the household and enterprise level provide a clear 'middle ground' for the Chinese reform process. In order to attain this middle ground, the central government must find its way toward a stable macroeconomic policy that would reduce industrial investment and moderate macroeconomic stresses. This cannot be achieved through the banking system alone, but will require a reduction in the investable resources that accrue to manufacturing sectors. This can be accomplished either by a partial recentralisation of finances, or by price reforms that direct more of the surplus to energy and raw material sectors – ideally by both measures simultaneously. Such measures will be politically difficult, for they will involve the reduction in resources now controlled by the industrial sector, which has been a primary beneficiary of the reform process thus far, and also the acceptance of a lower industrial growth rate. However, by simultaneously reducing its short-term growth aspirations and increasing its resources, the central government would be in a position to sponsor a more balanced, sustainable – and ultimately accelerating – growth path. Only then will the Chinese central government be able to recast itself in the mould of a developmental state working through the medium of a reformed and increasingly marketised economic system.

NOTES

1. Macroeconomic Research Office, Economic System Reform Research Institute, 1987: 'The Macroeconomy in the Process of Reform: Distribution and Use of National Income', *Jingji Yanjiu* [*Economic Research*] 8, pp. 16–28. These and subsequent figures in this paper are calcu-

lated according to the Standard National Accounts (SNA) national income accounting system as used by the United Nations. The only exception is the discussion of target accumulation rates on page 4, where the reference is to Chinese policy discussions in an earlier period. SNA accounts are superior both because they account for all income streams in the economy, while material product accounts do not, and because they facilitate international comparisons.

2. This percentage is not directly comparable to the percentages of investment and saving discussed below. Accumulation includes some expenditures excluded from Western definitions of investment (such as purchases of military equipment), while the rate of accumulation is determined by dividing by a less inclusive concept of national income (net material product) than that used in Western definitions. However, the basic concept is similar to that of the rate of investment, and changes in the two measures are closely related. The idea that a 25 per cent accumulation rate is somehow optimal can be traced back to the Soviet textbook on political economy of the 1950s, and to a set of canonical ratios advanced by Bo Yibo in the 1950s and 1960s.

3. Annual accumulation rates are given in *1987 Tongji Nianjian*, p. 59, and updated in *1988 Tongji Zhaiyao*, p. 6. For authoritative policy statements, see Yao Yilin, 'Report on arrangement of the national economic plans for 1980 and 1981', *Beijing Review*, 22 September 1981, pp. 31–32; and Yang Bo, 'Accumulation and Consumption', *Hongqi* (1981), p. 6.

4. See the discussion in William Byrd, 'The Role and Impact of Markets', in Gene Tidrick and Chen Jiyuan, (eds), *China's Industrial Reform* (New York: Oxford, World Bank, 1987), pp. 237–76.

5. Barry Naughton, 'Macroeconomic Policy and Response in the Chinese Economy: The Impact of the Reform Process' *Journal of Comparative Economics* 11 (1987) pp. 334–53.

6. Note that profits retained by the enterprise but subsequently distributed to workers do not count as enterprise saving.

7. If we examine gross investment (including depreciation), the state system at present still generates a slightly greater flow than the non-state economy. However, by this standard, the shift in favour of the non-state economy has been even more dramatic, since depreciation in that sector has increased more rapidly than depreciation in the state sector.

8. For international comparison, see Raymond Goldsmith, *The Financial Development of India, Japan, and the United States: A Trilateral Institutional, Statistical, and Analytic Comparison* (New Haven: Yale University Press, 1983) p. 34.

9. Domenico Nuti, 'The Contradictions of Socialist Economics', *Socialist Register* 1979.

10. The process described is similar in some respects to the socialist economic cycles described in Tamas Bauer, 'Investment Cycles in Planned Economies', *Acta Oeconomica* 21 (1978) pp. 243–60.

11. There are many reasons for this difference. To some extent, it is due to

the fact that the central government was willing to contemplate an overall reduction in the rate of national investment at an early stage of the reform process, as described above. As a result, 'accumulation bias', was a less pressing short-run impediment to reform in China. Moreover, the central government has been acutely conscious of the failings of the centrally directed investment policy carried out in China, and thus may have been more willing to see the scope of that policy curtailed. This, of course, also increased the government's commitment to the reform process overall. Finally, political power was more decentralised in China than in other socialist countries at the outset of reform, so there were fewer political obstacles to decentralisation.

12. Here, as elsewhere in this paper, total state fixed investment is derived by summing the categories of capital construction, 'technical renovation' and 'other' fixed investment. See State Statistical Bureau, *Zhongguo Guding Zichan Touzi Tongji Ziliao 1950–1985* [China Fixed Investment Statistical Materials 1950–1985] (Beijing: Zhongguo Tongji), 1987, pp. 14, 59. *1983 Tongji Nianjian*, p. 360. *Tongji Nianjian* 1987, p. 473. Subsequent figures on financing of fixed investment are drawn from the same sources.

13. In this simple conception of political-economic cycles, changes in policy are seen as leading the cyclical process, followed by changes in economic (especially industrial) growth rates, which are in turn followed by changes in 'imbalance', generally inflation or shortages. Fundamentally, it is the lag structure between policy, growth, and imbalance that creates the cyclical process.

14. Ma Hong, 'Chinese Style Socialist Modernisation and Readjustment of the Economic Structure', *Gongye Jingji Guanli Congkan*, 1, p. 2; 'Review of Major Trends in Economic Research', *Jingjixue Dongtai* 1979: 11, pp. 1–5.

15. Wu Jinglian and Zhao Renwei, 'The Dual Pricing System in China's Industry', *Journal of Comparative Economics* 11:3 (September 1987), p. 311.

16. The experience of the reform through this period is reviewed in Barry Naughton, 'False Starts and Second Wind: Financial Reforms in China's Industrial System', in E. Perry and C. Wong, (eds), *The Political Economy of Reform in Post-Mao China* (Cambridge, Massachusetts: Harvard University Press, 1985), pp. 223–52.

17. Both cycles 2 and 4 were characterised by the promotion of 'profit contracting' as a crucial innovation in the reform process. In the author's judgement, such schemes are unlikely to contribute to a successful reform program, since they are based on a process of negotiation over financial resources carried out within the bureaucracy by each individual enterprise and its superior organ. Successful reform initiatives will require restructuring financial, ownership and price systems in ways that will apply uniformly to all enterprises. See the discussion in Naughton, 'False Starts and Second Wind'.

18. This episode is discussed in Naughton, 'The Decline of Central Control over Investment in Post-Mao China', in M.D. Lampton (ed.) *Policy Implementation in Post-Mao China* (Berkeley: University of California Press, 1987).

19. This account is drawn from discussions with Chinese economists who stressed that a major change in credit policy such as that which occurred in April 1986 could only be decided at the highest levels of the government.

20. *Zhongguo Tongji Yuebao* 1988: 5, p. 78.

21. Zhu Pingxiang, 'A few opinions on current monetary conditions and policy', *Zhongguo Jinrong* 1988: 1, p. 21.

22. An example of coercive relations is given in the journal of the banking system, 'Party and government leaders in some regions compel banks to make loans', *Zhongguo Jinrong* 1985: 9, p. 7, which describes how a vice-mayor in Xi'an locked the bank leaders in a room until they agreed to make a loan to his favourite project. See also Zhou Xiaochuan and Zhu Li, 'China's Banking System: Current Status, Perspective on Reform', *Journal of Comparative Economics* 11:3 (September 1987), p. 404; and Gordon White and Paul Bowles, 'Towards a Capital Market? Reforms in the Chinese Banking System', Institute of Development Studies, China Research Report no. 6, 1987, especially pp. 26, 42, 46, 53 and 64.

23. Zhou Zhengqing, 'Contract the Scope of Credit and Adjust the Structure of Lending'. *Zhongguo Jinrong* 1987:12, pp. 15–17.

24. This is the case if all producers have equal access to capital during contractionary periods, which is never completely true in even the most fully marketised economies. Moreover, different sectors are differentially affected by contractionary polices in all economies.

25. Huang Yujun, 'The Focus of Industrial-Commercial Bank Work in 1988 should be Adjusting the Structure of Lending', *Zhongguo Jinrong* 1988:1, pp. 6–8.

26. Statistics are not available to calculate this figure for earlier years. Figures are derived from State Statistical Bureau, *Zhongguo Guding Zichan Touzi Tongji Ziliao 1950–1985* [China Fixed Investment Statistical Materials 1950–1985] (Beijing: Zhongguo Tongji), 1987, pp. 14, 59, 64, 218–19; *1987 Tongji Nianjian*, pp. 473–74, 506; *1988 Tongji Zhaiyao*, p. 67. I have taken the portion of 'other' investment going to oilfield development as expenditure on a central government project.

27. *1987 Jingji Nianjian*, p. v-36. Fertiliser production during 1985 tumbled to 63 million tons, but 22 million tons of unsold fertiliser piled up in warehouses. Zhang Yu'an, 'Fertiliser industry needs more help from the state', *China Daily Business Weekly*, February 28, 1988, p. 1.

28. *Beijing Review* August 24, 1987, p. 14.

29. For a general discussion of enterprise objectives in China, see William Byrd and Gene Tidrick, 'Factor Allocation and Enterprise Incentives', in Tidrick and Chen (eds), pp. 60–102.

30. Barry Naughton, 'False Starts and Second Wind', pp. 235–36.

31. Song Guoqing and Zhang Weiying, 'Several Theoretical Questions of Macroeconomic Balance and Macroeconomic Balance and Macroeconomic Control', *Jingji Yanjiu* 1986: 6, pp. 23–35.
32. The decline in rents is due to the larger proportion of total housing provided by enterprises at low rates, rather than to a reduction in rents for any given form of housing.
33. *1987 Tongji Nianjian*, p. 656; *1988 Tongji Zhaiyao*, p. 91.

3 The Changing Role of the State in Chinese Agriculture

Zhu Ling

The current economic reform has touched all aspects of society – including the political system – so that a new framework seems to be emerging for Chinese socio-economic development. Initially, the reform started from the agricultural sector which involved 80 per cent of the population at that time. Thus the course of reform in agriculture has had a strong impact on the development of China as a whole. Institutional and organisational changes in agriculture are generally regarded as having made the most significant contributions to reform: instead of the production teams of the people's communes, individual peasant households have become the basic units of agricultural production and consumption. These changes have inevitably led to a change in the part that the government has played in agriculture.

This paper will first provide an overview of the operating mechanisms of agriculture prior to the reform; second, it will briefly discuss the effects of the changing role of the state on agricultural production, resource allocation and income distribution; and third, it will examine current problems which may substantially impair the further development of agriculture and suggest possible counter-measures.

1 GOVERNMENT ACTIVITIES DURING THE PERIOD OF THE PEOPLE'S COMMUNES

The people's communes were set up during the 1950s with the aim of helping to establish a centrally planned economy in China through a forced overcollectivisation in rural areas where agriculture always played a predominant role in the economy. The communes consisted of three levels in terms of ownership as well as economic and administrative management: communes, production brigades and production

83

teams. The production team was the basic economic unit and on average included approximately 24 peasant households (OECD, 1985). By means of the communes' organisational structure, a hierarchical system like a pyramid was formed for implementing national agricultural plans, as the following figure illustrates. Plans were drawn up by the central government for the choice of products and the volume of production, the amount of area planted and the quota of government procurement and administered through different levels down to the production teams.

Purchasing and marketing of farm products were basically monopolised by state commercial agencies. In accordance with the collectivisation process, the state monopoly tended to cover the whole agricultural trading sector. The monopoly was extended to include as many as 180 kinds of farm products during the period of the 'Cultural Revolution'. Farmers were required to sell products to the state commercial agencies and were paid prices fixed by the state. However, the purchasing prices of farm products were set so low that there was not much incentive for farm people to produce more.

Restricted by this kind of planning and implementation framework, the teams were not able to make their own management decisions in such a way as to use existing resources efficiently and to obtain maximum profits. The low pricing policy of farm products was also used as a means of transferring resources intersectorally from agriculture to industry. Consistent with this strategy, a system for food subsidies was set up which was designed to favour only the urban population because it was eligible to participate directly in industrialisation.

The strategy of developing industry at the expense of agriculture has been adopted by most developing countries. However, only the Chinese government virtually ruled the rural population out of urban industrialisation by means of prohibiting labour migration from rural areas to cities. Through a system of registration of people and their places of residence, the government directly controlled a rationing system for daily necessities, and within that subsidies were exclusively available for urban residents. The hierarchical commune organisations were also used to prevent rural-urban labour migration since farmers had to ask brigade leaders for permission whenever they wanted to travel – even to visit their relatives. Thus the government not only distributed national income between agriculture and other sectors, but also directly allocated labour resources between them.

Furthermore, the government has always been the major monetary investor in agricultural capital construction. Prior to the reforms, investment

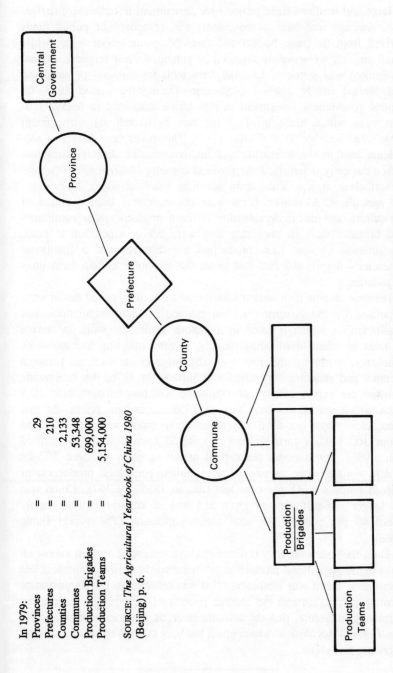

In 1979:

Provinces	=	29
Prefectures	=	210
Counties	=	2,133
Communes	=	53,348
Production Brigades	=	699,000
Production Teams	=	5,154,000

SOURCE: *The Agricultural Yearbook of China 1980* (Beijing) p. 6.

FIGURE 3.1   Administrative system for the Chinese agricultural sector during the period of the People's Communes

in large and medium-sized projects for agricultural infrastructure (irrigation, drainage and land improvement) was composed of public funds derived from the state budget and farmers' *gratis* labour input, while small projects were mainly financed by communes and brigades. Private investment was restricted to small farm tools for farmers' personal use and limited family sideline production. During the period 1953–78, central government investment in agriculture amounted to 63,592 million *yuan* which made up 11.5 per cent of overall state investment (*Statistical Yearbook of China*, 1987). This investment played a significant part in the formation and improvement of land infrastructure which basically determined the physical capacity of Chinese agriculture. Nevertheless, it was a far from adequate basis on which to modernise agriculture. Moreover, because of the extremely limited output of agriculture and the undervaluation of farm products, most communes and brigades were so poor that they were not in a position to make investments. Chinese farm production has then retained a traditional character – despite the fact that under the commune system farm units were large.

Personal income distribution within teams was also carried out in ways stipulated by the government. The essence of these stipulations was egalitarianism which resulted in a vicious circle: the work incentives of team members diminished steadily, thereby lowering average work efficiency, lessening the return of the brigades as well as personal income, and reducing incentives still further. In 1976, the nationwide average per capita income of commune members amounted to 62.8 *yuan* which was lower than that of 1956 at constant prices. At that time, more than one-third of peasant households were in debt and about 100 million farming people suffered from a shortage of food (Lu, 1986). The national per capital output of grain averaged 307 kg which was the same as two decades earlier; per capita production of oilseed crops was 41 per cent less than in 1956. By 1978, China was no longer self-sufficient in grain and had to import grain to supply about 40 per cent of the total urban population (The World Bank, 1986).

Thus, the state took over productive and commercial roles in almost all links in the agricultural production chain during the period of the people's communes, but it was inefficient. This was reflected in the stagnation of farming production and the chronic poverty of farm people. It was not surprising, therefore, that the reforms emerged in agriculture soon after the 'Cultural Revolution' whose effect has been to bring the whole national economy into crisis.

2   THE IMPACT OF THE CHANGING ROLE OF THE STATE ON AGRICULTURAL DEVELOPMENT

The beginning of economic reform arose from farmers' spontaneous attempts to break away from the restrictions involved in the egalitarian distribution of rewards. The 'household responsibility system' was the final outcome in terms of pattern of production organisation and personal income distribution. The system was later promoted by policy makers of the Chinese Communist Party and the central government. It can be considered as a kind of tenant-farming system in which public ownership of land is combined with private ownership of capital. Individual peasant households have the freedom as independent producers to manage their allocated plots of land and make their own decisions regarding economic activities. In this sense, family farms are now the basic agricultural production units.

In comparison with those in Western Europe and North America, family farms in China have two distinct characteristics: firstly, they have generally adopted simple equipment and techniques and continue to use traditional methods of farm management; secondly, the farms are small in size (on average 0.5 ha. of farmland) and have a mainly subsistence economy. In this paper, they are referred to as 'peasant farms'. With the emergence of peasant farms, the people's commune system was inevitably abolished. Those political and social functions which the communes had undertaken were taken over by the local government at the township (*xiang*) level. Instead of the former production brigade, a village committee was put in charge of social affairs (such as road construction, water management, and so on) within an administrative village. Production teams were replaced by villager groups which were established to facilitate administrative management at the grass-roots level in rural areas.

Following these institutional and organisational changes, the instruments which the state used to manage agriculture at the macro level have gradually been modified. The main tendency of these modifications is that, instead of direct involvement, the state manages agricultural development mainly by means of public policies designed to influence farmers' behaviour. Policies which have been radically changed fall into three categories:

(1) National mandatory plans regarding sown area, variety of products and volume of output were abolished while price and marketing policies were introduced to induce farmers to produce more. With the removal of the state monopoly on the purchasing and marketing of farm products (except tobacco), restrictions on free trade in those products in rural areas were lifted and urban fairs were opened for farmers. In 1978,

TABLE 3.1   *Composition of gross agricultural output value (in per cent) 1978–1985*

Year	Crop production	Forestry	Animal husbandry	Fisheries	Total
1978	79.3	3.6	15.5	1.6	100.0
1979	78.8	3.3	16.4	1.5	100.0
1980	77.4	3.7	17.4	1.5	100.0
1981	75.0	5.0	18.0	2.0	100.0
1982	74.7	4.8	18.4	2.1	100.0
1983	75.2	4.9	17.8	2.1	100.0
1984	74.4	5.3	18.1	2.2	100.0
1985	71.3	5.4	20.8	2.5	100.0
1986	70.4	5.1	21.5	3.0	100.0

NOTE: Calculated according to the data in *Statistical Yearbook of China*, 1986, p. 167.

China had 33,302 rural fairs while in 1985 the number had increased to 53,324 (*Beijing Review*, no. 19, 1987). By July, 1987, the sum of urban and rural fairs was already about 67,000. In addition, the central government directly controls the purchasing and marketing of only two kinds of key farm products, grain and cotton, but business is carried out according to contracts signed between state commercial bodies and farmers. For purchases under contract, two-tier prices were set by the central government. For 30 per cent of the grain sold, farmers are paid at a normal state purchasing price and the rest at a higher 'above quota' price. After supplying the quota fixed in the contracts, farmers are left to sell the surplus of both products on the market. This development made it possible for state purchase prices to rise after 1979, having been fixed at a low level for twelve years. The general purchasing price index of farm and sideline products increased by 77.5 per cent between 1978 and 1986.

(2) Structural policies were made for stimulating diversification of the farm economy since prior to the reform the main emphasis had been on promoting grain production. The extent of this structural readjustment can be seen from changes in the composition of gross agricultural output value (Table 3.1).

(3) Rural non-agricultural economic development policies were designed in order to shift surplus labour from agriculture into other sectors which had a labour demand within the rural areas. In 1987, more than 80 million surplus farm labourers, which constituting 20 per cent of the total labour force, were either employed by village or township-owned industrial enterprises or worked as specialists in businesses outside the realm of

TABLE 3.2 *Per mu yield of three key farm products in Henan Province in 1978–1985*

Year	Grain (kg/mu)	Cotton (kg/mu)	Oil-bearing seeds (kg/mu)
1978	153	24	35
1979	157	24	39
1980	175	43	43
1981	171	37	50
1982	166	28	42
1983	208	53	57
1984	214	50	60
1985	200	45	81

NOTE: The yield per unit area was calculated from the data in *Statistical Yearbook of Henan*, 1985 (Source), pp. 73–74.

traditional farming. The output value of rural industry amounted to 330 billion yuan in 1986, for the first time exceeding that of agriculture (300 billion yuan). In 1987, the gross output value of non-agricultural sectors already formed 50.8 per cent of the total gross output value of the rural economy.

An unprecedented growth in agricultural production and an increase in the income of farmers' families in recent years indicates that these policies have been successful. The gross output value of agriculture increased at an average rate of 2.9 per cent yearly during 1957–78, but by 8.9 per cent in 1979–84 at constant prices. (Since 1985 growth has become slower; this will be discussed in Section 3.)

The increase in the national output of some key agricultural products can be seen from Table 3.4. The rapid increase in the supply of farm products

TABLE 3.3 *Composition of annual net income per capita of nn average peasant household in China in 1978–1985*

	1978	1980	1981	1982	1983	1984	1985
Farm income (yuan)	114	149	171	204	222	250	264
Per cent	92.7	89.8	87.7	86.1	81.3	79.4	75.4
Nonfarm income (yuan)	9	17	24	33	51	65	86
Per cent	7.3	10.2	12.3	13.9	18.7	20.6	24.6
Total (yuan)	123	166	195	237	273	315	350
Per cent	100	100	100	100	100	100	100

NOTE: The data in this table was calculated from official statistics in *Statistical Yearbook of China 1986*, p. 674.

TABLE 3.4 *The national output
of some key agricultural products during 1979–1987*

Unit: million tons

Year	Grain	Cotton	Oilseed Crops	Pork, Beef Mutton	Aquatic Products	Tea
1979	332	2.2	6.4	10.6	4.3	0.28
1980	321	2.7	7.7	12.1	4.5	0.30
1981	325	3.0	10.2	12.6	4.6	0.34
1982	355	3.6	11.8	13.5	5.2	0.40
1983	387	4.6	10.6	14.0	5.5.	0.40
1984	407	6.3	11.9	15.4	6.2	0.41
1985	379	4.1	15.8	17.6	7.1	0.43
1986	392	3.5	14.7	19.2	8.2	0.46
1987	405	4.2	15.3	19.9	9.6	0.51

SOURCE: *Statistical Yearbook of China 1988*, The State Statistical Bureau of China, Beijing, pp. 248–66.

improved the diet of both the urban and rural population. At the same time, farmers have also benefited from the accelerated growth of agriculture. Per capita net income of peasant households increased at an average rate of 13.1 per cent a year between 1979–87, compared to only 3 per cent in the period 1954–78. Although income inequality has grown, it is not very pronounced. This can be supported by looking at the variations in the value

TABLE 3.5 *Composition of peasant households
by per capita net income group in China*

Income Group (yuan)	1978	1980	1981	1982	1983	1984	1985
100.00 and below	33.3	9.8	4.7	2.7	1.4	0.8	1.0
100.01–150.00	31.7	24.7	14.9	8.1	6.2	3.8	3.4
150.01–200.00	17.6	27.1	23.0	16.0	13.1	9.4	7.9
200.01–300.00	15.0	25.3	34.8	37.0	32.9	29.2	25.6
300.01–400.00	8.6	14.4	20.8	22.9	24.5	24.0	
401.00–500.00	2.4	2.9	5.0	8.7	11.6	14.1	15.8
501.00 and over	1.6	3.2	6.7	11.9	18.2	22.3	

SOURCE: *Statistical Yearbook of China 1986*, p. 673.

of the Gini coefficient referring to peasant households in China as a whole (State Statistical Bureau, 1986):

Year	1978	1980	1981	1982	1983	1984	1985
Values of Gini	0.2124	0.2366	0.2388	0.2318	0.2459	0.2577	0.2636

The basic cause of these achievements is thought to be the improvement in the economic operating mechanisms. As the state has gradually withdrawn from its direct involvement, the initiative and entrepreneurship of farmers have been released. Since farmers won the right to manage family farms – the prosperity of which serves to increase their family income – they were strongly motivated to allocate both human and physical resources efficiently. Furthermore, the introduction of market mechanisms has enabled farmers to make the most use of their local advantages to adapt to changes in demand. This has apparently improved the utilisation efficiency of local resources. Moreover, the rapid growth of agricultural production was achieved at a time when state investment in agriculture decreased both relatively and absolutely. Thus, the growth could be regarded as an outcome of a considerable improvement in efficiency. This may also reflect the main effects of the changing role of the state in agriculture.

3 CURRENT PROBLEMS IN THE DEVELOPMENTAL ROLE OF THE STATE IN AGRICULTURE

Together with this unprecedented agricultural development, various problems have emerged which were often thought to be caused by failures in the reform programme. In fact, they arose mostly from contradictions between:

- the existing ideological framework of Marxist orthodoxy and changing practices in the real world;
- the mandatory planning mechanism and the market mechanism;
- government interference and individual initiative;
- sectors which have experienced reform to varying degrees;
- enterprises which are doing business within the same sectors but have different patterns of ownership and operation;
- interest groups which have gained benefits from the reform and those which have lost some advantages;
- introduction of a competitive environment and people's behaviour patterns based on egalitarianism, dependency on the state, etc.

Nevertheless, these contradictions indicate a dynamic development. The new problems may have provided a motivating force for the Chinese people to find a new way out. Based on this understanding, the following discussion will focus on current problems which have substantially retarded the growth of agriculture.

In comparison with the period 1979–84, the growth rate of agriculture slowed down from 1985 onwards: the gross output value of agriculture increased by 3.4, 3.5, 4.7 and 3.2 per cent in 1985, 1986, 1987 and 1988 respectively. The output of several key products, including grain, cotton, oilseed crops, and pork, has fallen from a peak record output in 1984, although the decrease in output of some key products was reversed in 1987. Some authors argue that these phenomena indicate a transition in agriculture from 'super-conventional' growth to 'conventional growth' (Chen, 1987). Others regard them as a sign of possible stagnation which resulted mainly from faults in the design and implementation of certain policies, such as reducing public investment, limiting the volume of state purchased grain and depressing state purchase prices (Gao, Li and Zhou, 1987). In fact, this fluctuation in the growth of agriculture during 1979–1987 may be evidence that agriculture in China has reached an equilibrium characteristic of a poor traditional economy. In order to break this equilibrium and so further the development of agriculture, China must establish an appropriate institutional and physical infrastructure for transforming traditional agriculture to modern agriculture. However, there is a lack of incentive for farmers to participate actively in constructing such an infrastructure. This can be seen from the present situation in agricultural production, marketing and investment.

With regard to farm production, the extremely small farm size and the division of farmland[1] has become a barrier to obtaining the best from today's technology. It is important to note that farmland in China plays a role not only as production factor but also as food security for farmers and their families, since a social insurance system for the mass of the farming population has not yet been completed. In a situation where 800 million farm people are squeezed into about 106 million hectares of arable land, the allocation of farmland in the introduction of the responsibility system was carried out according to the size of peasant households. Apparently, the principle behind this allocation was equity rather than efficiency.

Nevertheless, a rapid growth in agriculture did take place as the system of family farms replaced the commune system. As this growth was an outcome of using existing resources more efficiently rather than of any technological breakthrough, the achievements since 1978 may only indicate progress in production organisation, which does not involve a change in the nature of traditional agriculture. Traditional agriculture has been characterised by Schultz as 'poor but efficient' (Schultz, 1964). According to this hypothesis the situation of resource allocation and utilisation in the communes can be summarised as 'poor and inefficient'. Thus, although the situation was improved by organisational changes, the inherent limitations of traditional agriculture prevented further growth.

The fundamental solution for agriculture lies in modernisation. However, it seems to be inconceivable so long as agriculture is based on 'market gardens by the million' (*The Economist*, 1987). Expansion of farm size is thus inevitable, but there are three crucial problems which impair the achievement of this. Firstly, farmland is virtually a non-marketable factor. Although the transfer of the right of land use has been officially permitted, the price (rent) system for such a transition seems to be difficult to envisage since a land evaluation system has not been set up as yet. Furthermore, there is a lack of necessary legislation concerning leasing and subleasing of farmland which would serve to monitor and control this kind of deal. Secondly, due to the limited development of industrialisation and urbanisation at the present stage, neither the rural non-agricultural sectors nor the urban economy can create enough employment opportunities to absorb surplus labour from agriculture. Consequently, farms are actually viewed as security against unemployment, so that even the farmers who already have a job in non-agricultural sectors will not give up their right to contracted land. Thirdly, according to official regulations, farmers involved in non-farm sectors still have to supply themselves with their own grain rations. It is important to note that they can cheaply produce enough foodstuff for their home consumption by expending a small amount of physical input and not much time rather than purchase food from the market. This is because land is used almost free of charge while food supplies on the market are unstable and market prices are comparatively high.

The contradictions which were referred to at the beginning of this section have emerged in the area of pricing and marketing of farm products, in particular foodstuffs. Firstly, since the previous strategy regarding industrialisation and urbanisation has not been basically changed and the state is still directly involved in the purchasing and marketing of a few key farm products – of which grain is a major item – the state has been in a dilemma in terms of raising the purchase price of foodstuff for producers and keeping down the selling price for urban consumers. Although state purchase prices have been substantially raised since 1979, they are actually still kept artificially low (Lardy, 1983 and Ma, 1987). This is reflected in the fact that market prices of farm products have generally been above state purchase prices. However, following the raising of farm product prices, the subsidies for food consumption by the urban population have significantly increased. In 1985, the subsidies amounted to 27.5 billion *yuan*, which is equivalent to a fourth of the wage bill of state employees. Today, the budgetary burden of the subsidies is so large that the commitment to fixed nominal prices for food supply to urban consumers is a substantial constraint on the ability of the state to offer incentive prices to producers. Nevertheless, the state has not abandoned such a system, mostly owing to the possible social disturbances which might arise from the urban population.

Secondly, the whole state machine has been accustomed to conducting economic affairs by means of mandatory plans and administrative control. This has led to an acute contradiction between administrative and market mechanisms and it has also resulted in a conflict between farmers and government institutions. Because of the unfavourable prices, farmers today are not willing to sign delivery contracts with the state. Under these terms state purchase orders were divided into quotas at different levels. Since 1985, each farm received a quota to fulfil which specified volume and type of commodity. This was in effect a compulsory purchase by government. In addition to this, a kind of producer subsidisation was introduced, executed by an 'administrative pyramid' similar to the one operating during the period of the communes. According to the contracted delivery volume of grain, farmers are entitled to obtain a certain amount of purchased inputs such as chemical fertiliser and diesel oil, at prices lower than the normal listed prices. What was not anticipated, however, was that the subsidy would be intercepted in part at different administrative levels, so that there are not many benefits left for farmers. The worst case of this misuse occurred in the implementation of the two-tier price system with reference to inputs, as some speculators took advantage of the price disparity between the two tiers.

Thirdly, a rudimentary market mechanism also constitutes a constraint on the envisaged transition of the agricultural sector from a subsistence to a market-oriented economy. Apart from the restrictions of the partly existing mandatory planning system, there are also some other decisive factors which impair the development of the market: (1) shortage of physical infrastructure such as roads, means of transport, packaging, processing, warehouse and market buildings (An, 1987); (2) lack of a service and support system and legal regulations; (3) growing protectionism and interference by local governments have become one of the main barriers to the formation of a unified nationwide market.

TABLE 3.6   *Development of Agricultural Commercialisation in China,*
1978–1985

Year	Gross agricultural output value[1]	Value of purchased farm products[2] (100 mill. yuan)	Commer- cialisation rate (p. c.)	Proportion of purchase of three key products to the total production respectively (p. c.)		
				grain	edible veg. oil[3]	cotton
1978	1288.7	530.1	41.1	14.0	55.9	94.3
1979	1386.3	677.6	48.9	15.6	62.1	97.8
1980	1964.5	797.7	41.0	15.0	71.1	99.0
1981	2091.4	908.0	43.4	15.0	76.4	98.0
1982	2327.6	1031.0	44.3	16.7	71.9	97.2
1983	2508.2	1206.0	48.1	22.0	65.4	97.1
1984	2815.6	1371.0	48.7	23.2	67.4	95.3
1985	2912.2	1600.0	54.9	15.4	68.4	84.4

NOTES:

1. The data regarding 'gross agricultural output value' did not include output value of village industry.

2. 'Value of purchased farm products' refers to the value of the products which all purchasing bodies brought from farmers.

3. 'Edible vegetable oil' includes soybean oil, rice bran oil and maize-plumule oil as well as oil-bearing crops equivalent to oil.

The problems in pricing and marketing of farm products make the pressure of supply shortage heavier. It can be seen from national statistics that the commercialisation rate of grain has always fluctuated around 20 per cent although grain output has increased.[2] For example, shortage in pork supply became so serious that several large cities reverted to a rationing system in 1987. One way of alleviating such pressure is to increase supply. The fundamental solution for increasing supply is to modernise agriculture by introducing more advanced technologies. A prerequisite for achieving this is adequate investment in the human and physical resources of agriculture.

However, capital investment in agriculture has apparently been depressed during the reform. Although production organisations have tended to become adapted to a market oriented economy, the previous system of agricultural investment has not as yet substantially changed. The government still plays a predominant part as a monetary capital investor but it has drastically reduced investment in agriculture in terms of both absolute and relative value. State agricultural investment amounted to

5,792 million *yuan* in 1979, constituting 11.1 per cent of total government investment, but decreased to 3,506 million *yuan* (3.0 per cent of the total) in 1986.

Three factors are essential to explain this tendency. Firstly, apart from a general limitation of funds and strong demands on investment from every sector – in particular, energy and communications – the return to agricultural investment seems too low to be given a priority. In fact, the low return has partly resulted from the undervaluation of farm products. Secondly, the rapid growth in the agricultural economy during this period may have led to an overestimation of the effects of economic reform and a neglect of the contribution of the existing physical capital to growth. Thirdly, a new organisational system for effectively executing government-invested capital construction projects has not been established since the disintegration of the commune system. As a result of the decrease in capital investment, the effectively irrigated area in China decreased by 3.4 million hectares between the years 1983–87 which led to a loss of grain totalling 10 million tons.

Peasant farms might have been expected to play a part as a major investor in agriculture. Nevertheless, they have not yet undertaken this task. When

TABLE 3.7   *Volume and Growth Rate of Per Capita Average Consumption Expenditure, Bank Savings and Investment of Peasant Households in China, 1978–1986*

Year	Consumption expenditure (yuan)	Growth rate (p. c.)	Bank savings (yuan)	Growth rate (p. c.)	Investment (yuan)	Growth rate (p. c.)
1978	116.09	–	2.09	–	•	•
1979	134.51	15.9	3.40	62.68	•	•
1980	162.21	20.6	6.73	97.94	•	•
1981	190.81	17.6	8.92	32.54	9.09	–
1982	220.23	15.4	11.42	28.03	14.51	59.63
1983	248.29	12.7	15.24	33.45	25.65	76.77
1984	273.00	10.0	19.54	28.22	39.44	53.76
1985	317.42	16.3	17.55	-10.18	31.86	-19.98
1986	356.96	12.5	•	•	•	•

NOTE:

1. '•' = missing value
2. Source: Sample survey made by the rural survey teams of The State Statistical Bureau, quoted from Jiang and Luo, a paper presented in the 'International Symposium for Rural Development Strategies', 25-31 October 1987, Beijing.

the capital stock of the production teams was equally allocated according to household size, most peasant households received such a small share that they had to make an investment – in the form of purchasing draught animals and farm tools – in order to enable the individual farm economy to subsist. Since then they have not shown a strong preference to invest in their farms but have tended to increase consumption. With regard to capital construction on farmland, the general problem is not only that farmers have used land without making investment in it, but even worse, they have intentionally expropriated the existing soil fertility. The outcome can be seen from a survey carried out by The Chinese Academy of Agricultural Sciences: soil fertility has generally declined (*People's Daily*, 28 January 1988).

There are two kinds of barrier to farmers' investment in agriculture. The first is the bitterness that farmers feel about their experiences during the political instability of the past – it seems that at present they have no confidence in the future. As a result, their decisions have been made in pursuit of an immediate increase in current income and rapid improvement in living standards rather than to make intermediate and long-term investments to increase future income. It is calculated that the marginal saving rate of farmers' families (0.371) is much higher than that of urban residents (0.291), despite the fact that the former are at a considerably lower income level (The Institute for Rural Development Research, 1987). However, in a list outlining reasons for saving, 90 farmers interviewed (in three counties of Henan province) in a study made by the author, gave housing and children's marriage as the most important reasons instead of reasons related to capital investment in production. The arguments supporting their choices can be seen in the fact that private ownership in housing in the rural sector has never been affected by the various political campaigns since the revolution, while private capital goods have always been in danger of expropriation. Moreover, marriage is, in the farmers' view, also a means of increasing labour, which can substitute for certain amounts of physical capital and definitely belongs to their own family. With regard to the three studied counties, farmers' spending on housing constituted 40.6, 62.2 and 33.1 per cent of the total investment in capital construction of each county in 1985 (Zhu, 1987).

In relation to farmland, the rights of owners and users have not been clarified as yet in both theory and practice. There are no institutions which effectively represent ownership of farmland so that collective ownership has virtually become an empty concept. In fact, the contracted area of farmland is temporarily owned by individual farmers since they have a right to till it free of charge. Farmers are aware that this situation involves problems which will be settled sooner or later by means of changing farmland policies. Thus, in order to procure as much return as possible from farmland before the anticipated changes take place, farmers expropriate soil fertility without caring what kind of resource they will leave for the future.

The second type of barrier to agricultural investment by farmers is its low return. Low productivity keeps the profitability of this sector correspondingly low. The undervaluation of farm products has forced agricultural profitability down to an even lower level, so that the sector has not been in a position to attract investment in order to enhance the productivity of factors of production. Clearly, this is a vicious

TABLE 3.8 *Per Capita Average Net Income and Living Expenditure of Peasant Households in Henan Province, 1955–1985 (in yuan)*

Year	per capita net income	Total living expend- iture per capita	Food	Clothing	Housing	Fuel	Daily articles	Cultural
1955	65.8	62.6	40.7	4.8		7.4	8.8	0.9
1956	68.2	66.1	41.6	6.8	0.1	7.2	9.4	1.0
1957	64.6	63.0	41.4	6.2		7.2	7.3	0.9
1963	77.2	75.9	48.2	6.7	4.1	8.8	6.2	1.9
1964	71.8	67.7	46.3	5.9	2.4	5.6	5.4	2.1
1965	73.7	66.9	47.3	6.9	3.0	2.8	5.1	1.8
1978	104.7	81.7	52.9	9.9	6.3	4.9	5.8	1.9
1979	133.6	110.8	67.3	14.3	8.7	5.6	11.1	3.8
1980	160.8	135.5	78.5	18.5	14.5	6.9	13.8	3.3
1981	206.9	165.6	89.1	24.5	19.9	8.7	19.2	4.2
1982	206.9	177.9	101.2	23.2	20.2	8.5	20.5	4.3
1983	261.6	196.2	113.7	24.2	22.1	10.2	21.6	4.3
1984	288.8	219.7	122.5	27.7	27.2	10.6	26.2	5.5
1985	329.4	259.6	145.3	29.1	35.0	16.6	26.2	7.4

NOTES:
1. The data of years 1958–1962 and 1966–1977 are not available.
2. 'Per capita net income' for 1981–1985 does not include transfer income.
3. Source: *Statistical Yearbook of Henan 1985*.

TABLE 3.9 *Average per mu net receipts referring to one harvest (yuan)*

Grain	Cotton	Oil-bearing seeds	Tobacco
62.61	187.55	72.39	223.66

Average net receipts per head of pigs (*yuan*): 15.75

SOURCE: *Agricultural Statistical Yearbook of China, 1986.*

circle. In a situation where industrial development is at the expense of agriculture, agricultural profitability has become increasingly inferior to that of other economic sectors. This continuing low level of profitability – either viewed in an absolute or a relative sense – has given a discouraging signal to farmers and leads their investment towards non-farm sectors.

The profitability of the key subdivisions of farm productivity may apparently be indicated by the data for 1984 (Table 3.9). However, average per member net receipts of 'new economic co-operatives'[3] amounted to 1,730 yuan in rural industry, 1,338 yuan in construction, 2,922 yuan in transportation and 1,949 yuan in commerce, catering and service trades. It is then not surprising that, in accordance with the disparity in profitability between sectors, the capital stock (in terms of value) increased by 56.5 per cent in transportation, 40.5 per cent in industry and 13.45 per cent in agriculture in 1985 compared with 1983.

Consistent with the depression of investment in physical capital construction, the investment in human resources of agriculture also does not seem to be encouraging. Up to now about one-quarter of farm people remain illiterate, and the school attendance rate in rural regions has tended to decline. A sample survey made in 1988 showed that around 30–50 per cent of children aged 13–15 dropped out of the education system (*People's Daily, Overseas Version*, 3 June 1988). This is because a number of farmers let their children leave school in order to assist in farming. Such a choice is determined, firstly, by the existing traditional farming system which does not require an educated labour force and, secondly, it is actually a response to deficiencies in the Chinese education system which is overwhelmingly academically oriented. Farmers prefer to choose vocational schools which are in extremely short supply in the whole country. From this analysis it can be predicted that, in regard to investment, agricultural development will be impaired by present problems if effective counter-measures are not taken.

4   SOME TENTATIVE CONCLUSIONS

The previously stated problems showed that China has not yet succeeded in creating a political and economic framework which can continuously provide incentives to farm people to modernise agriculture using their own initiative. In order to achieve such a framework, an envisaged economic operating model was announced by the 13th National Congress of the Chinese Communist Party (October 1987), that is: the state regulates the market and then the market regulates the economy. According to this design, the essential role of the state in agriculture is to provide legal regulations for economic activities, to manage agricultural development at the macro level by means of policies and economic instruments such as taxation, credit and public investment, and to promote further improvement of institutional and physical infrastructure in rural regions, especially in poor areas.

However, the state is still heavily involved in the kind of activities that economic enterprises should undertake, while the necessary operating rules for a changing socioeconomic environment have not yet been completed, despite the fact that only the state is in a position to devise these rules. Clearly a starting point for achieving the envisaged model should be that the state must continue to withdraw from its direct involvement. At the same time, in order to solve the problems which substantially retard current agricultural development, it is suggested that the following measures should be taken as a part of a reform programme:

- Undervalued farm product prices should be adjusted by means of market-mechanisms, so that state purchase and marketing prices can be adjusted according to market prices. However, such a system cannot be financed unless state subsidies for urban food consumers are removed and the lower income groups among those consumers are supported by public welfare.
- With regard to agricultural input goods, it is necessary to abolish the two-tier price system. The key point of this measure is to replace the administrative distribution system with a market-allocation system. In this way, farmers might be able to pay cheaper prices and get input goods of a higher quality. since enterprises would have to produce those goods more efficiently if they were under pressure of competition in the factor market.
- In order to increase the profitability of farms, the mobility of all factors of production including farmland should be intensified by means of introducing factor markets. Thus, a structural adjustment in farm size

can be anticipated. Moreover, a social insurance system must be set up so that hardships for the old, the physically or economically less competitive people can be dealt with.

- For the purpose of improving investment possibilities of farms, a political framework in favour of manifold cooperatives in the service sector (for example, supply of credit, purchase and marketing, utilisation of machines) should be established. Furthermore, private and public investment, vocational and short-term technical training should be promoted.

These measures will, to a certain extent, weaken the existing power of the administrative machine but they have to be implemented by means of an organisational network of the existing administrative system. Since this is already a contradiction arising at the very beginning, it can be predicted that China has still a long way to go to achieve the goal of reform.

NOTES

1. According to the national sample survey, a Chinese farmer on average cultivates 0.56 hectares of farmland which is dispersed in 9.7 plots, *Nongcun Jingji Wenti* [*Agro-economic Problems*] 1986, no. 6, Beijing).
2. An empirical study made by the author in Luoyang region, Henan province, in 1985, showed that the commercialisation rate of grain remains low – almost regardless of the income group to which the farmers belong.
3. The new economic cooperatives are joint ventures set up by groups of farmers in recent years. The enterprises are run in the form of joint operations and management by members – on the basis of their own private investment and work performance.

REFERENCES

An (1987), 'The Development and Improvement of Agricultural Marketing in China', paper presented in the *International Symposium for Rural Development Strategies* October 25–31, 1987, Beijing.

Chen (1987), 'The rural economy in China is transferring from supra-conventional growth to conventional growth', *Jingji Yanjiu* (*Economic Research*) no. 12, 1987, Beijing.

Gao, Li and Zhou (1987), 'A moderate growth or a sluggish development', *Economic Research* no. 9, 1987, Beijing.

Lardy, (1983), *Agricultural Prices in China* (Staff Working Papers, no. 606), World Bank, Washington DC.

Lu (1986), *Research on Systems of Responsibility* (The People's Publishing House of Shanghai: Shanghai, 1986).

Ma, Calkins and Johnson (1987), 'Technical and Allocative Efficiency vs. Equity in Shuyang County, Jiangsu'. Paper presented in the *International Symposium for Rural Development Strategies*, October 25–31, 1987, Beijing.

OECD (1985), *Agriculture in China* (Paris).

Schultz (1964), *Transforming Traditional Agriculture* (Yale University Press, 1964, New Haven).

State Statistical Bureau, *Statistical Yearbook of China 1986* (Beijing, 1986).

State Statistical Bureau, *Rural Statistical Yearbook of China 1986* (Beijing, 1987).

State Statistical Bureau, *Statistical Yearbook of China 1987* (Beijing, 1987).

State Statistical Bureau (1988) 'Statistical Bulletin Regarding National Socio-Economic Development in 1987', *People's Daily* (overseas edition), 25.2.1988.

'China's Economy', *The Economist* (London), August 1, 1987.

The Institute for Rural Development Research (1987), *A New Growth Stage of the National Economy and Rural Development* (The People's Publishing House of Zhejiang, 1987, Hangzhou).

The World Bank, *World Development Report 1986* (Oxford University Press, 1986).

Zhu (1988), *Income Development Among Peasant Households Through Rural Economic Reform in The People's Republic of China*, a thesis prepared for a Ph.D in Economics at the University of Hohenheim, Stuttgart, 1988.

4 A Soviet Specialist's View of the Chinese Economic Reforms

David Dyker

A comparison of the Soviet and Chinese economic reforms as of 1988 encounters an intriguing mixture of similarities and contrasts. Let us checklist the specific operational elements within the reform programmes of both countries, moving from the general to the particular.

THE EXTENT OF ECONOMIC DECENTRALISATION

Generally speaking, the Chinese reform has been more radical than the Soviet on key issues like freedom of contract and freedom of price formation. The Soviet programme for introduction of 'wholesale trade in the means of production', which means making industrial supplies available on an over-the-counter basis without the requirement of an allocation certificate, envisages gradual extension over the period up to 1992. Even after that date, however, key commodities will still require allocation certificates. In any case, the experience of 1988 suggests that it will be far from easy to orchestrate a smooth extension of wholesale trade, with the industrial ministries once again in the dock charged with obstructionism. At the present time wholesale trade accounts for at most 15–20 per cent of total Soviet industrial supply turnover. In China, by contrast, market allocation appears now to be the rule rather than the exception. As a general principle, only key commodities in deficit like steel, cement, timber, fertiliser, etc., are still subject to central allocation, and even here the dual price system, which permits free procurement at higher prices, allows a degree of flexibility. There is no parallel to the dual price system in the Soviet Union.

The same pattern is evident when we look at price systems as a whole. In the Soviet Union, Gorbachev has emphatically pronounced that it is not only impossible, but actually undesirable, for the central authorities to try to

103

set every price in the economy. Outside the area of private and co-operative enterprise (of which more below), however, operational developments have been fairly slow. Nevertheless the new category of 'contract prices' is beginning to add some new flexibility to the Soviet price structure. In China the majority of prices are in principle market-formed, though with the central authorities continuing to fix prices for key agricultural and industrial supplies, and retaining the right to impose ad hoc price controls, as they did in the autumn of 1988 in response to a rising inflation rate.

Yet with all these differences we can spot some crucial areas where Chinese and Soviet experience have been strikingly similar. Both systems have attempted to move towards greater reliance on the price mechanism in their approach to planning. Both systems have found that this movement is anything but a smooth linear progression.

Perhaps the best way to illustrate this point is to look at attempts in both countries to introduce stronger price incentives for deficit agricultural products. The whole tenor of Gorbachev's agricultural reforms, fruit of his years of experience as an agricultural administrator in Stavropol', has been to move away from the classic Stalinist system of output quotas, and towards a more parametric system. But this, in a sense, is where the problems begin:

> Natural and economic conditions in the Estonian republic are most suitable for the development of the beef and dairy industry and the cultivation of potatoes. But with the present structure of procurement prices, production of these relatively capital- and labour-intensive lines is not profitable enough. You can make much higher profits per unit costs, and with a lot less trouble, if you stick to pork and egg production, using fodder brought in from other regions. The only way to maintain output levels of less profitable categories of produce is through administrative measures, setting targets for sales of all product lines, profitable and unprofitable, to the state. *That is why sowing plans and plans for head of livestock are still being imposed in some parts of the country, despite a number of government pronouncements condemning the practice.* (emphasis added; Bronshtein, 1986, p. 81)

We find the same pattern in China, in connection with the pork shortage which developed in 1987. The number of pigs fell by 4.4 per cent in that year, by comparison with 1986, and the supply of pork by 0.4 per cent. The number of families involved in animal husbandry dropped from 860,000 to 770,000 (Zhang, 1988). Rationing had to be introduced in Beijing, Shanghai and other major cities. For the combination of low pork procurement prices and sharp increases in grain prices meant that farmers were making minimal profits, or even losing money on pig-raising. Pork prices did rise a little in 1987, and elements of subsidisation were introduced, but these measures were insufficient to reverse the basic trend.

The moral of the story is obvious enough. 'If farmers earned as much profit from animal husbandry as they do from manufacturing, the current meat shortages would not exist at all' (Zhang, 1988, quoting the Ministry of Agriculture). The way that local governments and townships have attacked the immediate problem, however, is by the reimposition of production quotas, directly or indirectly, through threats that key supplies would be cut off (interview with chairman of the Sino-Japanese Friendship township, Beijing in March 1988). Thus we find the same perverse pattern that is evident in the Soviet case. If you try to place more stress on prices, but fail to get the prices right, short term pressures will build up which will push the system back towards traditional output targets.

THE PROBLEM OF MACRO-ECONOMIC BALANCE

These agricultural problems are closely linked to budgetary problems. We can trace much of the difficulty with agricultural procurement prices back to food price policies. In the Soviet Union beef sells in state shops (if you can get it!) at less than half its collective farm market price. In China, pork is only half the price of chicken in state shops. It has simply proved impossible to reconcile a policy of cheap meat for the workers with adequate incentives for the peasants. Indeed, both Soviet and Chinese governments seem almost to have ended up with the worst of both worlds – massive subsidisation of retail food prices which has still not been enough to close the gap with a 'fair' procurement price. Some 10 per cent of Soviet National Income goes on subsidies for meat and dairy products alone (Gorbachev, 1987, p. 3). In China, 13.8 per cent of total state expenditure, 3.6 per cent of National Income, went on basic consumer good subsidies in 1987. Another major burden on budgets is subsidisation of loss-making enterprises – officially reported in the Soviet Union to represent some two per cent of National Income, but possibly adding up to much more than that. During the Brezhnev years the Soviet Union never admitted to having a budget deficit, and there, as elsewhere, *glasnost'* has brought a welcome breath of statistical fresh air. In his budget speech in November, 1988, Finance Minister Gostev, stated that the total Soviet budgetary deficit in 1989 would be Rb 36 bn – that would represent some 6 per cent of National Income. A few months later, it was admitted that the true figure is over Rb 100 bn. For China, the overall budgetary situation is difficult to pin down, because of complications with regional and local budgets, but the situation seems at the moment to be one of deficit, though not on the Soviet scale, the official budget deficit figures for 1987 and 1988 ('Quarterly Chronicle and documentation', 1988, p. 321) representing rather less than one per cent of National Income.

In the Soviet case it is clear that the budget deficit is a major source of inflationary pressure. Price control still ensures that the pressure is largely repressed, with a rate of open inflation of no more than 2–3 per cent. But there were signs towards the end of 1988 that the rate will increase as relaxations of price controls take effect. In the Chinese case the rate of open inflation is much higher – over 20 per cent towards the end of 1988 – but the main pressures here seem to come from the consumption and enterprise investment dimensions, rather than from the budget as such.

INVESTMENT PLANNING AND FINANCE

The purpose of central planning for extensive development is to mobilise the abundant resources – labour, and, to varying degrees, primary materials. The instrument of that mobilisatory impetus is capital investment. The politics of Stalinism helps to make capital more abundant than it would be 'naturally'. But even a Stalin cannot square the circle, and capital can never be anything else but a very scarce resource in a developing economy, particularly in circumstances where large-scale foreign aid is not available. It is one of the weaknesses of the classical Stalinist approach to development planning that this most precious of resources is often used wastefully. That weakness can be attributed partly to ideological hang-ups about the rate of interest and conventional procedures for project choice, partly to a characteristic gigantomania which may reflect a misunderstanding of the history of Western capitalism rather than anything specifically Marxist. Perhaps more importantly, it is attributable to organisational malfunctioning within the centrally planned system. Ministries and enterprises which do not have to pay for their investment resources will inevitably tend to overbid for those resources, the more so to the extent that prevalent supply uncertainty makes it advisable to have as many projects as possible on the go. Supply uncertainty also induces a powerful tendency to organisational autarky, as ministries and enterprises are forced to set up their own capacities to manufacture supplies they cannot reliably procure from elsewhere. The result of all this is a strongly delineated tendency to excessive lead-times and cost overruns. As the Soviet economy became increasingly complex during the post-war period, so these problems seem to have grown in severity (Dyker, 1983, 1985, chapter 1).

In his restructuring programme Mr Gorbachev has addressed the investment planning issue on two fronts. Firstly, he has introduced a new sobriety into Soviet project appraisal, publicly condemning the gigantomania of the past. Secondly, he has sought to revolutionise the organisation of the investment process through the *self-financing principle*. The line of argument is a simple one. Inefficiencies in the process stem primarily from two things – the bureaucratisation of decision-taking, and the fact that it is always someone else's money. The Soviet reform package shifts the locus of investment decision-taking for all projects except major green-field site projects from centre and ministry to enterprise. In addition, it posits that the primary source of investments for upgrading and expansion should be enterprise profits, supplemented where necessary by bank loans taken out on a commercial basis. Some Soviet exporters are now even being allowed to keep a portion of their hard-currency earnings to spend freely (in principle) on equipment imports. This decentralisation initiative in investment planning is being backed up by a reform of the banking system which seeks to create a network of commercial banking institutions which will be actively involved in the process of project choice.

The Soviet investment reform is still at too preliminary a stage for us to pass any final judgement on it. To date, two main problems have emerged. Firstly, to the extent that financial decentralisation has run ahead of decentralisation of supply, self-financing enterprises have found it difficult to convert rubles into bricks and machines (Dyker, 1987, pp. 74–77). Secondly, there has been a great deal of sheer bureaucratic obstruction, particularly of the hard-currency retention quota innovation, by banks and planners (Zverev, 1987; Valovaya, 1988). This, indeed, was one of the reasons why Gorbachev abolished the old Foreign Trade Bank in January, 1988. What further problems can we expect investment planning reform to run into as *perestroika* develops? We can go some way towards answering that question by looking at the evolution of investment policy in China.

There is evidence that 'excessive investment spread' was a substantial problem in pre-reform China, but with the adoption of the post-1978 new course there has been a major shift in the direction of self-financing, as Table 1 shows.

Perhaps even more important, that shift has been accompanied by a broadly-based transition to market-based allocation procedures for the bulk of investment supplies, in line with the general trend towards marketisation in the Chinese economy. Some key construction items are still centrally

TABLE 4.1 *The evolution of the pattern of investment finance in China*

	1979	1985
Budget	75.9	26.4
Bank loans	1.0	23.0
Enterprise profits	20.1	47.4
Foreign capital	3.0	2.8

SOURCE: Department of Economics, People's University, Beijing, 23 March 1988.

allocated, but again it is always in principle possible to buy supplies of them across the counter at a higher price.

This does not, of course, mean that the centre has abandoned investment planning in China. Enterprises are still obliged to deposit their retained profits with the Construction Bank, which gives the Bank a degree of leverage. And investment projects still have to be approved by the State Planning Commission or the State Council, wherever the finance comes from. Mechanisms do still exist, therefore, for the implementation of central priorities in the sphere of decentralised investment. The presumption is, however, that these mechanisms are used sparingly.

The Chinese case presents little evidence, then, of the perennial Soviet problem of matching financial with allocational decentralisation. Chinese investment planning reform appears to have been a consistent package, consistent internally, and with the reform programme as a whole. But that is not to say that it has not run into problems. Rather, the more consistent impetus of Chinese investment reform has served merely to highlight a point which we discussed earlier in general terms. The more a socialist economy moves towards market-based procedures, the more crucially important it becomes to get the price structure right. Officials of the Chinese Investment Bank are quite clear that the strategic goal should be to increase further the role of the market mechanism in the allocation of funds. They are ready to admit, however, that the trend in 1988 was in exactly the opposite direction. Deepening problems of structural balance forced the Bank to reimpose sectoral quotas in that year. The reason? Quite simply that without such quotas some sectors would not have received any investment funds at all (Discussions at the Chinese Investment Bank, 16 March 1988). No doubt this state of affairs may in part have reflected some reluctance by the centre to accept fully the implications of economic logic, to close down unprofitable and inefficient operations. It seems primarily, however, to have reflected deep flaws in the price system. Once again, then, wrong prices force you back, willy-nilly, into command planning. And the principle of self-financing may exacerbate the problem by inducing profit-maximising behaviour in actors who enjoy a quasi-monopolistic position, and can therefore use any flexibility in the price system to *distort it further*. As one Soviet citizen put it in relation to the early Soviet self-financing experiments: 'Give autonomy and command over resources to real enthusiasts, and they will, of course, work efficiently to the advantage of the state. But give the same freedoms to botchers, layabouts and cowboys . . . ' (Ronichev, 1985).

FOREIGN TRADE

The Soviet foreign trade system has certainly changed a great deal since Gorbachev came to power. In 1986 the time-honoured, Leninist monopoly of foreign trade was abolished. Up to that time all trade had to go through the bureaucratic intermediation of the Ministry of Trade. Now a limited number of Soviet ministries and enterprises would be allowed direct access to world markets, and the right to make their own contracts with foreign partners. Dominant and strategically crucial trade flows like energy exports and grain imports were excluded from the reform. Even so, over the first three months of 1988 organisations operating under the new dispensation accounted for 18 per cent of Soviet exports and 30 per cent of imports (Economist Intelligence Unit, 1988, p. 16). As we saw earlier, those exports carried with them the right to a hard-currency retention quota. In 1987 a law was passed which permitted, for the first time, foreign ownership of equity in the Soviet Union. The maximum foreign share in a joint venture was initially limited to 49 per cent, but was raised to 80 per cent at the end of 1988. Joint ventures are not subject to the authority of domestic Soviet planning bodies. By the end of 1988 over 100 (mostly small) joint venture agreements had been signed, without there being any sign of dramatic take-off in the new business form. A new law passed in December, 1988, to take effect from 1 January 1989, extended access to the new foreign trade system, in principle, to all enterprises. It also specified new tax concessions on joint ventures.

Momentous though these changes have been in the Soviet context, they seem modest enough by comparison with the 'open door' policy which China has adopted as a key element of the economic reform programme. In setting up a series of Special Economic Zones along the Chinese coast, Beijing has effectively allowed many of the most populous and economically developed parts of the People's Republic to 'join the world economy'. The state continues to finance infrastructural investment in the Special Zones, and exercises nominal control over matters like working conditions. But there is completely free access for foreign capital, and in practice foreign firms enjoy a great deal of freedom of action in relation to their Chinese labour forces. The currency system in the Special Zones is complex, involving simultaneous circulation of Hong Kong dollars and Chinese foreign exchange certificates (both convertible) and Chinese RMB (inconvertible). The position is confusing and unsatisfactory, but there is no doubt that hard currency talks in the Special Zones. Companies operating in SEZs are obviously expected to place the priority on exporting. They are also expected to import the bulk of their inputs – on a self-financing basis.

On balance, the Chinese Special Economic Zones could be described as a success and that success has not gone unnoticed in Moscow. Here, as in other respects, Gorbachev does, indeed, appear willing to try to learn from his Chinese comrades. But what exactly is he looking for? After all, the trading configurations of the two countries could not present a bigger contrast. The Soviet Union, a major world industrial power, obtains some 70 per cent of its total export revenues from the export of oil and gas. China, a poor, developing country exports mainly manufactures, with equipment deliveries making up some 40 per cent of total exports. Clearly, absolute advantage has a good deal to do with the 'perverse' pattern of Soviet exports, and the USSR has shown, in its arms export trade with the Third World, that it is perfectly capable of competing in quality- and technology-intensive export sectors. The fact is, though, that this remains an isolated success. Against the background of the 1985–86 collapse in oil prices, Gorbachev has perceived a pressing need to learn how to export civilian manufactures to the West, and has seen foreign trade reform as a vehicle for such a transformation. In China, by contrast, the Special Economic Zones, for all their radicality, have essentially picked up a tradition of export-orientated manufacturing which goes back to the nineteenth century and the age of the treaty ports. The Soviet leadership is likely to discover that foreign trade restructuring is no *substitute* for restructuring of the domestic economy, that Soviet economic reforms would have to go very much further before we could expect external stimuli to have an automatic impact on domestic investment patterns.

Still, the Special Zone idea does offer partial solutions to many of the planning problems which the new Soviet foreign trade arrangements run into. How exactly are Soviet 'national champions' supposed to relate to the economic hinterland? Enterprises doing their own export deals and joint ventures will want to order materials from 'ordinary' Soviet enterprises, sometimes at short notice. How is that going to fit in with plan fulfilment, and what incentive is there for ordinary enterprises to take on 'special orders'? How are Soviet enterprises working for both foreign and domestic markets to translate inconvertible rubles into dollars for purposes of accounting, wage payments, and so on? How is the joint venture initiative to be sold to the world business community as long as the Soviet side is reluctant to permit free repatriation of profits in hard currency except on the basis of exports for hard currency?

The Chinese model of the SEZ addresses all of these problems. Transactions are carried on mainly in convertible currency. The Zones are big enough to allow the development of whole *complexes* of economic activity working under the special dispensation. Thus for the great bulk of ancillary supplies and services an enterprise located in a SEZ can go straight to another enterprise working on the same ground rules as itself. Profit repatriation regulations are liberal. Yet the Chinese model is no panacea for Soviet ills. Repatriation of profits is not a serious problem in the Chinese case essentially because the Special Economic Zones have been so export-orientated right from the start. And while the Zones do much to resolve the characteristic supply difficulties of centrally planned systems, they do not obviate the problem all together. For, as the Chinese have discovered, where Special Zone enterprises do have to obtain their raw materials from the hinterland, they may encounter very Soviet-style problems, with 'ordinary' enterprises perceiving little self-interest in anything beyond the fulfilment of the plans imposed by their local authorities. As a *reductio ad absurdum* we may cite the case of the tobacco industry, where cigarette manufacturers have experienced serious difficulties with their tobacco leaf suppliers in the hinterland. Beijing's solution to the problem was to impose delivery targets on the tobacco growers! (conversation with Professor Liu Youqin, Economics Department, People's University, 24 April 1988). Finally, foreign businessmen could not expect to find the same abundance of cheap labour in the Soviet Union that they find in China.

Be that as it may, the Soviet Union is moving steadily, if cautiously, towards something like the Chinese model. The coverage of the foreign trade reform is being extended, some kind of convertibility for the ruble has been promised by the year 2000, and there are reports that Moscow is to set up its first Special Economic Zones in the Soviet Far East, in the area around Vladivostok, and in the Baltic region, near Leningrad.

AGRICULTURE

This is the area where the history and traditions of Soviet and Chinese Communism diverge most sharply. It is also the area where Mr Gorbachev faces his most pressing economic problems. Food shortages there certainly are in China, but the first thing a visitor from Moscow to Beijing would notice, and indeed marvel at, is the general absence of food queues. That is what Gorbachev would like to see in the Soviet Union, and he is clearly quite prepared to break with virtually every Bolshevik agricultural tradition in order to bring it about.

Since the abandonment of the Maoist commune in the late 1970s, the Chinese have reverted to a not unfamiliar pattern of agricultural organisation. In the majority of townships, as they are now called, peasants rent land, and produce for autoconsumption, and for the market. Some elements of compulsory output planning remain, but they are generally not onerous. The authorities have not as yet permitted the development of any kind of market for land itself, though that may come in the future.

The history of Soviet agriculture since 1965 has essentially been one of totally unsuccessful attempts to reform the collective/state farm system without actually abolishing it. Experiments with autonomous work-teams bearing a strong resemblance to the Chinese responsibility system have produced impressive enough immediate results, but have been prevented from making any significant general impact on agricultural efficiency by bureaucratic inertia, even hostility, the persistence of output targets and the (extremely inefficient) central allocation of agricultural inputs.

It is against this background that the Soviet President, in October, 1988, made a series of dramatic pronouncements which seem to herald something approaching the reprivatisation of Soviet agriculture (Gorbachev, 1988). Under the rubric of the *leasehold system* (*arenda*), he proposed a pattern of independent, medium-sized farms freed of the tutelage of quotas and free to purchase their own inputs on a market basis. Existing collective farm managers and specialists could either join the leasing collectives or offer consultancy services to those collectives – on a market basis. It was not for the centre, Gorbachev went on, to prescribe universal patterns of leasing, and if, for example, someone wants to go off to set up a self-contained family farm, with its own separate farmhouse – so be it. The Soviet leader also promised a new law on land utilisation, which could make it possible for farmers to bequeath their leases to their children.

The debt to the Chinese example is so obvious here that it hardly needs pointing up. But we should be careful not to be too hasty in seeing these proposals as a panacea for all the USSR's agricultural ills. The current Chinese leadership, with its deeply pragmatic bent, has been able to build on a centuries-old tradition of highly sophisticated, intensive techniques of cultivation which may have been set aside, but were certainly not forgotten during the Mao period. In the Soviet Union, by contrast, the collective-state farm system, now in place for nearly sixty years, represents the only system of which the great majority of Soviet peasants have any personal experience. And the pre-1930 experience was largely of extensive cultivation methods responding fairly stubbornly to the pressures of over-population. Of course, we should not forget the private subsidiary sector that has always coexisted with the socialist agricultural sector, still accounting for around one quarter of total Soviet agricultural output, and which shows very much higher productivity indicators than the socialist sector. So there is a contemporary Soviet tradition of intensive agriculture. But it is a *subsidiary* one, and we should not assume that the average Soviet peasant can, in 1989, just go off and set himself up as an independent farmer without any adjustment problems whatsoever.

There is another dimension to the Soviet agricultural problem. Since the late 1960s colossal funds have been invested in the development of agricultural infrastructure and land improvement. The bulk of these investments have yielded virtually no return. This problem of investment effectiveness is, of course, intimately related to the general problem of organisation and motivation under the collective/state farm system, but we should not assume that the transition to the leasehold system will automatically improve the quality of Soviet irrigation systems. The Chinese experience is very interesting in this connection. While the responsibility system has flourished in terms of bringing food to the people, it has left enormous gaps on the infrastructural side of agriculture. The sector's share of state investment has declined dramatically; irrigation systems have been neglected, with total farmland under irrigation shrinking by 66,000 hectares from 1981 to 1986; the machinery park has not been properly maintained; and the number of agricultural technicians has shrunk to a dangerously low level ('Call for . . . ', 1988). It will not be possible to revolutionise Soviet agriculture without first revolutionising the effectiveness of irrigation and drainage work. The Soviets are unlikely to learn from the Chinese how to do this.

THE PRIVATE SECTOR

So much for the *de facto* privatisation of agriculture. What about the private sector proper? Both countries have been through periods in which any form of private enterprise, with the partial exception of subsidiary agriculture, have been looked upon with the utmost suspicion. Things

began to change in the Soviet Union in 1987, with the promulgation
of a slightly disappointing law, bearing all the marks of a political
compromise, on private enterprise as such. The following year saw the
appearance of a much more important piece of legislation on co-operatives.
The new co-operatives would operate on a limited liability basis, would be
allowed to employ non-co-operant labour, apparently without any upper
limit, and with wages and working conditions subject to individual contract.
Distribution of co-operative income is to be decided exclusively by the
members of the co-operative, and co-operatives have complete freedom
as far as sales and purchase contracts, including international ones, are
concerned. They are, however, subject to elements of central price
control. Cooperatives may raise capital by issuing shares, but only for
sale to members and employees of the co-operative. As of mid-1988
co-operatives were employing between 100,000 and 200,000 people,
mainly in service sectors, and some Soviet economists have suggested
that they could ultimately account for as much as 10–12 per cent of
Soviet GNP.

The new course in China has led to a much more emphatic reappraisal of
the place of private enterprise outside agriculture. While in Beijing I visited
'Computer Road', with its dozens of computer companies and shops, many
of them privately owned. I was fortunate enough to be shown round the
Stone Computer Company, which can be taken as fairly representative of
the leading edge of private enterprise in China today. Stone employs about
500 people, and engages in the import and manufacture of computers.
It makes its own Chinese language word-processor. While it is not
subject to state planning, or any state-imposed limits on the number
it employs, it sells mainly to organisations in the state sector, and
rents a (previously loss-making) factory from the state. It is heavily
involved in international trade, and operates a joint venture with a
Japanese company of which it owns 51 per cent. It finances imports
both through exports and by buying foreign exchange (at above the
official exchange rate) on the foreign exchange market. Stone started
off by taking on unemployed people with few formal qualifications.
Now it employs mainly graduates. Recruitment is by interview and/or
competitive examination, and employment contracts are for one year, with
no automatic renewal.

While the direction of changes is the same, the contrast in the content
of policy on private enterprise between the Soviet Union and China is
almost total. In the Soviet Union, we have seen a cautious, on the part of
many grudging, movement towards liberalisation, as a way of bringing the
second economy out into the open, as a way of filling the great gaps in the

provision of consumer goods and services by the state. During Gorbachev's September walkabout in the Siberian city of Krasnoyarsk, he was anxiously quizzed by people involved in co-operatives. 'Mikhail Sergeevich, are you personally in favour of co-operatives or against?' (Gorbachev, 1988, p. 1). In China, by contrast, private enterprise has a place in the sun. It plays a crucial role, not only in the provision of consumer goods and services, but also in the development of high-technology sectors where the main customer is the state. That is not to say that there are no policy problems and tensions in relation to private enterprise in China. But the Chinese leadership does seem to have a much clearer idea of the *dynamic* role the private sector can play.

CONCLUSION

Despite the manifold differences in the situations of the two countries, then, there are many points of contact between the reform programmes being implemented. It follows that there must be lessons to be learned on both sides. Chinese economists and policy-makers must already be benefiting from the flowering in the USSR of the critical literature on reform themes which has emerged as one of the most valuable products of *glasnost'*. On the practical side, however, most of the lessons go in the opposite direction, for the simple reason that Chinese reforms have gone so much further than Soviet on nearly every dimension. As we have seen, Chinese models have in a number of connections been used quite explicitly in recent Soviet policy formulations.

Of course, there are negative as well as positive lessons. If Gorbachev is anxious about the problem of price reform, he will find in Chinese experience only further grounds for anxiety, rather than any formula for allaying it. However sturdy the common sense that underlies privatisation and quasi-privatisation policies in China, there is plenty of evidence to support the thesis that privatisation is as tricky a beast to handle under socialism as under capitalism. As the decay of Chinese agricultural infrastructure in recent years has shown, self-financing family farms are a necessary, but not a sufficient condition for a stable and efficient socialist agriculture. Up to now, the Chinese new course has simply not addressed the problem of indivisibilities and externalities in agriculture. We can perceive similar contradictions in policies on education and human capital. We should certainly applaud the forthright recognition on the part of the Chinese government that world technology is indivisible, that effective technology transfer is only possible where international business links are untrammelled by bureaucracy, and that technology is ultimately the engine of growth in international trade. We must at the same time question the stinginess of the Beijing authorities towards higher education, however much it may have contributed to the soundness of the finances of the state. Here, indeed, there is a curious contradiction in the policies of the new course. On the one hand, higher education is being liberalised beyond the dreams of most East Europeans. On the other hand, Chinese professors and lecturers are barely paid a living wage. Survival for China's intellectual elites requires location on some part of the spectrum that runs from moonlighting through to emigration, and that is no basis for the efficient allocation of human capital.

We can see the same tyranny of short-term over long-term considerations when we look at the style of labour relations under the new course. I was very struck by the pride of the Stone Computer Company management in their system of employment contracts – everyone is on a one-year contract, and many contracts are not renewed. It is easy enough to understand this as a reaction against the ethos of the iron rice bowl, but once again it seems to reflect an obsession with short-term pressure and short-term results which bears little resemblance to the way the great corporations of the West are organised. A large proportion of the employees of those corporations enjoy a substantial degree of *de facto* tenure, and in Japan, China's closest cultural cousin amongst the industrial Great Powers, most employees stay with their firm for life.

I would suggest, then, that there is still a good deal of misunderstanding in China about the nature of the corporatism of the industrialised market economies. And this is the more striking in that it finds a strong echo in the Soviet Union, where successive attempts to create some kind of Soviet 'corporation' (the Russian word *ob"edinenie* is usually translated as association), as a vehicle for the integration of production and research and development, have uniformly failed. Behind these problems, it seems to me, there lies a problem of mind-set, a continued failure to break with the priorities of the past. Central planning was developed as a vehicle for imposing maximum pressure for short-term output results. Initially it worked well enough, at least in the Soviet Union. Subsequently, it showed itself less and less able to produce the goods in terms of its own priorities. I have the impression that the Soviet and Chinese authorities, to a degree at least, are looking to decentralisation and privatisation to provide a more effective alternative way to *maximise short-term output results*. The fact is, however, that governments and firms in the developed capitalist world view output as an essentially dependent variable, with technology and marketing taking pride of place in the context of corporate planning. Economic reform will only work, and continue to work, if it is seen as a basis for genuine transition to intensive growth, rather than just as something which gives a new lease of life to extensive growth.

Finally, a few remarks on the political and geo-strategic limitations to Soviet imitation of Chinese new course policies. Modern China has never been as consistently isolated as Russia has been throughout the nineteenth and twentieth centuries. Even at the height of the Cultural Revolution, there were major focal points of Chinese international entrepreneurship – in Taiwan, Hong Kong and Singapore – which would later provide the model for the Special Economic Zones. Significantly, the geographical coverage of the Zones is partially coextensive with that of the Treaty Ports of the age of imperialism – only this time they are under Chinese control. Russia has never had a Hong Kong, never had an alternative model of how Russians could do things, and this is reflected at the level of mass culture as well as that of grand international strategy. The caution with which private and co-operative enterprise has been liberalised in the Soviet Union reflects not only sheer conservatism on the part of the elites, but also very substantial public suspicion of independent entrepreneurship. Such suspicion is certainly not absent in the People's Republic, but the Chinese mercantile tradition has survived the test of Maoism to resume its 'rightful' place in the reformed system. In the Soviet Union the notion that you cannot get rich unless you are exploiting someone is still deeply embedded in popular consciousness.

The problem of popular attitudes does not stop there for Mr Gorbachev. While China is nearly 90 per cent Han, the Soviet Union is barely 50 per cent Russian. While all of China's Special Economic Zones are in Han areas, most of the candidates for SEZ status in the Soviet Union are in national minority areas, such as the Baltic and the Caucasus, where Gorbachev's political liberalisation has opened up a Pandora's box of local tensions and problems over the past year or so. While that may help to explain why Moscow seems to have chosen as its first Special Zones the Far East and Leningrad regions – which are ethnically predominantly Russian – we are left wondering about the strategic implications of such a move. It is only five years since a Korean airliner was shot down after straying over the Far Eastern region. There is considerable evidence that Mr Gorbachev would, indeed, favour a major strategic disengagement vis-à-vis the West. But a very great deal will have to change before we will see a ring of Special Economic Zones, buzzing with foreign capitalists, around the rim of the Soviet Union. For the time being, the odds must be against anything except a very partial convergence of Soviet and Chinese economic systems.

NOTE

This article is based on a visit to China in March, 1988, when I taught a month-long course on 'Socialist Economic Development Patterns in Eastern Europe' at the People's University in Beijing. was allowed a degree of freedom of access to undergraduates which I could never dream of having in the Soviet Union, and might obtain with difficulty even, say, in Yugoslavia. While in Beijing, I was able to observe the Chinese reforms in action and discuss them with Chinese colleagues. My study of Soviet reform trends over a period of some twenty years suggested an intriguing yardstick against which to assess the more technical aspects of the Chinese economic reforms.

REFERENCES

Bronshtein, M. (1986) 'K kontseptsii khozyaistvennogo mekhanizma APK', *Voprosy Ekonomiki* [Problems of Economics], no. 2.
'Call for agricultural laws' (1988) *China Daily,* March 15, p. 2.
Dyker, D. A. (1983) *The Process of Investment in the Soviet Union,* (Cambridge University Press); (1985) *The Future of the Soviet Economic Planning System,* (London: Croom Helm); (1987) 'Industrial planning – forwards or sideways?', in D. A. Dyker (ed.), *The Soviet Union under Gorbachev: Prospects for Reform,* (London, Croom Helm).
Economist Intelligence Unit (1988); *Country Report USSR,* no. 2.
Gorbachev, M.S. (1987) speech in Murmansk, published in *Ekonomicheskaya Gazeta,* no. 41, 1987; (1988) speech to meeting of lease-holders, published in *Ekonomicheskaya Gazeta,* no. 42.
'Quarterly chronical and documentation' (1988) *The China Quarterly,* no. 114, June.
Ronichev, I. (1985) 'Gol ne v te vorota', *Literaturnaya Gazeta,* no. 45, p. 11.
Valovaya, T. (1988) 'Rekonstruktsiya idei', *Ekonomicheskaya Gazeta,* no. 1.
Zhang Yu'an (1988) 'More investment needed for animal husbandry', *China Daily,* March 13, pp. 1–2.
Zverev, A. (1987) 'Valyutnye fondy predpriyatii', *Ekonomicheskaya Gazeta,* no. 15, p. 21.

5 The Impact of the Open Door Policy on the Chinese State

Jude Howell

With the consolidation of Deng Xiaoping's position at the Third Plenum in 1978, the reformist leadership was able to embark upon a programme of reforms which entailed greater reliance on market forces, both domestic and foreign. The Open Door Policy refers to the set of policies adopted since 1978 in the spheres of foreign trade, foreign investment and foreign borrowing. The process of opening up has not only led to a rapid expansion in China's economic ties with the West and Japan but has also had repercussions in the socio-political domain. These can be observed in the changing role of the state with regard to foreign economic relations.

There is a common view amongst Chinese theorists and policy-makers as well as overseas academics that the state in the Special Economic Zones (SEZs) is fundamentally the same as elsewhere in China. This view rests on the assumption that the word 'special' in SEZs refers only to the economic policies prevalent in the zones. In a study of Shenzhen SEZ, for example, Chang maintains that the system of government in the SEZs is the same as in the rest of China:

> As far as the Party organisation and state apparatus are concerned, the principle of governing is no more 'special' than elsewhere in China for the SEZs are not special 'administrative' zones. Party discipline, the state constitution and laws and state administration all remain the same.[1]

It will be argued, however, that whilst the politico-administrative system is still basically the same in the SEZs as elsewhere in China, elements of a new type of state are emerging which have their economic base in the special economic conditions in the zones. The introduction of market forces, both international and domestic, has given rise to a new 'market-facilitating' state. Although this has been particularly evident in the SEZs where the concentration of foreign capital is highest and domestic

119

economic reform has proceeded furthest, it can also be observed in varying degrees in other parts of China where the process of reform and opening up is underway. This redefinition of the state has been reflected in the restructuring of state institutions and changes in their operational mode as well as in their social composition.

This chapter is divided into three sections. The first section examines the character of the state prior to 1978, with particular reference to that part of the state dealing with the external economy. The second part deals with the impact of the Open Door Policy on the state at the national level, whilst the final section considers the effects of the Open Door Policy on the state in Xiamen SEZ.

1 THE STATE AND THE EXTERNAL ECONOMY PRE-1978

Since Liberation in 1949, the overall character of the Chinese state has been heavily influenced by the Soviet Model. The Party has been the chief policy-making body with the government bureaucracy acting as its executive arm and the army serving, inter alia, the purpose of national defence. Apart from some short periods of decentralisation in 1958 and 1970, the defining features of the state have been centralisation, vertical integration and central financial responsibility. Although the criteria governing recruitment to the state have fluctuated, the importance of 'redness' has tended to dominate, especially during the Cultural Revolution. These features also characterised those sections of the state dealing with the external economy.

In the early 1950s the management of foreign trade was centralised under the Ministry of Foreign Trade. Due to the Western embargo on trade with China, the China Council for the Promotion of International Trade (CCPIT) was established to negotiate non-governmental trade agreements. With the socialisation of all privately-run trade companies in 1957, foreign trade fell wholly under state control.

The provincial foreign trade bureaux were assigned import and export quotas from the central Ministry which were in turn passed down to the various import/export companies. Neither export-producing enterprises nor import/export companies were deemed financially responsible for the outcome of their foreign trade activities. As in other sectors of the state, political criteria were important in recruitment to foreign trade organs. Although training in foreign trade and economics was provided in the 1950s and early 1960s, during the Cultural Revolution such 'bourgeois' subjects enjoyed little prestige.

The expansion of foreign economic relations since 1978 and the subsequently increasing demands on foreign trade organs has brought into relief some of the shortcomings of the pre-existing foreign trade system. The following have been of particular concern to the reformist leadership. Firstly, the Ministry of Foreign Trade exerted excessive and rigid control over its subordinate bodies. As a result, export-producing enterprises had little control over the level or direction of exports. Secondly, there was inadequate integration between production and marketing. As foreign trade bureaux and production enterprises had minimal contact with their suppliers or customers, apart possibly from annual meetings at the Guangzhou Trade Fair, their marketing skills and knowledge about alternative suppliers and international prices was severely constricted. The experience of exporting and importing production enterprises with foreign trade was even more limited. Thirdly, there was no clear division of functions between the 'government and enterprise'. Administrative trade organs took decisions on economic matters concerning the trading companies. Moreover, a maze of innumerable formalities and procedures reduced efficiency.[2] Finally, as a result of the Cultural Revolution the bulk of foreign trade personnel at the dawn of the Open Door Policy were poorly versed in the art of foreign trade, especially in relation to the international capitalist economy.

With the rapid increase in foreign trade and other forms of external economic links since 1978, the imperative for reform in the state sector dealing with the external economy became more urgent.

2 EFFECTS OF OPEN DOOR POLICY ON THE STATE SINCE 1978

The expansion of China's economic relations with the capitalist world economy has contributed towards the emergence of a 'market-facilitating' state. The key features of this new type of state are as follows: firstly, it is flexible, i.e., bureaucratic procedures are minimised so as to ensure quick responses to changing market conditions; secondly, it is entrepreneurial, that is, the state itself engages in entrepreneurial activity for the sake of profit; thirdly, it is legalistic, that is, economic relations with foreign companies are legally defined and economic disputes are settled according to existing laws by specialised legal bodies; finally, it is technocratic, that is, the state is staffed by technically and professionally qualified people. The emergence of this market-facilitating state has required changes in its structure, operational mode and social composition, each of which will be examined in turn.

(a)   Restructuring of State Institutions

The Open Door Policy has brought the creation of new state institutions at both central and lower levels as well as *the adaptation of existing institutions*. This restructuring of the institutional fabric has not occurred instantaneously, but has evolved gradually in accord with the spiral evolution of the Open Door Policy.[3]

In order to deal with the expansion of foreign economic relations, the reformist leadership has created new central administrative institutions in the spheres of foreign trade and foreign investment. These included the Foreign Investment Control Commission, which was to manage the introduction of foreign investment; the State Import and Export Commission which was to make policies concerning technology imports and new trading arrangements; the General Administration of Customs, which was to formulate preferential customs policies as well as the China International Trust and Investment Company (CITIC) which was to facilitate the establishment of joint ventures.

Furthermore, the tasks of the Foreign Trade Bureau were split between the Ministry of Foreign Economic Relations (MOFER) and the Foreign Trade Corporation, with the former concerned chiefly with planning and policy formulation and the latter dealing mainly with the actual activity of foreign trade. Apart from MOFER, the non-governmental China Council for the Promotion of International Trade (CCPIT) has also played a key role in arranging trade negotiations between China and potential trading partners, mounting trade exhibitions and providing consultancy services. However, in March 1982, as part of a general reform of the State Council's organisations, the Commission for Import and Export Control, the Ministry of Foreign Trade, MOFER and the Commission for the Control of Foreign Investment were merged to form the current Ministry of Foreign Economic Relations and Trade (MOFERT).

The establishment of four SEZs in mid-1979 also required the creation of appropriate administrative institutions. As initially the supervision of the zones was considered the prerogative of provincial bodies, SEZ Administration Offices were set up in Guangdong and Fujian Provinces. Growing national concern for developments in the SEZs in 1981, however, led to the establishment in June 1982 of the State Council's Office of SEZ Affairs under the leadership of the two reformers Gu Mu and Zhao Ziyang. The relations of authority between this central office and the SEZ Management Committees in Guangdong and Fujian were not, however, well-defined.

Although MOFERT assumed responsibility for foreign investment in 1982, concern amongst reformist leaders about the decline in foreign investment in 1986 led to the setting-up of the State Council Leading Group for Foreign Investment in August 1986, again headed by State Councillor Gu Mu. As this group involves not only members of the State Council but also officials from a wide range of state institutions connected to the Open Door Policy, it indicated that the deepening of the Open Door Policy required greater coordination across institutions.[4] Its functions include making policy recommendations to the State Council, arbitrating in the problems of foreign-invested enterprises, supervising both departments and regions in their use of foreign investment and drafting legislation for foreign investment procedures. Local level leading groups with a similar structure to the national groups have also been established in coastal provinces and municipalities with substantial foreign investment.

As well as these changes at the central state level, there has also been a proliferation of trading and investment companies at lower levels. By breaking up the monopoly of the large national Foreign Trading Corporations, reformers hoped to remove some of the rigidities inherent in a centrally and vertically integrated system. The mushrooming of these institutions has been most pronounced during upswings in the Open Door Policy when decentralisation policies were implemented. However, in downswings of the Open Door Policy, when central control over the economy is reimposed, the growth in these institutions has been stemmed and may even have contracted.

The first wave of new institutions began in 1980 when 17 new import-export corporations were established and foreign trade corporations were set up on an experimental basis in Beijing, Tianjin, Shanghai, Guangdong and Fujian. Following the success of these early initiatives foreign trade corporations were set up in other provinces. The process was accelerated with the further decentralisation of the economy in early 1984. By August 1984 the number of import-export companies under the Foreign Trade Corporation at provincial level and above had risen from 120 in 1978 to 600, excluding those in the SEZs and in special districts and municipalities and below.[5] The following month industrial ministries and provinces were permitted to set up medium and small foreign trade companies. As a result the number of foreign trade companies rose to 1,900 in 1987.[6] Provincial branches of CITIC were also set up to facilitate the negotiation and financing of joint ventures.

Not only has the expansion of foreign economic ties led to the creation of new institutions within the spheres of foreign trade and foreign investment, but it has also prompted the emergence of a new part of the legal system dealing with external economic relations. The legal system has expanded partly in response to the concern of foreign capital for legal protection.

Since the promulgation of the Joint Venture Law in 1979 several laws and regulations have been passed on taxation, patents, foreign exchange management, accounting, customs, entry and exit formalities and wholly-owned foreign enterprises.

The growth of foreign investment and foreign trade has also required the creation of arbitration committees to resolve disputes between Chinese and foreign parties. The CCPIT has, for example, set up an arbitration committee for foreign economic relations.[7] These arbitration bodies coupled with the expansion of legislation imply a shift in the mode of conflict resolution. Conflicts in China have tended to be resolved through mutual negotiation between the concerned parties rather than with reference to laws and courts. However, closer links with the capitalist world economy as well as the introduction of the contract responsibility system have bolstered the importance of a 'legal' state.

The implementation of the Open Door Policy has entailed not only the creation of new state institutions at central and lower levels but has also led to the adaptation of existing institutions. As the Open Door Policy becomes more entrenched, the process of adaptation has extended to a wider range of institutions. Financial and labour institutions, customs, the Party, army and other institutions have all had to adapt and expand parts of their structures and methods of operation to accommodate foreign capital. This phenomenon reflects the 'snowball effect' of the Open Door Policy whereby changes in one part of the economy and administration entail alterations in other parts of the overall system.

The banking system has had to adapt considerably to the new demands of foreign trade, foreign investment and foreign borrowing. The Foreign Exchange Control Bureau of the People's Bank of China is not only in charge of foreign debts but also the regulation of the foreign exchange transactions of foreign-invested enterprises. The opening up of certain areas to foreign capital has also prompted the decentralisation of certain banking functions. In July 1984, Chinese banks in the SEZs and the 14 coastal cities were granted greater power, putting them on par with provincial banks.

The Ministry of Finance has also broadened its activities; not only has it had to devise regulations on finance and taxation for foreign-invested enterprises, but has also determined their access to the domestic market. It has also decentralised some of its functions. By November 1985, the number of financial institutions authorised to act as guarantors in China had increased to 41.[8] With the sprouting of foreign-invested enterprises the work of accountants and auditors has not only expanded but also altered in content.

The opening up of China has also contributed to changes within the Party. Whilst the structures of the Party have not been directly affected, the methods of operation as well as the social basis of the Party betray some influence from the Open Door Policy. For example, as some foreign-invested enterprises have banned political meetings during production hours, the Party has had to devise other means for disseminating Party policy amongst both its members and the 'masses'. Both the reforms and the Open Door Policy have also encouraged the recruitment to the Party of younger, more educated candidates with scientific and technological skills.

The army, too, has had to make adaptations in its functions and scope of activities in response to the Open Door Policy. In the SEZs and open coastal cities, the army has had to yield land to the construction of factories and the development of tourist spots. As the army has been required to acquire some degree of financial autonomy, earning foreign exchange through military factories converted to civilian production to finance the import of military equipment has increased in importance. With the demobilisation of the army, troops have been deployed in the construction of the SEZs and factory sites.

In sum, the implementation of the Open Door Policy has contributed to a restructuring of that part of the state dealing with foreign economic relations. This has been reflected in the creation of new institutions at central level, the proliferation of trading companies and investment corporations at provincial level and below, as well as the adaptation of existing institutions. The snowball effect of the Open Door Policy has also served to extend the agenda of reform required for opening up from the foreign trade system to other state sectors.

However, this process of restructuring has not been complete. Whilst new institutions have been created to deal with foreign investment, there is a lack of coordinating institutions at central and lower levels to ensure that the introduction of foreign investment follows unified plans. Similarly, there is no coordinating institution, either centrally or regionally, responsible for foreign borrowing.

Although progress has been made in the development of a legal system, the pace of legislation has, however, lagged behind the needs of foreign companies. The Contractual Joint Venture law, for example, was only passed in 1988, ten years after opening up. Similarly, a law on wholly-owned foreign enterprises was only drafted in mid-1986. The immaturity of China's legal framework has been one of the chief obstacles to foreign investment, particularly US and Japanese. Moreover, even where laws have been introduced, the problem of enforcement has limited their efficacy.

This unevenness in the process of institutional restructuring is related in part to the tendency for institutional change to lag behind policy change, and in part to the political reverberations of institutional change. Clearly the development of a legal system governing foreign economic relations requires time and expertise. As the forms of trade and foreign borrowing have become more diverse since opening up, this process of legislation has also become more complex. Moreover, the dearth of professionally trained lawyers, as well as the lack of supervisory bodies ensuring the implementation of laws, put significant constraints on the realisation of the 'legal state'.

As the restructuring of the state entails the redistribution of power and resources, the process has also been shaped by resistance from potentially 'losing' institutions. The rise in importance of economic institutions has been parallelled by the decline in influence of ideologically-orientated institutions. The latter have frequently formed the backbone of ideological campaigns directed against the Open Door Policy. Delays in the granting of import and export licences or the approval of joint ventures may reflect not only lengthy bureaucratic procedures but also resistance by planning institutions whose former powers have been partly redistributed. Similarly, the adaptation of institutions such as the army, which has effectively yielded some of its resources and privileges for the construction of the SEZs, may also have fuelled resentment amongst some army members concerning their loss of power since the Third Plenum.

(b) Changes in the Operation of State Institutions

Whilst these changes in the institutional landscape provide the structural foundations for a potential market-facilitating state, the development of a more flexible and entrepreneurial state requires crucial changes in the way state institutions operate. The attempt to create a more dynamic state institution responsive to market change has been reflected in the decentralisation of authority over foreign economic relations from central to lower levels, the emergence of *quasi-state institutions* and the recruitment of professionally and technically skilled persons to state positions. Each of these will be examined in turn.

The proliferation of state institutions at provincial level and below has been accompanied by the decentralisation of some authority over foreign trade, foreign investment and foreign borrowing. By granting lower-level trading agencies as well as production enterprises greater authority in managing foreign trade, the central government hoped to stimulate local initiative and dynamism. Decentralisation has mainly been administrative, whereby power is devolved to lower levels of the state machinery, although some economic decentralisation, whereby power is redistributed from state administrative organs at all levels to economic units, has also occurred.[9]

The authority to conduct foreign trade has been decentralised in varying degrees to the branches of national corporations under MOFERT, to the provincial branches of MOFERT and industrial ministries, as well as to the newly established provincial trading companies. The granting of 'special policies and privileges' to Guangdong and Fujian Provinces in July 1979 enabled these two provinces to export all products, apart from a few exceptions, without central approval. Following the success of the experimental General Foreign Trading Corporations set up in Beijing, Tianjin and Shanghai in 1980, the right to engage in foreign trade and approve contracts was extended over the next four years to other areas in China including the inland cities of Wuhan and Chongqing. Some large industrial enterprises in coastal areas were even authorised to export their own products directly, thus bypassing Foreign Trade Corporations. According to some estimates, the ability to bypass the national Foreign Trade Corporations could reduce by half the time required to fulfil an export contract. Although the central government has been willing to decentralise some authority over exports, it has been more reluctant to unleash control over imports.

The heyday for provincial and branch trading entities came in 1984. In January provisional regulations for the issuing of import licences were introduced, giving the go-ahead to decentralisation. Foreign Trade Corporations under MOFERT as well as those run by ministries and provincial authorities were permitted to import unrestricted items without central approval, leading to a fall in the percentage of imports accounted for by MOFERT from 87 per cent in 1981 to 65 per cent in 1984.

In September 1984 the State Council approved the further decentralisation of the foreign trade system. Whilst MOFERT and its regional branches were to focus on the administrative management of foreign trade, importing and exporting was to be conducted independently by the foreign trade companies. However, the subsequent import boom and decline in foreign exchange reserves led to the recentralisation of foreign trade in 1985 and 1986 and the concomitant removal of various foreign trade privileges from provincial and local organisations. The number of commodities categorised as restricted import items was increased whilst an export licensing system was introduced. Similarly, in January 1986, foreign trading companies were required to fulfil the foreign exchange quota set by the state.

Closely linked to foreign trade is the more thorny issue of foreign exchange decentralisation. In order to encourage provincial exports a system of foreign exchange retention was introduced in 1979.[10] With the formalisation of this system in January 1984 most provinces were entitled to retain 25 per cent of their foreign exchange earnings from planned exports for their own use. The special status of Guangdong and Fujian allowed these two provinces to retain 30 per cent, whilst minority areas such as Ningxia could keep 50 per cent. The SEZs were permitted to retain between 70 per cent and 100 per cent of their foreign exchange earnings. In order to motivate producing enterprises to export, new regulations were introduced in January 1985 requiring the retained foreign exchange to be shared equally between enterprises and foreign trade companies.

The decentralisation of some authority over foreign exchange management gave provincial authorities more independence by allowing them to undertake projects without central financing and approval. Whilst it encouraged the development of export-oriented industries, it also contributed towards the import boom in 1984 and 1985. The reimposition of central control led to the reduction in the foreign exchange retention rates in the SEZs to 30 per cent, though this was raised again in early 1986 following the severe financial difficulties facing the SEZs. In April 1986, the regional allocation of foreign exchange was further reduced.

Authority to establish foreign-invested enterprises has also been administratively decentralised to regions. Thus the 14 coastal cities and the four SEZs all enjoy to differing degrees the right to approve joint ventures. Tianjin and Shanghai, for example, were permitted in April 1984 to approve projects up to US$ 30m, Dalian up to US$ 10m and other coastal cities up to US$ 5m.[11] Whereas, initially, wholly-owned foreign enterprises were confined to SEZs, since 1984 coastal cities have also been permitted to set up such enterprises. Moreover, certain trust and investment corporations at provincial level are permitted to negotiate joint ventures, though approval from the provincial MOFERT is still required.

The decentralisation of some authority over foreign economic relations to branches of Foreign Trade Corporations under MOFERT, to provincial trading and investment companies as well as to the branches of industrial trading companies is indicative of a trend towards a more flexible and entrepreneurial state, able to respond rapidly towards opportunities in the marketplace. However, foreign trade still remains under administrative control, even though the agents of authority are at lower levels of the state hierarchy.

The implementation of these decentralisation policies has been neither even nor smooth. The unevenness in this process is linked in part to the unintended consequences of decentralisation such as the duplication of imports, the introduction of inappropriate technology and the rapid upsurge in consumer imports in mid-1985, which led to the enormous foreign trade deficit. Whilst the market-facilitating state unleashed local level initiative, it was nevertheless not able to regulate or coordinate the economic actions of the numerous new trading companies. Moreover, the competition for export goods amongst trading agencies in turn affected the ability of national and provincial Foreign Trade Corporations to procure goods for their own export plans. Provincial and subprovincial trading companies and branches thus tended to pursue local rather than national interests.

In order to redress these economic imbalances, the administrative medicine of the commandist state was applied. However, as decentralisation redistributed power and resources to provincial and municipal authorities and line-branches, thus creating its own web of interests, the process of recentralisation involves a conflict of interests between the centre and lower-level state institutions.

The provincial and municipal trading authorities are unlikely to readily cede their newly acquired powers. Moreover, the proliferation of new trading companies at provincial level and below changes the process of recentralisation. Whilst prior to the creation of these new agencies recentralisation would have involved only already-existing provincial and branch companies, the spawning of institutions which have not previously experienced central control might make the process of recentralisation more difficult. As a result lower-level trading and investment authorities still fare better in 1987 than in 1978, even though their wings have been considerably clipped compared to the heyday of 1984. The development of a market-facilitating state thus raises crucial issues of control – not only of the market-facilitating state over the market but also of the commandist state over the newly emerging market-facilitating state.

Closely linked to the decentralisation of authority over foreign economic relations has been the emergence of a layer of *quasi-state institutions* mediating between the state and foreign capital. They are quasi-state in that they are set up by the state but are supposed to behave like business enterprises. These cross-breed institutions have been set up not only to create greater flexibility and initiative in the way the state interacts with market forces but also to promote a more profit-conscious state responsive to economic rather than administrative principles. These institutions are symptomatic of what Blecher describes as an emerging 'entrepreneurial state', whereby semi-autonomous enterprises are created to engage in profit-making activities.[12]

Although these quasi-state institutions are founded by the state, their organisational structure as well as operational mode resemble those of a business enterprise. As they are, in theory, responsible for their profits and losses, enjoying some leeway in the use of their earnings, they should relate to higher authorities and their subordinate enterprises according to economic rather than administrative principles. Compared to other state trading entities, they display greater initiative and innovation in their economic activities.

The China International Trust and Investment Corporation (CITIC) was one of the first such hybrid institutions to be set up at the national level. By 1981 22 ITICs and Overseas Chinese Investment Corporations had been set up in 16 provinces and municipalities. Although CITIC supposedly operated as a business entity, employing methods and techniques common in the capitalist world, it nevertheless enjoyed the status of a government ministry directly accountable to the State Council. However, the degree of authority and autonomy in foreign economic affairs CITIC enjoys as well as its relation to MOFERT or the Foreign Trade Corporation is not entirely clear. As it answers directly to the State Council, it would seem that it had in theory equal power to MOFERT, at least until mid-1989 when its administrative status was demoted.

Although this type of structure is aimed at decentralising micro-economic decisions, thus enabling these institutions to respond rapidly to market changes and take opportunities for profit-maximisation, to the extent that the directors are political figures appointed from outside, it is likely that the corporations will be subject to the influences of outside administrative agencies, thus restricting their degree of autonomy and flexibility.

Nevertheless, it is significant that the head of CITIC, Rong Yiren, was a former Shanghai capitalist, whose experience with the capitalist world would presumably facilitate the development of a profit-conscious enterprise. Compared to other state trading companies, these investment and trust corporations have a much wider scope of business ranging from the establishment of joint ventures to the issuing of bonds overseas. As CITIC disposes of its own funds and is able to raise its own money overseas, it enjoys greater financial autonomy than other trading entities.

Although it is difficult to assess to what extent CITIC and its branches as well as provincial investment corporations behave like business enterprises, there is considerable evidence of greater innovation and initiative in their economic activities than other state institutions.[13] This initiative is in turn related to the greater financial autonomy enjoyed by these institutions, which can raise their own funds through, for example, commission and overseas bonds.

The expansion of China's foreign economic relations has thus prompted the emergence of an intermediary layer of quasi-state institutions mediating between the state and foreign capital. The rise of these quasi-state institutions has been linked to the ebb and flow of decentralisation policies. Whilst they are supposed to operate like business entities, further research is required to establish to what extent their relations with subordinate companies and enterprises are determined by economic rather than administrative principles. As criticism has been levelled against the comparable industrial corporations, which, contrary to expectations, evolved often into 'administrative' rather than economic organisations, it is possible too that these quasi-state institutions dealing with foreign economic relations may also inherit features of the commandist state.

The emergence of these quasi-state institutions also raises key issues of control. As they dispose of considerable funds, earned in part through fees charged to their clients, and do not require the approval of MOFERT for some of their activities, they have greater room for manoeuvre than other state organs. Although these quasi-state institutions may have proven more dynamic than their administrative counterparts, their business initiatives have also contributed towards the periodic imbalances in the economy.

The shift towards more flexible and entrepreneurial state involvement in the economy is also reflected in *changes in the social composition of the state*. The Open Door Policy has required the cultivation of a layer of technical and professional cadres. Qualified staff are needed not only to make decisions about what technology to transfer but also to facilitate the process of technology absorption. The expansion of foreign trade has required more people with negotiation skills who are familiar with the workings of international trade. Similarly, the establishment of foreign-invested enterprises requires trained managers familiar not only with domestic business but also with Western or Japanese business culture.

The importance of these new skills at the same time heralds the demise of political qualities and activity as criteria for recruitment to the state. Whilst in the Cultural Revolution 'redness' was considered a greater virtue and quality than 'expertise', in the post-Mao period the 'colour of the cat' is not so important. The beneficiaries of the newly emerging market-facilitating state are thus the technocratic cadres, whilst the losers are the politicocratic cadres. Nevertheless, the changes in the structure and operational mode of the state involve the creation of new sources of power such as access to foreign exchange and foreign goods, overseas business trips and opportunities to study abroad. Party membership is still an asset, especially for those going for trips abroad or receiving training overseas.

In order to meet these new technical requirements the government has not only offered retraining courses for those whose education was forfeited during the Cultural Revolution, but also has introduced new subjects into the curriculum such as English language, economics, foreign trade, computers, etc. The reformers have simultaneously encouraged the recruitment of younger, more educated people to the Party and the early retirement of older, less educated cadres. Key policy-making think-tank organisations are increasingly staffed by young, Western educated economists and social scientists.

Although the reformist leadership has been keen to recruit reform-minded technocrats to the state administration and Party, this has been constrained both by the time-lag in training as well as the reluctance of politicocrats to make way for the better-educated and technically skilled technocrats. In order to accelerate the 'technocratisation' of the state, MOFERT laid down in early 1987 that Party and government officials could not work for both trade companies and government-Party institutions at the same time.[14] This stipulation reflects not only the commitment of certain central leaders to the reform of the state but also the degree of resistance from the politocratic cadres, who owe their positions of authority to political rather than economic credentials, to cede some of their power over economic decisions.

The emergence of the market-facilitating state is thus highly politicised. The losers under the market-facilitating state may obstruct, delay or reinterpret the Open Door Policy in their favour, whilst the beneficiaries will try to push the Open Door Policy forwards. Evidence that 'experts' have not been able to assert themselves in the policy-making process is reflected in the criticism made by some leading scientists that the opinions of experts are often neglected.[15]

Not only are younger, more professionally and technically qualified people being recruited to the state, but the Open Door Policy has also witnessed the resurrection of former capitalists to positions of power. The rationale for this is clearly that such people possess particular business skills and, more importantly, an understanding of the international capitalist economy – something which is in short supply. Thus Wang Guangying, who was a successful joint owner of a chemical works in Tianjin before 1949, was elected vice-mayor of Tianjin in 1980 and appointed chairman of the Board of Directors of the Everbright Industrial Corporation in Hong Kong. The appointment of former capitalists to power might also lead to dissatisfaction amongst both former revolutionaries as well as those cadres who came to power during the politically-charged period of the Cultural Revolution. These cadres would then form part of the social base of the leftist opposition.

To summarise, this section has examined the effect of the Open Door Policy on that part of the state dealing with foreign economic relations. The creation of new institutions at the central level, the mushrooming of trading entities at the provincial level and below as well as the adaptation of existing institutions provide the structural conditions for greater flexibility in state economic activity.

However, the restructuring of the institutional terrain is not a sufficient condition for the state to take maximum advantage of market opportunities. The post-Mao era has also witnessed a change in the way parts of the state behave in the sphere of foreign economic relations. The emergence of a layer of quasi-state institutions acting according to economic principles such as profit-maximisation exemplify a new entrepreneurial mode of operation on the part of the state. The development of this entrepreneurial and flexible state has been aided by the promotion of both former capitalist and technically-skilled personnel to positions of authority.

Although the nurturing of a market-facilitating state has entailed greater initiative at the local level, it has also created its own problems of economic imbalance, uncoordinated imports and exports as well as a predominance of small-scale, non-productive investment. Moreover, the redistribution of economic power to a proliferation of lower level institutions has also strengthened the independence of local level authorities, raising key issues of central political control. As the development of a market-facilitating state is both politically and economically complex, it is likely that its future course will continue to parallel the spiral evolution of the Open Door Policy. Whilst these changes in the character of the state can be observed in all parts of China where reform and opening up are underway, the process has been most advanced in the SEZs. The next section focusses on the case of Xiamen SEZ.

3 EFFECTS OF THE OPEN DOOR POLICY ON THE STATE: XIAMEN SEZ

Situated in Fujian Province on the South East coast of China, Xiamen SEZ was one of the first SEZs to be set up in July 1979 (see M1).[16] Chinese policy-makers in Xiamen SEZ also adhere to the view that the state in Xiamen is no different to elsewhere in China.[17] It will be argued in this section, however, that there is evidence of an emerging 'market-facilitating' state in Xiamen SEZ. Moreover, this redefinition of the state is more apparent in Xiamen SEZ than in non-zone areas where the concentration of foreign capital is not so great.

(a)   Restructuring of State Institutions

In order to deal with the changing conditions resulting from the introduction of market forces, both domestic and foreign, the state in Xiamen SEZ is undergoing a process of restructuring. This has involved the creation of new coordinating institutions, the proliferation of trading companies and voluntary trade associations and the adaptation of existing state institutions. These changes in the structure of the state have evolved in rhythm with the spiral course of the Open Door Policy. As up till 1984 the economic affairs of Xiamen SEZ fell under the administrative jurisdiction of the provincial government, the analysis necessarily covers changes at the provincial level as well.

In order to manage the establishment of Xiamen SEZ, a new SEZ Administration Office was created in Fujian Province. However, it was not until 1984 when Xiamen was granted greater autonomy that a SEZ Committee was also set up in Xiamen. Although the Xiamen SEZ Committee then fell directly under the State Council, the exact nature of this relationship is not clear.

As well as the creation of special institutions to manage the SEZ, there have also been considerable changes, as at the national level, in the management of foreign trade. Up till 1980 the Fujian Foreign Trade Bureau was the most important foreign trade entity in Fujian. This was related vertically upwards to the Ministry of Trade in Beijing and downwards to its branches in Xiamen and other cities. In 1980, however, as part of a national strategy to break up the monopoly of the Foreign Trade Bureau, two new trade institutions were established, namely, the Fujian Import/Export Office and the Fujian Foreign Trade Corporation. These changes were parallelled at the local level in Xiamen SEZ. As a result the powers of the Fujian Foreign Trade Bureau were considerably reduced.

The Fujian Import/Export Office took over not only the policy and planning functions of the Foreign Trade Bureau but also took responsibility for the allocation of foreign exchange within the province, thus usurping the administrative authority of the Foreign Trade Bureau. At the same time the Foreign Trade Corporation, which was responsible for its own profits and losses, weakened the control of the Foreign Trade Bureau over the branch foreign trade corporations.[18] The coexistence of the Foreign Trade Bureau, Import/Export Office and the Foreign Trade Corporation meant there was considerable overlap in functions.

Following the merger of several institutions into the national MOFERT, the administration of foreign trade was taken over by the newly founded Fujian Foreign Economic Relations and Trade Commission (FJFERTC).

Similarly, the Xiamen SEZ Economic Relations and Trade Commission (XMFERTC) was set up in 1983 to administer and plan foreign trade, foreign investment and supervise overseas labour exports. As Xiamen FERTC was directly responsible to MOFERT in Beijing, it became in theory at least autonomous from the provincial FERTC. The establishment of the zone has thus entailed a redistribution of power away from the province to Xiamen SEZ.

Following the expansion of the area covered by Xiamen SEZ in March 1984 further institutional changes were made. The Municipal Economic Commission, MOFERT and Finance Office were merged into a single Municipal Economic and Trade Commission, handling Xiamen's economy.[19]

As the reimposition of central control over the economy in mid-1985 had deleterious effects on the level of foreign investment, further adjustments in the institutional fabric of the foreign investment system were made. As at the national level several new institutions were established both in Fuzhou and Xiamen to deal with the specific needs of foreign capital, thus furthering the development of a market-facilitating state. The Xiamen SEZ Foreign Investment Leading Group Office, for example, was set up both to take charge of the planning and approval of joint ventures in Xiamen SEZ and to facilitate relations between joint ventures and government.

The Open Door Policy has also prompted the development of a new arm of the state, namely a legal structure dealing with foreign economic relations. Xiamen set up a Foreign Economic Lawyers' office which provides legal services for both Chinese and foreigners. Xiamen has also promulgated almost 50 administrative and economic laws since opening up.

Apart from the creation of new administrative institutions at provincial and SEZ levels, there has also been a proliferation of institutions at subprovincial level involved in foreign trade. Provincial branches of new national specialist trading corporations such as the Fujian Footwear and Headgear Branch Corporation have been set up, whilst cities such as Sanming, Putian and Quanzhou have been permitted to set up new Foreign Trading Corporation branches and foreign trading companies. As a result in 1987, there were 208 local foreign trade companies authorised to export locally supplied products outside central control, of which 105 were accounted for by Xiamen SEZ.[20] The proliferation of trade companies and the subsequent loss of central control over foreign trade led, as at the national level, to their reappraisal in early 1986.

As well as the creation of new institutions, existing institutions such as the banks, customs and educational institutions in Xiamen SEZ have also adapted their structures and operations to accommodate foreign capital. The Bank of China has, for example, through its Trade and Consultancy Department, become involved in the formation of joint ventures. Moreover, the role of foreign exchange management in the bank has increased in importance. The recruitment of labour through advertisements has also altered the role of newspapers, reflecting both the commoditisation of labour and the media. As a result of tourism and the establishment of the SEZ, the work of the customs has increased. Not only has the quantity of goods requiring inspection risen, but the incidence of smuggling has also spiralled.

The Party has also had to adjust its methods of operation. As wholly-owned foreign enterprises and many of the joint ventures in the SEZs ban the Party and trade unions from holding political meetings during production hours, alternative means have to be employed for the dissemination of Party and trade union formation in Xiamen. Educational establishments in the zone have also adjusted their curricula to suit the needs of the special economic environment. The Lujiang University, for example, has set up specialist vocational courses for training secretaries, interpreters and technicians to work in the zone. Two electronics high schools have been set up to train people for the local electronics industry. Xiamen University has also expanded its foreign trade, law and management departments.

Although there has been a restructuring of state institutions in Xiamen to accommodate the introduction of foreign capital, the new institutional framework is still only partially developed. As at the national level there is no particular institution responsible for coordinating and administering foreign loans. Similarly, although the right to negotiate joint ventures has been decentralised to a number of state agencies, there is no exclusive institution which deals with the coordination and planning of foreign investment projects. Moreover, although progress has been made in the development of economic legislation, Xiamen still lacks laws in the fields of auditing, real estate and management as well as in specific sectors such as agriculture, transport, communications, resources, market and financial services.[21]

The development of a market-facilitating state has been constrained both by the time required to make institutional changes as well as the political reverberations of the redistribution of power and resources within the state. As the importance of economic institutions in Xiamen SEZ has increased *vis à vis* political institutions and the army, resistance from the latter to such changes, in particular through support of ideological campaigns against the Open Door Policy, has been an important constraint on the pace of institutional change.

(b) Changes in the Operational Mode of the State

The development of a more flexible and entrepreneurial state has been facilitated not only through the restructuring of the institutional terrain but also through decentralisation, the mushrooming of quasi-state institutions and the recruitment of technically qualified personnel.

The decentralisation of some authority over foreign economic relations has been a key feature of changes in the operational mode of the state in Xiamen. The process of administrative decentralisation in foreign economic relations has proceeded from centre to province and then from Fujian province to Xiamen. The provincial government has thus had to cede some of its power over foreign trade, foreign investment and foreign exchange allocation to Xiamen SEZ.

In 1979 Fujian and Guangdong were granted greater autonomy in both their local economy and foreign trade. Compared with other provinces, they enjoyed greater authority in devising and implementing provincial plans, more favourable terms and conditions in the allocation of funds, loans, foreign currency and tax relief, permission to set up a SEZ and a greater degree of direct trading between provincial authorities and foreign partners. This strengthened their economic independence *vis à vis* central government, enabling them to undertake construction projects and import technology that would otherwise have required central approval.

In the initial stages of the construction of the zone the provincial government was closely involved in its development.[22] Following the support given to SEZs by reformist leaders at the Party Congress in September 1982, Gu Mu called for greater autonomy for Xiamen. This reflected an awareness on the part of central leaders that the concentration of power and resources within the provincial government was a significant constraint on the pace of opening up in Xiamen SEZ. Although in September 1983 Fujian People's Government decided to increase Xiamen's autonomy, it was only after the visit of Deng Xiaoping in 1984 that Xiamen's autonomy from the provincial capital of Fuzhou began to be implemented.[23] This was related in part to the reverberations of the Spiritual Pollution Campaign launched by the leftist opposition which cast a momentary shadow over the future of the zones and in part probably to a reluctance by the provincial government to cede power immediately.

Although the autonomy of Xiamen SEZ from the provincial government with regard to its foreign economic relations was increased in 1984, it has still been subject to central restrictions. Whilst Xiamen municipal authorities can approve joint ventures, business licences in 1984 were still issued by the respective central authorities. Similarly, in May 1984

Xiamen Municipal Economic and Trade Commission was given authority to examine and approve investment projects for the import of technology, but only under Y 1 m.[24]

Following Deng Xiaoping's visit to Xiamen in 1984 Xiamen Municipal Economic and Trade Commission was permitted to approve joint ventures with a total investment of up to US$ 10m, whilst previously provincial approval was required. However, for projects over this amount as well as wholly-owned foreign enterprises Xiamen had to obtain central government approval. The provincial government had thus lost its authority over Xiamen SEZ to approve foreign investment.

With regard to foreign exchange, considerable administrative decentralisation of authority has occurred. In 1980 the provincial government could only retain all export earnings above a level fixed according to the value of trade the previous year, whilst Fuzhou and Xiamen municipal governments could only retain 20 per cent of above-target forex earnings.[25] Certain enterprises were also permitted to retain some of their foreign exchange earnings, depending on their output volume and exports. The restrictions over foreign exchange retention were considerably relaxed in 1984. Whilst Fujian can retain 70 per cent of above-plan export earnings, Xiamen SEZ can retain 100 per cent. Both Xiamen and Fujian can only retain 30 per cent of foreign exchange earned from planned exports, the remaining 70 per cent being passed on to central government.

The right to retain foreign exchange strengthens the independent of provincial and municipal governments. As foreign exchange is allocated administratively in China and not through market forces, local governments attach great importance to the right to retain and use foreign exchange. Possession of some foreign exchange enables exporters both to have easier access to imported inputs and to reduce the administrative costs of applying for foreign exchange through regular channels. Moreover, it enables local governments to undertake some projects without central approval and funding. Thus the decentralisation of foreign exchange retention to both Fujian and Xiamen SEZ authorities has granted them greater power than previously in imports, the planning of the economy as well as technology introduction. Moreover, the Overseas Chinese link in Fujian Province also provides it with an extra source of foreign exchange through Overseas Chinese remittances.

Although the decentralisation of authority over foreign economic relations from centre to Fujian Province and from Fujian to Xiamen SEZ, particularly from 1984, enabled local governments to respond more flexibly to opportunities in the domestic and international market, it also contributed towards serious imbalances in the economy. This in turn led to the reimposition of central control over the economy in mid-1985. As a result the number of technological trade companies in Fujian permitted to assist enterprises with the introduction of technology was reduced from 100 to 18.[26] This was probably achieved through the requirement in early 1986 that all trading companies register with MOFERT. There was thus a rise in the power of the commandist state and a step backwards in the emergence of a market-facilitating state. These fluctuations in Xiamen's authority are linked in part to the contradictory effects of decentralisation. Whilst on the one hand decentralisation increased local initiative, it at the same time contributed towards the rapid surge in consumer imports and the concomitant fall in foreign exchange in 1985.[27] As decentralisation strengthened the position of the provincial government in relation to the central authorities and of Xiamen in relation to the provincial authorities, the process of recentralising has become more complicated as lower level authorities seek to defend their newly-acquired privileges. To the extent that decentralisation of authority over foreign economic relations creates its own set of interests at lower levels, there is the risk from the point of view of the central government that the market-facilitating state serves local rather than national interests and market rather than plan interests.

Whilst this decentralisation of authority to the provincial and SEZ levels has contributed towards the creation of a more flexible state, the mushrooming of numerous *quasi-state trading institutions* in Fujian Province has been symptomatic of greater state entrepreneurialism. Similar to the national quasi-state institutions referred to in the previous section, they are intended to operate as economic agencies, enjoy some financial independence and cover a broad range of tasks.

The most prominent quasi-state institution in Xiamen SEZ is the Xiamen Construction and Development Company (XCDC), set up in January 1981 by the Xiamen Municipal Government and the Administration Committee of Xiamen SEZ.[28] Its activities are broad, including the establishment of joint ventures, import-export business and leasing. XCDC has been involved in around half of all joint ventures in Xiamen SEZ and is a shareholder in about one third of these. It is thus an important and relatively accessible source of finance for state-owned enterprises seeking to import technology or set up joint ventures with foreign companies. As its name suggests, it is a crossbreed institution, harbouring features of both a state organ and an economic enterprise. Although the XCDC enjoys considerable financial autonomy compared with other state organs, it is not totally autonomous. According to informal sources, XCDC was severely restricted in early 1987, probably by the municipal authorities, from extending any loans to state-owned enterprises for technology imports or joint venture projects.

Partly to facilitate trade with Taiwan and partly to manage the infrastructural development of Huli District, XCDC set up a joint venture, namely
the Xiamen SEZ United Development Corporation (XUDC), in October 1983
in conjunction with the Trust and Consultancy Company of the Bank
of China and five Hong Kong banks.[29] As there are no governmental
trade relations between Taiwan and China, XUDC, as a non-governmental
enterprise, was better equipped to manage business with Taiwan. Xiamen
UDC is in theory at least an independent economic entity, responsible for
its own profits and losses. Other quasi-state institutions include the Xing
Xia Company, Xiamen Investment and Enterprises Company and Xiamen
International Trade and Trust Company.

Although the structure of these quasi-state institutions resembles on the
surface that of a business enterprise, with the highest level of authority
being, in theory at least, the Board of Directors, there is some evidence
to suggest that the recruitment of leaders follows a similar pattern to state
institutions. For example, as in state-owned enterprises, there can still be
considerable duplication of posts both within and between organisations.
Liu Shouming, for example, was both chairperson and executive director
of the Fujian Foreign Trading Corporation, whilst the director of Fujian
was also chairperson of the quasi-state Fujian Investment and Enterprise
Corporation. The occupation of key posts in these organisations by leading
political figures in the province, who are highly likely to be Party members,
implies the continued involvement of outside administrative bodies, casting
a shadow over their supposed independence.

To the extent that these political figures are reform-minded, this might
provide important political support for these new institutions. On the
other hand, as they are politically rather than professionally qualified,
the potential tendency to seek administrative solutions to economic
problems might be greater. Moreover, as their interests extend beyond
the corporations, the economic transactions of these companies may
be constrained by the competing interests of external administrative
bodies.

The development of a more entrepreneurial state in Fujian is reflected
not only in the rise of quasi-state institutions but also in the emergence
of *voluntary trade associations* set up by local businessmen and
Overseas Chinese. The Sanlian Economic Development Company, a
non-governmental economic entity, was established by some members
of the Fujian Provincial Federation of Industrialists and Businessmen
and Fujian Provincial Federation of Returned Overseas Chinese to attract
foreign investment, introduce advanced technology and conduct foreign
trade. Similarly, the Fujian Overseas Chinese Investment Company was

also set up in March 1984 following Deng Xiaoping's visit to Xiamen one month earlier.

Whilst the quasi-state institutions share similar features to other such bodies in the rest of China, the voluntary associations are distinctive in that they reflect the interests of a particular social group, namely, Overseas Chinese. On the one hand, this may be linked to deliberate policies of both central and local government to tap this lucrative source of foreign capital, on the other hand, it is an expression of mutually recognised interests based on family and historical ties. The potential political implications of these associations is far-reaching, particularly with respect to the issues of reunification and Overseas Chinese policy.

Whilst the mushrooming of these quasi-state institutions and voluntary trade associations has lent greater flexibility to the structural base of foreign economic relations, it has also contributed its own problems. In particular, the complexity of the institutional fabric has not only made coordination of the activities of the individual parts more difficult but has also led to cut-throat price competition between foreign trading companies both in the purchasing of export goods as well as in the sale of these in the international market. By 1984, non-trade organisations accounted for almost 40 per cent of all trade activity in Xiamen whilst foreign-invested enterprises laid claim to 20 per cent.[30] The proliferation of foreign trade companies in Xiamen as well as the concomitant cut-throat price competition led, as at the national level, to a 'rectification' of such companies in early 1986.

The development of a market-facilitating state is reflected not only in decentralisation and the spawning of quasi-state institutions but also in *changes in the type of person recruited to state institutions* dealing with foreign economic relations. The lack of suitably qualified personnel in Xiamen has required the import of technicians from other provinces. Thus in 1984 Huli Management Committee recruited 260 specialised, technical cadres from Beijing, Shanghai, Tianjin and Nanjing, some of whom took up positions as managers and supervisors in joint ventures.[31] At the same time, various courses have been set up in Xiamen's numerous educational institutions designed to train young people in relevant skills such as Japanese, English languages, catering, hotel management, tourism, business studies and foreign trade.

The employment patterns in local foreign trade institutions suggest that professional qualifications have become a significant recruitment criterion. In the quasi-state Fujian Investment and Enterprise Corporation, 80 per cent of the staff had college or university education.[32] The percentage of tertiary educated employees in intermediary organisations interviewed in Xiamen was relatively high. Although compared to 1978 there were more young people with university education and language skills in the General Foreign Trade Corporation in Fujian, it seems that newly founded organisations are more able to adopt professional criteria in recruitment.[33]

To conclude, the establishment of a SEZ in Xiamen has prompted the partial emergence of a market-facilitating state at the local level. The strong Overseas Chinese links in Fujian Province have been a significant factor stimulating greater economic entrepreneurialism in the form of voluntary trade associations. The development of this new form of state has been constrained, however, by the inevitable time-lag involved in institutional change, resistance by individuals and institutions losing out in this process as well as economic imbalances arising from greater micro-level initiative.

CONCLUSION

The process of reform and opening-up has led to a redefinition of the state in post-Mao China. The introduction of market forces, both domestic and foreign, has stimulated the emergence of a 'market-facilitating state', which is more flexible, entrepreneurial, legalistic and technocratic than its predecessor. This has entailed the restructuring of state institutions, changes in its operational mode as well as its social composition. Although this chapter has focussed on that section of the state dealing with the external economy, similar changes are occurring in other parts of the state concerned with the domestic economy. Moreover, this redefinition of the state can be observed in varying degrees in all parts of China, where reform and opening up are underway, though the process has proceeded furthest in the SEZs, where the concentration of foreign capital is greatest.

The ongoing nature of these changes implies that the state is in a process of transition. As a result the state assumes a polymorphic character, whereby features of the former institutional matrix co-exist with the seeds of a new matrix. In particular, the web of the commandist planning state is receding whilst the web of the market-facilitating state is advancing. Institutions with structures and operational principles appropriate to the previous central command economy coexist with new institutional forms designed to meet the needs of domestic and external market forces. Whilst the 'old-style' commandist institutions continue to operate according to administrative logic, the new institutional generation responds to the economic imperatives of the marketplace. Similarly, state cadres who owe their positions to political credentials cohabit the corridors of power with the new 'professional-technocratic' strain of state employees. Moreover, there is a temporary vacuum where the pace of institutional change lags behind the transformation of the economy.

The development of the market-facilitating state has been shaped by a combination of economic and politico-institutional factors. As the process of institutional change and professional training requires time, there is clearly a time-lag between the policies designed to reform the state and their implementation. As the micro-economic activities of the market-facilitating state have contributed towards periodic macro-economic imbalances, the ensuing reimposition of central control over the economy has implied the strengthening of the central commandist state. Subsequent decentralisation in turn gives impetus to the growth of the market-facilitating state.

Furthermore, as the development of a market-facilitating state implies a redistribution of power and resources between institutions and between social groups within institutions, the process is highly politicised. The chief beneficiaries of the market-facilitating state are branches of ministries, provincial and municipal authorities and technocratic cadres, whilst the 'losers' have been the central government, minstries and politocratic cadres, even though the boundaries between 'losers' and 'winners' are not always clear-cut. The ensuring conflict and cooperation between potential 'winners' and 'losers' has contributed towards the periodic fluctuations in the development of the market-facilitating state.

These vacillations in the development of the market-facilitating state have parallelled the spiral trajectory of the Open Door Policy. Thus during upswings in the Open Door Policy the market-facilitating state gathers momentum whilst in the downswings the commandist state reasserts itself. As each new cycle in the Open Door Policy entails the extension and deepening of the policy, the roots of the market-facilitating state likewise become deeper and stronger. There is thus an 'institutional' spiral shadowing the Open Door Policy spiral.

The current transitional character of the state has ambiguous effects on the implementation of the Open Door Policy. The proliferation of institutions due to decentralisation combined with the continued existence of commandist institutions has not only created an impression of overlapping bureaucracy amongst foreign investors but has also confused lines of authority both for Chinese cadres as well as for foreign companies. This has been exacerbated by the periodic fluctuations in the development of the new form of state.

To the extent that the market-facilitating state gains a firm foothold, the institutional environment for opening up becomes more favourable. The resurgence of socio-political unrest in the spring of 1989 amongst intellectuals and workers, and in particular the events of June 4th, however, have brought about the reassertion of control by the commandist state. The future prospects for the Open Door Policy, and by implication the continued growth of the market-facilitating state, hinge crucially on the specific conjuncture of interests within the leadership and society in the immediate years to come.

ABBREVIATIONS

FBIS   Foreign Broadcast Information Service
SWB   Summary of World Broadcasts: Far East, from the BBC
CBR   *China Business Review*

NOTES

I have used the term 'Open Door Policy' since it is more familiar to Western readers. The Chinese use the term 'open policy' (*kaifang zhengce*).

1. C. Y. Chang, 'Bureaucracy and Modernisation: A Case Study of the Special Economic Zones in China' in Y.C. Jao and C.K. Leung, *China's Special Economic Zones* (OUP 1986) pp. 108–109.
2. Zheng Tuobin, 'The Problem of Reforming China's Foreign Trade System' in *Chinese Economic Studies* (Summer 1987) pp. 31–33.
3. For a full account of the spiral evolution of the Open Door Policy, see the unpublished DPhil thesis by this author, entitled 'The Political Dynamics of China's Open Policy' (Institute of Development Studies, University of Sussex, 1989).
4. Institutions involved included, for example, the State Planning Commission, State Economic Commission, Ministry of Foreign Economic Relations and Trade, Bank of China, Ministry of Finance, China Customs Administration, China Foreign Exchange Administration Bureau and the State Council Special Economic Zones Office.
5. *Zheng Tuobin* (Summer 1987) p. 130.
6. *Hong Kong South China Morning Post*, 30 June 1987.
7. This Committee was a development of the Foreign Trade Arbitration Commission established in 1956.
8. *South China Morning Post Hong Kong*, 8 November 1985 in FBIS, 8 November 1985, W1.
9. There are two types of decentralisation: administrative decentralisation whereby power is devolved to lower levels of the state machinery; and economic decentralisation whereby power is redistributed from state administrative organs at all levels to economic units. On administrative

and economic decentralisation, see G. White's chapter in this volume. This is similar to Schurmann's concepts of Decentralisation I and II – see F. Schurmann, *Ideology and Organisation in Communist China* (University of California Press, 1966), pp. 175–178, 196–199.

10. See World Bank, China 2 External Trade and Capital (World Bank, Washington, USA, 1988) p. 20.

11. In July 1985, however, the privileges of ten of the coastal cities were restricted again.

12. See M. Blecher, 'Developmental State, Entrepreneurial State: the Political Economy of Socialist Reform in Xinji Municipality and Guanghan County', in this volume.

13. For example, in order to secure supplies of timber and obtain forestry experience, CITIC set up a forestry company in the USA.

14. *Guoji Shangbao* 16 January 1986 in SWB 8182/C1/3–7, February 13 1986.

15. Xinhua 17 March 1987.

16. The other zones are Shenzhen SEZ, Zhuhai SEZ and Shantou SEZ, which were also set up in July 1979. In August 1987, it was revealed that Hainan Island would become China's fifth SEZ.

17. For example, in an introductory pamphlet to Xiamen SEZ published by the Fujian FERTC, it was stated: 'Xiamen SEZ, neither a political zone nor a special administration zone like Hong Kong . . . is a so-called SEZ because it practises the SEZ policy, special economic management system and special flexible measures'.

18. E. Terry, 'Decentralising Foreign Trade', CBR, Sept./Oct. 1980, pp. 10–23.

19. *Guangzhou Wanfang Jingji*, no. 6, 1986.

20. *China Trader*, (February 1987).

21. See *Hong Kong Macao Economic Digest*, 6, 1986.

22. See Almanac of Xiamen's Economy Editorial Board, *Almanac of Xiamen's Economy 1986* (China Statistical Publishing House 1986).

23. *Fujian Ribao* 22 March 1984, p. 1.

24. *Beijing Ribao* 24 April 1984.

25. In 1980 this level was US$ 200m. See E. Terry, CBR, Sept./Oct. 1980, p. 11.

26. Interview, Fujian FERTC, June 1987.

27. For further details of this, see unpublished DPhil thesis by author, entitled 'The Political Dynamics of China's Open Door Policy', pp. 128–136, IDS, University of Sussex, 1989.

28. Interview, Xiamen Construction and Development Corporation, April 1987.

29. H. Topper, 'Xiamen SEZ: Poised for Take-off' in CBR, November 1988, p. 16.

30. Almanac of Xiamen's Economy Ed. Board (1986) p. 94. Although it is not clear what 'non-trade organisations' refers to, it probably refers to production enterprises and possibly investment corporations.

31. *Fujian Ribao* March 26 1985, p. 1.
32. Interview, Fujian Investment and Enterprise Corporation, June 1987.
33. Interview, Fujian Foreign Trade Corporation, June 1987.

BIBLIOGRAPHY

Primary Sources

Almanac of Xiamen's Economy Editorial Board, *Almanac of Xiamen's Economy 1986* (China Statistical Publishing House 1986)
Guoji Shangbao, Beijing
Beijing Ribao
China Business Review
China Trader
Fujian Ribao
Hong Kong Macao Economic Digest
Nanfang Jingji, Guangzhon
South China Morning Post, Hong Kong
New China News Analysis

Secondary Sources

Blecher, M., 'Developmental State, Entrepreneurial State: the Political Economy of Socialist Reform in Xinji Municipality and Guanghan County, in this volume.

Chang, C. Y., 'Bureaucracy and Modernisation: A Case Study of the Special Economic Zones in China' in Jao, Y. C. & Leung, C. K., *China's Special Economic Zone – Policies, Problems and Prospects* (Oxford University Press, 1986).

Howell, J., 'The Political Dynamics of China's Open Policy', unpublished DPhil thesis, Institute of Development Studies, University of Sussex, 1989.

Schurmann, F., *Ideology and Organisation in Communist China* (University of California Press, 1966).

White, G., 'Basic-Level Local Government and Economic Reform in Urban China', in this volume, Chapter 9.

World Bank, *China: External Trade and Capital* (World Bank, Washington, USA, 1988).

Zheng Tuobin, 'The Problem of Reforming China's Foreign Trade System', *Chinese Economic Studies* (Summer 1987) pp. 27–49.

Part 2
Politics and the
National State

6　Much Ado About Nothing: Party Reform in the 1980s

Tony Saich

The student demonstrations that took place in April–May 1989 and their brutal suppression in June, exposed in tragic fashion the central problem of the reform movement during the eighties. Key CCP leaders have taken the un-Marxist position that economic reform can be isolated from the consequent pressures for political change. There has been a consistent refusal by China's top leaders to come to terms with the processes of change which their own economic reform programme had set in motion. Indeed the whole question of political reform became a major issue of division. However, as the CCP prepared to end its fourth decade in power, it had become increasingly clear to some leaders, including the then General Secretary, Zhao Ziyang, that a major shake-up of the Party's organisational structure and a re-think of its role were necessary. Without such a shake-up, the economic reforms would slide further into trouble. At the Thirteenth Party Congress (1987), Zhao presented a series of proposals that tried to deal with the key issue of the Party's role in society, to define more precisely the relationship between the CCP and the state sector and to limit the role of the Party in the work-place. These issues together with reforms of internal Party organisation are dealt with in the following.[1]

THE PARTY AND REFORM OF THE POLITICAL SYSTEM

The most important question in reform of the political system is that of the correct role for the Party and its relationship to other organisations. CCP dominance has been felt in all walks of life as the Party sought not only to control the legislature and executive but also to dictate the nation's moral and ethical values. The Party took over the traditional role of the state in China. Unchallenged by other organisations, such as the Church, the imperial state had assumed an all-embracing role that included defining correct ethical values.[2] Through its penetration of the state sector, the Party has taken over this role. This view is reinforced by its guiding ideology which asserts that human activity is governed by certain objective laws that only the Party can discern.

Not surprisingly, suggestions for reform have focused on the need to decrease the Party's influence over the day-to-day affairs of other organisations. Talk about political reform was legitimised by Deng Xiaoping in August 1980 when he proposed that a mere tinkering with the system and a removal of what were seen as irregularities in Party work caused by the Cultural Revolution were not enough.[3] The new development strategy adopted at the Third Plenum of the Eleventh Central Committee (December 1978) accentuated the need for change. The policies introduced to stimulate the use of market mechanisms combined with attempts to decentralise economic decision-making were not readily served by a rigid, over-centralised political system dominated by the Party and staffed by personnel who felt at home hiding behind administrative rules and regulations. Leaders such as Deng Xiaoping and his supporters began to realise that the demands of a modern economy required a greater differentiation and clarification of roles for China's institutions.[4]

During the early eighties, a number of initiatives were undertaken to reform the political system, including the adoption of new Party and State Constitutions, measures to trim the bureaucracy, attempts to improve the quality of the cadre force, and steps to promote more effective citizen participation. The Party even changed its self-definition. The 1982 Party Constitution refers to the Party as the 'vanguard of the Chinese working-class' rather than as the 'political Party of the proletariat and its vanguard'. The term working-class is more neutral than that of the proletariat, the latter term conjuring up visions of class struggle. This suits the emphasis which was placed on the tasks of economic modernisation and the down-grading of the role of class struggle. Also, importantly, the CCP now defines intellectuals as an integral part of the working-class. This attempt to reach out to broader groups in society is shown by the fact that the 1982 Constitution claims that the Party is the 'faithful representative of all Chinese people'.[5] This claim did not appear in any of the previous Party Constitutions.

Although restructuring of the Party and state apparatus continued throughout the eighties, a major overhaul was resisted. In particular, the question of the Party's dominant role was not tackled and many cadres balked at the idea of any curtailment in their power. Even the most reform-minded members of the establishment realised that there would be limits to the permissible. As in other periods of liberalisation in the PRC, as indeed in all state-socialist societies, there were differences of opinion about just how much the grip of the Party could or should be relaxed. Recognition that the Party cannot control everything, and trying to define what its leading role means in practice, leaves plenty of room for disagreement.

The notion of continued Party leadership was enshrined in promotion of the slogan of adherence to the 'Four Basic Principles'. These principles were first put forward by Deng Xiaoping in March 1979 at a Central Theoretical Work Conference.[6] This was in response to the Democracy Movement of the late-seventies. After initially using the movement in his political struggle against his opponents in the Party leadership, he had no further use for the movement and wished to set limits to non-Party sanctioned Party activity. Adherence to the 'Four Basic Principles' indicated that there were limits to the reforms and suggested a range of obligations for those engaged in discussions about political reform.

A further limit to wide-ranging reform was the general consensus among top Party leaders that political reform was dictated by the needs of economic reform.[7] Only such reforms would be initiated as were necessary to keep the motor of economic reform running smoothly. Further, as the eighties progressed and as economic success began to restore its confidence, the Party began to reassert its role as the guardian of the ideology. It discovered that socialism had a moral spiritual goal as well as a material goal, and that these goals could only be defined by the Party. At the Twelfth Party Congress (1982), Hu Yaobang, then General Secretary, reversed the listing of the Party's tasks placing the building of 'spiritual civilisation' before democratisation, thus making it a prerequisite for democratisation.

By Summer 1986, it was clear that political reform had become a severely divisive issue within the Party leadership. A Hong Kong newspaper report from Summer 1986 referred to a meeting at Beidaihe at which some leaders had expressed the view that, on the whole, the current political system was basically suited to the needs of economic development and that reform could lead to the negation of the Party's leadership and the 'Four Basic Principles'. To counter the perceived 'liberal' tendencies of the time, they suggested a strict set of obligations for those engaged in discussions about reform. Disagreements led to the postponement of an expected decision on political reform until the Thirteenth Party Congress (October 1987).[8] In fact, the Sixth Plenum of the Twelfth Party Congress (September 1986), instead of discussing political reform, passed a resolution on the need to improve work in the ideological and cultural spheres. These are issues more closely identified with those seeking to limit the extent of political reform. The opponents of too radical reform continued to link wide-ranging changes with bourgeois contamination. In November 1986, [then] Politburo member Peng Zhen warned against those who yearned for bourgeois democracy 'as if the moonlight of capitalist society was brighter than our socialist sun'.

The student demonstrations in late 1986, provided these opponents with their chance to launch a counter-attack and remove Party General Secretary, Hu Yaobang. The much larger student demonstrations of April–June 1989, provided them with the chance to remove Zhao from the same function. It is important to note that both rounds of student demonstrations took place after a perceived defeat for the proponents of further political reform within the top Party leadership. The demonstrations of 1989 have to be seen in light of the meeting of the National People's Congress held from late-March until early-April 1989. The decisions adopted by the Congress made it clear that Zhao and his pro-reform allies had lost the policy debate. Premier Li Peng and vice-Premier Yao Yilin, put forward a programme of tight economic austerity combined with attempts to curtail political liberalisation.[9] Indeed, China's most pro-reform newspaper Shanghai's *World Economic Herald* was barred from sending reporters, other journalists were told only to dwell on the brighter things of socialist life, and delegates were asked to refrain from being too critical and to confine themselves to patriotic displays of unity.

Within the top leadership, opinions on political reform crystallised into two main viewpoints: the *pragmatic reforming* and the *traditional orthodox*. These two viewpoints served as points on a continuum around which different opinions clustered at crucial moments. Certainly they were not the only views expressed and some individuals such as Deng Xiaoping moved between the two viewpoints. These viewpoints are linked to the question of the extent of economic reform. Clearly the nature of the Party depends on the kind of economic system over which it is to preside. The pragmatic view was presented by Zhao Ziyang at the Thirteenth Party Congress. The term pragmatic is used as the reforms proposed are designed primarily to improve economic efficiency. Picking up the theme first put forward by Deng Xiaoping in August 1980, Zhao contended that political reform was indispensable if economic reform was to continue. In linking the two processes, he stated, 'The process of developing the socialist commodity economy should be a process of building socialist democratic politics'. As a result, the Central Committee had decided that 'it was high time to put political reform on the agenda for the whole Party'.[10]

In addition, Zhao took over the idea of the pro-reform intellectuals who had begun arguing in the Summer of 1986 that the problems of China's political system derived from its feudal heritage as well as its own revolutionary experiences. The fact that he did not refer to the 'Four Modernisations' in his speech is also significant.[11] This slogan had emphasised concern with economic reform and ignored the need for an accompanying 'modernisation' of other aspects of society. Those concerned to push ahead further with political reform referred rather to 'socialist modernisation', a term that included 'modernisation' of culture and ways of thinking.[12]

Zhao's proposals called for a redistribution of power both horizontally to state organs at the same level and vertically to Party and state organs lower down the administrative ladder. The intention was for the Party to exercise political leadership but not to become directly involved in the routine work of government. Moreover, breaking with the monistic view common to CCP thinking and the idea of uniform policy implementation, Zhao acknowledged both that 'specific views and the interests of the masses may differ from each other' and that 'as conditions vary in different localities, we should not require unanimity in everything'.[13] However, his acknowledgement of a limited pluralism was not intended to accommodate factions within the Party, something which had been suggested by some reform-minded intellectuals, still less a 'loyal opposition'. This was evident when Zhao decided to close down the conservative Party theoretical journal *Hongqi* (*Red Flag*) and replaced it with a flagship for reform entitled *Qiushi*. It would have been feasible to allow both to function to provide an outlet for different policy preferences within the party leadership.

The market oriented reforms required that new groups in society be given the chance to participate in the process of both formulating and implementing the reforms. In this changing environment, the pragmatists realised that the Party had to find a new role for itself and devise new institutions to mediate between the Party and the officially sanctioned sections of society. Pragmatic reformers did not see this as weakening Party control, far from it. Such reforms were seen as the way to strengthen Party leadership.[14] The economic reforms are, in fact, giving rise to new forces within Chinese society. If the Party continues to pursue economic reform, it will have to adopt strategies to accommodate the demands of these new forces. In addition, the Party will become dependent on new strata such as professional managers, traders and entrepreneurs as well as the technicians and scientists who were already important for the functioning of the centrally planned economy, to implement more market-oriented policies.

However, any increase in political activity should not be allowed to disrupt stability or the overriding goal of achieving economic modernisation would be undermined. This, in turn, produces the need to 'institutionalise' such activity in order to prevent the increased heterogeneity in society leading to instability.[15] Further, tacit recognition by the Party of the existence of other groups should not be interpreted as the emergence of a 'pluralist' political system.[16] Indeed, the attempts to integrate these groups can be interpreted as an attempt to prevent that plurality by revising the structure of the regime and the Party's relationship to state and society.

To this end the Party can pursue two policies. First, it can recruit as Party members those new groups on which it has become reliant for its continued rule. This allows the Party to expand its presence in significant sectors of society while maintaining its privileged ruling position. Of course, this has the effect of importing the interests of these groups into the Party with the possibility that they prove a threat to the formerly dominant ethos. Secondly, it can seek to influence key groups in society more indirectly by binding them into organisations that become dependent on regime patronage. To head off mass opposition, the Party will seek to extend its organisation and supervision of as much of the population as possible.

Traditionally, for this purpose, the Party has relied on what it terms mass organisations such as the Trade Unions and the Women's Federation. This is, of course, a two-edged sword since it provides a mechanism of participation to officially sanctioned groups. However, it makes the formation of autonomous union organisations or women's organisations extremely difficult. Further, it ensures that sectoral interests are subjugated to general Party policy. The Party allows such organisations the autonomy to organise their own activities, within a broadly defined framework, and to support the pursuance of legitimate rights of their members in so far as they do not override the common good, as defined by the Party. In return, the Party expects unconditional support for its broader political, economic and social programmes. However, even at times when control, economic and political, has been much tighter these organisations have proved themselves to be unwieldy for serving this purpose.

While neither Hu Yaobang in late-1986 nor Zhao Ziyang in mid-1989 saw the student protests as a major threat, the traditionalists in the Party saw them as a challenge to the very fundamental principles of Party rule. Crucially, Deng Xiaoping decided to side with the traditionalists. Whereas Zhao appeared willing to make concessions to the students' demands, his opponents felt that no retreat was possible as it would lead to a collapse of socialism.[17] Their reaction to the events and their brutal repression of the students only serves to highlight their fear of spontaneous political activity that occurs outside of their direct control.

The group Deng sided with opposes wide-ranging political reform for a variety of reasons. First, there are those who are worried about the consequences of liberalisation for the social fabric of China. For them, the economic policies combined with a relaxation of ideological education were the causes of the increased corruption and the emergence of 'unhealthy' ideological tendencies. This group includes veteran leaders such as Wang Zhen, Peng Zhen and Hu Qiaomu. Secondly, there are those such as Chen Yun and Bo Yibo who represent the old central state planning and economic apparatus and are concerned about the economic consequences of current policy. Chen Yun, having been a major sponsor of the more market-based reforms is not, against reform *per se*, but argues for greater caution and the primacy of plan over market. Thirdly, there are senior military officers many of whom were imbued with 'leftist' ideology and worried about the erosion of Mao Zedong's legacy. They are products of the old peasant army who have opposed the shift to a less political and more professional army that was a part of the reform programme.

These groups seek to limit the scope of change and to run the Party and its relationship to society along orthodox Leninist lines. Efforts to relax the Party's grip over state and society are resisted and they seek continually to institutionalise Party dominance. In particular, they have been concerned about attempts to loosen the control of the Party in the work-place. With the decentralisation of some of the decision-making powers to the work-units, it is felt important that the Party retains a strong role in the enterprises to stop the work-units deviating too much from central Party policy.

The drive to maintain institutionalised Party dominance provides stability and assurances as well as status for Party cadres. However, at the same time, this drive does much to explain the stifling of initiative that has been increasingly apparent during the reform period. In combination with the dual-pricing system, it provides the structural basis for corruption that has been heavily criticised not only by student demonstrators but also in the official Chinese press. The concentrated nature of power and the lack of a genuine system of accountability mean that Party officials at all levels are in a unique position to turn professional relationships into personal connections for financial gain. For example, they can arrange the permits to purchase scarce goods at controlled prices. The product is then sold on to one of the new enterprises or a foreign venture at the full market price. Given this structure, the idea that the problem can be resolved by the punishment of a few middle-ranking officials and an ideological campaign to instil correct behaviour in cadres is a non-starter.

The tendency towards intrusiveness in all spheres of life has been increased by the student demonstrations of mid-1989. The disturbances are blamed on the emergence of bourgeois ideas in Chinese society along with the economic reforms. Former Party secretaries Hu Yaobang and Zhao Ziyang are blamed for not taking this problem seriously enough at an early stage and thus allowing it to get out of hand. As early as October 1983, the 'open-door policy' had been identified as a source of problems within the Party. An official decision on Party Consolidation, while stating that the 'open-door policy' had been entirely correct, noted that there had been an increase in the 'corrosive influence of decadent bourgeois ideology and remnant feudal ideas'.[18]

To combat the influx of such heterodox ideas, the traditionalists favour the launching of intensive ideological campaigns. In the process, such campaigns become a cover for attacks on various other aspects of the reform programme that are considered unsuitable in a socialist country. In turn, they create an air of concern and uncertainty about the future direction of reform and thus began to undermine the economic programmes that Deng Xiaoping has been consistently keen to pursue. Thus, the campaign against 'spiritual pollution' launched in October 1983 was reined in by February 1984 and the campaign to combat 'bourgeois liberalisation' launched after Hu's dismissal in January 1987 only had a shelf-life of about one month. Both the launching and the quick termination of these campaigns were sanctioned by Deng Xiaoping, thus revealing the continual dilemma with which he and his like are confronted. He stands in the tradition of the mid-nineteenth century reformers who wanted to use the West's technology to stimulate economic growth at home but who were not prepared to accept the political consequences.

The student demonstrations of mid-1989 have given veteran leaders such as Peng Zhen and Wang Zhen another chance to re-launch such an ideological campaign and this time, despite Deng's expressed wish to push ahead with economic reforms, he will find it much more difficult to contain it. Only another major change in the leadership will prevent the campaign broadening out into a major attack on key elements of the economic reforms. When Hu Yaobang fell from power, Zhao Ziyang was able initially to use his position as General Secretary to limit the extent of the political campaign and to continue to exert influence over economic policy. The manner and circumstances under which Jiang Zemin was appointed as Zhao's successor give him no room for manoeuvre on these issues even should he wish to influence them. Traditionalist leaders recognise full well that certain aspects of the economic reform programme not only create the basis for 'disruptive ideas' but also call into question traditional notions of socialism. They challenge what the Hungarian economic theorist, Kornai, calls the 'ethical goals' of socialism such as equality, solidarity and security.[19] Thus, it is not surprising that despite calls for continuing the economic reforms, in August 1989 attacks began in the official press on the private economy and the inegalitarian consequences of Zhao's (not Deng's!) policies.

Both Hu Yaobang and Zhao Ziyang have been criticised for being too weak on ideological affairs and even of 'surrendering to the bourgeoisie'. One of the specific accusations against Zhao is that in his speech to commemorate the 70th anniversary of the patriotic May 4th Movement (1919), he refused to include the need to 'oppose bourgeois liberalisation' as had been requested by Premier Li Peng and various other 'comrades'.[20] Should the proposed long-term campaign to combat 'bourgeois liberalisation' launched in the summer of 1989 continue, it will lead to a reassertion and strengthening of the Party's role throughout the Chinese political system. While careful not to conjure up visions of a new Cultural Revolution, the new leadership has also given a renewed emphasis to the role of 'class struggle' in socialist society. This calls up a more traditional role for the Party to launch and manage an ideological and political campaign.

The strengthening of the Party's role throughout the system is signalled by the prominence given to the need to uphold the 'Four Basic Principles'. These vague principles are used by the traditionalists to extend their control over society by Party organisations and give them the chance to criticise anything with which they disagree as negating socialism and the Party. After Zhao's fall, to strengthen discipline within the Party, the principles of democratic centralism began to be mentioned explicitly in the Party press. It was noticeable that from the mid-eighties, mention of democratic centralism in official publications declined. Where it was mentioned, emphasis was laid on the democratic rather than centralist component. The reassertion of democratic centralism as the guiding principle of Party life will be used to ensure that all Party members obediently follow the line of the faction that dominates the top party leadership.

This approach to the Party's role in the political system is clearly out-dated in a context where economic reform and technological development are creating a more diversified and sophisticated society. Zhao's acknowledgement that a limited plurality is inevitable is rejected and the traditionalists prefer to think in terms of a single undifferentiated mass of people who work harmoniously for the creation of socialism. The Party's role, of course, is to tell the masses what their interests are as they strive to build socialism. Should the current leadership decide to push ahead with the economic reforms, inevitably they will be confronted by precisely the kinds of problems that they so manifestly refused to deal with in April–June 1989.

Eventually, the Party will have to move back to the kind of relationship between Party and state and society that was envisaged by Zhao Ziyang and his supporters.

RE-DEFINING PARTY–STATE RELATIONS

Overlap and confusion about the division of responsibility between policy formulation and implementation have been a constant feature of political life in the PRC. On occasions, the overlap of Party and state has led to the Party actually implementing policy. Normally, this is condemned but during the Cultural Revolution, it was positively encouraged. Some of the resulting confusion was removed by the abolition of 'revolutionary committees' in 1979, and initial moves to abolish the concurrent holding of Party and state posts. In July 1980, Hua Guofeng announced that he would hand over his post of Premier to Zhao Ziyang while retaining the position of Chairman of the Party. At the Third Session of the Fifth National People's Congress (August–September 1980), the practice was extended to the provincial level to prevent the 'over-concentration of power and the holding of too many posts concurrently by one person' and to separate effectively and clearly Party work from government work.[21]

Such moves were more of symbolic importance given that all key officials in the state apparatus were, and still are, leading Party members. There was never the intention that such measures should lead to autonomy for the state sector, and institutional dominance was retained through Party groups in all state organs. Certainly changes fell far short of the kind of administrative shake-up called for by reformist Party intellectuals. Highlighting the problem, the former adviser to Zhao Ziyang, Yan Jiaqi, wrote that in practice Party organisations had undertaken work that should have been handled by 'organs of state power, namely the executive branch and the legislative branch'.[22]

As early as October 1980, Liao Gailong had outlined an extensive programme for reform of the administrative structure. One proposal was that the National People's Congress be turned into something more than a 'rubber stamp' by reducing the number of delegates and splitting it into two chambers that would supervise the work of the State Council and act as a check on one another. Local government was to be strengthened at the expense of central government, an independent judiciary was to be set up free of Party influence and a freer role was to be given to the media to give it a watchdog function.[23] As the eighties progressed, separation of powers became a key demand of reform-minded Party intellectuals.[24] However, the idea of a separation of powers is seen as a 'bourgeois' disease by all of China's top Party leaders. At the Thirteenth Party Congress, Zhao Ziyang commented that China will 'never indiscriminately copy the Western system of the separation of the three powers'.[25]

Party domination of the legislature, executive and judiciary is worsened by the fact that the Party has no effective regulatory mechanism. The system of 'discipline inspection commissions' revived in the late-seventies has not concerned itself with this kind of problem, concentrating on internal Party discipline. As a result, when the interests of the state or of the individual are infringed, the legal system cannot automatically intervene as it is controlled by the Party. Numerous cases are reported in the press of high-handed Party secretaries acting in defiance, or perhaps in ignorance, of the law. To improve this situation some reform-minded intellectuals have even suggested that a Constitutional Court of Law be set up to adjudicate whether decisions taken by central and local Party and government leaders are in line with the law of the land.[26] However, as long as 'rule by man', in this case 'Party man', rather than 'rule by law' is the dominant ethos, the creation of new rules and regulations will not fundamentally resolve the problem.

The problems with such a confusion of roles are evident and good practical reasons exist for trying to create a real division of responsibilities. As the American social scientist, Schurmann, has pointed out, the more an organisation becomes a 'command-issuing body' the more it must 'grapple with the concrete technicalities of command'. This would lead to increasing bureaucratism and inflexibility thus thwarting the Party's ability to innovate and adjust to changing circumstances.[27] This point was recognised by former General Secretary, Zhao Ziyang. Speaking in October, 1987, he warned that if the Party took on the work of other organisations, it would turn into an interested party leaving it with little room to manoeuvre in resolving conflicting interests that arise. Zhao was also concerned that if the Party became so involved in routine government work it would be unable to look after its own Party affairs. Zhao felt that Party members would allow 'their own land to go barren while tilling the land of others'.[28] Given the reported lack of discipline, increasing corruption and ideological confusion among Party members, there is certainly enough work for Party members keeping their own 'land' under control.

While his proposals were designed to reduce the interference of the Party as an institution within state organs, they were not to grant these organs autonomy. The Party was to retain its political leadership over the system. In line with policy-making in other areas in recent years, the Party returned to the tradition of designating certain places as trial areas for reform, summing up their experiences before introducing the measures as national policy. In March 1986, the State Council approved 16 cities to begin political structural reform on a trial basis. It is interesting to note that one the cities was Anyang, Zhao's home town.[29]

The most important measure proposed by Zhao Ziyang at the Thirteenth Party Congress was the abolition of leading Party member groups in units of state administration. Previously it had been the normal practice for Party members who were leading members in state administrative units, enterprises or research establishments to hold caucus meetings to discuss policy within their organisation. These groups became increasingly powerful, taking over more and more work of the organisation concerned. They were established by the Party committee at the next highest level and were responsible to that committee. The abolition of these Party groups was interpreted by scholars in the Chinese Academy of Social Sciences as a major weakening of Party power in their research institutions.[30]

Further, most Party committees that parallel a department in the state sector appoint one of the members of the Standing Committee to take charge of work in the state sector even if the person concerned holds no official position in that sector. Zhao Ziyang announced that this practice would be halted.[31] Thus, the Organisation Department of the Central Committee informed all provincial Party Committees in January 1988 that in the forthcoming elections to their committees the post of fulltime deputy-secretary or standing committee member taking charge of government work without holding a government post should be abolished. The number of standing committee members of Provincial level Party committees was to be reduced accordingly.[32]

In the same spirit, all CCP work departments that carry out overlapping functions with those of state departments were to be abolished. In April 1987, the Anyang city Party committee closed all departments that overlapped with government departments, including the economic and rural work departments. Further, the city government took over the cultural, educational, sports, health, national affairs and overseas Chinese work that had been formerly controlled by the city Party committee's propaganda and united front departments. The list of these departments indicates just how far the arms of the Party reached. Also, the Party committee's organisational department's role of managing over 800 cadres above the section level was transferred to the city government. The transfer of cadre management out of direct Party control could have a significant impact. A common complaint of government officials is that often they cannot make decisions concerning their own personnel as this is an area where the Party exerts ultimate authority.

The pragmatists also made an initial attempt to spell out the duties of Party committees during this transitional period. These duties clearly show the continued political leadership that the Party still thinks to maintain. At the same time, their vagueness suggests that even they do not have a clear idea about exactly what the Party should be doing in a time of change. The Central Committee of the CCP is to retain leadership over the 'political principles and orientation' in major policy decisions concerning domestic and foreign affairs, the economy, national defence, and so on. Importantly, it will retain its power of *nomenklatura* by recommending the officials for major posts in the central state organisations. Given that the Organisation Department is headed by a Chen Yun supporter, Song Ping, the traditionalists have retained considerable say over official appointments. The same range of powers are granted to the local Party committees. The vagueness of the functions means that whoever is in control of the Party apparatus at whatever level has considerable leeway for interpreting just to what extent the Party can interfere in other areas.

With the removal of Zhao Ziyang as General Secretary in 1989 and the campaign by the traditionalists to reassert Party dominance, the question arises whether these nascent reforms will be pursued or whether they will be allowed quietly to drop.

THE PARTY AND THE NEW ENTERPRISE LAW

Party interference at the grass-roots levels is said to have impaired economic efficiency and as a result efforts have been made to loosen the grip of the local Party committee. The pragmatists' intention is to aid the policies of economic reform by shifting decision-making power in production units from Party secretaries and committees to enterprise managers.[33] This shift in power has been difficult to achieve and has been strongly resisted by the traditionalists.

Given the fear of the consequences of making a wrong decision, the tendency in all PRC organisations is to push decision-making on even the most trivial matters to the highest levels. The potentially adverse consequences of making an incorrect decision have far outweighed the potential gains of displaying initiative. In practice, this has meant referring all decisions to the Party committee, which means that Party committees become overloaded with minor matters and are called on to make decisions for which they are not trained. The example of a Party committee in a Shenyang enterprise shows how much irrelevant work such committees could become engaged in. In a three month period in 1980, the Party committee met 32 times to discuss 150 issues only about 30 of which concerned the Party. Virtually all of the remainder were specific issues that should have been handled by the relevant administrative departments.[34]

In the past, this tendency has been compounded by the all-embracing notion of the Party's 'unified leadership', which has been taken to mean total Party dominance in all spheres. This has been the case in PRC history with the exceptions of the early-fifties under the 'One-Person Management System', when power was concentrated in the manager's hands and in the early years of the Cultural Revolution when the Party as an institution was under attack.

The identification of this problem has led to two types of reform measures being adopted to try to improve the decision-making process in enterprises, research institutes and other institutions. First, reformers in the Party have tried to ensure that more experts are appointed to run such institutions and, second, that once appointed they have the necessary powers to carry out their decisions. In May 1984, experimentation was begun in six cities with a new managerial form for Chinese enterprises referred to as the 'factory director [or managerial] responsibility system'. The following year, the scope of experimentation was extended and it was made clear that reformers were pushing for this form of management to be adopted nationwide.

This new system was to replace the former system described as the 'managerial responsibility system under the leadership of the Party Committee'. The new system emphasises the need for the manager to act on certain matters without always first asking for the approval of the Party committee. This removes the Party committee, often in reality the Party Secretary, from being the key decision-making body for all the enterprise's work. As Chamberlain has pointed out, while the Party committee's primary responsibility does not change (it is still to ensure adherence to the Party's general line, policy and plans), its powers are 'severely curtailed'. They are restricted to the realms of strengthening ideological and political work among Party members as a part of 'Party construction'.[35]. Under this scenario, the Party in the enterprise would be reduced to little more than playing out a formal, ritualistic role. A more radical response to the question of this relationship would be to remove Party committees from the enterprises entirely. However, such an option is not politically feasible.

Not surprisingly, these attempts at reform have met with stubborn resistance from local Party officials who fear that their former dominance would be undermined. Within production units and research institutes, there have been cases of conflicts between Party officials who owe their position to their political and administrative skills in the old system and those who derive power from their technical knowledge. While those with the technical skills push for greater autonomy, many Party officials push for greater control over the enterprise in order to maintain their own position.

At the enterprise level, even where those with professional knowledge achieved leadership positions, they were not necessarily in a position to implement their decisions if the Party secretary disagreed. The latter could always invoke the ultimate authority of the Party to get his or her own way. One way around this problem is to recruit more managers and entrepreneurs into the Party, a phenomenon that has taken place. Two strategies have been adopted to blunt the influence of these recruitment drives. First, once a Party member, the individual is subject to Party discipline. Party secretaries have used appeals to party discipline to bring independent managers to heel, thus thwarting the pragmatists' intentions of bringing more such people into the Party into the first place. Secondly, by contrast, on occasions jealous local officials have blocked applications of technically qualified people or have put them on unlimited probation periods while their 'complicated' backgrounds are investigated.[36] Local Party officials fear that such people will take all the best jobs if they are allowed to join the Party.

The ability of Party secretaries still to lord it over enterprises and the managers has been helped by the confusing signals sent out by the Party centre. Changing alliances at the top have led to shifts in central policy concerning how Party secretary-manager relations should be interpreted. It is noticeable that at times when conservative forces have had more influence at the centre, messages sent down to the enterprises have encouraged Party secretaries to believe that they still rule the roost. This was evident in 1985 when the urban reform programme came in for criticism, in late 1986/early 1987 and in late 1989. During these periods, enterprise managers' entrepreneurial instincts could expose them to criticisms of corruption, and so on. Such accusations were accompanied by appeals to Party secretaries to tighten up on their leadership of enterprises. For example, the campaign launched after Zhao's removal to strengthen the Party at all levels restores if not formally, at least in practice, supreme power to Party secretaries in enterprises. In a tense political environment, managers would not dare go against the orders of a Party secretary. On 20 July 1989, Party General Secretary, Jiang Zemin, called on Party committees in enterprises to set up organisations to strengthen ideological and political work.[37] Given such vacillating signals from the Party centre, it will not be surprising if some managers are afraid to step out from the shadow of the Party secretary or if the latter takes expressions for more autonomy for managers with a pinch of salt.

At the national level, the opposition is best demonstrated by the enormous problems that the pragmatists encountered in getting the 'Law of the PRC on Industrial Enterprises Owned by the Whole People' [Enterprise Law] adopted.[38] A draft of the law had been circulating in the autumn of 1984 and was proposed to the Standing Committee of the National People's Congress (NPC) in January 1985. It met stiff opposition and had to be revised. Again, when discussions on this law were held at the Standing Committee meeting that preceded the Sixth Session of the NPC (March 1987), it was made clear the correct relationship between managers and their Party committees was a key point of division. Opponents of change argued that it would undermine Party and leave it without any proper role. As a result of the disagreements the Standing Committee did not put forward the draft of the law to the full session of the NPC.

Shortly before the Thirteenth Party Congress, a clear signal was given that Deng Xiaoping supported reforms to remove the Party committee from involvement in 'routine affairs'. Deng's August 1980 reform speech was republished by *Xinhua* in June 1987, but this time it contained a new point four that discussed the need for major reforms in the administration of Chinese enterprises.[39] Taking his cue, at the Thirteenth Party Congress Zhao Ziyang indicated that the intention was still to move ahead with reducing formal Party power in the enterprise. In his report, he stated that Party organisations should support managers in their overall leadership and only play a 'supervisory' role while 'guaranteeing' implementation of policy.[40] At the same time adjustments were made to the Party Constitution in anticipation of the Enterprise Law being adopted. Additions were made to Article 33 of the Constitution to outline the Party's reduced role in the enterprise.[41] The break-through came in April 1988 at the Seventh NPC when the law was adopted.

As the opponents of the Enterprise Law feared, one of the main intentions was to limit as far as was politically possible at the time, the scope of Party work in the enterprise. It made clear that as enterprises were not political organisations, the functions of enterprise Party committees were fundamentally different from those of central and local Party committees that undertake political leadership. Within the enterprise, the main role for the Party organisations was simply to be directed towards building stronger Party organs. However, Party organisations were still allowed to present views and suggestions on major issues to ensure and supervise the implementation of Party principles and policies and government laws.[42] How the Party functions in the future will depend on how these particular phrases are interpreted.

In addition, accountability on the part of Party officials was to be increased and Party organisation in the enterprise to be streamlined. Prior to the introduction of the law, accountability of Party secretaries in enterprises went no further than laying stress on the principle of collective leadership. The law stipulates that members and secretaries of enterprise Party committees should be elected in multiple candidate elections. With enterprises being encouraged to make more profits which can improve employees' material conditions, the expectation was that Party officials unsympathetic to the market-orientated reforms would not be elected. The change of political climate after the removal of Zhao Ziyang might ensure precisely the opposite result.

The number of full-time staff and offices of Party committees were also to be reduced. Party offices involved in administrative affairs were to hand their work over to the enterprise's administrative departments. While large enterprises would retain fulltime secretaries and deputy secretaries, in small enterprises such work was only to be done on a part-time basis. Superfluous personnel were to take up fulltime jobs in the enterprise itself.

The Enterprise Law goes a long way towards defining separate roles for managers and, if implemented fully, would herald a radically reduced role for the Party. Whether it is properly implemented in the short-term will depend largely on whether both managers and Party officials alike can overcome the ingrained mentality regarding the superiority of the Party and the belief that the Party 'takes the lead in everything'. The stress on the need to strengthen the Party, and its ideological and political work in the aftermath of the student demonstrations in mid-1989, may well legitimise a greater interference by party secretaries and their committees in all aspects of enterprise work. Even were the law to be properly implemented, it is important to remember that a manager of a major enterprise will almost certainly be a Party member and most probably a deputy secretary of the enterprise committee.

INTERNAL PARTY REORGANISATION

Reforms of the internal Party organisation have been intended to restore predictability to Party life, clearly define institutional roles and tackle the tricky problem of succession. The reforms were, in Deng Xiaoping's phrase, to return the Party to 'a conventional way of doing things'.[43] Deng Xiaoping and his supporters (including Zhao Ziyang until April 1989) have been at pains to stress that the lawless years of the Cultural Revolution were over and that China was now entering a period of predictability governed by the rule of law. To this end the correct functioning of principles such as democratic centralism and collective leadership, and the rights and duties of individual members have been outlined. Similarly to ensure the maintenance of Party discipline, Party Schools and the discipline inspection commission system were revived.[44]

Both the Party schools and the discipline inspection commissions were resurrected to overcome what are termed 'bureaucratism' and 'bad work-style' and opposition to agreed Party policy. The schools are expected to provide Party members with a proper education in the way that they should behave and the way in which the Party should be run. The use of the commissions represents an important part of the attempt to re-establish an institutionalised system for monitoring abuses by Party members. This system replaced what the post-Mao leadership saw as the more arbitrary and unpredictable system that developed during the Cultural Revolution. However, during the eighties while under the leadership of Chen Yun, these commissions formed a power base for those opposed to the full implementation of Den Xiaoping's market-orientated reforms, particularly insofar as they were seen to lead to a rise in corruption.

The stress placed on traditional Leninist notions were intended to come to terms with the problems of over-concentration and hence abuse of power, and especially the 'personality cult'. Collective leadership is interpreted as a basic principle of democratic centralism and the 1982 Party Consitution clearly stipulates that all major decisions shall be decided upon by the Party committees after democratic discussion.

The events of mid-1989 clearly underlined just how far the Party was from devising institutional mechanisms capable of dealing with major policy divisions among its elite. Under stress from outside and divided internally, the Party returned to its own 'unconventional' way of doing things. Individual power relationships built up over decades proved to be more important than the rule of law and the formal functions people held. Even after their 'retirement', it was clear that the two most politically powerful figures remained Chen Yun and Deng Xiaoping. Indeed, the decision to implement Martial Law in May 1989 was not taken by a formal Party body but by *ad hoc* meetings held at Deng Xiaoping's home following discussions between Deng and other veteran Party leaders.[45] It was only after the veteran leaders took their decision that it was presented to the Standing Committee of the Politburo for its formal approval. In fact, according to the PRC's constitution, only the Standing Committee of the National People's Congress or the State Council can decide on the implementation of martial law. To provide a veneer of legality, the published martial law order was signed by Li Peng in his capacity as Premier of the State Council.[46]

In the absence of institutional mechanisms for accommodating serious divisions, the system still desperately needs a Deng-like figure to fulfil the role of final arbiter in policy debate, a role formally filled by Mao Zedong. Indeed, Zhao Ziyang told Gorbachev during the latter's visit (15–18 May 1989) that a secret decision had been taken in 1987 that all important decisions had to be referred to Deng.[47] This pivotal role of Deng's explains why it is necessary, after the massacre of June 1989, to build up a cult of personality around him to restore his shattered prestige and to extricate him from the Party's factional fighting in which he had become embroiled. This inability to institutionalise policy debate and succession suggests another debilitating struggle in the near future. No-one in the present leadership has either the stature or the power-base to take Deng's position.

The attempts to institutionalise life at the Party Centre led to changes in the relationship between the Party's leading organs. In the last decade, institutional power in the Party has shifted between the Politburo, its Standing Committee and the Secretariat under the General Secretary. This formal power structure competed with the aforementioned individual power bases and the Central Advisory Commission, which provided veteran cadres opposed to many aspects of the reform programme with their own institutional power base.

At the Thirteenth Party Congress, Zhao Ziyang announced an important adjustment in the relationship between the Politburo and the Secretariat. The Party Constitution adopted at the Twelfth Party Congress (1982) had legislated that the Politburo, its Standing Committee, and the General Secretary and the Secretariat were all to be elected by the Central Committee. This resulted in the Secretariat and the Politburo acting as competing sources of power. This is not surprising given that one of the reasons for the resurrection of the Secretariat may have been because at the time Deng Xiaoping and his supporters could not gain a natural majority in the Politburo. In fact, there was even talk of the Politburo being abolished. In theory, the Secretariat was to handle the day-to-day work of the Party, becoming the Party's administrative heart. The Politburo and its Standing Committee would be freed to concentrate on taking important decisions on national and international issues. In practice, it placed the Secretariat in an extremely powerful position, as it supervised the regional Party organs and the functional departments of the Party that should, in theory, be responsible directly to the Central Committee and the Politburo. This access to information and its control functions meant that it could function as an alternative power-base to the Politburo.

Zhao Ziyang announced a clear change in this relationship, down-grading the Secretariat in respect to the Politburo. It was reduced in size from

10 to only four full members (excluding the General Secretary) and one alternate and was made the working office of the Politburo and its Standing Committee. Instead of being directly elected by the Central Committee, its membership is now nominated by the Standing Committee of the Politburo and approved by the Central Committee. A practical indication of the decline of the power of the Secretariat was the announcement that in the future agendas raised by the State Council for policy-making by the Politburo or its Standing Committee would no longer be 'filtered' by the Central Secretariat. However, in practice, it functioned as Zhao Ziyang's support base in the Party Centre. Zhao and three of his supporters in the Secretariat were removed at the Fourth Plenum of the Thirteenth Central Committee on 24 June, 1989.[48]

The dispensability of institutionalisation is clearly seen with regard to the composition of the Standing Committee of the Politburo, now the Party's most powerful formal organ. Attempts to institutionalise membership on the basis of functional occupation as stated in the 1982 Party Constitution had already been abandoned at the Thirteenth Party Congress. According to the Constitution, the heads of the Military Affairs Commission (Deng Xiaoping), the Discipline Inspection Commission (Qiao Shi) and the Central Advisory Commission (Chen Yun) must be members of the Standing Committee of the Politburo. Deng presumably felt it was better to face ridicule for yet again ripping up the Constitution, than to have his strongest opponent, Chen Yun, still in the Standing Committee. Also, given Deng's and Chen's ages, it would have made the policy of introducing 'new blood' look utterly ridiculous.

It is clear that the Central Advisory Commission has wielded major influence behind the scenes providing an institutional power for veteran cadres opposed to certain aspects of the reform programme. The Commission was originally set up in 1982 at the Twelfth Party Congress in an attempt to relieve aged officials of their posts. The Commission was referred to as a 'temporary expedient' until a proper system of retirement for cadres was introduced. However, the Commission has shown no signs of fading away and its Standing Committee has become an alternative power centre to the Politburo's Standing Committee. Both Deng Xiaoping and the Central Committee congratulated members of this Commission for the 'decisive role' they had played in putting down the student demonstrations of mid-1989. Song Renqiong, the Deputy-Chairman of the Advisory Commission, clearly showed the intention of these veterans to become more involved in the daily work of deciding policy when he re-emphasised the fact that members of the Commission's Standing Committee had the right to attend Politburo meetings.[49]

CONCLUDING COMMENTS

It is clear that to date even the reforms suggested and introduced by Zhac Ziyang and his supporters have not succeeded in bringing about fundamental changes in the way the Party functions and its relationship to other organisations in society. First, the Party has not devised institutional mechanisms to deal with serious policy differences among its elite. The purge of Zhao and the subsequent witch-hunt scotched the idea that it was becoming increasingly accepted for dissenting views to be aired and accommodated within the Party. In line with its self-ascribed infallibility, the Party has resorted to the traditional Stalinist method of finding a scapegoat who led the Party and people astray by usurping power. Of course, the propaganda neglects to add that the last two usurpers, Hu Yaobang and Zhao Ziyang, were chosen personally by the 'true helmsman' of 'bold vision', Deng Xiaoping. With the purge of alleged Zhao supporters beginning to spread, Party members will think twice about putting forward dissenting views in the near future.

Secondly, the institutionalisation of the political system in the eighties has not gone as far as had been supposed and the power of the individual still dominates over any notion of collective rule and responsibility. Of particular danger here is the inability to deal with the problem of succession to Deng Xiaoping. At present, the only mechanism available is a debilitating power struggle which may spill over into broader social unrest. This danger is increased by the fact that the Party remains severely divided. Among the current victors, there are serious divisions of opinion between those wishing to follow Deng's orders to continue with economic reform and those who see these reforms as the source of the troubles and thus wish to blunt and even roll back key elements of them. Further, there are the vanquished forces of Zhao Ziyang who, although defeated at the Party top, retain positions of influence throughout the system. Comments in late-August 1989 by senior Party leaders concerning the 'shocking' state of affairs within the Party and the need to extend the examination and purge of Party members further shows that substantial opposition remains.[50]

Thus, thirdly, the Chinese political system is now extremely unstable and the Party leadership must rule without the support of key sectors of its urban population. Indeed, the Party faces a severe crisis of legitimacy. Deng's favoured route is to try to move ahead again on the economic front to restore people's faith in the Party. The traditionalists prefer a stepped up ideological campaign to reassert what they see as traditional communist values especially among the young. This latter view is clearly not an option for the long-term unless China closes its doors against to the outside world and rolls back key aspects of the domestic reforms. While control over cultural and educational affairs has been quickly reasserted, it will be much more difficult for the centre to reassert economic control over the localities and to squash the budding entrepreneurship.

Over the long-term, a return to the programme of economic reform is more likely. Yet this will confront the leadership with precisely the same kinds of problems that it showed itself unwilling to come to terms with in mid-1989. Even if the leadership was to return to Zhao's pragmatic political reforms, or even if Zhao himself were to return – a factor that cannot be discounted completely – it would still face major problems.

These political reform measures were designed ultimately to strengthen rather than weaken the Party's overall authority in the political system. The changes were designed to make the Party more efficient and the economic system more capable of responding flexibly to the new demands placed upon it. The longer term objectives of Zhao's proposals for reform of the Party structure and the attempts to redefine its relationship to other organisations in society were to institutionalise the political process in a way that accepted the increasing diversity within Chinese society without undermining political stability or the concept of single Party rule.

At the level of the enterprise, the ingrained mentality of the Party's superiority and the belief by individual Party officials in their own unchallengeable power remain major stumbling-blocks to the smooth implementation of the proposed reforms. Also, the view of many lower-level officials that political reform is at best a 'necessary evil' that has to be entertained in order to progress with economic development limits the scope for change.

Finally, the Party has not devised institutions for dealing with the new interests that are arising in PRC society. Much activity that takes place does so outside of the formal structures and has been to some extent anti-systemic. Unless the party is capable of devising a political system that is not only an efficient managerial machine but also one that can accommodate the demands of an increasingly complex society, it will have to resort continually to the use of force to maintain its 'leading role'.

NOTES

1. The ideas are developed from T. Saich, 'The Chinese Community Party at the Thirteenth National Congress: Policies and Prospects for Reform' in *Issues and Studies*, vol. 25, no. 1, January 1989, pp. 11–40.

2. On this point see the article by L. Vandermeersch, 'An Enquiry into the Chinese Conception of Law' in S. R. Schram (ed.), *The Scope of State Power in China* (Hong Kong: The Chinese University Press, 1985), pp. 3–26.

3. Deng Xiaoping, 'Reform of the Party and State Leadership System', in *Deng Xiaoping Wenxuan* (Selected Works of Deng Xiaoping) (Guangdong: Renmin chubanshe, 1983), pp. 280–302. The fact that this speech was not officially published until 1983 attests to its contentious nature.

4. For an analysis of the initial reforms of the Party see T. Saich, 'Party Building Since Mao – A Question of Style?', in N. Maxwell and B. McFarlane (eds), *China's Changed Road to Development* (Oxford: Pergamon Press, 1984) pp. 149–69.

5. For the 1982 Party Constitution see T. Saich, 'Introductory article and translation of the 1982 Party Constitution' in W. Simons and S. White (eds.) *The Party Statutes of the Communist World* (The Hague: Martinus Nijhoff, 1984) pp. 83–115.

6. The principles are adherence to the socialist road, the dictatorship of the proletariat, the leadership of the Communist Party and Marxism-Leninism and Mao Zedong Thought. See Deng Xiaoping, 'Uphold the Four Basic Principles' in *Deng Xiaoping Wenxuan*, pp. 144–70.

7. Influential intellectual Party members such as Liao Gailong and Su Shaozhi envisaged reforms of the political structure that would be an end in themselves in terms of greater freedom and accountability rather than in terms of economic pay-off. However, these views not come to dominate the thinking of top Party leaders. See the collection of essays in Su Shaozhi, *Democratisation and Reform* (Nottingham: Spokesman, 1988) and Liao Gailong, 'Historical Experience and Our Path of Development', *Zhonggong Yanjiu* [Studies on Chinese Communism] vol. 15, no. 9, September 1981, pp. 108–77. This text is translated in *Issues and Studies*, vol. 17, nos. 10, 11 and 12 (1981) pp. 65–94, 81–110 and 79–104 respectively.

8. Cheng Hsiang, 'News from Beidaihe', *Wen Wei Po*, 8 August 1986, translated in *Summary of World Broadcasts: the Far East* (SWB), 8335.

9. For Li Peng's report to the meeting see *Beijing Review*, no. 16, 17 April, 1989.

10. Zhao Ziyang, 'Advance along the Road of Socialism with Chinese Characteristics' *Renmin Ribao* [People's Daily], 4 November 1987, p. 3. An official English translation can be found in *Beijing Review*, vol. 30 no. 45, November 9–15 1987.

11. The 'Four Modernisations' were put forward by the then Premier, Zhou Enlai, in January 1985, but fell into disuse during the subsequent succession struggles. The early revival of the slogan after Mao Zedong's death (September 1976) and the arrest of the 'Gang of Four' (October 1976) indicated the new leadership's intention to deal with pressing economic problems.

12. See, for example, Jin Xiong, 'Socialism and Social Modernisation', *Guangming Ribao* [Glorious Daily] 21 September 1987; and 'Political and Ideological Reform in the People's Republic of China: an Interview with Professor Su Shaozhi', in *China Information*, vol. 1, no. 2, 1986.

13. Zhao Ziyang, 'Advance along . . .', pp. 3–4.

14. See, for example, Zhao Ziyang, 'On separating Party and Government – Part of a Speech at the Preparatory Meeting for the Seventh Plenary Session of the Twelfth Central Committee', *Renmin Ribao*, November 26 1987, p. 1. The meeting was on 14 October 1987.

15. For an outline of this kind of thinking see S. P. Huntington, *Political Order in Changing Societies* (New Haven: Yale University Press, 1968) and also S. P. Huntington and J. M. Nelson, *No Easy Choice: Political Participation in Developing Countries* (Cambridge, Mass., 1976).

16. The definition of a 'pluralist system' follows that of Dahl, i.e. one that has a plurality of relatively autonomous groups within the domain of the state. R. A. Dahl, *Dilemmas of Pluralist Democracy: Autocracy versus Control* (New Haven: Yale University Press, 1982), p. 2.

17. See for example Yang Shangkun's speech of 24 May 1989, 'Key Points of Comrade Yang Shangkun's Speech to an Emergency Enlarged Meeting of the Military Affairs' Commission' 24 May 1989, printed speech, p. 3.

18. 'The Decision of the Central Committee of the Communist Party of China on Party Consolidation' in *Beijing Review*, no. 42, 17 October 1983, p. I. The decision was adopted at the Second Plenum of the Twelfth Central Committee.

19. J. Kornai, 'The dilemmas of a socialist economy: the Hungarian experience', *Cambridge Journal of Economics*, no. 4, 1980. I am grateful to Gordon White for drawing my attention to this work.

20. See Li Peng's speech of 22 May 1989 in 'Key Points of Speeches by Li Peng, Yang Shangkun, Qiao Shi and Yao Yilin at the Meeting of 22 May', printed pamphlet distributed to Party members on 25 May 1989, pp. 2–3.

21. Hua Guofeng, 'Speech at the Third Session of the Fifth National People's Congress' in *Main Documents of the Third Session of the Fifth National People's Congress of the People's Republic of China* (Beijing: Foreign Languages Press, 1980), p. 196.

22. Yan Jiaqi, 'Our Current Political System and Political Democracy', *Jiefang Ribao* [Liberation Daily], Shanghai, 13 August 1986. Until 1987, Yan had been Director of the Institute of Political Science in the Chinese Academy of Social Sciences. In 1989, he was forced into exile in the United States.

23. Liao Gailong, 'Historical experience . . .'.

24. See, for example, Tan Jian, 'Reform and Strengthen China's Political System' in B. Stavis (ed.) 'Reform of China's Political System', *Chinese Law and Government*, vol. xx, no. 1, 1987, p. 49.

25. Zhao Ziyang, 'Advance along the road . . .', p. 3. Perhaps the use of

the word 'indiscriminately' is significant suggesting that some form of 'separation' might be possible.

26. 'Political and Ideological Reform in the People's Republic of China: An Interview with Professor Su Shaozhi', in *China Information*, vol. 1, no. 2, p. 24.

27. F. Schurmann, *Ideology and Organisation in Communist China* (Berkeley: University of California Press, 1968), p. 111.

28. Zhao Ziyang, 'On separating Party and Government . . .', p. 1. Ironically, one of the major accusations made against Zhao since his dismissal is that he ignored Party work and thus allowed internal discipline to disintegrate.

29. Lu Yun and Feng Jing, 'Anyang Begins Political Reform', *Beijing Review*, vol. 31, no. 12, 21–27 March 1988, p. 18.

30. Interview with members of the Institute of Marxism-Leninism and Mao Zedong Thought, the Chinese Academy of Social Sciences and with members of the Institute of Politics and Law, Jiangsu Provincial Academy of Social Sciences, June 1988.

31. Zhao Ziyang, 'Advance along the road . . .', p. 3.

32. 'CCP Guidelines on Forthcoming Elections', *Xinhua* in Chinese translated in SWB 0059 B2/1, 27 January 1988.

33. Limitations of space prevent discussion here of the changing relations of local Party officials to the production process in the rural areas. For an interesting account of how the ability of the Party-state apparatus to control and direct grass-roots rural life has been reduced see G. White, 'The Impact of Economic Reforms in the Chinese Countryside: Towards the Politics of Social Capitalism?', in *Modern China*, vol. 13, no. 4, October, 1987, pp. 411–40.

34. 'Reforming Existing Enterprise Leadership Systems Can Improve and Strengthen Party Leadership', in *Jingji Guanli* (Economic Management) no. 6, June, 1981, p. 61.

35. H. B. Chamberlain, 'Party Management Relations in Chinese Industries: Some Political Dimensions of Economic Reform', in *The China Quarterly*, no. 112, December, 1987, p. 646.

36. Sun Jian and Zhu Weiqun, 'What is the Current Situation in Implementing Policies on Intellectuals?', *Renmin Ribao*, 8 July 1984, p. 4.

37. 'CPC to Boost Ideological Work', in *Beijing Review*, vol. 32, no. 31, 31 July 1989, p. 5.

38. For the rest of the law as it was finally adopted on 13 April 1988 see SWB 0136/C1/9–14, 27 April 1988.

39. *Xinhua* in Chinese, 19 June 1987.

40. Zhao Ziyang, 'Advance along the road . . .', p. 3.

41. 'Revisions to the Party Constitution', *Xinhua* in English 1 November 1987, in SWB 8714/C1/3, 2 November 1987.

42. CCP Central Committee Circular on the Enterprise Law, *Xinhua* in Chinese, translated in SWB 0150 B2/3 13 May 1988.

43. Deng Xiaoping, 'Reform of the Party . . .'.

44. For a description of these early measures to reform the Party's internal organisation see T. Saich, 'Party Building Since Mao – A Question of Style?', especially pp. 153–58.
45. Deng had already consulted with Chen Yun, Li Xiannian, Peng Zhen, Wang Zhen and Deng Yingchao, See Yang Shangkun's speech of May 22, p. 3.
46. The order can be found in *Renmin Ribao*, 21 May 1989, p. 1.
47. See SWB 0459 i, May 17 1989. In criticising Zhao, Premier Li Peng did not refer to the illegality of this decision but merely the fact that Zhao had brought it out into the open. See Li Peng's speech of 22 May 1989 in 'Key points of speeches . . .', p. 3.
48. These were Hu Qili, Rui Xingwen and Yan Mingfu. Only Qiao Shi remained.
49. *Wen Wei Po*, 24 July, 1989, translated in SWB 0518 B2/4, 26 July 1989.
50. See, for example, Jiang Zemin's and Li Peng's comments to a national conference of organisation department heads on 21 August 1989. *Xinhua* in Chinese 21 August 1989, translated in SWB 0543 B2/3, 24 August 1989.

7   A Janus-Faced Army? The Military and Reform Policies in the PRC

Eberhard Sandschneider

Throughout the 1960s and 1970s it was hardly necessary to justify a continuously high academic interest in the political role of the Chinese People's Liberation Army (PLA). The representation of military leaders in central and regional leadership bodies of party and government organs in the People's Republic of China (PRC) was – even for Chinese standards – high, and so was the academic output of work on the subject.[1] As soon as the army's extensive representation started to decrease, the academic interest of western China watchers followed proportionally. Today, the major interest in studies on the PLA focuses primarily on questions of technical modernisation and technology transfer.[2] Observation of the army's political role has been reduced to a sideline occupation.

However, as a military force the PLA – even after an approximate 25 per cent reduction between 1985 and 1987 – still ranks among the largest armies of the world with some 3.2 million men in active service.[3] In political terms, moreover, the army still wields enormous power. One may, therefore, conclude that it must have political capabilities beyond its mere representation in leadership bodies. Several questions follow from this. While – in very broad terms – reform policies implemented since 1978 clearly have affected almost every aspect of military politics in China, what are these effects in detail and how does the military react to their intentional and non-intentional results? Throughout China and especially among Chinese intellectuals there is a deep-rooted fear that current reforms might finally fail due to the military's resistance. Is the army (ground, naval and air forces) really to be regarded as a major obstructionist force against reforms, both military and civilian, or has it accepted the major priorities underlying these policies? What is, after all, the military's base of political power? Is the 'pillar of the State' perhaps turning into a 'challenge for the Party'? Finally, what role does the army play in the enigmatic process of top level leadership succession?

These are the questions which will be addressed in the following paper. It starts with a synopsis of different analytical approaches and interpretations which clearly influence academic results and therefore deserve a closer and critical look.

1 MILITARY REACTIONS TO REFORM POLICIES

Conflicting Analytical Views and Interpretations

The study of the complicated and at times conflict-laden relationship between military and civilian powerholders in China is located at the crossroads of at least three sub-disciplines of social and political sciences – between the study of international military regimes focussing on interdisciplinary aspects of military behaviour in politics,[4] comparative communism and its study of the political role of military leaders in communist systems,[5] and, finally, Chinese studies.

Although China-watchers usually try to shield their work from the nuisance of comparative questions by pointing to the 'fact' that China – or in our case the PLA – is 'special', the field has nevertheless taken over basic analytical concepts from the neighbouring disciplines mentioned above. First, there is the 'civil-military' dichotomy taken from research on international military regimes: second, we find a 'Party-army' dichotomy inherited from comparative communism; and third, there is the specific 'Chinese' topic of political control over the armed forces, best expressed in Mao's famous statement that the Party controls the 'Gun' and the 'Gun' should never be allowed to control the Party.

These intellectual heritages have led the majority of scholars to follow three basic, but somewhat misleading views:

(a) Political Control

In theory the concept of political control over the army – expressed in Mao's dictum and repeated again and again in official Chinese publications – has always been valid. In political reality, however, it was never clearly defined or consistently implemented. The heterogeneous character of political control may be described as follows. Before, during and after the Cultural Revolution, political control over the army was never exerted by a monolithic and united party leadership, or by different monolithic and united party leaderships, but by different groups within this leadership. Attempts to control the army were not directed towards the military as an institution, but towards different parts of the military leadership.

The content and instruments of political control differed considerably and often left remarkable leeway for the military's interpretation and reaction.

Let me give two prominent examples. First, Lin Biao's attempt during the early 1960s to shape a 'political' army which could be used as reliable instrument in political confrontations failed because the professional commanders, who were not among Lin's principle objects of indoctrination, turned out to be more powerful than political commissars and the army's rank and file. When the Cultural Revolution swept the military right into the centre of political confrontation, it soon became clear that the instruments of personal and ideological control could successfully be matched by the political opposition of professional commanders. Second, the strongest attempts to establish a functioning system of political control over the army were made by the Cultural Revolutionary Left around Mao's wife, Jiang Qing, between 1973 and 1976. Their endeavours to reduce and counter the army's opposition took place on three different levels: control from above was exerted through the General Political Department under Zhang Chunqiao; control from below was attempted through political agitation among the army's rank and file; and, finally, there were even attempts at external control through the build-up of the urban militia as a direct rival to the PLA. The obvious failure of this policy towards the army became evident during the events of September/October 1976 with the purge of the so-called 'Gang of Four'.

The decisive question in Chinese politics never was: who controls the army? It always was: who controls the party? At least during and immediately after the Cultural Revolution proper (1966–69) and – if with declining importance – also for the better part of the early 1970s, the answer had to be given according to the following equation: the army leaders controlled the party which in its turn controlled the army. Although still valid in theory, the ideological principle was in practice out of order.

Historically, all attempts of direct control over the military through political commissars, ideological indoctrination and personal penetration failed whenever the aims of control were at loggerheads with the military leadership elite's specific political interests.[6] One may, therefore, conclude that the army and its politically active leadership can only be controlled if they accept the major aims of control. Otherwise political conflicts are to be expected.

In consequence, one may argue that in a situation where the different groups within the political leadership disagree on central issues, the military's parameters of political participation increase while mechanisms of party control are doomed to failure.

(b) 'Mao in command'?

The myth of political control over the army has – at least in the case of China – also led to an overestimation of the role of individuals in top of control structures, especially the CCPCC Military Commission, and in particular the myths of 'Mao in command' up to 1976 and of 'Deng in command' since 1978.[7]

Stripped of the effects of official propaganda until 1980/81, historical evidence shows that Mao Zedong never was in a position of absolute control over the army establishment.[8] Like Deng Xiaoping since 1978, he had always to compromise with powerful military leaders (especially among the regional and career commanders) on decisive issues. Those who still believe military power in China to be in the hands of one man will find it difficult to explain the ups and downs of Deng's political manoeuvring towards the military leadership since 1978.

(c) Opposition or subordination

Representatives of the third view tend to regard the army and its leadership as a – if not the – decisive obstacle to a continuation of reform policies.

Without any doubt, the initiative of reform policies after 1978 marked a watershed for the political role of the PLA as the Cultural Revolution had done in the 1960s. It was not only the fact that military representation in leading bodies was drastically reduced, but there was also a cluster of material and non-material losses which led to repeated complaints and dissatisfaction from military representatives. Not only did military leaders lose their undisputed, direct access to central and regional decision-making bodies in the party and government, they also had to cope with heavy losses of military reputation, social prestige and socio-economic appeal.

There is certainly no way of denying the widespread dissatisfaction among those cadres and soldiers who must be counted among the losers of reform policies. Their spectrum of oppositional motives has been summarised by June Teufel Dreyer as follows:

> Deng's reforms aroused a great deal of resistance. Leftists resented what they felt to be the denigration of people in favour of military hardware and resisted attempts to repudiate a Maoist military legacy they believed had retained its validity. *Soldiers* who feared demobilisation felt that they had given long, hard years of their lives in support of a party

and a government that were planning to discard them ungratefully. Some staged antigovernment demonstrations; others resorted to looting and banditry. *Civilians* worried about the effects that a million former soldiers would have on the already glutted job market. *Uneducated soldiers* were uncomfortable with what they considered the haughty airs of those who were better educated. They also believed that years spent in the classroom had softened the better educated, making them unfit for the hardships of military life. *Educated soldiers*, many of whom had not wished to join the military, were frequent targets of ridicule and harassment. An active 'back door' system immediately began to help people avoid Deng's regulations if they could not or would not conform to them.[9]

It is exactly because of these losses and the published reactions by different military spokesmen that an influential group of Western and, above all, Taiwanese China-watchers again concentrates on aspects of the traditional conflict approach – a Party-Army conflict – in order to explain the present status of the PLA in Chinese politics.[10]

The military leadership is regarded as one of the most important oppositional forces against the continuation of reform policies. Consequently, the future of reforms in the PRC is seen as a direct function of the reformers' ability to control the military and its influence on politics.

Gordon White, in a letter to the present author, very aptly summarised this view as follows:

> First, the PLA's revolutionary background makes it a kind of guardian of ideological rectitude and thus critical of some aspects or effects of the reforms (e.g. the salvos fired by the Army newspaper *Jiefang Junbao*; second, given the army's particular form of organisation, much of the market 'logic' of the reform programme seems at best irrelevant and at worst disruptive. One would therefore expect the military to be pretty sceptical of reforms.

If we, nevertheless, do not follow his overall estimation, i.e. that the army may be a major obstacle against reform policies, it is because of the considerations unfolded in the following parts of this article.

Another group of China-watchers, led by Ellis Joffe and Harlan Jencks, follows the military-professionalism approach and argues that, considering the positive effects of military modernisation policies and the furtherance of military professional interests, there is not much reason for the PLA leadership fundamentally to oppose the present reform policies.[11]

Between the two views outlined so far, the present article takes a medium position: it neither regards the present PLA leadership as only guided by strictly military interests, nor accepts the 'civil-military' dichotomy on which the first school of interpretation is based.

2 THE MILITARY AND REFORM POLICIES: THE 1980s

Even if it is quite obvious that the PLA belongs to the net losers of reform policies, its actual political behaviour shows opposition only against certain non-intentional effects of reform. Here, some general remarks seem appropriate. If we can learn anything from 40 years of analytical experience with the PRC, its political ups and downs and its information policies, it is what one can perhaps best call the 'two golden rules of China-watching', namely:

1 Never take official documents at face value! And
2 Never say never – policies and politicians tend to come back, as the political career of Deng Xiaoping clearly demonstrates!

So never regard any policy as 'irreversible'! Despite a fairly consistent general direction, the ups and downs of reform policies since 1978 should be sufficient evidence. What we need, then, is a clear distinction between different information levels and an even clearer idea of their respective analytical validity. One possible – and hopefully fruitful – suggestion is outlined in the following paragraph, where a distinction between three different analytical levels of observation is suggested:[12]

The First Level: Political Propaganda

On the first level, mainly comprising published political propaganda, we find all types of documents which represent the system's (or in our case the military subsystem's) wish to appear in absolutely flawless perfection. Examples can be found in speeches, communiques and official documents as they are published in newspapers and radio broadcasts. Especially important in this context are e.g. the so-called 'Joint Editorials' (of *People's Daily*, *Liberation Army Daily* and *Red Flag* – as long as the latter appeared) which are published regularly on the 1st January (New Year), the 1st July (Army Day) and the 1st October (National Day) every year. These articles are reprinted in press organs all over the country and serve as important guidelines for political discussion, especially in political training for the armed forces. Whenever they deal with army affairs, these publications perhaps best represent the official effort to shape an unrestricted positive public image both for the Party and for the army.

Nevertheless, documents of this kind are not completely useless for the observation of Chinese politics. They may be used as a general framework for directing our research interests, but they have to be interpreted against the background of the following two levels in order to lead us to reliable analytical results.

The Second Level: Internal Discussions

On the second level we find all kinds of internal (*neibu*) documents and critical press reports distributed only to selected readers as well as speeches of civilian and military leaders dealing with detailed and specific problems of every-day work.[13]

It is difficult to assess the complexity of issues under debate within the leadership elite and especially within the military elite. From the observation of regularly recurring topics in these documents, one may conclude that the focus in recent debates lay on at least four major subjects:

First, there was a heated debate on how best to employ limited budgetary resources.[14] One group of military leaders criticised the idea that national defence should entirely rely on state financial investments; they complained that the actual costs of national defence were not taken seriously into consideration and that the results of research were rarely well translated into production. In consequence, they postulated 'that national defence no longer be monopolised by the state, that there be more careful cost-accounting, that more emphasis be placed on producing more concrete results from theoretical research, and that these results be extended to the civilian sector, to build up the national economy'.[15] Their opponents argued that such measures failed to concentrate on the army's really essential tasks – on strengthening the national defence sector without contributing more than necessary to its intrusion into the civilian sector while at the same time raising money for specific military needs.

A second focus of intra-PLA debates was centered on the legacy of Mao Zedong Military Thought, which ever since 1981 has been an important theme, especially given the army's strong heritage of relying on Mao Zedong Thought as a major guideline for army building and its sluggish process of overcoming outdated strategic theorems.

The change from the Maoist doctrine of 'People's War' to a new doctrine hopefully better adapted to the conditions of modern warfare has been remarkably slow and there is no systematic explanation of what the new theorem 'People's War under modern conditions' really means. 'Emerging as a by-product of current strategy and operations problem-solving[16] it characterises the difficulties in overcoming the army's traditionally strong adherence to Maoist military principles.

The third problem which has been under discussion for several years until September/October 1988 was the introduction of military ranks. This debate is particularly useful as an indicator of intra-military differences ever since the revision of the Military Service Law in May 1984. According to an article published in *Mingbao*, Hong Kong, the rank system was to be introduced during 1988 according to a three-stage plan: first, a civilian post system for non-military personnel working in army institutions would be instituted; second, a reward of decorations for veteran military cadres was intended to appease those who were not to be assigned to expected positions; and finally, on October 1, 1988, the military rank system itself was introduced.[17]

A fourth major intra-military debate concentrated on an exchange of heated arguments about morale problems centering on complaints that soldiers were 'unstable in their consciousness, lax in their style, do not set high demands for their work and lack an enterprising spirit'.[18]

Despite our growing knowledge on debates of this kind centering on the army's general political, economic and social role, its historical legacies and its military ethic and style, they still do not necessarily provide a reliable picture of the PLA's actual political behaviour. This can only be analysed by a piecemeal comparison of central, regional and local reports and broadcasts outlined in the following section.

The Third Level: Military Actions and Behaviour

Writing as long back as 1937, Mao Zedong characterised the communist armed forces as being a military, political and economic force at the same time. This characteristic still holds true today. Given our available information, it remains doubtful whether the army is really 'back in the barracks'. In several very important aspects of political change, the army not only accepted new political priorities but also took a vanguard position in implementing them.

Since the de-Maoisation campaigns of the early 1980s, army units have continuously been acting as promoters of a change of political values from egalitarian to meritocratic principles through organisational restructuring and rectification. The PLA also took the lead in certain areas of institutional change by gathering and propagating intra-military experiences for civilian institutions in the crucial fields of rationalisation and raising of efficiency. Finally, the army also contributed to economic and technological change by copying the modernisation drive of other Third World armies in production and basic research.

These aspects of military behaviour will be briefly analysed in three respects:

(a) Military aspects

Despite continuing difficulties in such important fields as military strategy, weapons development and innovation and technology standards, there have been slow but distinct improvements in most areas of hardware *equipment*.[19] With limited budgetary resources, the PLA meanwhile can register limited modernisation successes which are primarily due to a combination of cost-cutting policies. While it has to do without much high technology imports from western countries, the main stress lies on cost reduction, diversified investments and technological improvements of older equipment.[20]

Furthermore, as a *major arms supplier* especially to Third World countries, the PLA not only helps to gain access to the worldwide domain of the two superpowers, but at the same time contributes to the difficult process of financing the costs of its own technical modernisation programs.[21]

And finally, since the beginning of the 1980s, the PLA has been undergoing a sustained programme of *demobilisation* whose results have been described by June Teufel Dreyer as follows:

'There has been a notable reduction in the size of the PLA during the past two years ... The median ages of commanders have been lowered an average of eight years, with the newer people in general better educated than their predecessors. Certain units have been disbanded, and the officer-to-soldier ratio has been lowered significantly'.[22]

Although positive results of military reforms cannot be denied, the army is far from being satisfied with the effects of these reforms, and recurring complaints and intra-military dissatisfactions indicate growing problems for future success.

(b) Political aspects

Although – in quantitative terms – there have been substantial changes of *military representation* in political leadership bodies, the army's share of political leadership positions as of 1988 – with 2 out of 21 Politburo members and 32 or 18.2 per cent out of 175 members of the Central Committee – is far from being negligible. It would certainly be too simplistic to conclude from a general reduction in direct political representation since the mid-1970s that military leaders have lost their influence on political decision-making. A more plausible explanation may be found in the following cluster of arguments:

First, a by now younger military leadership elite which directly and personally witnessed the negative effects of a politicisation of the army during the Maoist era is all in all less prone to become directly involved in political issues beyond its specific interests. Second, the political retreat of army leaders was followed by concessions in other fields of military interest (e.g. the political and historical assessment of Mao Zedong, the army's public image, etc.). Third, military opposition is by now too fragmented to be fully successful. Finally, political decision-making in a period of relative stability is based on cooperation and compromises instead of factional conflicts and allows the army to concentrate on its own affairs.[23]

Furthermore, the PLA's political power and importance is impressively underlined by the fact that the successful transition from Deng Xiaoping to Zhao Ziyang as Chairman of the CCPCC Military Commission primarily depends on Zhao's ability to find support within the PLA leadership.[24] And it was only very slowly that Zhao gained acceptance among the military establishment.

In political terms, the army leaders are far from being negligible actors in Chinese politics, although the changes described above have gradually reduced their position to that of spokesmen of one interest group among many, which has to compete and compromise for political advantages.

(c) Economic aspects

While improvements in military education rank among the first priorities in present military modernisation policies, the continuing stress on *dual purpose education* is meant to raise the army's appeal to educated young people and to contribute to the country's general efforts in raising the educational standards necessary for all aspects of modernisation.[25]

And, last but not least, the Maoist tradition of involving the army in *civilian economic production* has not been discarded, but instead been increased. In a comment in the *Liberation Army Daily*, this policy is summarised with the words: ' . . . by grasping well production and operations within military units, we both support state economic construction and create more wealth for the people, as well as making up the shortfall in military expenditures, improve the material and cultural life of the cadres and fighters, and give our PLA greater appeal'.[26]

This short summary of the major aspects of the PLA's role in present reform endeavours can, of course, not be complete and comprehensive. One may, however, find it hard to reduce the political, economic and social functions of the PLA in the mid-1980s to a purely obstructionist role. Military critics of reform policies have by now lost much of their former influence. Due to Deng Xiaoping's strategy of personnel changes, they have been replaced by cadres who generally accept and support the principal aims of economic reforms in China, although they still come out with public criticism whenever basic military interests are at stake.

By the mid-1980s, therefore, the military leadership in the PRC, may come very close to the late Marshall Ustinow's position in the Soviet Union. The political task of such prominent leaders as Yang Dezhi (former chief of the PLA General Staff) and Yang Shangkun (President of the PRC and Vice-Chairman of the Party and State Military Commissions) in the PRC seemed not only to be characterised by their representation of military interests *within* the party's top level leadership organs, but also by their extremely important function to represent, defend and implement the party's decisions towards the military.

The army still plays a vital role in Chinese politics. However, as compared to the early 1970's, the character of its interest articulation and aggregation has been adjusted to the general features of present politics in the PRC. Top level political leaders in China – including the military elite – can no longer simply be pigeonholed along factional lines. The CCP's top leadership is presently made up of individuals still sharing a broad range of common attitudes and convictions, while at the same time competing with each other on the basis of specific interests. Thus, Chinese politics today are primarily characterised by a continuous and at times difficult search for political compromises, in which army leaders still take an important, but not necessarily obstructive position.

CONCLUSIONS

It has become fashionable to view China's present top leadership in the context of two conflicting groups: one being the 'reformers' and the other the 'conservatives' or 'orthodox' forces.[27] For the military's role in politics, this view can be reduced to the two extremes of a postulated obstructionist versus supportive military behaviour towards reforms and their non-intentional effects (budget cuts, loss of social prestige, etc.).

Quite contrary to this dichotomous view, we would argue that China's top leadership group – including the military elite – is made up by people

– who all share the belief that the system must be reformed in order
to increase its legitimacy and efficiency;

– who all share the aim to build a strong, prosperous and internationally
influential socialist system with a flourishing economic sector, while at
the same time repeatedly coming into conflict over the fundamental
question of which consequences of reforms can still be tolerated and
which not.

It is in this sense only that one may regard the present PLA leadership as
being Janus-faced in its political behaviour. Given the slow but continuous
improvement in military modernisation, the army has accepted the priorities of reform policies, while at the same time heavily criticising presumed
or actual negative or destabilising effects of those reforms.

The key factors in determining the overall behaviour of China's present
military leadership towards reform policies and their specific effects will be
found in the outcome of a twofold success: first in the success of personnel
changes within the army, and, second, in the success of economic reforms
as such, which will help to appease military (and not only military)
critics.[28]

The military's base of power can be described as a politically important
combination of its monopoly of national defence, its still remarkable top-
level leadership representation, its considerable and probably still growing
economic importance and, finally, its ability to articulate and push through
its vested interests without too much intra-military friction.

Instead of being a 'challenge to the Party', the PLA still has to be regarded
as a comprehensive military, economic and political service system for the
Party, which in times of relative political stability reacts towards violations
of its vested interests as a veto-group. While still trying to push their own
favourite political alternatives, PLA leaders can at best reach acceptable
compromises or postpone certain disliked policies, but they are no longer
in a position to block or dominate political decision-making.

Remembering that one should never say never, a major return of the
army into politics should not be completely excluded. Such a development
could be assumed on the basis of an international comparison which shows
that any army, once it entered politics, tends to return as soon as the 'fruits'
of its former intervention(s) again seem to be endangered. In China,
this could happen first, in the case of a full-scale return to leftist and
Cultural Revolutionary policies; second, in a situation of serious systemic
instability; and finally, in the case of serious and extended violations of
the army's vested interests.

Given our present state of information, the highest plausible consideration, however, is that the PLA and its leadership will continue to exert considerable political influence, even up to a point where it can decisively influence the overall outcome of national policies.

NOTES

1. For the most important works, see Joffe 1965, Gittings 1967, Griffith 1967, Whitson 1973, Nelson 1981 and Jencks 1982.
2. E.g. Stuart and Tow 1982; Segal and Tow 1984 and Teufel Dreyer 1989, esp. chap. 8–10.
3. Cf. IISS 1987/88, p. 145.
4. E.g. Huntington 1957; Finer 1962.
5. E.g. Herspring and Volgyes 1978.
6. See the two examples quoted above and Sandschneider 1987, pp. 32–7 and pp. 133–7 for further details and evidence.
7. Esp. Yü 1986 and 1988.
8. See, for example, his attempts to win over regional military commanders for a political coalition against Lin Biao in August 1971.
9. Teufel Dreyer 1984, p. 269.
10. Esp. Yü 1986 and 1988.
11. Joffe 1978, 169 ff; Jencks 1982.
12. For the following analytical approach see Wagenlehner 1988.
13. Most important in this group of documents are the Central Committee Directives (*zhongfa*) which are regularly published by Taiwanese sources, but also internal information services such as *Cankao Xiaoxi* [Reference News], *Xuexi Wenjian* [Documents for Study] and *Dangfeng yu Dangji* [Party Style and Party Discipline].
14. The PLA's share of fiscal appropriations has been reduced from 17.5 per cent (22.3 billion yuan) in 1979 to 8.3 per cent (20.4 billion yuan) in 1987: i.e. by an average 7 per cent drop per year. See Cheung 1988, p. 771.
15. Dreyer in Yang 1988, 2 and Cheung 1988, pp. 760–8.
16. Godwin in Lovejoy/Watson 1986, p. 4.
17. Obviously, opposition arose not so much against the introduction of the rank system itself, but against the distribution of ranks among older military cadres fighting among each other for better positions under the new system. For a survey of the rank system, see *China Aktuell*, July 1988, p. 507.
18. *Jiefang Junbao* [Liberation Army Daily] [hereafter JFJB].
19. Cf. Yang 1988.
20. Cf. Sandschneider 1987, pp. 204–6; Yang 1988, pp. 39 ff, 51 ff, and 169 ff.
21. Cf. Lee 1987.

22. Teufel Dreyer 1988, p. 105.
23. Cf. Johnson in Lovejoy and Watson 1986, pp. 120–1.
24. Cf. *Far Eastern Economic Review*, 7 April 1988, p. 20.
25. 'Dual purpose personnel' (*liangyong rencai*) means personnel trained for military and civilian jobs – helping them to return to civilian life while at the same time supporting the civilian economy's need for sophisticatedly trained personnel.
26. JFJB, 23 September 1987, p. 2; for more details see Wang in Yang 1988, pp. 135–52.
27. Cf. e.g. Yü 1988, 15, note 7.
28. See also Larrabee 1988, 1002–25, esp. p. 1025 for a description of similar structures in the USSR as far as the attitudes and expectations of Soviet military leaders towards Gorbachev's reforms are concerned.

BIBLIOGRAPHY

Cheung, Tai Ming (1988) 'Disarmament and Development in China: The Relationship between National Defence and Economic Development' *Asian Survey*, vol. XXVIII, no. 7 (July) pp. 757–74.

Finer, Samuel E (1962) *The Man on Horseback: The Role of the Military in Politics* (London).

Gittings, John (1967) *The Role of the Chinese Army* (London).

Griffith, James B. (1967) *The Chinese People's Liberation Army* (New York).

Herspring, David R. and Volgyes, Ivan (eds) (1978) *Civil-military Relations in Communist Systems* (Boulder: Colorado) .

Huntington, Samuel P. (1957) *The Soldier and the State: The Theory and Politics of Civil-Military Relations* (Cambridge, Mass.).

International Institute for Strategic Studies (IISS) (ed.) (1988) *The Military Balance 1987/88* (London).

Jencks, Harlan W. (1982) *From Muskets to Missiles: Politics and Professionalism in the Chinese Army, 1945–1981* (Boulder, Colorado).

Joffe, Ellis (1965) *Party and Army: Professionalism and Political Control in the Chinese Officer Corps. 1949–1964* (Cambridge, Mass.).

Joffe, Ellis (1987) *The Chinese Army after Mao* (Cambridge, Mass.).

Larrabee, Stephen F. (1988) 'Gorbachev and the Soviet Military', *Foreign Affairs* (Summer) pp. 1002–25.

Lovejoy, Charles D. Jr. and Watson, Bruce W. (eds) (1986) *China's Military Reforms, International and Domestic Implications* (Boulder/London).

Lee, Wei-chin (1987/88) 'The Birth of a Salesman': China as an Arms Supplier' *Journal of North East Asian Studies* vol. VI, no 4 (Winter 1987/88) pp. 32–46.

Nelson, Harvey (1981) *The Chinese Military System: An Organisational Study of the Chinese People's Liberation Army* (2nd ed., revised and updated; Boulder, Colorado).

Robinson, Thomas W. (1982) 'Chinese Military Modernisation in the 1980s' *China Quarterly*, 90 (June) pp. 231–52.

Sandschneider, Eberhard *Militär und Politik in der Volksrepublik China, 1969–1985*, Mitteilungen des Instituts für Asienkunde 160. (Hamburg, 1987).

Segal, Gerald and Tow, William T. (eds) (1984) *Chinese Defence Policy* (Urbana, Ill.).

Stuart, Douglas T and Tow, William T. (1982) 'Chinese Military Modernisation: The Western Arms Connection' *China Quarterly* 90, June 1982, pp. 253–70.

Teufel Dreyer, June (1984) 'China's Military in the 1980's', *Current History* (September).

Teufel Dreyer, June (1988) 'The PLA: Demobilisation and its Effects', *Issues and Studies*, vol. 24, no. 2 (February).

Teufel Dreyer, June (ed.) (1989) *Chinese Defence and Foreign Policy* (New York).

Wagenlehner, Günther (1988) 'Militärdoktrin und Glasnost. Die drei Ebenen des sowjetischen Militärwesens', *Osteuropa* June 1988, pp. 435–46.

Whitson, William W. (with Huang Chen-hsia) (1973), *The Chinese High Command* (New York).

Yang, Richard H. (ed.) (1988) *SCPS Yearbook on PLA Affairs 1987* (Sun Yat-sen Centre for Policy Studies, National Sun Yat-sen University, Kaohsiung, R.O.C.)

Yü Yü-lin (1986) 'The Role of the PLA in Mainland China's Power Transition', *Issues and Studies*, vol. 21, no. 12 (December) pp. 76–92.

Yü Yü-lin (1988) 'The PLA's Political Role after the CCP's Thirteenth National Congress: Continuity and Change', *Issues and Studies*, vol. 24, no. 9 (September) pp. 11–35.

8 The Law, the State and Economic Reform

Donald C. Clarke

1 INTRODUCTION

A study of the role of law in economic reform in China is hampered by the difficulty of knowing what exactly we are talking about. The legal system, if we can call it that, is not the direct institutional descendant of a European system, and we cannot assume in advance the equivalency of various terms. To translate *fa* as 'law' and *fazhi* as 'legal system' can only be the beginning of understanding, not the end. Indeed, the meaning of *fazhi* in China itself is not yet complete. Its linguistic limits are still fluid and ill-defined. What it comes to mean will depend on what people want it to mean, and that in turn will depend in large part on the political consequences of defining certain institutions and practices as inside or outside the territory of law.

The proper role of law and legal institutions in the implementation of state policy has never been conclusively settled in China. For many years, so-called legal institutions have been distrusted by many on the grounds that they hamper the freedom of the government to act and tend to freeze the *status quo*, thus blocking further revolutionary change.[1] Others have argued that this understanding confuses specifically bourgeois legal instructions with legal institutions generally, and hold that there can be socialist legal institutions with socialist content. These are not only desirable, but indeed indispensable in China.[2]

For the time being, at least, the latter school holds sway. Many of China's past problems are blamed on a lack of law, with 'law' understood to mean a restraint on the uncontrolled exercise of arbitrary power by individual leaders. The government recognise a need for specifically legal reforms[3] to accompany reforms in other areas of social, economic, and political life, and many of those reforms are to consist of bringing the area in question under legal regulation.

It is not enough, however, simply to call for the regulation by law of some activity, for the legal system in China is itself in the midst of transformation. It does not stand passively outside of politics and economics, waiting for problems from those realms to be consigned to it. How the law and legal institutions regulate activities will depend upon the types of activities they are called upon to regulate. Frequently, the government's idea of what legal institutions should look like is much less clear than its idea of how an activity consigned to legal regulation should be conducted. The imperatives of demands made upon law and legal institutions will shape what law and legal institutions come to look like.

Since 1978, the Chinese government has undertaken a series of potentially far-reaching economic reforms. While the pace of reform has been significantly slowed, and perhaps even in some places reversed, by the retrenchment following June, 1989, it does not yet appear to be the government's intention to return to the old system in its entirety. Nor does the post-June leadership appear inclined to abandon the view, expressed in 1979 in the *Beijing Review*, that law has an important role to play in promoting economic development:

> Development of the productive forces in China will necessitate major changes in the relations of production as well as in the superstructure, of which laws, decrees and rules and regulations form an important component. To this end, various laws and regulations on economic work, including those for the people's communes and factories [and] fulfilment of contracts ... will be drafted and gradually perfected. Judicial organs will be established to arbitrate lawsuits and disputes between enterprises.[4]

But the Chinese legal system does not already exist in a strong and well defined form, able to force economic activities along a straight and narrow path. Instead, the requirements of economic reform will shape the way legal institutions perform their regulatory function, and will thus shape perceptions of what law is and can be. This paper is an examination of this shaping process with particular reference to the reform of urban enterprises.

2 THE ROLE OF THE LAW

The general burden of the reforms is to replace direct controls with indirect controls – that is, to replace to a large extent production and allocation according to a mandatory plan with production and allocation according to market forces. The state does not propose to give up control over economic activity; it proposes to replace control by orders with control by costs, some imposed by impersonal market forces and some imposed deliberately by state law or economic policy. To understand the legal ramifications of this shift, let us look at the pre-reform system of state control of enterprise behaviour.

The Idea of State Control

Urban enterprises are commonly grouped into two categories: state-owned and collectively-owned. In many cases the distinction is merely one of history: a municipal government may, for example, control the operations and the personnel of both a state-owned enterprise and a collectively-owned enterprise. The difference in practical terms may be minimal or it may be significant. As a first approximation, one might say that the planned sector of the economy corresponds roughly with the 'state-owned' sector, while the unplanned (market) sector corresponds with the collective and private sectors. This approximation must be immediately qualified, however, with the observation that some small state enterprises have been virtually outside the plan, while some collective enterprises (notably large ones) have been routinely included. My discussion in this paper will focus on state-owned enterprises, because the legal issues are more difficult in that sector. If we can understand the problems there, those of the collective sector become much more tractable.

The fundamental fact of state-owned enterprises at present is that they are controlled by the state in the service of the plan. This control is vital in the absence of effective market forces. Where there is no invisible hand, the plan must provide a visible one. From the stand-point of the controlled enterprise and its managers, 'the state' is simply that administrative entity that has the power to engage and discharge senior personnel and that provides them with targets for production, profits, and so on, while being responsible for ensuring that the enterprise receives the necessary supplies.

From the stand-point of the controller, however, the concept of 'state control' is problematic. It may mean nothing more than that it is not the managers who decide. On the other hand, the members of the State Planning Commission obviously cannot collectively exercise direct control over every enterprise in the planning system. 'The state', as far as the enterprise is concerned, can be any institution from a central ministry to a local government. The concept of 'the state' in this, context therefore becomes fragmented. Put simply, if we insist on speaking of 'state control of enterprises', we must conceptualise the state as an entity that is capable of pursuing contradictory and inconsistent policies.[5] This is one of the aspects of state control through planning that has been perceived as unsatisfactory and in need of reform.

Methods and Nature of State Control

There are many ways in which the state might wish to exercise control over enterprises in general and over state-owned enterprises in particular. A conceptual problem is posed by the fact that the state is both the owner of state-owned enterprises and the lawmaker for them. The state can exercise control through ownership because, as the owner, it stands in a relationship of hierarchical superiority to the enterprise. It can exercise control through law because the enterprise, like all other enterprises and persons within the territory of the People's Republic of China, is subject to its jurisdiction. When a state agency gives an order to an enterprise under it, is it the order of an owner or of a government, and does the answer to this question matter?

Consider the difference between the state as owner and the state as government. The owner possesses proprietary rights and the government possesses sovereign rights. As owner, the state has the right to all the profits if it wishes. The state as government has no right to the profits *per se*, but can of course impose taxes. As owner and sole shareholder, as it were, the state has the right to decide on management personnel and operational strategies down to the last detail. As government, the state can pass laws dictating these matters provided that such specific and detailed legislation is not barred by constitution or custom. What happens, then, when the state taxes the profits of an enterprise at 100 per cent and controls through legislation many details of its operation? For all intents and purposes the state now has all the incidents of ownership, and indeed, one should say that such measures constitute the *de facto* expropriation of the enterprise by the state.

In short, there is nothing in the *nature* of legal regulation, broadly defined, that dictates the degree of generality of the rules or the amount of autonomy that will be given to enterprises. The logic of economic reform, however, does suggest that regulation by the state as owner will have to yield to regulation by the state as government. This is another way of saying that regulation by enterprise-specific directives, whether we call them laws or administrative orders, will have to yield to regulation by rules of general applicability. This is because the difference between laws of general application and enterprise-specific directives, whether or not we call them law, is that enterprise-specific directives need to be guided; they need to have some rationale behind them to make sure that they have the desired effect; in short, they have to be part of a plan. But the government is trying to reduce the scope of the plan; it is trying to enlarge the autonomous powers of management. Prices and interest rates can function as economic levers only when they apply to all enterprises indifferently. High-priced inputs are now supposed to go to those enterprises which, because they produce a valuable product, can afford them. The task for law in economic reform is to play a similar role: to function as an aspect of the environment in which enterprises operate. If all economic law is enterprise-specific, there can be no hope of making its content rational and internally consistent without something like a plan. If law is to be used as an economic lever, it must apply indifferently to large numbers of enterprises.

Types of General Rules

It is not enough merely to identify generality as a necessary feature of law in the service of economic reform. We must now look at the various types of regulation that might plausibly be called 'legal' in China and to distinguish the ways in which they operate even though all can share the characteristic of generality. The Chinese government has, over the last several years, issued vast quantities of documents and instituted many new practices relating to urban economic reform. Many of these documents and practices have legal-sounding labels: 'laws', 'regulations', 'courts', etc.[6] They operate in widely different ways, however, and some of those ways are not 'law-like' as the lawyer would conceive the term.

Ostensibly 'legal' government documents in China can be usefully analyzed by appeal to ideal types, three of which are set forth below. Because these are ideal types, I do not claim that all or any Chinese legislative material necessarily fits neatly into one of three categories. What I suggest is that we can have a better idea about what is important and interesting about Chinese legislation and the accompanying institutions and practices if we can see *to what extent* they partake of certain ideal types. I hope to show that certain types of legislation do in fact fit some of the categories closely, but it is not necessary to the argument that they do.

(a) Policy law
'Policy-law' might look like a law – it might be called the 'Law on XYZ' and be divided into chapters and articles – but in fact it is nothing more or less than the written expression of government policy. It could be argued that all statutory law anywhere is just the expression of government policy, in the sense that a ceiling on civil liability for nuclear accidents represents a

'policy' that civilian nuclear power should be encouraged. But policy-laws are different. They do not seek to further a policy so much as they are the policy themselves. In many legal systems, legislators often attempt to achieve a policy through granting rights or imposing penalties, and legal analysis consists of the study of the system of rights set up by the law. But the notable feature of policy-laws is that they do not grant rights and are not justifiable by courts.[7] At most, they express values that are expected to inform judicial decision-making.

Some of China's recent legislation on the management and activities of state-owned enterprises contains a strong flavour of policy-law. For example, the 1985 State Council rules on enlivening state-owned enterprises (the 'Enterprise Rules')[8] merely express some generalised wishes and policy goals, such as that enterprises should obtain good leadership, increase their ability to reform themselves, and take effective measures to cut costs and raise productivity. The Enterprise Rules are clearly directed at the various national and local government departments directly in charge of state-owned enterprises, and it is unimaginable (at least at present) that anyone could go into a Chinese court with a claim that some right he had was violated by the improper implementation of these 'rules'.

(b) Bureaucratic law

By 'bureaucratic law' I mean the regular procedures, written or unwritten, used within a bureaucracy to deal with its internal management and to deal with outsiders. Bureaucratic law is promulgated by the bureaucracy itself (or by a superior body that permits the bureaucracy to draft the rules), and it can be changed by that bureaucracy. The outstanding characteristic of bureaucratic law is that it governs the behaviour of bureaucrats, not that of the public at large. Like policy-law, it is not intended to be handled by courts. Unlike policy-law, however, it is conceivable that disputes could occur based on some concept of entitlement under the terms of the bureaucratic law. The employee of a government department can claim that the department has not followed its own rules in ruling on his application for retirement benefits, for example. Similarly, an enterprise that is regulated by an agency can claim that it has submitted all the proper documents in the course of some proceeding and that the agency under its own rules should grant its request.

In all these cases, however, the agency will be the judge of whether its own procedures have been or should be correctly followed in the case at hand. The agency formulated the law in the first place and it can always amend it, whether the amendment is by formal means or is carried out merely as a matter of bureaucratic practice.

Much of China's legislation relating to foreign trade and investment tends strongly toward the model of bureaucratic law. Generally, such laws should not be understood as rights-granting instruments. If the law says that X 'shall' be done, you do not necessarily have a right to redress if X is not done and you are thereby damaged. If one is looking for rights, many of these laws appear very poorly drafted indeed. 'Should' is used liberally alongside of 'must'; laws frequently state that X 'should in general'[9] or 'should in principle' be done, but give no indication of when exceptions can be made.

The intention of the drafters becomes clearer, however, if one considers the law as a set of bureaucratic rules directed to administrators. Most foreign economic contracts, for example, must be approved by these administrators: it is they, as much as the parties to a contract, who must 'obey' the Foreign Economic Contract Law. Where the law says that contracts 'should in general' contain a certain provision, is a contract without that provision invalid? Have its signers violated the law? The question is impossible to answer. The relevant question, for the state, is whether, when one looks at all of the contracts approved by the relevant authority, the rule of 'in general' or 'in principle' has been satisfied. What the law aims to establish is a kind of sta.istical regularity, not any particular individual's right to something.[10]

(c) Juridical law

The third ideal type to be defined is that of 'juridical law'. By juridical law I mean rules that are intended to govern relations between parties who are more or less juridical equals.

These rules impose duties and grant entitlements that can be sued on in court. Generally speaking, only courts have the jurisdiction to pass on and to enforce these laws. At a minimum, no body regulated by the law also administers the law. In other words, this is the type of law we are familiar with in the West. The only reason I specify it as a particular type is that much of what in China goes under the name of 'law' is not in fact of this type.

A key difference I wish to define between juridical law and the other two types is that juridical law is regular in its application. Policy-law can be rescinded at any time, and a bureaucracy has great discretion over when and where to use its bureaucratic law. But juridical law is not controlled by the party that made it. Once promulgated, it stays available for use by anyone who has standing under it, although of course where juridical law is regulatory the only party with standing to mobilise the law may be a government agency.

Within the scope of juridical law, it is useful to distinguish public law from private law. Public law can be understood as the rules governing the state and governing hierarchical relations between the state on the one hand and natural or legal persons on the other; private law comprises the rules governing relations between persons of equal juridical status. Public law can be juridical law if the state agency involved is judged by a neutral arbiter and the citizen can invoke the rules on his or her own. Juridical law certainly includes what we would call private law – the rules of tort and contract, for example, that apply between private citizens. In China, the best example of private juridical law is probably the General Principles of Civil Law (the 'GPCL').[11] promulgated in 1986. The GPCL set forth general rules governing such matters as agency and tort liability, and are to be passed on and enforced by courts.

The distinction between public and private law is often criticised as illusory – Lenin, for example, is often quoted to the effect that under socialism, all law is public law.[12] This is true in the sense that the rules of private law, such as those governing contracts or torts, can be consciously molded to serve particular social ends. For example, labour law in Western countries is a conspicuous area where the 'private' rights governing employer-employee relations are consciously manipulated by the state to serve particular social ends. American antitrust law allows victorious private plaintiffs to recover three times their actual damages in order to encourage suits and thereby deter genuine violations that government regulatory agencies might be unable to act upon merely through lack of funds. Nevertheless, it is useful to distinguish between public law and private law because of the different role for 'private', non-governmental parties in each.

The key to the use of juridical law as 'private law' is that it can bring 'private parties' into the picture. In China, the term 'private party' must be used with caution, because major economic actors are generally tied in some way to some governmental body. But we can usefully distinguish actions instigated directly by the central government from actions instigated by parties not under the direct control of the central government. An enterprise may be owned by the state but under provincial or municipal control. And enterprise management may in fact attain a large degree of autonomy through an alliance with its immediate supervisory agency, similar perhaps to the familiar phenomenon of regulatory capture.[13] In short, there are many significant economic actors in China that do not march obediently to orders from the State Council or the Party Central Committee. And, of course, if individually insignificant economic actors like consumers are permitted to bring suit in large numbers, they will become economically significant actors not under central government control.

The use of private-law juridical measures to regulate the economy indirectly will be controversial in China. Such measures highlight the continuing tension in Chinese development policy between centralised control and decentralised initiative. It is not merely a question of reducing the power of the state over enterprises. It is a question of putting the power and authority of the central government, through the court system, at the service of parties not genuinely controlled by the centre.[14]

This is less of a problem if regulation is accomplished through public-law juridical measures. With such measures, a governmental body is always involved and has some measure of control over the outcome. To say that a governmental body is involved, however, begs the question of who controls the governmental body. Different state organs are perfectly capable of pursuing inconsistent policies. In addition, if there is to be real progress away from comprehensive planning and toward enterprise autonomy, even public-law juridical measures will have to be accompanied by notions of regularity, generality, and rights.

3 'LEGAL' VERSUS 'NON-LEGAL' MEASURES

In China, as in most countries, the government cannot hope to implement a policy merely by passing a law and waiting for it to work. There must at a minimum exist some means of publicising and enforcing the terms of the law. Chinese courts and some administrative agencies are at present generally weak and frequently encounter problems in enforcing judgements and orders.[15] The effective implementation through courts or other agencies of legislated rules can by no means be taken for granted.

Legal institutions, therefore, are just one means of policy implementation. Others are possible: in the past, for example, mass campaigns were often used.[16] Another possible channel is the Communist Party structure. It is thus important to see Chinese law and legal institutions in their political context. Legal institutions serve particular bureaucratic interests and harm others. They promote certain ways of governing and disfavour others. If the government chooses to implement a policy through the use of legal institutions, one should ask why that method was chosen. Why was the Communist Party structure not used? Why was a different bureaucracy not used? How effective can legal institutions be in implementing the policy?

A prominent example of what appears to be a legal measure in the service of enterprise reform is the national Enterprise Bankruptcy Law.[17] passed in December, 1986. This law was passed to achieve certain goals, notably the elimination from the economy of inefficient, money-wasting enterprises. The interesting question is why those who wanted to achieve these goals sought to achieve them through the passing of legislation in the National People's Congress. The law is to apply only to state-owned enterprises. Yet state-owned enterprises are already under the discretion of a government administrative department, either on the central or the local level. These departments have always been capable of ordering the closing of an enterprise under their jurisdiction – clearly not every state-owned enterprise that has existed since 1949 is still operating today,[18] and in 1985 the *China Legal System News* reported what can only be termed a 'common law' bankruptcy and closure.[19]

If there were no bankruptcy law, the department in charge of an enterprise could adopt one or more of the following measures in the face of losses:

1. change the enterprise's leadership on the theory that losses are due to bad management;
2. provide subsidies, either directly or perhaps through ordering a bank to make loans on easy terms;
3. merge it with another enterprise;
4. change the product line; or
5. close the enterprise down.

The decision is not a legal one; it is a bureaucratic one guided by whatever standards the department in charge wishes to use. Nevertheless, it would be possible for the goals of the bankruptcy law to be met by the system basically as it now exists.

The explanation for the passage of the bankruptcy law must be sought outside of the particular goals it seeks to achieve. A key feature of the law is that it attempts to change the locus of decision-making power over enterprises. Evidently there is a perception on the central level that local departments in charge have been coddling inefficient enterprises. In the bankruptcy rules of Shenyang (the 'Trial Rules')[20], the determination of bankruptcy is made by the local administrative department for industry and commerce, not by the department in charge. The decision is appealable to a court. In the national Enterprise Bankruptcy Law the entire process from beginning to end is under the jurisdiction of the people's court of the area where the enterprise has its offices. Similarly, the Shenyang Trial Rules provide for a Supervisory Committee (whose job it is to preside over the near-bankrupt enterprise) to be headed by the local administrative department for industry and commerce and not, as might have seemed natural, by the department in charge.

Finally, both the Trial Rules and the Enterprise Bankruptcy Law are noteworthy for the fact that, unlike many other economic laws, they do not say that the power of interpretation shall rest with such-and-such administrative organ. It lies instead with the courts.

The national bankruptcy law thus in effect proposes a major shift in the power to make decisions affecting the national economy. This is no doubt one reason why the law ran into so much opposition. The real difference between a future bankruptcy system and the present system is that bankruptcy law promises – or threatens – a system of enterprise closings administered by courts instead of by local departments in charge. Whoever controls the courts will decide whether enterprises live or die, with the attendant consequences for production and employment. Evidently those in favour of court-administered enterprise closings are confident that national economic policy can be better effected through courts than through other local government bodies.

Another important aspect of the Enterprise Bankruptcy Law is that it puts the initiative in the hands of what might be called 'private parties' – the creditors. As noted above, the use of the term 'private parties' can be misleading, because most of the creditors, at least the ones to whom anybody is likely to pay any attention, will be state- or collectively-owned enterprises or government departments (most notably banks). But it is a useful term because it brings out the fact that an enterprise's fate is to a certain extent being taken out of the hands of the department in charge of it – taken out of the planning system – and being made hostage to the anarchic forces of the non-plan economy. Any single creditor who is not getting paid now has some kind of right to take action that may result in the whole enterprise's being shut down. Moreover, that creditor is not required to consider the interests of anyone else: it can apply to the court simply because it wants to get its money. When we view the law in this light, it is easy to see why it would be extremely unattractive to those leaders who favour central planning and distrust anything not under the control of the central bureaucracy.[21]

No matter what the motivations behind this transfer of power, in order to be successful it will require a quantum leap in the power of courts over Chinese society. Courts have hitherto exercised their power primarily over individuals – for example, in criminal cases and property disputes. Now they are to be given the power to decide the fate of large collectivities and to put hundreds of workers out of work. Whether they can exercise that power effectively will be considered briefly in the conclusion.

Bankruptcy law illustrates a major problem with the use of law in economic reform. It aspires to be a juridical law. It is to be activated by private parties (as I have qualified the term). It is to operate with regularity and predictability; if it did not, it would not accomplish its purpose of putting the staff of inefficient, wasteful enterprises in fear for their jobs. And enterprises must be made to worry about losses – prices must be made to matter – if price reform is to be successful.

The demands of law, however, seem to conflict with the demands of justice. As noted above, bankruptcy law uses losses as an indicator of unworthiness. If it did not do so, losses could never be made to matter. Yet to do so, in an economy of planned allocation and fixed prices, is clearly unfair. It is this perception of unfairness, irrationality, and injustice that has held up the implementation of the Enterprise Bankruptcy Law. One of the first local bankruptcy laws operating, the Trial Rules of Shenyang City, has not in fact operated in a juridical way. It has operated almost as a policy-law. The municipal government passed the regulations, then looked for enterprises to which to apply them. The number of eligible candidates turned out to be too large, the government feared social disruption,[22] and so it was decided to hand out bankruptcy warnings to only three enterprises. The decision eventually to close down one of those three – the Shenyang Explosion Prevention Equipment Plant – was a quintessentially political decision, not a legal one in any sense. It was taken at a meeting of the municipal government presided over by the mayor.[23]

Another example of the frustration of law by justice can be found in the practice of taxation of state-owned enterprises. Until recently, state-owned enterprises simply turned over their profits, or a portion thereof, to the state. They thus had little incentive to increase profits, since the increase would not be distributed to the staff. The amount of retained profits would be negotiated between the enterprise and the state. This system was then changed. Enterprises were to pay taxes instead of turning over profits.[24] The intent was that enterprises would then have an incentive to maximise profits, since the tax rate was supposed to be fixed. But in fact, little changed, and the reform seems to have been suspended, if not dropped entirely. It was unfair to tax all enterprises at the same rate, because different sectors of the economy may have widely varying average profits that have nothing to do with the merit of enterprises in those sectors. Tax rates thus became as negotiable as retained profits had been.[25] Both the enterprise and the authorities could argue respectively that an extra subsidy or tax was needed because the original profitability did not express a social gain. This is a legitimate argument, but it subverts the ideal of a uniform tax rate.[26] As one writer has remarked,

In China, the treatment of every enterprise and problem as a special case leads to collusion between local governments and enterprises, with the local governments often acting as patrons rather than regulators. The lack of universally applicable rules diverts the energies of enterprises to bargaining from improving efficiency and product quality. Enterprises seek rents rather than profits. They look for ways to manipulate the rules to their financial advantage rather than taking the rules as given.[27]

In short, there appears to be a tendency for laws aspiring to juridicality to be undermined by the injustice of a regularly operating law that distributes rewards and punishments on the basis of (at least partly) arbitrary economic endowments. The regularity of tax law has been undermined by the negotiability of tax rates. The regularity – indeed, the hoped-for merciless operation – of bankruptcy law has been undermined by the theory that enterprises should pay a penalty only for 'business losses', and not for 'policy losses'.[28]

4   THE NEED FOR JURIDICAL LAWS

The basic strategy behind China's economic reform is the substitution of indirect for direct controls. Because the controls are indirect, enterprise autonomy and initiative can be maintained. But because they are, after all, controls, the state can continue to guide the economy and induce desired behaviour. Such, in any case, is the idea.

For this idea to be realised, the state has to make use of such economic levers as interest rates, taxes, credits, financial rewards and penalties, pricing, state orders for goods, and subsidies granted for policy considerations. But for these measures to have macro-economic effect, enterprises must also be reformed so that they will respond to such signals.

So far, it would appear that enterprises have not been so reformed. In other words, even while the state expands its manipulation of, for example, interest rates and taxes, enterprises if left to themselves remain relatively unresponsive.

Under these circumstances, the role of law (if one can call it that) in regulating the economy seems largely to have become one of providing a substitute for the market pressures that are felt as yet imperfectly by enterprises. Instead of being punished in the marketplace, managers and enterprises will be punished by taxes, fines, demotions, or even criminal sanctions if they make undesirable decisions.[29] So, for example, there has been a tax on fuel oil to promote conservation[30] and taxes on bonuses to discourage excessive payments to workers by management.[31] In one regulation, the giving of excessive bonuses is made directly punishable as a violation of financial discipline.[32] The State Council has promulgated special regulations requiring state and collective enterprises to keep their wage bill down and attempting to control their expenditures through the banking system.[33] The degree of oversight felt necessary is perhaps best exemplified in a rule issued by no less than the State Council prohibiting state-owned enterprises, among others, from wasting money by sending wall calendars to favoured customers.[34]

In addition, the government has felt it necessary to issue direct regulations to prevent enterprises from responding too well to market forces. This is what all price regulation attempts to do.[35] The State Council also viewed with alarm the tendency of small state-owned shops to cut back on items for daily use and to concentrate on stocking larger items with bigger profit margins. It issued a regulation forbidding such shops to change their line of business or to decrease the number of items stocked without the approval of their superior administrative department.[36]

The problem with such measures is that they reinforce the system of direct and detailed regulation of enterprise behaviour that the government is otherwise trying in large measure to abolish. Even regulations which appear fairly general on the surface (all small state-owned shops, for example, are forbidden to decrease the number of items stocked) often require detailed administrative oversight for enforcement (the department in charge of a small shop will have to check its compliance and pass on requests for exemptions).

Moreover, such direct regulations are particularly subject to negotiation, and hence weakening, in their application. This is because the administering authorities have neither the incentive nor the information necessary to stand up to pleadings that a particular enterprise constitutes a special case.

Private juridical law, however, is not under the control of an interested bureaucracy. It is controlled by economic actors who may have antagonistic interests. One side will have an interest in seeing the law enforced as written, even if that brings about an unfair result to the other side. To the extent that laws tend to be juridical laws, they have the potential to be more effective as regulators of enterprise behaviour. But this effectiveness is at the constant risk of being undermined – and indeed, the prestige of legal institutions as regulators of enterprise behaviour runs a similar risk – because of the perceived and often real unfairness of using universal standards instead of the more familiar case-by-case negotiation. Enterprises are to be held equally to such standards when in fact they are often unequal, even when that inequality has been imposed on them by the system itself.[37] If the law is to work, it must at least begin by being unjust.

5 CONCLUSION

The Chinese are discovering that the proper role for law and legal institutions in economic reform is by no means self-evident. On the one hand, laws and regulations must be of more general application than specific *ad hoc* directives if the system of comprehensive planning is to be replaced in anything but name. On the other hand, there are few institutions in China with an interest in the enforcement of such general and uniform standards *per se*. The most likely candidate for this challenge would be the courts, but their ability to take on the task is open to question. Formidable obstacles remain to be overcome.

First, the central government must challenge and defeat local authorities over control of local courts. It has long been the practice in China for local Party secretaries or Party committees to review and approve the disposition of cases by courts.[38] This was the concrete manifestation of the principle of Party leadership. The official theory now is that Party leadership is to be exercised at the level of legislation, not adjudication,[39] and the Central Committee explicitly abolished the practice in September, 1979.[40] But it has proved difficult to break old habits. As recently as February, 1988 the *Legal System Daily* saw the need to report in a major article that the Beijing Municipal Party Committee had in recent years stopped the practice of approving individual cases.[41] The term 'recent years' might be construed to stretch back to 1979, but if there were no problem it is unlikely the report would have appeared. Local court officials are appointed by people's congresses on the same level,[42] so they are in effect answerable to the Party at that level. For courts to be more independent, the tenure of court officials will have to be taken out of the hands of the local Party organisation. There is an avenue through which this could occur. In his report to the 13th Congress of the Chinese Communist Party,[43] Zhao Ziyang called for the formulation of a law on public servants. This would classify public servants in two categories: political and professional. Political cadres would have specified tenures and would in general be subject to government and Party organisations at various levels. Professional cadres, on the other hand, would have permanent tenure, subject no doubt to some concept such as good behaviour in office, and would gain their places through examination. They would be regular bureaucrats. If legal work is classed as professional and not political work – and it will be very interesting to see how or indeed whether this question will be resolved – then we might see more security of tenure for judges and more independence for courts. The experience of Japan, which saw a bureaucratised and fairly independent judiciary very soon after the Meiji Restoration,[44] suggests that such a solution need not be unthinkable for an authoritarian government.

The second challenge is that of raising the power and prestige of local courts. It is not enough that court officials should be able to render judgements that displease local authorities. Many lower level people's court judges, often demobilised army officers, are not especially well trained. The courts find it difficult to get their judgements enforced, as the press frequently reports. It may be that local court power is directly proportional to local Party influence on the court. The local Party organisation is willing to support the court to the extent that it is consulted in the court's activities. Even where the local Party organisation supports the court, however, defendants from other localities often appear able to ignore adverse judgements at will, probably because of the local political support they enjoy.[45]

Laws and regulations in China can be effective only to the extent that some agency has the power to enforce them. Unless the above obstacles can be overcome, then the kind of laws that are typically assigned to courts for enforcement – juridical laws – will be ineffective, and the programme of economic reform will not be able to rely on such laws. Effective legal regulation will not be able to move beyond bureaucratic laws. Such laws are most effective within the bureaucracy responsible for them. As a result, disputes crossing bureaucratic boundaries will have to be resolved in the traditional way: by bargaining. But the bargaining power of the parties will be determined by the political and economic resources available to them, not by a set of legal entitlements.

ABBREVIATIONS

BR	Beijing Review
CD	China Daily
CQ	China Quarterly
FBIS	Foreign Broadcast Information Service, *Daily Report: China*
FEER	Far Eastern Economic Review
FZRB	Fazhi Ribao [Legal System Daily]
GWYGB	*Zhonghua Renmin Gongheguo Guowuyuan Gongbao* [People's Republic of China State Council Gazette]

JJF	*Jingji Fa* [Economic Law]
JLDX	*Jilin Daxue Shehui Kexue Xuebao* [Jilin University Journal of Social Science]
JNXB	*Jinan Xuebao (Zhexue Shehui Kexue)* [Journal of Jinan University (Philosophy and Social Sciences)]
JPRS: PSMA	Joint Publications Research Service, *China Report: Political, Sociological and Military Affairs*
RMRB	*Renmin Ribao* [People's Daily]
RMWX	*Renmin Wenxue* [People's Literature]
SHKX	*Shehui Kexue* [Social Sciences]
SWB	British Broadcasting Corporation, *Summary of World Broadcasts, Part III: The Far East*
ZFYJ	*Zhengfa Yanjiu* [Political and Legal Studies]
ZGQYJ	*Zhongguo Qiyejia* [The Chinese Entrepreneur]
ZGFZB	*Zhongguo Fazhi Bao* [Chinese Legal System News]
ZXYJ	*Zhexue Yanjiu* [Studies in Philosophy].

NOTES

1. The locus classicus for this view is Lenin:
   Dictatorship is rule based directly upon force and unrestricted by any laws.

   The revolutionary dictatorship of the proletariat is rule won and maintained by the use of violence by the proletariat against the bourgeoisie, rule that is unrestricted by any laws.
   V. I. Lenin, 'The Proletarian Revolution and the Renegade Kautsky', in Robert C. Tucker (ed.), *The Lenin Anthology* (New York: W.W. Norton & Co., 1975) p. 466.
2. See, for example, Wang Jiafu and Hsia Shuhua, 'Carry Forward Democracy, Establish a Sound Judicial System, and Speed Up the Realization of the Four Modernizations', ZXYJ, no. 8, 1979, translated in FBIS: PSMA, no. 39, 3 December 1979, pp. 9–23.
3. It might be more appropriate to speak of the formation of the legal system rather than its reformation. The word *jianshe* ('establishment' or 'construction') is applied to the legal system far more often than the word *gaige* ('reform'), while *gaige* is the favoured word used to describe changes in the economic or political system.
4. 'China's Socialist Legal System', BR, 12 January 1979, p. 30.
5. One writer characterises 'the different branches, vertical or horizontal, of the administration . . . as many little independent 'kingdoms' each following its own objectives . . .' Wojtek Zafanolli, 'A Brief Outline of China's Second Economy', in Stephan Feuchtwang, Athar Hussain and Thierry Pairault (eds.), *Transforming China's Economy in the Eighties*, vol. 2 (London: Zed Books, 1988) p. 150.
6. One consequence of the newness of the government's stress on

legislation and other types of formal rule-making is that the legal consequences of attaching a particular label to a document cannot be spelled out with certainty. Chinese government usage has frequently been inconsistent. The following can be no more than a superficial guide.

Theoretically, the constitution (*xian fa*) is supreme. Next in authority are laws (*fa*) and decrees (*faling*) issued by the National People's Congress or its Standing Committee. Then come regulations (*tiaoli*), rules (*guiding*), or *banfa* (procedures), in descending order of generality, enacted by the State Council or its ministries. The generic term for such administrative rules and regulations is *fagui*. (Regulations governing State Council documents were issued only in 1987 – see 'Provisional Regulations on the Formulation Process for Administrative *Fagui*', 21 April 1987, ZGFZB, 11 May 1987, p. 2). Finally, local governments may issue their own rules and regulations provided they do not conflict with any of the above.

This neat formal structure has several problems, but limitations of space do not allow me to discuss them here.

7. In a similar vein, an article in the *Legal System Daily* pointed out that many laws were virtually unenforceable because they were so vague and general as to amount to little more than mere 'declarations'. See 'A discussion of the problem that 'law has no effect when it is violated by the multitude', FZRB, 27 June 1988, p. 1.

8. 'State Economic Commission and State Commission on System Reform Provisional Rules on Several Problems relating to Enlivening Large and Medium-sized State-owned Industrial Enterprises', GWYGB, no. 28 (20 October 1985) p. 951.

9. See, for example, Article 12, 'Law of the PRC on economic contracts involving foreign interests', RMRB, 22 March, 1985, p. 2 (hereinafter the 'Foreign Economic Contract Law'.)

10. See, for example, Article 26 of the 'Provisional Rules on the Contracting-Out Management System for Industrial Enterprises Owned by the Whole People', GWYGB no. 5 (15 March 1988).

11. 'Min fa tong ze' [General principles of civil law] GWYGB, no. 12 (20 May 1986) p. 371.

12. See John Hazard's comments in his 'Socialism, Legalisation and Delegalisation', in Terence Daintith (ed.), *Law As an Instrument of Economic Policy: Comparative and Critical Approaches* (Berlin & New York: de Gruyter, 1987) pp. 277–78.

13. See William Byrd and Gene Tidrick, 'Factor Allocation and Enterprise Incentives', in Gene Tidrick and Chen Jiyuan (eds.), *China's Industrial Reform* (Oxford University Press 1987) p. 81. Regulatory capture is the term used to describe what happens when a regulatory agency ends up representing the interests of those it is ostensibly regulating.

14. Note that whereas the central government does not purport to guarantee the implementation of decisions made by, say, a *xian*-level people's

congress, it does make this guarantee with respect to decisions of *xian*-level people's courts. See, for example, the case reported in 'Dawu *Xian* court persists in local protectionism, delays for three years and refuses to co-operate in executing a judgement from an outside locality', FZRB, 4 June 1988, p. 1.

15. Numerous press reports make this complaint. See, for example, 'Enforcement of Law Urged'. CD, 12 April 1986, p. 5; 'More Muscle Waged [sic] in Enforcing Laws', CD, 3 October 1985, p. 1; 'Legal adviser', ZGFZB, 21 October 1985, p. 3; 'The antennae of stopping the unlawful occupation of land have extended into every corner', FZRB, 14 June 1988, p. 1.

16. See the review article by William Jones, 'On the Campaign Trail in China', *Review of Socialist Law*, vol. 5 (1979) p. 457.

17. 'Enterprise bankruptcy law of the People's Republic of China'. GWYGB, no. 33 (20 December 1986) p. 979.

18. For instance, the State Council's 1983 'Provincial Regulations on State-Owned Industrial Enterprises' provided for the closing of loss-making enterprises (Article 20) and contemplated the cancellation of contracts and obligations (Article 21). See *Guoying gongye qiye zanxing tiaoli* 1 April 1983, in *Zhonghua Renmin Gongheguo Fagui Huibian 1983 nian 1 yue–12 yue* [Collected Laws and Rules of the People's Republic of China, January–December 1983] (Beijing: Falüchubanshe, 1986) pp. 383–399.

19. See Xiao Genbao, 'How the court handled a case of enterprise liabilities exceeding assets', ZGFZB, 10 July 1985, p. 3. In this case, the court took charge of the assets, assigned priorities among various classes of creditors, and paid off claims proportionately.

20. 'Shenyang City trial rules concerning the handling of the bankruptcy and closing of urban industrial enterprises under collective ownership'. ZGQYJ, no. 1 (1986) p. 55 (hereinafter the 'Trial Rules'). The trial rules were promulgated on 9 February 1985. See Qiao Mai, 'The "explosive" experiment of the explosion prevention [equipment] plant', RMWX, no. 4 (1987) p. 82.

21. Even before the demonstrations of spring, 1989, and the subsequent crackdown and purge of reformers, the Bankruptcy Law had already shown itself to be essentially a dead letter. Its prospects were not enhanced by the disappearance and probable arrest after June 4th of its leading advocate, Cao Siyuan. See Nicholas Kristof, 'Turmoil in China', *New York Times*, 13 June 1989, p. A1, col. 2.

22. As Barrington Moore points out, 'urban workers resemble a praetorian guard for socialism, and it is risky to discipline the praetorian guard'. Barrington Moore, Jr., *Authority and Inequality Under Capitalism and Socialism* (Oxford: Clarendon Press, 1987) p. 99.

23. A detailed account of the prelude to and aftermath of the bankruptcy of the Explosion Prevention Equipment Plant can be found in Qiao Mai, *op. cit.*

24. See *Caizheng Bu guanyu guoying qiye li gai shui shixing banfa* [Ministry

of Finance trial procedures for (the implementation of) the tax-for-profit system in state-run enterprises], 12 April 1983, in *1984 Zhongguo Jingji Nianjian* [Almanac of China's economy 1984] (Beijing: Jingji guanli zazhishe, 1984) sec. IX, pp. 83–84; also *Zhonghua Renmin Gongheguo Jingji Da Shi Ji (1949 nian 10 yue–1984 nian 9 yue)* [Record of important events in the economy of the People's Republic of China (October 1949–September 1984)] (Beijing: Beijing chubanshe, 1985) p. 614.

25. See Max Wilkinson, 'The Next Stage After Profit and Incentives', *Financial Times* (London) 18 December 1987, sec. II, p. 12, col. 5; Fred C. Hung & Calla Wiemer, 'The Course of China's Economic Reforms 1978–1985', *Journal of Oriental Studies*, vol. 23, no. 1 (1985) p. 73.

26. See Janos Kornai, 'The Dual Dependence of the State-Owned Firm in Hungary', in Gene Tidrick and Chen Jiyuan (eds), *op. cit.*, p. 327.

27. Gene Tidrick, 'Planning and Supply', in Gene Tidrick and Chen Jiyuan (eds), *op. cit.*, pp. 198–99 (emphasis added; footnote omitted).

28. See Enterprise Bankruptcy Law, *op. cit.*, Article 3 (applying the law to enterprises that have suffered losses due to poor management); Trial Rules, *op. cit.*, Article 2 (applying the law to enterprises with severe 'non-policy losses'). Policy losses are those due to the economic structure, such as the deficits caused by irrational prices, or caused by managers' lack of control over the quality of raw materials the enterprise receives under the plan or the size and quality of the work force. Business losses are losses due to the incorrect use of what decision-making power the management does have. Needless to say, there will be considerable room for argument over how to characterise any particular loss item.

29. For this line or argument, see Xu Guanglin, 'An inquiry into relevant problems of legal methods in economic management', JLDX, no. 6 (1986) p. 59, reprinted in JJF, no. 2 (1987) p. 33.

30. See *Guanyu zhengshou shaoyou tebie shui de shixing guiding* [Trial rules concerning the collection of special taxes on fuel oil], in *1983 Zhongguo Jingji Nianjian* [Almanac of China's economy 1983] (Beijing: Jingji guanli zazhishe, 1983) sec. VIII, p. 64.

31. See *Guowuyuan guanyu guoying qiye fafang jiangjin youguan wenti de tongzhi* [State Council notice on questions relating to the issuance of bonuses by state-owned enterprises], GWYGB, no. 8 (10 May 1984) p. 251; *Guoying qiye jiangjin shui zanxing guiding* [Provisional rules on the taxation of bonuses in state-owned enterprises], GWYGB, no. 20 (30 July 1985) p. 723; *Guoying qiye gongzi tiaojie shui zanxing guiding* [Provisional rules on the wage adjustment tax in state-owned enterprises], GWYGB, no. 20 (30 July 1985) p. 725.

32. See 'Ministry of Finance notice on resolutely preventing the use of holidays as an excuse for the excessive issue of bonuses, subsidies, and materials', GWYGB, no. 25 (20 September 1985) p. 862.

33. See 'Provisional procedures for the control of wage funds', GWYGB, no. 29 (30 October 1985) p. 979.

34. See 'State Council Office notice on firmly prohibiting the mutual sending of wall calendars', GWYGB, no. 7 (30 March 1987) p. 264.
35. See 'Several rules on strengthening control over the price of means of production and prohibiting the uncontrolled raising of prices and collection of fees, GWYGB, no. 12 (25 May 1987) p. 435.
36. See 'Ministry of Commerce notice on correcting the practice of small state-owned commercial enterprises of changing their line of business at will and neglecting trade in small commodities'. GWYGB, no. 19 (20 July 1985) p. 716.
37. The problem is a familiar one in Western jurisprudence and political philosophy. Is it fairer to treat unequals as if they were equals, or to recognise the inequality? Does the source of the inequality make any difference? The issue has perhaps been posed most poignantly in the debate over affirmative action in the United States. See *Regents of the University of California v. Bakke*, 438 U.S. 265 (1978), and especially Justice Blackmun's dissent, where he holds that '[i]n order to get beyond racism, we must first take account of race . . . . And in order to treat some persons equally, we must treat them differently'.
38. This practice, far from being irregular, has in fact been given a name: '*shuji pi'an*' (approval of cases by the [local Party] secretary). See generally Shao-chuan Leng and Hungdah Chiu, *Criminal Justice in Post-Mao China* (Albany: State University of New York Press, 1985) pp. 22–24.
39. For example, see Dong Likun, 'Nobody can be above the law', SHKX, no. 1 (1980) p. 10.
40. See Shao-chuan Leng and Hungdah Chiu, *op. cit.* p. 99. In his report to the Beijing City Conference on Criminal Adjudication Work, Jiang Hua, the President of the Supreme People's Court, noted that the abolition of the practice had been called for in a Central Committee document entitled 'Directive of the Central Committee of the Chinese Communist Party on Resolutely Guaranteeing the Genuine Implementation of the Criminal Law and the Criminal Procedure Law'. See 'Abolish the practice of the Party Committee examining and approving cases, guarantee independent adjudication by the courts according to law', RMRB, 25 August 1980, p. 1.
41. See The Beijing Municipal [Party] Committee in recent years no longer examines and approves cases, FZRB, 1 February 88, p. 1.
42. See Articles 35 and 36 of the Organic Law of the People's Courts of the People's Republic of China, *Zhonghua Renmin Gongheguo Fagui Huibian 1979 nian 1 yue–12 yue* [Collected Laws and Regulations of the People's Republic of China, January–December 1979] (Beijing: Falü chubanshe, 1986) pp. 37–38.
43. Zhao Ziyang, 'Advance Along the Road of Socialism with Chinese Characteristics', BR, vol. 30, no. 45 (9–15 November 1987) pp. I–XXVII.
44. See Barbara Teters, 'The Otsu Affair: The Formation of Japan's Judicial

Conscience', in David Wurfel (ed.), *Meiji Japan's Centennial: Aspects of Political Thought and Action* (Lawrence, Kansas: University of Kansas Press, 1971) pp. 36–63.

45. Guangdong defendants seem to be particularly brazen in this regard. See 'Uphold the dignity of the law; do not fear a thousand difficulties and ten thousand dangers'. FZRB, 23 May 1988, p. 1. For an example from Hubei, see 'Dawu Xian court persists in local protectionism, delays for three years and refuses to co-operate in executing a judgement from an outside locality', FZRB, 4 June 1988, p. 1.

Part 3
Decentralisation and the Local State

Part 3
Decentralisation
and the Local
State

9 Basic-Level Local Government and Economic Reform in Urban China

Gordon White

1 INTRODUCTION: THE ECONOMIC REFORM PROGRAMME AND THE ISSUE OF DECENTRALISATION

The central focus of this paper is on the relationship between China's market-oriented economic reforms and the changing role of urban local government. One would expect that the radical changes envisaged in the operation of the economy would have major implications for government in general and for local government in particular especially so in a country the size of China where 'local' governments often oversee communities larger than most national governments elsewhere. How have the economic reformers perceived the links between changes in the economic and governmental system in China's cities and what changes have taken place in the role and structure of urban local government during the era of post-Mao economic reform since 1978?[1]

'Decentralisation' has been one of the central features of the programme of economic system reform launched by the Chinese Communist Party (CCP) leadership at the cardinal Third Plenum of its Central Committee in December 1978. However, the exact meaning of 'decentralisation' has remained somewhat elusive and the attitude of economic reformers has been markedly ambivalent. We can distinguish two basic types of decentralisation: administrative decentralisation whereby powers are devolved to lower levels of administration (local governments and/or local branches of central agencies) and economic decentralisation whereby powers of planning, coordination and management are devolved from administrative units at any level to enterprises.[2] During the Maoist period (1958–76), *administrative decentralisation* was the major method adopted to tackle perceived problems arising from over-centralisation in the system of

215

economic planning and management, the period being characterised by an undulation between phases of administrative decentralisation (1958 and 1970) and recentralisation (the early 1960s); *economic decentralisation* gained a tenuous foothold in the early 1960s but was then washed away by the Cultural Revolution (for critical reviews of this experience, see Ji and Rong 1979 and He 1979).

Post-Mao economic reformers tend to view administrative decentralisation, the transfer of power to local governments and branch agencies, with suspicion: as an expression of the previous 'Maoist' approach to reform which, in their opinion, lost some of the advantages of centralisation while at the same time both creating dislocation and duplication in the planning system and maintaining the economically irrational principle of bureaucratic domination over enterprises.[3] In their mind, the direct subordination of enterprises to government was unwise, regardless of the level of government involved. The key link in meaningful reform, therefore, was economic decentralisation, increasing the decision-making power of enterprises.[4]

On the other hand, reformers have recognised that a measure of administrative decentralisation to local governments can play some role in remedying the defects of the previous system of central planning. While certain key areas of macro-economic decision and regulation should still be reserved for the Centre, reformers admit that there are economic benefits to be reaped from devolution of certain decisions which Beijing is unable to handle, and from a clearer and more rational division of labour between levels of government. On the other hand, they emphasise that administrative decentralisation should not be accorded the prime priority and, to the extent that it did take place, should be accompanied by a process of economic decentralisation at the local level, so that local governments should exercise their economic powers in a new way, indirectly rather than directly, using economic policy mechanisms not administrative fiat. Implicit in the thinking of the economic reformers, therefore, was a notion of reforming local government itself, specifically in the way it engaged in economic planning and management. Without such changes, greater power for local governments might well pose greater obstacles to the economic reform process.

The issue of a more rational division of labour between central and local governments (and between layers of local government) goes beyond mere questions of economic planning and management. Implicit in the arguments of reform spokespeople was the idea that local governments should be neither an instrument nor a replica of central government. If they opposed local subordination to the dictates of centralised economic planning, they also opposed the tendency for local government to set up 'independent kingdoms' which led to regional autarky and a fragmentation of the national planning system. Liu Shinian (1980, p. 17), for example, argues that local governments have functions different from central government: first, responsibility for forms of production other than state, i.e. collective or private business. Since one of the basic goals of the economic reformers has been to create a more balanced economic structure by encouraging non-state enterprise, the regulatory burden of local governments would be expected to increase in tandem; second, 'services related to the daily life of the people', a diverse category which includes the need to encourage the service sector which had long lagged behind industry and to provide urban public utilities such as water, energy and housing; third, to handle physical planning of urban areas with attention to environmental issues. The logic of the economic reforms, moreover, also meant that local governments would take on greater welfare functions in addition to their traditional responsibility for education and health. Reformers argued that welfare functions previously undertaken by enterprises – such as housing, labour insurance, pensions and health insurance – should gradually be 'externalised', becoming the responsibility of local governments.

A successful economic reform, therefore, would embody sweeping changes in the nature, role and context of local governments, especially in the urban areas. Their economic environment would become more complex and their welfare responsibilities would increase. Moreover, they are on the front line in the implementation of the reform programme and thus responsible for handling the social tensions which have arisen from some of its ill effects – inflation, unemployment, bankruptcy, 'speculation', corruption and so on. These tensions mounted as the reforms ran into increasing difficulties in the mid-1980s, culminating in the traumatic events in Beijing during April–June 1989, which found expression in most large cities across the nation.

The implications of economic reform are highly complex, therefore, and for reasons of economy and precision, this study has limited its attention in three ways: first, to the urban sector because the situation in the urban and rural areas is substantially different and because the issue of urban local government is itself highly complex; second, within the multi-layered system of local governments, to basic-level local government, a category which is itself difficult enough to pinpoint, as we shall see; third, to the issue of links between local government and economic reform. The issue of reforming local government has many facets, of which some of the most important are proposals and/or attempts to change local political institutions, notably the people's representative congresses. Benewick addresses these issues in his paper in this volume, so I shall concentrate here on the role of basic-level urban government in planning and managing the local economy.

Systematic thinking in China about either local government in general and its changing role in the context of economic reform was scarce until the mid-1980s. In 1986, the issue received some attention during the debate on 'political system reform' in the latter part of the year. One important impediment to systematic analysis of this issue has been the lack of an intellectual constituency with the responsibility to investigate the issue. In the early years of reform, thinking about government-economy relations was dominated by two groups: the proliferating economists who have concentrated on economic analysis and have had little systematic to say about government and still less about local government, and party spokespeople who have reserved the right to monopolise discussion of 'political' issues and, with a few exceptions, have been slow to investigate avenues for the throughgoing reform of political and administrative institutions. In the mid-1980s, however, a small group of political scientists emerged across the nation, one of whose research foci was the issue of local government. Writing on administrative and political reform expanded gradually, for example, in new journals such as *Political Studies Research* [Zhengzhixue Yanjiu], edited by the Institute of Political Studies of the Chinese Academy of Social Sciences in Beijing. The issue of local government reform was the subject of two large symposia, one in Wuhan in December 1984 on the subject of 'Local Government and People's Representatives' and the other in Chongqing in December 1985 on the general issue of local government reform.[5] In 1986, the issue of the relationship between 'economic system reform' and 'political system reform' was for the first time given a major role on the official agenda, an event which encouraged an outpouring of opinions and proposals. In spite of this recent activity, however, analysis of local government reform still remained in its infancy and few systematic proposals for reform received a public airing.[6] With the onset of the anti 'bourgeois liberalisation' campaigns of 1987 and 1989, moreover, the progress on this issue has come to a standstill. However, some changes have already taken place and many of the important issues have at least been put on the table. This paper will be dealing with this initial phase of intellectual development and policy review in the mid-1980s, basing itself on a research trip to China in mid-1986[7] and on the writings of Chinese scholars and other experts during the period.

2   THE NATURE OF BASIC-LEVEL URBAN GOVERNMENT

China's state system is complex and the term 'local government' covers a number of levels, as we can see in Figure 9.1, from province down to street

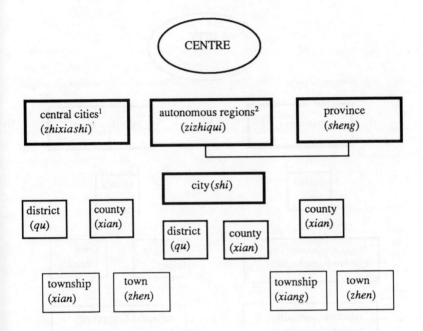

NOTES:
1. There are three large cities which are directly administered by the Centre (Beijing, Shanghai and Tianjin) and thus equivalent to the province.
2. These are the equivalent of the province in the national minority areas. There are similar differences in labelling at lower levels but these have been ommitted for the sake of simplicity.

FIGURE 9.1 *The structure of China's governmental system*

or neighbourhood office (*jiedao banshichu*) in the cities to the township (*xiang*) or town (*zhen*) in the countryside. To simplify matters, we have only included in Figure 9.1 those levels which are units of both politics and administration – by politics, we mean that they have a people's representative congress (PRC). There are or have been certain levels – between centre and province ('districts', *diqu*), province and county ('special districts' or 'prefectures', *zhuanqu*), county and township (also 'districts', *diqu*) and under the urban district (the street or neighbourhood office) – which are bureaucratic extensions of the level immediately above and have no corresponding organs of political representation.

This distinction is important in defining the main focus of this paper, 'basic-level urban government'. Formally speaking (i.e. according to Article 95 of the state Constitution of 1982), [8] 'basic-level government' (*jiceng*

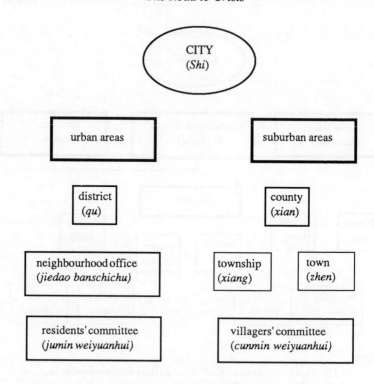

FIGURE 9.2 *The structure of urban local government*

zhengquan) is at the urban district level (*qu*) in large cities (and counties responsible for suburban areas) and the city itself (*shi*) in small cities. Since this research has mainly been conducted in larger cities, we are thus mainly interested in the urban *district*. This is a unit of local government in both political (it has a people's congress) and administrative senses. Below it, however, is the urban street or neighbourhood office which formally speaking is a bureaucratic organ subordinate to the district, an 'agency' (*paichu jigou*) not an instrument of political and governmental power in its own right. The situation is further complicated by the presence of another level of urban organisation beneath the neighbourhood, the 'residents' committees' (*jumin weiyuanhui*) which formally (according to Article 111 of the state Constitution) are 'mass self-managing organisations at the basic level' i.e. not organs of governmental but popular power (the equivalent of 'villagers committees' [*cunmin weiyuanhui*] in the countryside). Figure 9.2 depicts these levels in a typical large city.

These formal distinctions, however, are a rather feeble guide to reality. From the political point of view, the key institution at the local level is the party not the people's congress and this permeates the hierarchy; from an administrative point of view, each level is enmeshed in a hierarchical bureaucratic system regardless of its formal status as governmental or non-governmental. Thus each qualifies, in different ways, for the title of 'basic-level local government'.

This ambiguity has not escaped the attention of China's new generation of political scientists. A debate about the nature of basic-level urban government has sparked several important issues. Since the realities of urban government diverge from the formal situation, they have inquired as to how they can they be brought into closer harmony. The *role of the neighbourhood office* is of particular importance here since its role has expanded enormously since its formal tasks were set out in 1954 and, in the words of one commentator, 'it no longer has the character of an agency; in reality it plays the role of basic-level urban government' (Bai Yihua, 1986, pp. 389–90). This author continues by citing the case of a neighbourhood office in Xian:

> [It has] sixty-five work tasks in all: from productive construction to the people's livelihood, from public order and security to environmental health, from culture and education to employment, including everything from politics to economics, culture, health, etc. Whatever organs the city or district has, the neighbourhood office has as many tasks; whatever departments the district has, the office has as many organisations. According to investigations in all localities, the situation of neighbourhood offices across the nation is basically the same. Some office cadres say: 'Apart from not having a people's representative congress, we handle as much work [as levels which do]'.

The most commonly proposed method to remedy this anomaly is the establishment of a fully constituted 'people's government', including a representative congress, at the neighbourhood level. Thus the neighbourhood would become a distinct political, administrative and financial level of government. This proposal is not only designed to recognise the wide-ranging governmental functions of the neighbourhood offices, but also argues that the neighbourhood is a more appropriate scale for basic-level urban government, the district being far too large.

Bai Yihua (1986, p. 388) cites statistics to support this argument. In 1984 there were 149 small cities (without subordinate districts) and 595 urban districts, each with an average of ten subordinate neighbourhood offices and with populations ranging from 200,000 to 500,000. In Beijing, for example, each district supervised nine neighbourhoods on average and had an average population of 547,600 – the largest district, Chaoyang, had a population of over one million. In the smaller city of Shijiazhuang in Hebei province, each of the six districts (with an average of 5.3 neighbourhoods each) had an average of 175,000 population (the smallest being 130,000). The results of this local gigantism were that basic-level governments found it difficult to deal with the complexity of tasks they faced. Most Chinese commentators agree that the functions of urban governments had gradually intensified since their establishment in the 1950s. As we have already suggested, moreover, the economic reforms of the post-Mao era have accelerated this process, not only increasing the regulative burdens of urban governments but making their environments more complex and difficult to manage. In consequence, the inadequacies of urban governments have become more obvious and the level of discontent among the urban population has increased (for example, Bai 1986, p. 388), a not inconsiderable impetus behind the popular protests of April–June 1989.

While the issue of scale is important to economic reformers who are concerned about the regulative capacities of urban government, it is also important to political reformers bent on increasing democratisation and governmental accountability who feel that district governments are 'too far from the masses'. The establishment of a people's congress at the street/neighbourhood level and the latter's formal constitution as 'basic-level urban government' is seen as an important step towards these political goals.

Clearly there are different views on this issue and as of mid-1986 the matter was still in the early stages of investigation and discussion (for a review, see White and Benewick 1986). Answers vary according to the extent to which the issue is being analysed within the narrower framework of economic reform or the broader framework of both economic and political reform – as late as 1986 discussion still tended to focus on the former. As an official of the Shandong Province Civil Affairs Bureau remarked, 'there is a desire to send power down in the cities, but so far it has been concentrated on economic issues, not political-administrative' (ibid.). There are also differences within and between people in different institutional contexts: academic experts, experts in government bureaux charged with handling the issue (notably civil affairs departments), cadres in various levels of urban government and urban residents themselves. In the 1985 Chongqing symposium on local government, for example, Bai Yihua's emphasis on the need to reconstitute the neighbourhood was not shared by other participants. For example, Li and Niu (1986) stressed the need to strengthen the operation of the urban district, particularly in relation to its superior, the city government, and to clarify and reform the division of labour between the district and its neighbourhood offices in ways which give the latter more power and responsibility – however, the neighbourhood office would still remain a mere 'agency' of the district. From their perspective, greater autonomy for the neighbourhood office combined with a more rational organisational set-up and a better personnel system could improve the managerial capacity of existing basic-level institutions; problems of responsiveness and accountability could be tackled through a more effective people's representative congress at the district level.

Moreover, there is clearly concern, shared by people in different circles, that the establishment of the neighbourhood as a level of government in its own right would 'damage the unity of city government'. Experts in the Institute of Jurisprudence of the Shanghai branch of the Chinese Academy of Social Sciences, interviewed in mid-1986, thought that it would make urban planning, economic management and financial coordination more difficult (White and Benewick 1986, p. 65).

In our opinion, if [the neighbourhood office] becomes a level of government, there will be contradictions between neighbourhoods, for example about widening roads, sewerage, housing, and so on. Each neighbourhood can decide and this may be against the interests of other neighbourhoods, therefore more trouble.

Neighbourhood cadres seem divided on the issue. For example, the middle-aged director of the Yuyuan Neighbourhood Office in Shanghai's Jingan District opposed the reform but admitted that some of his younger colleagues were in favour.

Most comrades don't approve of this because of the convenience of transportation which depends on unified planning. If we become a unit of government, the masses will raise many opinions which we could not deal with within this small area . . . For a simple example, take the problem of a new toilet. It needs land which involves the District Real Estate Bureau and Environment Bureau, and so on. At present, it is the district head who convenes a conference of relevant agencies and he can take the decision.

Proponents of the reform have argued on the contrary that the closer proximity of the neighbourhood to the people will enable local government officials to meet the needs and solve the problems of their constituents more effectively. It is also argued that it will facilitate management of local business and enable the constituent Residents' Committees to play a greater role in 'supervising government organs' (Chen Hefu 1986, p. 383).

By mid-1986 the argument had not been resolved and experiments were under way to provide evidence on potential costs or benefits. An experiment in Nanjing has devolved certain financial powers and governmental functions (such as looking after small roads, house and school repairs, and administration of some primary schools) to the neighbourhood office. It appears that the constituency against reform was still very strong. Some of the reformers, moreover, recognise that such a reform at the neighbourhood level cannot be undertaken before reforms at higher levels, notably in relations between the city and district levels (White and Benewick 1986, p. 65) – I shall deal with this question below.

Another important issue involved in the debate about what constitutes the 'basic-level' in the cities is the *role of the residents' committees* and their relationship with local government institutions at the neighbourhood and district levels.[9] As we clarified earlier, urban residents' committees are formally classified as 'non-governmental' institutions, organs of direct as opposed to representative democracy, theoretically operating according to the three principles of 'self-service, self-management and self-education' (White and Benewick 1986, p. 33). From a long term point of view, they are nascent tutelary institutions which will create a 'democratic spirit', *minzhu yishi*, and train the population to bring about the ultimate abolition of the state (ibid., p. 38). Like neighbourhood organisations, their formal functions are defined by regulations issued in 1954 and were originally confined to maintaining public order and basic welfare; like neighbourhood offices, their functions have proliferated since the 1950s. They have also in effect become *agents* of local government; in other words, their relationship to the neighbourhood office has become rather like the latter's relationship with the district, as yet another level in an integrated bureaucratic hierarchy. In financial terms, most of their revenue comes from the neighbourhood office. In consequence, their independence has been compromised and they have fallen under the direct 'leadership' (*lingdao*) of neighbourhood offices rather than indirect 'guidance' (*zhidao*) as originally intended.[10] A researcher in Shandong CASS put the matter as follows (ibid., p. 38):

> Our research concentrates on the relationship between [residents' committees] and local government. The Constitution says it is guidance, i.e. the latter cannot give them direct orders. But in reality some tasks cannot be done through guidance (taxes, production planning, family planning) – they need orders. But this is hardly 'self-government', is it?

In short, they have become the 'hands and feet of local government, an agency for everything and everyone'. Where their functions have proliferated, moreover, they have become 'bureaucratised' (*jiguanhua*), their internal structure taking on the formal characteristics of a government organisation (Liu Lansheng 1985, p. 302). In effect, it was the residents' committees which had become 'basic-level government' in the cities. This process of 'governmentalisation' apart, moreover, residents committees are not constituted so as to strengthen their formal function of democratic 'self-government': their cadres are overwhelmingly retired people, particularly older women. This reflects the fact that for most economically active people, the most important sphere of life is their place of work not their place of residence; they are thus unlikely to get involved in residents' committees which, from the point of view of establishing viable basic-level democratic institutions, are marginalised in consequence.

From the point of view of the system of urban government, however, they are important institutions. They vary in size (in large cities such as Beijing and Tianjin they have an average of about 2 000 inhabitants) and consequently in degree of structural diversification (larger ones have an array of committees and subcommittees for specific functions). Their functions are *very* wide-ranging, as wide if not wider than the neighbourhood office: since the residents' committee not only has its own responsibilities, but has to implement tasks sent down not merely by neighbourhood offices but other 'systems' such as family planning and public security. Hence the phrase used to describe their role; 'On top a thousand threads, at the bottom a single needle' (Chen Hefu, 1986, p. 383). Residents' committees have responsibilities which are economic (running small-scale services and providing employment for local youth, housewives and retirees), political (disseminating current propaganda, 'reflecting the opinions of the masses' to higher levels of government and assisting the public security bureau to keep order), legal (notably the organisation of mediation committees to adjudicate local disputes and avoid recourse to the legal system proper) and social (providing basic health-care, carrying out campaigns for public health, keeping their area clean, implementing the official 'one-child family' policy in family planning and making special provisions for the needs and problems of target groups, notably children, the disabled and old age pensioners) (for a detailed account of a residents' committee in Jinan, see White and Benewick 1986, pp. 46–8).

Academic reformers see the problem of reforming residents' committees as quite the opposite of the neighbourhood office: in the latter case, reforms are designed to constitute it as a distinct unit of local government; in the former case, they should aim to 'deconstitute' it as a unit of government, by simplifying and codifying its functions and attempting to free it from the grasp of local government and establish its originally intended character as a 'self-governing' organisation.[11] They also propose that its aging cadre force be replenished by younger, more educated cadres drawn from local schools and industry (Liu Lansheng 1985, pp. 303–4, White and Benewick 1986, p. 38). It appears that, while these ideas may find some favour with overburdened residents' committee cadres, officials in local government are unsympathetic since the residents' committees are a convenient, indeed irreplaceable, instrument of policy implementation; the latter favour the directness and certainties of 'leadership' over the subtleties and hypotheticals of 'guidance', though they are of course willing to preach the latter while practising the former. Some hedge their bets and argue that the residents' committee has a dual role, as a 'mass self-governing organisation' and as 'agency of basic-level local government' (Liu Lansheng, 1985, p. 302). Given these constraints, the political impetus for any significant 'emancipation' of the residents' committees seems unlikely. Thus when the draft organic law for residents' committees was made public in August, 1989, in the wake of the urban disturbances of April–June that year, their role as an *instrument* of urban government received particular stress (*SWB* 0550, September 1989).

We must conclude, therefore, that our search for 'urban basic-level government' is not an easy one: formally it is the district level but in real terms it must include the neighbourhood offices and residents' committees. This confusion reflects the anomalous evolution of urban government over the past three decades, a process intensified by the post-Mao economic reforms, for as their environments have grown more complex and the demands upon them more pressing, the functions of basic-level urban governments have expanded far beyond their original remits established in the mid-1950s. There is a pressing need to reassess the situation and initiate reforms which clarify and codify the respective roles of different organisations against the background of an evolving urban 'socialist planned commodity economy'.

It is in this context that I shall investigate certain dimensions of local government reform in the sections that follow. I intend to explore the changing context of, and challenges to, basic-level urban government in the era of economic reform; to describe the structural reforms proposed and initiated to meet these changes and assess their impact on policy and institutions; also to discover the extent of actual changes which have occurred in an *ad hoc* incremental way rather than as a result of conscious policy. Though the analysis will of necessity range across the various levels described above – from residents' committees up to municipality – I shall focus on the specific role of the urban *district* given its formal importance as the basic-level of urban government, its real importance as the crucial link between the city-level administration and its component parts, and the comparative lack of previous scholarly work on the subject.

3 ECONOMIC REFORM AND REFORM OF URBAN GOVERNMENT

There is wide agreement among both analysts and local officials in China that the economic reforms have increased the administrative and managerial burdens of local governments in general and urban governments in particular. The programme of economic 'readjustment' since the late 1970s has changed the structure of urban economies in ways which make them more dynamic and diverse: by encouraging a shift from industry to commerce and services, and from state to collective or private firms. Urban districts and their subordinate neighbourhood offices and residents' committees have prime responsibility for the new priority sectors. The 'readjustment' has also brought a reallocation of public investment priorities away from industry and production generally towards social consumption, the main priority being housing but also attention to basic urban services and environmental issues. Again, these are a prime responsibility of urban governments.

In the face of these burgeoning tasks, reformers have recommended changes in the role and nature of local governments along several dimensions: (a) strengthening the general principle of the horizontal (*kuai*) as opposed to vertical (*tiao*) principle of administrative coordination by increasing the financial and managerial autonomy of local governments; (b) restructuring the organisational systems of local government to produce a more streamlined, relevant and efficient administrative apparatus; (c) changing the role of the government in economic management from direct control of the micro-economy to indirect macro-economic regulation by 'separating government and enterprise'. Let us discuss these areas of reform in turn.

(a) Decentralisation and Local Autonomy

It is generally accepted that the economic reforms have led to greater power for local authorities in a number of respects, though the situation has varied over phases (Wong, 1987). This not only reflects the desire for selective decentralisation on the part of central decision-makers but also the ambitions of local governments themselves who see the reforms as both the reason and the opportunity to increase their sphere of operation and autonomy.

The issue of local decentralisation is complex. First, it is important to clarify which particular activities and powers are being devolved: managerial responsibilities for enterprises formerly under central control; control over the allocation of material supplies; or greater fiscal and other financial resources. Chinese analysts emphasise the importance of fiscal/financial autonomy and we shall focus on this aspect here. Second, given the basic structural principle of 'dual rule', administrative decentralisation does not necessarily mean devolution to a local entity in the sense of a geographical locality (*kuai*) but may be to a subordinate branch of a central agency within a vertical bureaucratic hierarchy (*tiao*). The relationship between local governments and local functional branch offices is ambiguous and may be contradictory (Shue, 1984a). Third, there is a significant gap between formal and informal decentralisation – notably between the official budgetary system and the existence of various kinds of local 'extra-budgetary funds' not subject to formal controls.

Previous scholarly work has suggested that the economic reforms have brought about a significant increase in both the 'official' and 'unofficial' financial powers of local governments, focussing on the provincial, county and municipal levels (Shue, 1984a; Naughton, 1985; Ferdinand and Wang, 1987; Wong, 1985). A new system of revenue sharing between central authorities and local authorities (province, municipality and county) was introduced: in 1980 this was based on different sources of revenue; in 1983 the principle of division changed to fixed ratios.[12] This led to the retention of greater resources at local levels (particularly city and county) to the detriment of central finances. Central concern over this situation led to efforts at financial recentralisation and a new attempt to define central-local relations based on different kinds of taxes, which came into operation in 1985.[13] The scope of local 'extra-budgetary funds' has also expanded as the economic basis of local governments, light industry, has expanded rapidly, and local authorities have sought to tax or otherwise drain away the 'retained funds' of enterprises which have increased greatly over the past eight years (for the statistical trends in the size and distribution of 'extra-budgetary funds', see State Statistical Bureau 1987, p. 526). Our knowledge of these trends is so far confined to the higher levels of local government – the province, municipality and county. We wish to inquire here whether this process has extended to include urban basic-level government, notably at the district level.

Our research suggests that the trend towards decentralisation, of both functions and finances, has operated between the city and its component parts but that this process, as of 1986 at least, seems more attenuated at the district level than at other levels of local government, notably city and province. Participants in the late 1985 Chongqing forum on local government reform complained that urban districts might be requiring more responsibilities but they were not acquiring more power, particularly financial power (Li and Niu 1986, pp. 393–4). There have been tentative moves, in some larger cities at least, to expand both the responsibility and power of the district. An official in Shanghai's Jingan District described this process of decentralisation as follows:

[In future] we will have functions which originally were exercised by the city: education, culture, sports, real estate, environmental hygiene, gardens and parks, urban construction. These eight bureaux have already had power decentralised to them. Before, the city organised – through *tiao* – urban construction, living quarters construction, health and hygiene, gardens and parks – we had no say. For example, if people wanted a toilet in the past, the district-head had to apply to the city bureau for it. We didn't have the money or the personnel or materials, but we had the duty to maintain environmental sanitation, order, etc. From 1985, this decentralisation began *re* the environment, so our initiative was enlarged. (White and Benewick 1986, pp. 68–9)

1985 also had important implications for the financial powers of this district. First, though their budget was still allocated by the city, they were given discretionary power over a certain proportion. Second, a new revenue-sharing arrangement meant that, if the district's revenue increased in a given year (from greater tax revenue, from increased profits of local enterprises) they were allowed to retain 23.2 per cent for their own use. Similarly, officials of Heping District in Tianjin referred to 'a policy of encouraging the role of the district government' which was able to retain about one-sixth to one-seventh of its income for its own projects (ibid., p. 33). Similarly, officials of Lixia District in Jinan, Shandong province, reported a small increase in their financial powers while recognising that these were still negligible (ibid., p. 44). In each of these cases, moreover, district officials indicated that the trend was towards greater autonomy. In at least one city, Beijing, this process seems further advanced; officials of Xi Cheng district claimed (ibid., p. 18) that their finances were 'relatively independent' with 'a basic right to decide on our expenditures', though this basic right still operated within a context whereby all district income went to the city government and the district received a certain percentage from the latter, this depending on the overall balance of city finances.

There is clearly pressure for greater financial autonomy at the district level (and below it at the neighbourhood office and residents' committee levels). In part this reflects the perennial budgetary appetites of governmental units anywhere, the desire to retain as great a part of local revenue as possible and to extract as much as possible from high levels with as few strings as possible. Tensions between levels are likely to mount as the economic base of urban basic-level administrative agencies (residents' committee, neighbourhood office and district) expands along with the economic reforms: their specific economic bailiwicks have shown particularly vigorous growth as against those of the city government, namely services as opposed to industry, small-scale collective and private enterprises (including industrial and commercial) as opposed to state. These enterprises are golden-egg geese and are the object of an intra-governmental tussle for revenue: for district enterprises, between district and city; for neighbourhood enterprises, between neighbourhood and district; for enterprises under residents' committees, between them and the neighbourhood office (ibid., p. 71). In the past, there was a tendency that, when these geese grew bigger and fatter, they were taken over by higher levels of government. For example, officials of Lixia District in Jinan reported losing enterprises to the city government in 1979 which were transformed thereby from 'small' to 'big collectives' (i.e. statised in effect) (ibid., p. 44). Though the official reason for transfer was the inability of the district to manage them properly, officials maintained that this was only the case under the traditional division of managerial labour between city and district which was breaking down as the district took on more responsibilities for developing industry and commerce. It is increasingly likely that entrepreneurial governments at each level – and 'local entrepreneurship' is a phenomenon easily visible in China today (for vivid examples, see Blecher's article in this volume) – will seek not merely to fatten their geese and increase their numbers through increased investment, but also prevent them from being taken to another pond. From the point of view of the economic reformers, such local entrepreneurship and inter-level/inter-local competition are at best ambiguous phenomena and at worst downright counter-productive, since they foster excessive and unwise investment, impose local fetters on the natural flows of a commodity economy and increase depredation on the real producers, the enterprises. Small wonder that local governments often figure as the villains in the dramatic scenarios of disgruntled reformers. As we shall see later, however, a political analyst might be inclined to a less demonic view.

(b) Institutional Changes at the District Level

There is clear evidence that the increased pressures on urban governments and their desire to acquire more operational autonomy are producing institutional changes in basic-level governments at the district level and below. As we have seen, the reformers have increased the size and complexity of local economic systems under district regulation and control; but they have also brought new functions for local governments which require institutional change. Evidence at the district level (including its component parts, the street offices and residents' committees) demonstrates this trend in detail.

Within the system of governmental organisation itself, one can detect three trends. First, there are certain areas of activity which are increasing in tandem with economic reform, leading to the expansion of existing organisations. Urban governments reported an expansion in their tax offices, in line with the increasing use of taxation as an 'economic lever', particularly in the context of the policy of substituting 'tax for profit' (*ligaishi*) as the means for generating state revenue from enterprises. Increased commercial activity and the proliferation of collective and private business has led to an expansion of existing bureaux of finance and trade and industrial and commercial management at both city and district levels.

Second, the diversification of governmental functions has led to the formation of new organs, either splitting off from existing organisations or being established *de novo*. Some urban districts are taking on a planning role by establishing institutions to coordinate economic activity within their borders, a clear institutional expression of the expansion of the area principle. At the district level this takes the form of a planning committee (for example, in Shanghai's Jingan District); at the street office level, it may take the form of an 'economic work group' (for example, in Jingan District's Yuyuan Street Office). Separate auditing bureaux have also been established, usually beginning as a segment of the existing finance bureau. In Tianjin's Heping district, for example, the origin and functions of the auditing bureau were described as follows (White and Benewick, 1986, p. 132):

These new organisations reflect the expansion of the functions of local government after the Third Plenum [1978] . . . In the past, the functions of these new organisations were handled in other bureaux, but their functions have expanded, thus a need for new organisations. They reflect the reforms: for example, the district Auditing Bureau supervises the expenditures of enterprises (both city and district enterprises; the city level looks after the larger ones). The Auditing Bureau has two functions: to supervise the budget of the district government and enterprises. It is responsible to the district government and higher auditing departments, mainly the city.

Similarly, the reformers' desire to make price regulation more sensitive and flexible, as well as the recurrent need to clamp down on 'unwarranted' price rises which generate local discontent, have created the need for new (or expanded) price bureaux. Reform attempts to strengthen the role of economic law have also led to the establishment of new legal institutions or the expansion of existing ones. For example, the legal bureau of Tianjin's Heping District was established only recently. At the neighbourhood level, one office in Shanghai's Jingan District appointed a judicial assistant in 1985 to handle an increasing load of local disputes. One can also expect the activity of the economic sections of district-level courts to expand substantially, though some disputes will still be handled administratively by Industrial and Commercial Bureaux.

An aspect of the economic role of urban governments which is expanding rapidly is that of external 'economic cooperation'. This is particularly visible at the city level, but is also apparent of the districts in larger cities. For example, Lixia District in Jinan had established cooperative relations with ten other districts and counties outside the city, including other provinces; these links had not been possible – at least formally – before the reforms. In the smaller city of Zhenjiang in Jiangsu province, an economic cooperative committee was established in 1985 'to link economic departments with other areas'. These linkages *within China* should be distinguished from foreign economic ties which are handled by foreign trade committees or bureaux, the activities of which are also expanding along with the (uneven) spread of the Open Door policy.

Turning from the economic sphere, another broad area of rapidly expanding local government activity is that of spatial planning and environmental regulation. This reflects several policy innovations of the reform era: the shift in priorities away from 'productive' to 'non-productive' investment to favour social consumption and raise overall urban living standards, notably by improving public utilities and expanding the housing stock; the desire to rationalise urban assets and improve the efficiency with which they are managed – particularly important is the effort to reform the system by which urban real estate is categorised, valued and regulated. A glance through official statistical handbooks reveals these trends at the national level up to the mid-1980s: 'non-productive' investment,[14] as a proportion of total investment in capital construction, increased from 20.9 per cent in 1978 to 43.1 per cent in 1985, of which housing projects alone constituted 20 per cent (State Statistical Bureau 1986, p. 20; cf. pp. 54 and 373); living floor-space per capita increased from 4.2 sq.m. in 1978 to 6.7 in 1985 (ibid., p. 555); efforts have been made to improve urban public utilities such as tap water, public transport, paved roads, sewers, household energy, urban vegetation and environmental sanitation (ibid., p. 602). District governments reported the establishment of new departments to deal with these functions: city beautification and city construction committees in Tianjin's Heping district (which may be unrepresentative because of the need to rebuild earthquake damage), an urban construction management committee in Lixia District in Jinan which exercises new powers of construction (previously it had only been allowed to handle maintenance); in Shanghai's Jingan District they were setting up in 1986 a Living Quarters Bureau and Environmental Protection Office and planned to establish a Design and Project Office to engage in urban planning.

These examples suggest a proliferation of organisations in urban district governments, at least in the larger cities, specifically in response to the strategic and institutional changes introduced by the economic reform programme. These new organisations at the district level are the lowest rung in new 'branches', which extend up to the city level and above. At each level, therefore, the organ is subject to 'dual leadership' from its city branch superior and the district government. However, it is significant for our purposes to note the development of 'area' organisations i.e. organs whose specific responsibility is to coordinate across branch organs and assert local as opposed to sectoral priorities. It is the specific function of new 'committees' or 'commissions' to coordinate across sectors: for example, the foreign trade committee in Zhenjiang City in Jiangsu province replaced a foreign trade bureau which was formerly a branch department 'under unified leadership of the centre and province'. The change, said city officials, 'reflects the expansion of our independent power at the city level'.

This trend towards the emergence of new local government organs is not confined to the urban sector and there is no significant evidence that it has been countered effectively by periodic attempts at administrative reform.[15] For example, the party committee of Canxi county in Sichuan province reported that, before attempts at administrative reform in the early 1980s, the county had 64 organs (departments, committees, sections and bureaux);

by the end of 1984 after the reforms there were 84, an increase of 31 per cent, with a 15 per cent increase in staff.[16] A similar process may well be under way in the newly reconstituting township and town governments in the countryside, partly in response to an expansion of functions at that level, partly by taking over functions formerly exercised by village-level governments and partly through the establishment of 'provisional' organs under instructions from above (for example, the Ministry of Civil Affairs reported in 1985 that each of Shanghai's 17 townships and 2 towns had an average of 35 'provisional' organs, mostly established during the previous three years).[17] As we shall see below, moreover, this phenomenon of organisational expansion is not confined to the sphere of formal bureaucratic offices; there has also been an explosion of 'companies' or 'corporations' (*gongsi*), which are intermediate organisations between the state bureaucracy on the one side and basic-level units and enterprises on the other.

Organisational proliferation reflects the fact that, while new institutions are arising to take on new tasks, old institutions which are theoretically superseded and should either contract or disappear, have apparently not done so. This should hardly be a surprise to students of public administration who are familiar with the tendency of public organs towards immortality. Particularly interesting cases in China are those of local industrial departments (this phenomenon is most visible at the city level where industrial departments are responsible for state industry under local control, unlike the district level where enterprises are mostly collective) whose powers have been directly threatened by the reforms in industrial administration, notably the efforts to increase the autonomy of enterprises and to change financial relationships between enterprises and the state through the 'tax for profit' system. Local functional bureaux have sought to protect themselves by a variety of means: by simply dragging their heels and either implementing reform policies slackly or not at all; through a kind of institutional camouflage by which they simulate the appearance of change (for example, by changing from a bureau to a company, or devolving authority to subordinate companies) but retain the previous substance (by not changing their operational methods), or using their subordinate companies as instruments of continuing control over their constituent enterprises; by institutional 'creativity' to repair bureaucratic fortunes undermined by the reforms. An interesting example of this last phenomenon is the Shanghai City Textile Bureau (White and Bowles 1987, p. 74). Let an official of the Bureau tell the story:

Enterprises have their self-owned funds. This process went through three stages: (1) [the system of] retained funds from profits (9.5 per cent in 1979). This 9.5 per cent was redistributed by our Bureau to meet the bonus and welfare needs of enterprises and keep them at the same level as other trades in Shanghai. *We had a lot of power then.* (2) Then in 1982 'profit-to-tax' came in, but we did not implement this because the 1979 profit contract was for five years. (3) In 1984 came the second stage of 'profit-to-tax' which *took away our power to distribute,* so our fiscal role decreased greatly. [emphasis added]

The Bureau responded to the third stage by establishing a new agency, a Financial Allocation Centre (FAC) in an attempt to recapture at least part of their previous financial power by drawing off part of the retained funds of textile enterprises (ibid., p. 75).

Enterprises have increased their own funds; we want to pool some of these funds so we set up our FAC. Remember that before the reform, the [local] financial bureau went through us and our companies to the enterprises. Both our bureau and the company retained a portion of the funds. Now the enterprises have direct relations with the finance bureau.

The Bureau justifies its FAC on the grounds that its subordinate enterprises have differential profitability and needs for technical upgrading, so some form of redistributive financial agency is still required. An economic reformer might not agree but, regardless of the FAC's economic logic, it is a revealing example of protective institutional adaptation, perhaps reflecting a rich variety of such defensive entrepreneurialism which requires further research.

Now to summarise this section. I have been concentrating on the administrative agencies of urban, primarily district, government. We can conclude at this point that China's urban local governments are undergoing considerable structural expansion and diversification, partly in spite of the economic reforms but more significantly because of the reforms.[18] The latter involves two basic thrusts: first, the desire to remedy problems which had been neglected in the Maoist era (notably to improve the living conditions of urban populations); second, the need to adapt to the increasingly diverse requirements of a reforming economy which is becoming structurally more complex and the nature of whose relationships with government is changing, albeit slowly.

(c) Management of the Economy

If we focus here on the district level and its component parts (the street offices and residents' committees), the economic environment is substantially different from that of city level administration. While the latter is responsible for state-owned enterprises, the former mainly deals with collective and private enterprises, among which commercial and service units predominate over industrial. Though state industries may be situated geographically within a district, the powers of the district government are relatively marginal in relation to them and they are managed by their specific branch systems under the city government. Historically, relations between state agencies and collective enterprises (I use this term in the sense of 'small collectives' as opposed to 'big collectives' which are *de facto* state enterprises and tend to be the direct responsibility of the city level) have been in general looser and more distant, so that one would expect relations between the district government and the enterprises under its jurisdiction to have been already less rigid and directive than would be the case at the city level. During the reform period, there has been an attempt to change the process of economic regulation; in the words of a Jinan district official, 'to change from controlling the enterprises by management-type to service-type regulation' (White and Benewick, 1986, p. 45).

> In the past, we managed the plan, material, sales and appointments; now we are giving these powers to the neighbourhood companies. The economic sections of the government guide companies, companies guide enterprises – this is an experimental process and we don't have much experience.

The introduction of companies is one of the major institutional innovations of the reform era. They are a kind of 'half-way house' between a state organ proper (in this case of districts, an agency such as the Industrial and Commercial Management Bureau) and an enterprise. They are 'quasi-state' organisations in terms of ownership and responsibility. They are usually responsible to a district economic organ, though they will probably be under 'dual leadership' – responsible to both the district economic organ and to a higher level of company at the city level on the branch principle, the latter being responsible to a corresponding government organ at the city level. The division of responsibilities tends to be between administrative (handled by the 'area') and professional supervision (handled by the branch), the former involving the right to appoint managers and other skilled personnel and to arrange labour. Similarly, companies at the neighbourhood office level report to both neighbourhood office and district. At the same time, however, companies are supposed to be economic agencies, they have an 'enterprise character' (*qiyexing*), exercising a degree of commercial autonomy and interacting with their bureaucratic superiors and enterprises subordinates in terms of economic rather than administrative relationships.

The concrete institutional picture varies from area to area, but the following pattern seems common. Within the district, there are two levels of companies – at the district and neighbourhood levels. At the district level are the more specialised companies (for instance, transportation, labour service or housing development) while neighbourhood companies tend to group together disparate types of small enterprise under umbrella Industrial and Commercial Companies (either separate or fused) – in Beijing similar functions are performed by cooperative 'associations' (*lianshe*) at the neighbourhood level. The companies have an important role in planning the production of their constituent enterprises, in providing finance and in helping to find materials and sales outlets. Companies levy management fees or a percentage of profits from their constituent enterprises and taxes are also paid to the district finance bureau or tax office. If companies have not been established, then the neighbourhood office itself imposes a levy on the net profits after tax: Shanghai's Yuyuan neighbourhood office, for example, took 10 per cent of net profits as a 'management fee'. In places where private business activity is developing, a separate system of private industrial and commercial offices may be established, responsible to the district Industrial and Commercial Management Bureau. These in turn either deal directly with private concerns or with their representatives: in the case of Yuyuan Street Office, for example, there was a newly established Private Labourers' Association. This latter is an example of a wider trend towards the development of independent economic associations, formed by enterprises, households or individuals themselves rather than imposed by the state, perhaps the sprouts of an emergent 'civil society'.

To summarise, again the picture is one of institutional proliferation, in this case through the emergence of intermediate agencies with hybrid characteristics – both state and enterprise, administrative and economic. While the initial Chinese enthusiasm about the advantages of companies has receded, it would be too easy to see them simply as a new layer of state control. It is clear that they are subject to control and monitoring from superior state agencies and that successive layers of local government view them as important instruments to extract resources from enterprises to expand their own financial base. At the same time, however, an element of flexibility seems to have entered the system of economic management: companies do appear to have some autonomy from their bureaucratic superiors and to exercise some freedom of manoeuvre to the economic benefit of themselves and their constituent enterprises (I have made this argument in detail elsewhere, in the case of Labour Service Companies; see White, 1987). The institutional picture is further complicated by the rise of associations organised from below by collectives and private businesses. Overall, these phenomena imply a trend towards a system of economic management which is more indirect and mediated than previously, more decentralised and subject to bargaining and manoeuvre.

CONCLUSIONS

Analysis of the role of local governments in the post-Mao reforms has tended to paint them as obstacles. This may partly reflect a tendency to analyse them in narrowly economic terms and concentrate merely on their relationship with central government. If however, we broaden our analytical scope to include the local political environments in which they operate and their non-economic responsibilities, our attitude may become more sympathetic; indeed they may be more victims then villains of the reform piece.

Urban basic-level local governments face environments of increasing complexity and mounting demands on their services which they are at present hard-pressed to meet; at the same time they do not appear to have benefitted as greatly from the financial decentralisation of the early 1980s as their counterparts at higher levels (city and province). These changes, and the pressures they generate, reflect, first, a gradual accumulation of new functions since the establishment of the urban government system in the 1950s and the recent release of accumulated (individual and social) consumer frustrations among urban populations after the Maoist era; second, the impact of the economic reform programme itself in terms of its impact on urban economies and its new demands on governmental institutions, as well as its explicit encouragement of popular aspirations for ever higher standards of living. Moreover, the implementation of the economic reform programme has created mounting political tensions and social discontent, particularly in response to inflation, corruption, economic inequalities or the real or perceived prospect of unemployment. Little wonder that local officials put political and social 'calm and unity' at the top of their list of goals. To the extent, moreover, that economic reforms are in fact accompanied by political reforms (for example, in the people's congress system) which increase the channels for, and strength of, interest articulation, political pressures on local governments may be expected to increase, though passing through institutionalised channels. Since these political reforms have been slow in coming, however, urban tensions have been bottled up; from this perspective, the protests of April-June 1989 were not hard to explain (though their scale and intensity were).

In short, local governments are at the 'sharp end' – they are under pressure to perform more (and ideally better) yet face resource constraints in their attempt to do so. Some of their organisational responses have been creative and positive (indeed, entrepreneurial) when viewed within this context. The attempt to 'search' for a better level of urban basic-level government (the neighbourhood office) which balances conflicting needs for coordination, manageability and 'closeness'; the reorientation of existing institutions and the establishment of new institutions to perform the new governmental functions required by the economic reform programme; and the attempt to reinforce the *kuai* principle by strengthening the role of coordinating institutions to limit the segmental effects of branch (*tiao*) administration. Another response, of which reform economists are critical, is the attempt to expand their revenue base by developing the economy under their jurisdiction and levying revenue on it, while at the same time trying to extract more resources and power from the next higher level of government. Given the pressured environment of urban governments, such revenue-seeking behaviour is to be expected, particularly in a context where their real responsibilities are greater than their formal responsibilities, where popular aspirations and dissatisfaction are mounting, where higher levels of local government are reluctant to devolve financial power and where there is little clarity about the specific rights and responsibilities of successive levels of government.

Unless the issue of local government reform is given higher priority and unless a more systematic and determined effort is made to sort out the tangle of urban government, then the currently prevalent form of revenue seeking, which is defensive, competitive and economically problematic, threatens to turn local government into successive layers of leeches battening on the blood of caged enterprises, thereby generating greater popular resentment.

There would seem to be a strong case for the Chinese authorities to develop the expertise necessary to focus more squarely on the structure and content of state itself, rather than merely the nature of its relations with the economy. At the local as well as the central level, the desired change in China is not so much from 'more' to 'less' state (though, properly defined, this is an important element) but from one form of developmental state to another. It is probable that the latter will actually be larger and structurally more diverse than its predecessor, but would operate according to a different political and administrative as well as economic logic. Within this reappraisal and redefinition of the state lies the more precise area of the role of local governments, not merely in relation to the central government or the enterprise, but also to their own nested layers.[19]

The emergence of systematic thought on these problems in China has been slow in coming – still slower the move from thought to action. There are various reasons for this: the very complexity of the changing urban society and economy and of the institutional network of local government; the fact that the structure of local government is a pagoda of many levels and reforms at each level are interdependent; the fact that analysis and action goes beyond the relatively 'safe' sphere of economics to tackle the more sensitive areas of administration and politics; the fact that the objects of inquiry and action are themselves political actors with well established institutional interests which run counter to the dictates of reformist rationality, whether economic or administrative. Sadly, in the climate of the political reaction which has followed the Beijing massacre of June 4 1989, even the limited progress made in addressing the issue of local government reform now seems to be in jeopardy.

NOTES

1. Reform of rural local government has already received some Western scholarly attention, notably Shue 1984b on the transition from commune to township administration and Shue 1984a and Kueh 1983 on changes at the county level.

2. This distinction accords with that made by Franz Schurman (1968, pp. 175, 196) between decentralisation I (economic) and II (administrative); it is somewhat different from the distinctions devised by the World Bank (1983, p. 120): 'deconcentration' – transferring powers from headquarters to other branches of central government, 'devolution' – to autonomous units of government such as municipalities and local governments; and 'delegation' – to organisations outside the bureaucratic systems. The notion of 'administrative decentralisation' includes both 'deconcentration' and 'devolution' (reflecting the ambiguities of 'dual rule') while 'economic decentralisation' can be equated with 'delegation'. For a valuable discussion of the oscillation between the vertical (*tiao*) and horizontal (*kuai*) principles in Chinese administration, see Unger 1987.

3. Reformers were very critical of the ill effects of previous attempts to solve problems in the planning system. For example, see Ji and Rong 1979, p. 11:

    [When] there was suitable unified decentralisation of China's system of industrial administration, the coordination of supply, production and marketing were good, . . . and production developed rapidly. However, when enterprises were too often placed under the administration of lower levels, there occurred a chaotic fragmentation of production and a state of anarchy and the standard of enterprise administration declined.

4. For a review of different opinions on the issue and a resounding defence of economic decentralisation, see Liu Shinian 1980.

5. The results of these symposia have been published in book form, see Lu *et al.*, 1985 and Local Government Research, 1986.

6. However, experiments in urban organisational reform did begin in 16 medium-sized cities in May 1987 and, based on this experience, a report was issued by the CCP Central Committee and the State Council in August 1987. For a text, see BBC, *Summary of World Broadcasts: Far East* (hereafter SWB) 8663.

7. The research was conducted jointly with Robert Benewick of the University of Sussex who has a paper in this volume on the political reform of local government institutions. The field research involved three large cities – Beijing, Tianjin and Shanghai – and two smaller ones – Jinan in Shandong province and Zhenjiang in Jiangsu province.

8. For the Chinese text of the State Constitutions, see *Renmin Ribao* (People's Daily) (hereafter RMRB), 5 December 1982; for an English text, *Beijing Review* vol. 25 no. 52 (27 December 1982).

9. Research on the issue of basic-level mass organisations is being conducted by Shandong CASS in Jinan in cooperation with Shanghai CASS: Shandong concentrates on villagers' committees and Shanghai on residents' committees (see White and Benewick 1986, p. 38, p. 64). For a report on some of the research results, see Liu Chuanchen 1986.

10. For a discussion of the differences between 'leadership' and 'guidance', see Liu Lansheng 1985, p. 305.

11. The Party Centre and the State Council issued a document to this effect in 1983 (no. 53) and Peng Zhen made a speech on the subject (Liu Lansheng 1985, p. 303).

12. For more detail on the 1980 reform see the report by *Heilongjiang Radio* on 17 January 1980, *Jilin Radio* on 14 March 1980 (in SWB 6380), *Guangdong Radio* 22 May 1980, in *Foreign Broadcast Information Service* (hereafter FBIS) p. 110, *New China News Agency* (hereafter NCNA) (Chinese) 20 September 1980 re Anhui (in SWB W1112). For the 1983 reform, see Wong 1987, p. 15.

13. For an analysis of the need for a new system of revenue-sharing, see Wang Bingqian, 'Certain questions in financial work', RMRB, 26 November 1982 (in FBIS 229). For a more academic review of the issue,

see Cai Xun, 'Reforming and improving the socialist financial system
. . .', *Guangming Ribao* 29 May 1983 (in FBIS 116). Also see 'It is imperative
to centralise financial and material resources', NCNA (Chinese), 4 July
1983 (in FBIS 131) and 'Ten manifestations of excessive decentralisation
of capital', *Beijing Wen Zhai Bao* (Beijing Digest News) no. 98, 19
August 1983 (in FBIS 171).

For the new system in operation, see *Jilin Radio* 10 January 1985 (SWB
7859) and *Heilongjiang Radio* 19. June 1985 (in SWB 7984).

14. 'Non-productive' investment involves, to a large extent, 'construction
which meet the material and cultural life of people' and includes public
utilities, public health, social welfare, education, culture and residential
housing. For a full definition, see State Statistical Burea 1986, p. 750.

15. For an overview of attempts at administrative reform during the reform
era, see my 'Administrative reforms in post-Mao China', *IDS Bulletin*,
Institute of Development Studies, University of Sussex, vol. 19, no. 4
(Oct. 1988), pp. 12–18.

16. NCNA, domestic service, 7 July 1985, in SWB 8001.

17. *Ibid*, 22 July 1985, in SWB 8017.

18. There have also been changes in the organisation of people's representative congresses at both district and city levels, mainly through the
establishment of standing committees after 1979 and the growth of their
specialised committee system. For a detailed discussion, see Benewick's
article in this volume.

19. The last point raises the need for more research on that ecology of
political games which comprises local government – games between
layers and games within layers (notably the conflict between *tiao* and
kuai at the local level). This will allow us to break down the concept
and reality of 'local government' – which has been overly homogenised
in the past – into its component political actors, mapping the relative
power and interest of each actor and documenting the emergence of new
actors (such as the various kinds of intermediate organisation spawned by
economic reform). This will hopefully provide a clearer idea of the limits
and possibilities of both economic and administrative reform in China's
cities.

10 Political Institutionalisation at the Basic Level of Government and Below in China

Robert Benewick

1 A CRISIS OF INSTITUTIONALISATION[1]

Twenty years ago Samuel P. Huntington argued that a theory of political development had to be matched by a theory of political decay. Rapid mobilisation and participation which are political aspects of modernisation can also undermine political institutions and procedures, especially where there is no tradition of the rule of law. Communist states have an advantage because the Party can attempt to balance mobilisation with organisation. (Huntington 1965, 1968). When the party in Communist states is unable to maintain this balance, however, a result is political decay or a crisis of institutionalisation. That is, the legitimacy, efficacy and stability of the existing institutions is called into question. Moreover, this process is exacerbated if the party is seen to be the principal source of political decay by significant sections of the population.

In China, institutional development since 1949 was by and large unsystematic, uneven and unstable, as can be inferred from the need for four constitutions over the following 33 years. In so far as the Cultural Revolution decade (1966–76) was a dramatic manifestation of political decay we are in a better position to understand the tasks that confront the post-Maoist leadership. The failure, for example, to institutionalise participation, and the disruption caused by mass mobilisations and campaigns, left a political vacuum. Moreover, the priorities of a new and reforming leadership require institutional change. Although a radical set of economic policies and reforms have gained ascendance and widespread

243

acceptance, this has not been matched by political reforms. Where they have been introduced the reforms are often not fully implemented or, where institutions have been established, they are likely to be underused.

From our perspective, however, China's political reforms can be characterised as a movement from mass mobilisation towards institutionalisation. Following Huntington (1965, p. 394) institutionalisation is used here to describe 'the process by which organisations and procedures acquire value and stability'. China's leaders are determined to prevent a recurrence of the upheavals associated with the Cultural Revolution and many reformers are convinced that restructuring the state political system is necessary for the effective functioning of what they describe as a socialist commodity economy. Institutionalisation is also regarded as a concomitant to redefining the role of the Communist Party (CCP), discredited by the Cultural Revolution, as well as being important in its own right.

The goals have been articulated at a number of levels by reformers: the implementation of a set of economic reforms combined with an indictment of the policies and practices of the Maoist era to gain support, establish legitimacy, promote stability for development as well as to revitalise the economy; the principle of a separation of powers to distance the CCP from government, and government from administration; the ideological demotion of the class struggle and with it demarcating the political, economic and social spheres of society; a recognised need for reforms of administrative structures, procedures and personnel; and the undertaking, with varying degrees of intensity, of reform of the government and the Party. The introduction of fixed terms of office and the creation of advisory committees to foster elite mobility provide concrete examples of attempts to implement reforms. However, the response of the 'retired' and more conservative leaders to the urban protests of May/June 1989 suggest a failure in institutionalisation.

The above policies are of course interrelated, develop their own momentum and do so unevenly. They also focus upon and challenge existing political institutions. The presence of an emerging crisis has increasingly been recognised. Drawing upon the works of Deng Xiaoping, the report of the Third Plenary Session of the Eleventh CCP Central Committee (December 1978) and the Report of the Thirteenth National Congress of the CCP (October–November 1987), the authors of a 1987 article argue 'the lack of concrete institutional construction and a low degree of institutionalisation are major lessons in our country's democratic political construction', and observe 'that the basic principles set down for political structural reform by the 13th Congress are penetrated throughout by the principles and ideas of institutionalisation'. (Wu Guoguang and Gao Shan 1987, pp. 14,15). Thus institutionalisation is central to political structural reform and involves grassroots level democracy and participation (ibid. p. 16).

The purpose of this chapter is to examine empirically the post-Mao leadership's moves towards the institutionalisation of government and, taking account of Huntington's notion of political development and political decay, a process of re-institutionalisation. That is, the attempt to activate and develop structures that were in place but never achieved or lost value and stability. We will focus on institutions for representation and direct participation at the basic and grassroots levels of the political system.

There are people's congresses at the following levels of local government: provinces, cities directly administered by central government (Beijing, Shanghai, Tianjin) counties, cities, urban districts, townships, nationality townships and towns.[2] In addition, there are exclusively administrative levels such as the neighbourhood office and there are non-government 'mass organisations of self-management at the grassroots level', i.e. urban residents' committees and rural villagers' committees. Basic level government for the purposes of this research refers to the lowest level of government with a people's congress, small cities not divided into districts, districts in large cities and townships. We will however, also be taking into account the lowest level of government, where the people's congress has a standing committee, the county level, and examining in some depth, residents' and villagers' committees.

Our data is largely drawn from interviews with leading members at these levels, supplemented by discussions with social science colleagues in China, working on similar questions during the Spring of 1986, when institutionalisation was, as it is now, in an early and largely experimental stage. The research was conducted in three cities directly under central government, Beijing, Shanghai and Tianjin, two medium size cities, Jinan and Zhenjiang, and two provinces, Shandong and Jiangsu. The townships and counties visited were more properly suburban than rural. It is assumed that the reader shares with the author awareness of the methodological limitations inherent in carrying out this type of research. In particular, the diverse and complex nature of Chinese society and the difficulties in acquiring and verifying political data counsels cautious interpretation.

These levels have been selected at least in part because they have been targeted with good reason by the more liberal reformers. In the countryside this is where the economic reforms have had a dramatic impact. With the dismantling of the people's commune, what political institutions have emerged or re-emerged to accommodate the new situation, how well do they fit the stated goals of the reformers in Deng Xiaoping's leadership coalition for achieving political structural reform, i.e. how far have they advanced towards institutionalisation and achieving legitimacy, effectiveness and stability? These questions also apply to the urban areas, but the position is more problematic because of the differential nature of the reforms in an environment which is more complex. A seminar on comprehensive structural reforms in big cities, for example, reported in 1987 that urban reforms were far less advanced than those in the countryside (SWB 8533, 30 April 1987). Yet opposition and resistance occurred in both urban and rural areas, raising for the reformers the spectre of countervailing tensions and tendencies. For example in the countryside there have been expressions of resentment from disgruntled local cadres and there has been violence against those who have prospered from the reforms, while in the factories the introduction of bonuses has had divisive effects. On a wider scale there have been bureaucratic sectoral and regional conflicts over the control of resources (Perry and Wong 1985, chaps 6, 7, 8; Burns 1985–86; *The Economist*, 1987; Lampton, 1987). In this respect our enquiry is more narrowly directed towards the suitability and adaptability of existing institutions reflecting the discussions taking place in China.

In addition, our evidence indicates that considerable responsibilities have accrued to basic-level as well as local government consequent upon the economic reforms. This suggests an interactive spiral: as the activities of basic-level government expand and diversify, pressure for participation and interest articulation increases. In turn, the need to accommodate demands and interests, which may take place within or outside formal institutions, further increases the importance of basic-level government and promotes individual and group interests. Yang Baikui of the Political Science Institute of the Chinese Academy of Social Sciences wrote in 1987:

> . . . with the development of reforms in various aspects, social groups, which are independent to a certain extent, will be formed in our country, such as workers' groups in factories and mines, the groups of entrepreneurs, the groups of intellectuals, the groups of individual industrialists and businessmen, the groups of agricultural labourers, and so on. Some of them are shareholders and some are not. They are relatively independent. In particular, the relative independence and development of the 'intermediate strata' will bring changes to the social-ist political structure. They are the basic units of residents' participation

in politics, and the intermediate link, of democratic communications between residents and political power. (p. 9)

Three related points having to do with the form of government, the political and ideological environment and the pace of change require consideration at this stage. Huntington makes the point that it is the degree not the form of government that counts (1968, p. 1). In China the political reforms are characterised by a diversity of practices and a tentative, incremental approach. While caution may be necessary and experiment justifiable, the question is posed of the extent to which the changes are cosmetic, effective power remaining with the Party. This is at least recognised by the leadership when they proclaim the need to separate the Party from government and management: 'It is time for us to distinguish between the responsibilities of the Party and those of government and to stop substituting the former for the latter' (Deng Xiaoping, 1980, p. 303). Nevertheless, the relationship remains unclear, for, given the interests involved, it can only be a gradual process requiring more than just involving non-party personnel and restricting dual office holding by party members.[3] Even so, the reforms represent a shift away from the mobilisation of the Maoist period and a step towards institution building and the formulation of procedures. Examining the people's congresses, for example, should provide a guide to the progress towards institutionalisation.

The second point refers to the political and ideological environment for reforms. Political structural reforms have been on the agenda since the third Plenum of the Eleventh Central Committee of the CCP in 1978 as we have seen. They confirm our contention of an institutional crisis but they also indicate obstacles to its resolution. In what was regarded as the preceptive statement, Deng Xiaoping, in a speech delivered in 1980 and republished in an amended version in 1987 to include enterprises, called not only for the separation of party and government but for reforms to overcome impediments to modernisation, i.e. bureaucracy, over-concentration of power, patriarchal methods, life tenure in leading positions and various kinds of privileges (Deng Xiaoping, 1980, pp. 309–317). Recent refinement of these goals has been no more exacting. Administration is to be simplified and made more efficient, decision-making devolved, and the initiative of grassroots units, workers, farmers and intellectuals promoted (see for example, 'Outline of Deng Xiaoping's Ideas on Political Structural Reform', SWB 8613, 7 July 1987). These goals must be located in the inhibiting environment of a long established and firmly entrenched administrative system and of the hegemony of the largest political party in the world possessing the legitimacy of revolution. Both the CCP and the state bureaucracy are of course no strangers to resisting previous attempts at reform.

When viewed from this perspective, the debates and demonstrations of 1986 on the substance and extent of political structural reforms and at least, in part, the urban protests of 1989 come as no surprise. Yet the determination of the Chinese leadership to institute political reform should not be dismissed. While the dispute and delays in the Standing Committee of the National People's Congress in 1987 (SWB 0038, 1 January 1988) over the status of villagers' committees as the lowest level of government or, like residents' committees, 'self-governing mass-organisations', was indicative of resistance on the one hand, it is evidence of the determination of the reformers and the seriousness of the reforms as well as the recognition of opposition and conflict on the other hand.

Thirdly, it is clear that a cautious strategy towards reforms had been adopted and that the timetable for their introduction was to be tightly controlled. The statement of Bo Yibo, then Vice-Chairman of the Advisory Commission of the CCP Central Committee, in the summer of 1987 is typical:

> We can't copy Western Democracy with its bicameralism, multiparty system and separation of power among legislative, executive and judicial branches. Our democracy is practised in a guided and orderly manner. It is necessary to combine democracy with dictatorship and the promotion of democracy with the building of the legal system to ensure stability and unity. (SWB 8611, 4 July 1987)

In elaborating the restrictions on the exercise of 'democratic rights', one commentator set forth what can be accepted as an objective of the political reformers: 'At present, we should pay particular attention to building political power at grassroots level, to closely combining the building of democracy with the building of the legal system, and to bringing into play the initiative of the people' (Chi Fulin 1987). It is to the institutionalisation of this process that we must now turn, beginning with the formal constitutional position.

2 THE CONSTITUTIONAL POSITION

Constitutions reveal little political reality but the four constitutions of the young People's Republic (1954, 1975, 1978, 1982) reflect political discourse and policy changes. Constitutions are also a blueprint and a guide to institutional continuity, change and status. It is our contention that the 1982 constitution registers the crisis of institutionalisation consequent upon the Cultural Revolution. As Hsin-Chi Kuan (1984, p. 65) notes, its image of legality distinguishes it from its predecessors. In this sense the 1975 constitution which, for example, devotes only three short articles to local people's congresses and governments compared to 14 in 1954, 5 in 1978, and 17 in 1982, is important for what it does not say. The numerous references to the 1982 constitution in the course of our interviews also suggests its ideological and symbolic importance.

It is apparent that the dislocations of the Cultural Revolution have not inspired radical innovations but that the constitution makers have opted for restoration, stability and incremental development. The 1954 constitution formally institutionalised the system of local and basic-level government. The principle is that a local people's government is not only responsible to its people's congress but also subordinate to the government at the next highest level. Deputies are directly elected to people's congresses at basic- level government and indirectly at each level above it by the people's congress at the next lower level.

The 1982 constitution substantially restored the 1954 state structure and invested representative institutions with enhanced responsibilities if not powers. In doing so it underwrites commitment towards institutionalisation. Standing committees are established for local people's congresses at and above the county level and the direct election of deputies is extended upward to the county level congresses. Residents' Committees, which were being set up as early as 1951 (Schurmann, 1966, pp. 68, 374), along with villagers' committees, are recognised in the constitution for the first time. It is, of course, left to legislation to spell out the appropriate detail which can be contentious as in the case of the status of villagers' committees referred to earlier. Despite the fact that villagers' committees are universally established throughout China, the law was adopted on a trial basis.

Having briefly outlined the constitutional changes we are now in a position to describe the changes in institutional practice.

3 PEOPLE'S CONGRESS

It would be premature to devise measures for institutionalisation and in any event we are dealing with a stage of trial and experimentation which is under discussion and the subject for research and monitoring by state officials and academics in China. In the meantime, restored institutions vested with enhanced responsibilities are confronted with changing conditions and new circumstances, particularly the economic reforms at basic-level government. By describing this process it is possible to move beyond the formal constitutional expressions of intent to observe the extent of institutional implementation and development. This may well be a three stage process in which an institution is established and entrenched or secured, adapts or responds to changing conditions and becomes effective in executing its prescribed tasks. In this section we take up the question of representation at the basic level of government, as institutionalised in the people's congress, and the development of standing committees as instruments for improving the effectiveness of the people's congress to supervise government at the county level. In the following two sections we move from representation to describe a form of direct democracy or participation, that is, the self-governing residents' associations and villagers' committees.

Representation is indicative of the process of institutionalisation in so far as the pressure of economic reforms promotes notions of democratic accountability and practice. Elections, however, pre-date the founding of the People's Republic with the CCP conducting them in the revolutionary base areas. Worried by the high rate of illiteracy, elections were carried out by throwing beans rather than by secret ballot. (Zhang Qingfu and Pi Chunxie, 'Revise the electoral laws to institutionalise democracy', *People's Daily*, 22 May 1979, SWB 6128, 30 May 1979). An electoral law was enacted in 1953 and direct elections were held at the district level (Whyte and Parish 1984, p. 296). Three sets of direct elections have taken place since 1979. The third set was completed by the end of 1987 with elections having been held in 2,830 counties, county-level cities, and municipal districts and in more than 50,000 townships (SWB 0046, 12 January 1988). The elections are formalistic, ritualistic, directed, constrained and mobilising. The procedures can be even more elaborate than those prescribed in law. In the 1984 election Jiading County, Shanghai, for example, had a potential electorate of 414,000 entitled to elect a people's congress of 355. In the first stage 9,800 candidates were nominated by 9,500 electoral groups based on villages, factories and other units. For the second stage the county was divided into 277 electoral districts with some districts entitled to two delegates. However, rather than relying simply on residence, the election was combined with quotas in two ways: (1) units would nominate from their own membership, e.g. a school would nominate a teacher; (2) the outgoing standing committee of the people's congress would instruct each election district on what kind of candiate they should elect, an overseas Chinese for example.[4] The resulting composition of the people's congress was reported as follows: farmers 39 per cent; workers 17 per cent; intellectuals 19 per cent; cadres 18 per cent; overseas Chinese and other party representatives 10 per cent; others 5 per cent. Of these 59 per cent were party members and 69 per cent men and 31 per cent women (White and Benewick 1986, pp. 73–4). Despite its limitations the electoral system contributes to the process of institutionalisation and signifies a commitment to gradual political reform and participatory practices. This is apparent in the ways in which the system has been adapted since 1979 (Benewick, p. 1988).

Although local and basic-level government are formally responsible to their people's congress and to the next level of government above, the activity and effectiveness of the people's congress are circumscribed for they do not make laws. They meet once a year for a few days to review the work of their level of government. The responsibilities of the people's congress for Zhenjiang city were described in formalistic terms: to secure the implementation of state decrees and policies; to review the reports submitted by the city government, procuracy and the court; to review the financial work and the budget; to discuss the general socio-economic situation in the city; raise questions about the work of specific government agencies; elect the mayor, vice-mayors, heads of procuracy and the court, chair and vice-chair of the people's congress and representatives to the provincial congress; guarantee the democratic rights of citizens, sexual equality, securing the ownership of private property; and dismiss incompetent officials. This was an impressive recitation of the constitution and organic law and it was admitted that the responsibilities were not new.

These formalistic functions however are insufficient to legitimate or entrench such an institution. An alternative source of legitimacy could reside in the delegates themselves but one meeting a year and part-time status is not enough to establish a reputation, and despite relatively frequent elections the permitted amount of electioneering has been reduced. As informants argued, delegates may be model workers or have distinguished themselves in one way or another, but these are not necessarily the qualities needed for the task and which will enhance the institution. Legitimacy for people's congresses at these levels of government could be derived from the Party but this ignores its contribution to the crisis of institutionalisation in the first place and the difficult task of achieving a mutual accommodation between the Party and the state in the second place. The potential contribution of the Party must also be set against its own rectification campaigns, the rhetoric of separation of party and state and the determination of the reformers to broaden representation. In any event, institutionalisation is about institutionally derived legitimacy.

People's congresses viewed in the context of the political system could be better adapted to and more effective in its relations to government indirectly through their standing committees which were instituted at the county level after 1979. One academic researcher commented, 'The development of the standing committee is an important step towards law and democracy as an accompaniment to modernisation', while another argued that although people's congresses existed at the district level in the past, they had no power; now with standing committees they have more power to supervise government (ibid. pp. 66, 37).

There are variations in the nature of the standing committee according to level of government and different models apply. In Jiading county, Shanghai, for example, the 355 members of the county congress in 1984 elected the standing committee, the head and vice-heads of the county government, the head of the court, and the head of the procuracy. The standing committee is composed of 23 members of which the 6 directors and vice-directors are full time paid by their units. In this case no member of the Party committee is a member of the standing committee, although the county head is vice-secretary of the Party. They meet four times a year in between sessions of the congress. As might be expected, city level standing committees are more developed. Meetings are more frequent and they have a staff.

Standing committees are formally entrusted with the supervision of their respective governments. Non-standing committee members of the people's congress become involved in this process in two ways. First of all, delegates can make requests on behalf of their constituents to county agencies and bureaux and these are followed up, if necessary, by members of the standing committee. Secondly, the committee divides into functional groups, such as agriculture, law, finance and economics, culture and education, industry and transport and organise other congress members to visit the appropriate units to check on them.

The importance of the standing committee may be better understood by considering the town and township levels of government where there are people's congresses but standing committees have not been instituted. The people's congress for Xinqiao Xiang, Danyang county, Jiangsu, meets once a year for one day and the 91 delegates do not undertake any congress tasks in between meetings. The people's congress for Longhua Xiang, Shanghai, also meets only once a year for 2 to 4 days but in contrast to Xinqiao Xiang the 150 delegates divide in 12 groups according to village and meet every three months. In this way, they process opinions and pursue problems of their constituents. Certainly the standing committee enhances the influence and control of the people's congress over the government at its level. But this must be viewed in the context of the vertical appropriation of power downwards from the next level above together with the corresponding level of the Party structure. In regard to planning this means the economic role assigned to local government by the reformers through the allocation of funds.

In Jinan, district leaders claimed that there was no longer a clear division of labour between city and district governments since the latter had increasing responsibility for industry and commerce and the district was not an independent accounting unit. Similarly, academics in Shanghai reported that the district was acquiring more economic tasks and management responsibilities, and that this increases their powers informally; while in the Eastern district of Beijing the process is being instituted on a more formal basis as an experiment. In short, local government is becoming too complex for standing committees, as presently constituted, to exercise effective control. This is of course a part of a more general problem of legislative oversight which is not peculiar to this level of government or to China. What is apparent is that deputies do bring forward claims on behalf of their constituents and within the parameters of effective action attempt to oversee the work of government whether or not there is a standing committee at their level (McCormick 1987, pp. 407–11). For example, the people's congress was successful in persuading Wuxi city government to remove its tourist hotel construction away from Lake Taihu in order to prevent polluting the lake.[5]

Group claims, however, is a growing area of activity which may test the adaptability and effectiveness of people's congresses. The environment of reform since the Third Plenum of the 11th Central Committee of the CCP in 1978 has encouraged the re-emergence of private associations and the formation of new ones. In Guangdong province alone, over one thousand unofficial 'mass organisations' have been reported in existence (SWB 0041, 6 January 1988). The evidence suggests that the economic reforms in particular have encouraged the formation of interest groups at local and basic levels of government. Beijing, Shanghai and Shenzhen have so far promulgated regulations controlling their management. Shenzhen boasts of ranking first with over 160 organisations and this does not include what may be the most significant, that is, the 50 or more in the Shekou industrial zone.

The confusion caused by this mushrooming of relatively autonomous government and non-government organisations has prompted this need for regulation. In Shenzhen regulations apply to non-profit making mass organisations separate from the state. They are required to have a constitution, a fixed number of members, a standing committee, a permanent office and stable funding. The list is wide ranging and includes the federation of trade and industry, trade unions, Communist Youth League, Women's Association, Buddhist Association, Catholic Church, Association of returned overseas Chinese, and Association of Taiwan compatriots (SWB 8650, 27 August 1988). It is also apparent that at least some of these organisations function at the basic-level government as well. For example, a Private Labourers Association was active at all three of the levels of Yuyuan neighbourhood office, Jingan district and the municipality of Shanghai. While some of these would seem to be Party-led mass organisations, the sheer number and their separation from the state also suggests that there are many private associations, although the extent to which they are regulated is unclear.

It is our prediction that these organisations will also seek to promote their interests through the people's congress as well as other channels, in so far as such a body can adapt and provide a gloss of legitimacy for their activities. This is an interactive process in so far that interest participation heightens the activity and effectiveness of the congress.

The nagging question is why should individuals participate in an institution whose effectiveness is no match for the Party and is at best indirect unless election to the people's congress also provides a gloss of legitimacy for an individual's access and connections. A more likely explanation is that the majority of delegates are expected to participate as part of their Party careers. A third and complementary explanation assumes that one consequence of the economic reforms is that local government will be invested with increasing welfare responsibilities which would enhance the role of representative bodies. A fourth approach focuses on corruption, which gains a degree of recognition if not acceptance when viewed as a consequence of development. Zhao Ziyang when Party secretary was reported as saying that 'In a developing economy it is impossible competely to avoid various unhealthy tendencies in the society as a whole . . .' (SWB 0196, 6 July 1988). Participation can be seen as an opportunity for personal gain but it can also provide the opportunity to oppose corruption. Where the latter is the case reputations could be made or unmade with institutional legitimacy as an important spin-off. As it stands corruption is an impediment to institutionalisation.

The extent to which the people's congress adopts or responds to the economic reforms and whether market influences promote pluralistic representation suggests a fruitful area for research. In regard to the themes of this chapter what is at stake is the disjuncture between economic reform and political change and whether the people's congress acquires value and stability.

4   URBAN RESIDENTS' COMMITTEES

Turning from the issue of representation to that of direct participation and self-government, the urban residents' committees were set up during the period 1950–1954. They did not gain constitutional recognition, as distinct from being incorporated through organic law, until 1982 along with the rural villagers' committees. The residents' committee is a 'self-governing mass organisation' located at the grassroots or pavement level of urban organisation and in many ways its functions parallel those of the work unit.[6] It is however, under the leadership of the neighbourhood or street office and dependent upon it for finance and under the supervision of the Party committee at street office level. Since the role of the street office, which is an administrative organ of the district government, is under consideration and discussion in the context of the urban reforms proposals, changes will have a knock-on effect for the residents' committee.

It is not difficult to understand why the micro-politics of the residents' committee has been a relatively neglected area for research by social scientists. According to a notable exception, 'The most menial positions of general leadership in urban China are the residents' committee and residents' small group leaders in local neighbourhoods' (Whyte and Parish, 1984, p. 212). Our own research reinforces the conventional view of an organisation of housewives and retired workers, mainly women, tied to the neighbourhood because of the demands of their household circumstances. A visit to a residents' committee in Jinan revealed that the committee was elected from retired workers and that the Director had held her post for over 30 years. However, there were thirteen candidates for seven places in 1984 and one person new to the committee was elected. The Director and the two deputy directors are paid and are assisted by thirty volunteers. The unrepresentative character of the residents' committee is, however, less important than the main interests of the majority of residents being located in their work unit. This, of course, will vary according to the demographic features of the neighbourhood.

In summary then, the self-government of the residents' committee is significantly constrained: the principle remains supervision by, rather than separation from, the Party; the leadership of the street office casts the residents' committee in the role of agent; the availability of personnel is limited; there are alternative and thereby fragmented centres of responsibility particularly the work unit and at least in one neighbourhood visited parallel organisations for health and old age provision; and there are opportunities for citizens to by-pass their residents' committee in preference for the street office and above.

This catalogue, however, could give a misleading impression of their effectiveness for their responsibilities as distinct from powers are substantial in a context of urban growth at this micro level. These responsibilities derive from several sources. The first is its entrenched position. The original intention of the CCP was to install a system of social control (Whyte and Parish, 1984, p. 22 and chap. 8) and the residents' committee has survived institutionally throughout the upheavals of the last 40 years. Depoliticisation may alter the priorities of the residents' committee, but there is little likelihood of its presence being affected. The residents' committee viewed from this perspective provides an element of stability in an era of institutional crisis and during a difficult period of urban reform. Constitutional recognition entrenches this process – a fact of considerable value bearing in mind a certain fickleness in Chinese constitution-making. The presence of the residents' committee also serves to legitimate the 'newer' and potentially more powerful rural villagers' committee.

A second source as noted by White in his contribution to this book is its delegated responsibilities from a network of authorities. These include para-legal functions such as resolving local disputes through its mediation committee and assisting in the maintenance of public order; public health sanitation and family planning; social welfare provision for children, disabled and old age; and providing a two-way channel of communication between residents and government. This may well be a growth area if work units, with whom it shares some of these responsibilities, begin to shed them as a consequence of economic restructuring. A third source is its ambiguous relationship with the street office in so far as it is charged with implementing its policies and that the population has increased within the catchment area of the residents' committee as a result of urban growth. This relationship clouds its position as a self-governing mass organisation but the resulting tension provides opportunities to exert influence. Fourthly, the residents' committee as a provider of services, creates a local economy. This is not a new role but has expanded to include temporary employment for young people 'waiting for work' and has a still greater potential in the growth of private individual and cooperative enterprise. For example, within the catchment area of the Jingan District, Shanghai, there are 11 youth cooperatives. Six of the cooperatives had no links with the residents' committees but five turned over some income since they were provided with space. Private businesses paid no money to the residents' committees and although the latter make some attempt at regulation they rely mainly on persuasion since they were not well organised to exert controls. This is another area in need of systematic research.

Finally, as the institution of direct democracy the residents' committee is charged with what one researcher has described as 'fostering the democratic spirit (*minzhu yishi*) . . . [and] . . . training (*xunlian*) the people towards an ultimate abolition of the state'. But as the same researcher noted, residents' committees are not in practice self-governing so we are not talking about democracy in a developmental sense of acquiring democratic values and learning democratic procedures but socialisation into a political system.[7] Yet the degree to which the residents' committee has evolved from an effective instrument of social control to an institution for socialisation and training for citizenship also suggests itself for study.

More generally, the overall brief of the residents' committee could expand consequent upon the growth, diversification and decentralisation in urban organisations, economic reforms and market pressures, and increasing social and political pluralism. This raises the question of how well adapted is an organisation run mainly by retired cadres and workers who have become veteran local leaders to new and changing priorities? More fundamentally, the residents' committee which has provided continuity and stability during periods of political decay and institutional crisis may in turn engender political resistance or disruption in conditions of economic development and reform. In other words, political reforms have not kept pace with changes in the urban economic environment, and this mismatch along with the complexities of the economic reforms, many of which are disputed, harbours potential conflict. With this in mind we turn to villagers' committees.

5 RURAL VILLAGERS' COMMITTEES

Attempts at institutionalisation at the village level dates to the Republican period, and although roots of the present system can be located there, power was invested firmly in the hands of the local landowning elite (Burns, 1988, p. 4). The efforts in the 1950s and early 1960s to revive the tutelary structures of the Nationalists and to institute participatory practices including the establishment of local assemblies were demoted in favour of mass mobilisation by the commune system. The common denominator during this post-liberation period was the presence of the CCP which in effect meant control by a new Party elite. As this elite lost credibility during the Cultural Revolution political decay or a crisis of institutionalisation set in. As Blecher (1988 and 1986, pp. 129–31) has pointed out however, the commune system did not preclude lively participatory politics. What was affected was entrenchment, adaptability and effectiveness. In regard to village level elections from 1962 to 1984 Burns argues that they were not reliable because they were not institutionalised and that they were not effective because they were dominated by the Party elite. It is likely that the same argument applied to local assemblies (Burns, 1988, pp. 119,172).

Decollectivisation marked the shift away from political mobilisation and towards an incremental approach to institutionalisation. In 1982, the political and administrative functions of the peoples' communes were transferred to township governments and to villages. The 1982 constitution as we have seen, recognised villagers' and residents' committees for the first time and stipulates that their members be elected. But it was not until 1987 that the Standing Committee of the NPC was able to agree an organic law for the villagers' committees. This included provision for election including the 'appropriate' number of women, the establishment of a villagers' assembly in which all members of the village over 18 are entitled to participate either on a direct or representative basis and for the setting up of villagers' groups. Its responsibilities are similar to those of the urban residents' committee but it is charged with promoting and developing village industry and with managing the land and other collectively owned assets (SWB 0014, 1 December 1987). The Vice-Chairpersons of the Legislative Affairs Commission of the Standing Committee of the NPC described the organic law of village committees as 'an important legal guarantee of the institutionalisation of democratic life at the grassroots level in rural areas' (SWB 0038, 1 January 1988).

There are a number of considerations to take into account in distinguishing the villagers' committee from the residents' committee. First, the village differs from the neighbourhood in that work and residence are more likely to be coterminous. This may be in flux however in so far as the economic reforms have increased the need for mobility encouraging or forcing members of households to seek work in nearby towns or cities. Second, many villages and particularly those visited in the course of our research, have a greater stake in enterprises than do urban neighbourhoods, which at least initially increases the resources and function of the villagers' committee. Third, the economic reforms have had a more significant impact on the village than on the neighbourhood in transforming the nature of the local economy. Fourth, it follows that there has been a greater shift in the power relations both within and outside of the villages. The commune system vested considerable power in production brigade and team leaders. Although cadres lost powers as a consequence of the reforms, they acquired new powers under the responsibility system, especially in regard to negotiating and supervising household contracting.

These acquired powers however, are likely to dissipate in time as the responsibility system stabilises. More important, the agricultural reforms in shifting resources to the household has tilted the balance of power in that direction. Since these agricultural policies have also encouraged diversification, the changing nature of the local economy has profound implications for power relations and political institutions.[8]

It was reported that between the constitutional recognition of villagers' committees and the approval of the organic law in November 1987, 948,000 villagers' committees were established (*Beijing Review* 7–13 December 1987). This attempt at rapid implementation was the likely result of a centrally inspired mobilisation and commitment to institutionalisation at the village level in order to complement the economic reforms. The local response, however, was varied (Perry, 1985, pp. 175–92) and implementation was often perfunctory at best.

The degree of institutionalisation then is likely to vary according to location, resources and progress under the commune system, although subsequent research revealed the establishment of villagers' committees in remote and less developed minority nationalities areas in Xishuangbanna Prefecture in Yunnan province (Benewick 1987). This uneven institutionalisation is reflected in the functions performed by the more advanced villagers' committees, some of which derive from their former incarnation under the commune system. Liu Tan is a highly developed village and former production brigade, located in a suburb of Tianjin. In terms of output value, 60 per cent is derived from industry, 32 per cent from services and only 8 per cent from agriculture. Out of 700 households with a total population of 2,700, however, 455 are engaged in agriculture but there is no responsibility system and production teams still exist to provide specialised services. Instead, the agricultural households market their produce themselves and receive a subsidy from the village, including fertiliser, transportation and machinery. Collective enterprises include five industries, one manufacturing electric motors for washing machines, three engaged in commerce and two transportation teams. In addition, there are a number of small private businesses and some of the residents travel to work in state factories.

The village leaders then, describe themselves as in charge of agriculture, enterprises and the life of the village. The eight members of the villagers' committee are elected in a meeting and are full time, paid from the income of the village agricultural, industrial and tertiary sector. The former production brigade enterprises are now managed by an agricultural-industry-commercial company and there is some interlocking and overlapping of personnel rather than separation between the company, villagers' committee and Party. The company has one manager and one vice-manager each for industry, agriculture and commerce. All four are appointed by the villagers' committee and the manager is also one of the two deputy heads of the villagers' committee and one of the five members of the Party branch. Moreover, the second deputy head of the villagers' committee is also a Party branch member.

In terms of a developed local economy Liu Tan is an advanced village which has adapted well to the reforms. In regard to institutionalisation, although there are formal separations of power the interlockings are striking. This can probably be credited, at least in part, to the village's progress when a production brigade.

Shanzhoujia village is located in a suburb of Jinan. It is an advanced village which has also adapted well to the reforms but differs in a number of respects from Liu Tan. First it was one of four villages which made up a production brigade and were reconstituted a township during the initial period of the reforms. A villagers' committee was established under a reorganisation that took place in 1983 which amalgamated nine villages into a town. Second, agriculture figures more prominently with its 1,370 population primarily involved in the cultivation of 2,000 *mu* of land compared to 580 *mu* in Liu Tan. The village operates a household responsibility system, involving the villagers' committee, town government, the county department responsible for the particular product and in the case of cotton, the main crop, the procuring agencies as well as the household in the contract negotiations. As elsewhere, the villagers' committee supervises the implementation of the household contracts. For example, if a member of a household works elsewhere, the share of land is redistributed. It also has the responsibility for establishing and contracting with enterprises. The only exclusively village enterprise at the time of our interviews was a vehicle parts plant run by a member of the villagers' committee. The contract is reviewed each year but it was evident that the villagers' committee were experiencing difficulties in obtaining the necessary information to exercise proper supervision. Third, most of the village income is from 30 enterprises run as joint ventures with the other three villages with which it had previously made up the production brigade. A joint committee supervises the contracts.

Shanzhoujia's villagers' committee was established in 1983. It was elected by secret ballot in contrast to Liu Tan and there were 11 candidates for 9 places. The village head was the one with the most votes. The second election in 1985 resulted in two new members of the committee. All are full time members and in addition to the traditional portfolios of head, birth control, militia and public security, mediation, village construction and accounting, members were assigned responsibilities for land adjustment, small enterprises, electricity and water supply, and notably the Young Communist League. The village head is also the Party Secretary. Hence the interlocking is even more formalised than in Liu Tan.

There is little doubt that Liu Tan and Shanzhoujia are atypical in terms of location, resources and commune experience. Given their relatively high degree of development it was not unreasonable to expect that village assemblies had been established. Moreover, they have been described along with the principle of majority rule as important, 'in order to institutionalise democratic life at the grassroots level in rural areas and guarantee the position of villagers as masters . . .' (SWB 0038 1 January 1988). Yet no mention was made of them, although academic researchers confirmed that they were functioning in Shandong province. Indeed Taipingjie village in Laiwu city held 18 meetings in 1985 with an attendance of between 700–800 people at each meeting (White and Benewick, 1986, p. 36). Village small groups were also in existence with the group head vested with responsibility for forwarding opinion to the villagers' committees. Small groups were also reported in Shanzhoujia but not in Liu Tan, although the latter still had production teams. It is one thing however to establish villagers' committees, assemblies and small groups and invest them with responsibilities and quite another for those responsibilities to be executed let alone executed effectively. So there is evidence to suggest (Blecher, 1989) that these institutions are underused, and as such it is likely that they will fail to acquire value and stability. In so far as this proves to be the case village committees will differ little from urban residents' committees. One explanation for such a development is that the economic functions have passed on to the households, the villagers' committees do not have sufficient regulatory powers while the town like the urban street office retains financial control (Duan, 1989).

A second explanation, as already indicated, is that uneven institutionalisation is also apparent in the separation of government, Party and economy. This may, in part, be a matter of transition and the complexities involved in reorganisation involving higher levels of government, as well as the result of the ambiguous status of villagers' committees in practice and the difficulties of implementing such a politically sensitive policy. It is of course an issue of major concern. One commentator has noted however, that the separation of Party and government at the township and village will only be considered after it has been achieved at the county level (Cai Shangshui 1988). Whatever the explanations, uneven institutionalisation is likely to produce a variety of political styles at village level that suggest themselves for more research.

6   CONCLUDING OBSERVATIONS

We have attempted to describe rather than to measure the extent of institutionalisation at basic-level government and below. Our concern has been with representation and participation so that the focus has been on the people's congress, the residents' committee and the villagers' committee. Since the reformers have established standing committees for the people's congresses in local government, we have also included the county level where relevant. Although we have only scratched the surface, we have been able to provide modest observations as well as to suggest important areas for further research.

It remains to relate, albeit briefly, the themes of this chapter to the urban protests of May and June 1989. It has been argued that institutionalisation is a reflection of the determination of the post-Mao leadership to prevent a reoccurrence of the chaos of the Cultural Revolution decade. The reformers identified a crisis of institutionalisation and introduced forms of participation and representation moving away from the politics of mobilisation. What were described as political structural reforms, however, were linked to economic reforms with no clear agreement as to their value and priority. At the same time there was little progress in reforming the Party as a possible source of political decay. A consequence of this strategy was a developmental lag where political reforms were unevenly implemented and weakly institutionalised so that they have not kept pace with the rapid social and economic change. It is suggested in conclusion that this political lag is a crucial factor in understanding and explaining the urban protests.

NOTES

1. The main research for this chapter was conducted under the auspices of the British Academy/Economic and Social Research Council/Chinese Academy of Social Sciences and reported in White and Benewick (1986). This research has been supplemented by further visits by the author to Yunnan Province (1987) and Beijing (1989).
2. For a helpful chart of the structure of China's governmental system see White's article in this volume.
3. A recent article, for example, describing the progress of political structural reforms in Anyang city Henan province illustrates the cautious approach to separating government and party (Lu and Feng 1988, p. 19).
4. A similar procedure was reported in the Haidian district of Beijing (Benewick, 1989).

5. Similar interventions by people's congresses were reported in the Haidian district and Evergreen township in Beijing (Benewick 1989).
6. For a comparison between the two see Whyte and Parish, 1984, p. 25–6.
7. Note however that the Vice-Chairpersons of the Legislative Affairs Committee of the Standing Committee of the NPC described the villagers' committee as a 'democracy training class for 800 million peasants' (swb 0038 1 January 1988).
8. For a lucid exposition of this point see White (1987).

REFERENCES

Benewick, Robert, 1987, 'Field notes of a trip to minority nationalities areas in Yunnan province'; 1989, 'Field notes Beijing'.
Benewick, Robert, 1988, 'Political Participation' in Benewick, Robert and Paul Wingrove (eds), *Reforming the Revolution: China in Transition* (London and Chicago, Macmillan and Dorsey).
Blecher, Marc, 1986, *China: Politics, Economics and Society* (London, Boulder, Frances Pinter and Lynne Rienner).
Blecher, Marc 1988, 'The re-organisation of the countryside' in Benewick and Wingrove, 1988.
Blecher, Marc 1989, 'The contradictions of grassroots participation and undemocratic statism in Maoist China and their fate', a revised version of a paper presented at the Conference on Contemporary Chinese Politics in Historical Perspective celebrating Tang Tsou's 70th birthday, University of Chicago, 1988.
Burns, John, 1985–86, 'Local Cadre Accommodation to the "Responsibility System" in Rural China', *Pacific Affairs*, vol. 58, no. 4, Winter.
Burns, John P., 1988, *Political Participation in Rural China* (Berkeley, Los Angeles, London, University of California Press).
Cai, Shangshui, 1988, 'Correctly understand the scientific implications of party leadership', fbis 003, 11 February 1988.
Chi Fulin, 1987, 'The building of democratic politics in China is a process of gradual development', *Liaowang Overseas Edition*, 3 August 1987, in swb 8645, 13 August 1987.
Deng Xiaoping, 1980, 'On the reform of the system of party and state leadership', *Selected Works of Deng Xiaoping 1975–1982* (Beijing, Foreign Languages Press, 1984, pp. 302–25).
Duan, Shunchen, 1989, 'Fieldwork report concerning China's village leadership', unpublished manuscript.
The Economist, 1987, 'A survey of China's economy', 1 August 1987.
Hsin-Chi Kuan, 1984, 'New departures in China's constitution', Studies in Comparative Communism, vol. 17 no. 1, Spring.

Huntington, Samuel P., 1965, 'Political development and political decay', *World Politics*, vol. 17 no. 3, April.

Huntington, Samuel P., 1968, *Political Order in Changing Societies* (New Haven, Yale University Press).

Lampton, David M. (ed), 1987, *Policy Implementation in Post-Mao China* (London, University of California Press).

Lu Yun and Feng Jing, 1988, 'Anyang begins political reform', *Beijing Review*, vol. 31 no. 12, 21–27 March.

McCormick, Barnett L., 1987, 'Leninist implementation: the election campaign', in Lampton, 1987, pp. 383–413.

Perry, Elizabeth J. and Christine Wong (eds), 1985, *The Political Economy of Reform in Post-Mao China* (London, Harvard University Press).

Schurmann, Franz, 1966, 1968, *Ideology and Organisation in Communist China*, (2nd edn, London, University of California Press).

Weng, Byron, 1982, 'Some key aspects of the 1982 draft constitution of the People's Republic of China', *China Quarterly*, no. 91, September.

White, Gordon, 1987, 'The impact of economic reforms in the Chinese countryside', *Modern China*, vol. 13 no. 4, October.

White, Gordon and Robert Benewick, 1986, *Local Government and Basic-Level Democracy in China: Towards Reform?*, Institute of Development Studies, University of Sussex, China Research Report, no. 3.

Whyte, Martin King and William Parish, 1984, *Urban Life in Contemporary China* (Chicago, London, University of Chicago Press).

Wu Guoguang and Gao Shan, 1987, 'Promote the institutionalisation of socialist democratic politics in our country', *Hongqi*, no. 21, 4 November 1987 in FBIS 271, 16 December 1987.

Yang Baikui, 1987, 'Some questions on China's political structural reform', *Guangzhou Yanjiu*, no. 2, 1987 in FBIS 090, 11 November 1987.

Zhang, Qingfu and Pi Chunxie, 1979, 'Revise the electoral laws to institutionalise democracy', *People's Daily*, 22 May 1979 in SWB:FE 6128.

11 Development State, Entrepreneurial State: The Political Economy of Socialist Reform in Xinju Municipality and Guanghan County

Marc Blecher

In social science, the subject of study generally changes much faster than our ability to conceptualise, much less theorise, it. This has happened once again with respect to the problematic of reform of state socialism. Caught flat-footed by the phoenix of Dengism which rose not once but twice from the ashes of late Maoism, China studies was forced to cast about for an analytical framework appropriate to the radical changes in political economy. For state-society relations, totalitarianism was resuscitated, both in its familiar old dark visage and as a newly refined conceptual progeny shorn of the theoretical excesses and political biases of the progenitor.[1] At the level of development strategy and attendant political conflict over it, the paradigm of two-line struggle soon found itself confronted by the more hydra-like three-line struggle.[2] And for the study of the actual planning and administration of development, many returned to the language of decentralisation. Indeed, there was a virtual stampede back to the conceptualisation offered in the mid-1960s by Franz Schurmann of decentralisation I and decentralisation II, because it was the most sophisticated and powerful discussion of the topic available.[3]

The most significant effort to break new analytical ground in the study of the Chinese reforms has come from the IDS, where the problematic was formulated in terms of the 'developmental state'. By placing 'development' at the centre of attention, this paradigm has helped de-Sinologise the study of China, locating it in a wider universe of 'developing' countries and in particular in a sub-group, the newly industrialising countries (NICs) of East Asia.[4] It has incorporated but also gone beyond the plan/market dyad on which the literature on state socialism and its reform had fixed. It has offered valuable new distinctions, such as 'complementary' versus 'competitive' plan-market relations, 'porous' versus 'definitive' planning, planning versus administration and regulation, and 'state bias' versus 'urban bias'. The analysis in this paper is deeply influenced by the developmental state approach, in at least two general respects. First, it resists the tendency to see in the Chinese reforms a diminution of state power. Second (and this may also be a premise for the previous point), it poses the problem of the developmental state more in qualitative than quantitative terms. It seeks to examine (and, somewhat more ambitiously, reconceptualise) the specific roles which the state plays in development.

The need to reconceptualise stems from the fact that the decentralisation approach, whether drawn from Schurmann or elsewhere, could not overcome the conceptual constraints imposed by the analysis of bureaucratic systems. The essence of the latter lies in the realm of administration, planning, control and regulation. Initiative, creativity and innovation are foreign to the logic of bureaucracy. Thus, they are commonly assumed to be absent in state socialism. In economic terms, state socialism has planners, not entrepreneurs. Reform is about the reorganisation of planning; even the transfer of power down to enterprises whose relations and actions would be regulated by some kind of market are conceptualised as a form of decentralisation ('I') rather than as an opening to entrepreneurship. A small dose of linguistic deconstruction makes the analytical and ideological problems evident. Reform of state socialism can be expressed as a negation – de-centralisation. Enterprise – a word resonating to positivities like initiative and creativity – does not appear in the literature on state socialism even when enterprise reform or enterprise de-centralisation are the order of the day. Apparently 'enterprise' is always modified by the word 'free' at least implicitly. This is all the more troubling for the study of state socialism in China or elsewhere at moments of economic reform, when, as is evident to one and all, entrepreneurship is flowering as never before.

This tendency to exclude entrepreneurship from the developmental role of the state at the theoretical level has been carried over to the developmental state approach, at least as it has been applied to China. Though the 'Introduction' to *Developmental States in East Asia* does at one point speak of the state as 'a developmental elite supplanting the capitalist entrepreneurial class', by and large entrepreneurship is conceptualised as an activity undertaken by enterprises which are implicitly or explicitly viewed as distinct from the developmental state administration.[5] There is nothing wrong with this view *per se* or the policy consequences it envisions. Indeed, it fits the actual situation in at least one locality – Xinji Municipality in Hebei province – to be discussed here. The problem is that there are other Chinese realities which it does not fit. One is Guanghan County in Sichuan province, which presents a particularly troubling analytical problem since it is a positive exemplar of the reform programme.

This suggests a need to begin to theorise a developmental role of the state in a way which emphasises entrepreneurship by state administrative or bureaucratic agencies as a central activity. This theory of what will be called the entrepreneurial state will then be contrasted with a rather different developmental role for the state in which entrepreneurship is undertaken by enterprises. This will be termed the developmental state after the larger approach that inspired it. These ideas will be explored in the context of two case studies. An effort will then be made to explain why in each locality the state evinced its specific developmental role. Finally, some general theoretical conclusions will be drawn concerning the two models, their implications for development, and their places in the historical trajectory of Chinese state socialism both past and future.

Before proceeding, one methodological point should be underscored. As used here, the entrepreneurial state and the developmental state are not ideal types, but rather concepts which have been formed inductively in the course of trying to come to grips with the political economy of development in two Chinese localities. Studies of other localities or other periods may suggest the need for other theoretical approaches. Indeed, this paper is a plea for a more plural analytical approach to Chinese development – based not on macro-level theorising but on locally-based studies.

ENTREPRENEURIAL STATE, DEVELOPMENTAL STATE

The essence of the distinction between the entrepreneurial and the developmental state has to do with the locus of entrepreneurship and the relationship of the enterprise to the state. In both decentralisation and developmental state approaches, entrepreneurship is presumed to lie with enterprises – state, collective or private. The role of the state is variously to promote development (through planning, bureaucratic co-ordination, arrangement of finance, procurement of inputs, development of infrastructure, etc.) or to regulate it. But in the entrepreneurial state conceptualisation, bureaux of the state themselves undertake entrepreneurial activity. They start enterprises of their own, which are not independent (though they may be formally separate, like dummy corporations), but rather remain under bureau or agency control. To put the matter more starkly, they remain part of the bureau or agency. Of course, Chinese bureaux have long established their own production or commercial facilities. For example, grain bureaux have been running grain mills for decades. What is distinctive about the entrepreneurial state is the establishment and operation by state agencies of enterprises not merely to assist the agency in carrying out its assigned task, but in order to earn profits.

From this distinction flow a number of theoretical implications.

(1) State control over the enterprise and entrepreneurship would tend to be more direct under the entrepreneurial state and more indirect under the developmental state. In other words, the enterprise has greater autonomy under the developmental than the entrepreneurial state.

(2) State control over enterprises would be exercised more through vertical channels in the entrepreneurial state and more through horizontal ones in the developmental state. This could happen for two kinds of reason.

> (a) In the entrepreneurial state, the agency or bureau takes the initiative and responsibility for arranging financing, licensing, input procurement, marketing and so on, while in the developmental state the enterprise itself must deal with the various bureaux in charge of these functions.
>
> (b) Horizontally-orientated state agencies such as planning bureaux or even Party organs would be less likely to feel the impulse to make profits by establishing enterprises than would vertically-orientated bureaux, which are held responsible by higher levels of their bureaucratic systems for meeting profit targets.

(3) Consequently, the level of planning co-ordination could be greater under the developmental than the entrepreneurial state. This in no way contradicts the first proposition above. In fact, it flows therefrom.[6] In the entrepreneurial state, vertically-oriented bureaux and agencies operate on their own, sometimes even competing with each other, in pursuing entrepreneurial opportunities. But in the developmental state, horizontally-oriented state agencies engage explicitly in planning and co-ordination. In the Maoist period, they did so through direct administrative means.[7] In the post-Maoist period, such co-ordination could extend to other, more indirect forms (such as structuring markets or providing infrastructure).[8]

(4) Accordingly, the entrepreneurial state resonates more to the logic of the market, while the developmental state has more to do with some

combination of plan and market. The markets involved here are not for products, but also for labour and, of special importance, for capital. Thus, one specific policy consequence might be that the developmental state would have an easier time than the entrepreneurial state in controlling excessive accumulation and capital construction (which have been *bêtes noires* of the reform programme since it inception).

(5) The developmental state may be more capable of pursuing goals having to do with balanced growth and economic equality than the entrepreneurial state, whose orientation to market activity would cause it to ignore or even exacerbate inequality and developmental imbalance. This latter outcome could occur either because of the pure operation of market forces or because state bureaux could exercise more market power than the more autonomous enterprises with whom they might compete.

THE DEVELOPMENTAL STATE IN XINJI MUNICIPALITY

In May, 1986, as part of a national policy of elevating more economically advanced rural localities to an administrative status that reflected their regional centrality, Shulu County in Hebei province was redesignated Xinji Municipality. As of December 1986, this change was little more than nominal. Xinji Municipality is located approximately 70 km. east of Shijiazhuang City (the capital of Hebei Province): it is a rural rather than suburban area, situated well out into the North China Plain. With its agriculture engaged primarily in grain production, it is about average for its area in rural development. But it is relatively advanced industrially; in fact, it is the most industrially advanced county in the prefecture. In 1978, gross value of industrial output (GVIO) made up 55 per cent of total output value by official count, and by 1986 the figure was 63 per cent . Per-capita income was ¥88 in 1978, well below the national average though above average for Shijiazhuang Prefecture; in 1986 it was up to ¥522. Still, in 1978 only 4 per cent of the county's population was classified as 'non-rural householders', and by 1986 this figure had risen only to 6 per cent . With 537 persons per km. and 5.4 persons per cultivated hectare in 1978, it is densely populated. It had never been a national model of economic development, either in the Maoist or post-Maoist periods.

The Developmental State in Shulu during the late Maoist period

Gordon White has written:

In crude terms of industrial growth and structural change, Chinese economic performance since the mid-1950s had been very creditable. Clearly there was some positive dynamic in the old system which needs analysis.[9]

Insofar as Shulu County was a successful industrialiser during the Maoist period, analysis of it during those years can shed some light on this very important, if ideologically unpopular, question. Our explanation relies heavily on the flexibility immanent within the county government structure and the capacity of Shulu's leadership to make use of it to promote development through careful planning and wise investment of the county government's own financial resources, especially from its extra-budgetary fund, to develop infrastructure and productive enterprises.

An analysis of Shulu county government finance as a complex network comprised of three strands of administrative and authority relations (the state budget, the vertical systems [*xitong*], and the horizontal extra-budgetary fund) has been published already.[10] On the basis of research findings in Shulu County in 1979, it will be argued in a forthcoming book that this institutional setting provides the backdrop against which a county government with strong leadership and some financial resources under its own control could take the initiative to promote successful and balanced economic development.[11] The major basis of these locally-controlled financial resources was profits of the 'five small industries' established to support agriculture in 1970, which the county government deposited in its extra-budgetary fund. It used some of these monies to refinance the development of this sector, thereby expanding the county government's own financial base. Eventually the government could plan development projects of considerable scope using locally-controlled (horizontal) extra-budgetary funds as seed money to obtain other needed funding through the (vertical) state budget and ministerial systems. But the primary emphasis of Shulu county government was not on making these industrial profits, rather on expanding developmental horizons.

The best example of what is being called here the 'developmental state' in Shulu was a major water conservancy project built in 1978–79. Our discussion of it is reproduced here (in somewhat shortened form) to illustrate not only the financial aspects of the project but also to provide some flavor of the specific leadership and co-ordination of the 'developmental state' type that can be undertaken by a county government:

Twelve communes in the southern part of Shulu, with 30,420 ha. (43 per cent of the total) under cultivation, lie on the historically disaster-prone Heilongang, and have always had lower than average yields. In 1977, the entire area of these ten communes was flooded in heavy rains. The effect on the county's overall agricultural output was disastrous.

In the face of the crisis, the Shulu County Revolutionary Committee took the initiative in organising a survey team to ascertain what system of canals, ditches and other water works would be needed to assure adequate drainage as well as better irrigation of the area. At the same time, the Committee held a series of conferences with representatives from the various communes involved, to solicit their opinions and quickly to formulate a plan of work. It was decided to organise a very large force of workers to attack the project all at once, and to finish it in one season.

One hundred thousand people were mobilised to work on the project. Seventy thousand workers on the project came from the ten communes that would benefit directly from it. An additional 30,000 workers from other communes were organised to participate on the promise that when their communes undertook capital construction work sometime in the future, the ten communes would reciprocate by sending 30,000 of their own workers for commensurate periods of time.

The cost of the whole project was roughly ¥5 million, and the county government had to put funds together from several sources to pay for it. It received ¥1.5 million on credit from various county bureaux (for transportation, machine repairs, etc.) and from the ten southern communes (for food and food preparation). These debts had been almost completely repaid by the summer of 1979. Another ¥1 million came from higher organs of the state, presumably through the Water Conservancy Bureau. The remaining ¥2.5 million was drawn from the county's own extra-budgetary fund, thus making the county government itself the largest single contributor . . . [The] project did succeed in lowering the underground water table, and in bringing 12,700 ha. under irrigation while improving that of another 18,000 ha.

County officials were proud of the success of this major water conservation project, which illustrates what an important role the county government can play in co-ordinating and financing key local development undertakings that individual bureaux or communes alone do not have the means to carry out. Those ten flooded communes clearly did not possess sufficient resources on their own to finance such a comprehensive network of canals. But taking the whole county as a field for the mobilisation of capital, labour and administrative and technical skills, it was possible to make a selective injection of assistance where it was needed. This benefited a part of the county which, both historically and in contemporary times, had·been comparatively poor and disaster-prone. But the decision had a 'constituent'[12] character too, contributing to the development of the whole county as well as a poor part. This project, then, was an instance when local interests (from the affected rural collective units) and state concerns (as expressed by county government and higher level organs) coincided.[13]

At the risk of making this arduous reality sound even more like a Maoist-period fairy tale, they did live happily ever after: Xinji Prefecture officials interviewed in 1986 declared that the salinity problems which this project attacked had by then been completely solved.

If the Shulu County government undertook to plan, finance and implement development projects like this one, and to develop an industrial base under its own horizontal control in order to help finance them, it also played a more subtle and indirect developmental role by co-ordinating the activities taken by lower-level units. Sometimes production unit leaders persuaded county officials in one bureau or another to help them get started with loans, equipment or technical assistance. But far more often, it seemed, the unit first made its own inquiries or contacts. Once the unit made its own decision to go ahead with trial production and had some initial successes, usually with minimal or no assistance from the county, then it was able to obtain local government support in expanding its business.

Two examples may be of interest. In the first, the role of 'developmental state' was played both by the county government and also the prefecture and provincial governments above it. The story begins in the Chengguan Commune Agricultural Machinery Repair and Manufacturing Plant where one workshop was engaged in producing padlocks.

Commune officials explained somewhat apologetically that in the late 1960s . . . a need had grown up in the commune to secure warehouse doors, certain pieces of machinery, and other movable items. Using the profits from its diesel engine intake-valve production, the factory undertook to produce padlocks. Of course the investment could not be recouped by production for the commune's own needs alone. There was demand for locks in other parts of Shulu anyway, so a production contract was arranged with the Shulu Department Store, which distributed them in its main Xinji store as well as branch shops throughout the county. Serendipitously, officials of Shijiazhuang Prefecture and Hebei Province, in Xinji for a conference at the guest house across the street from the main department store, noticed the locks while out for a walk. Upon their return home, they dispatched officials of their own commercial departments to the Chengguan Commune plant and the Xinji store. Existing stocks were purchased, and a trial sales run proved successful. Production contracts under the state plan were then signed directly between the prefectural and provincial commercial agencies and the Chengguan plant. By 1979 Pingyuan (Plains) brand locks manufactured by Chengguan Commune were on sale throughout Hebei.

In this case the process by which production was undertaken, and then expanded had nothing at all to do with administrative fiat or the slow, grinding operation of bureaucratic machinery, the picture so prevalent in the literature on socialist planning. It had much more to do with attempts by local producers to invest profitably and produce for local demand, along with efforts of state officials to respond to a real, market opportunity. This example, in other words, testifies to the compatibility of state planning and a kind of market rationality commonly assumed to prevail only in capitalist economies.

In the second case, Jiujie Production Brigade leaders first thought of raising mink in 1974 when they read a local newspaper story about mink raising in Pingshan County, northwest Shijiazhuang Prefecture. Brigade leaders contacted the Native Products Company through their County Foreign Trade Bureau. They did not receive a loan to get operations under way at first, but the Company did supply them with some wood and wire for building cages. Three or four times the first year, company animal husbandry technical personnel came to the brigade to advise them. And the brigade frequently consulted company people by telephone during the first year when problems or questions arose. By 1979, brigade leaders felt they had mastered this new sideline. In this case, as in the case of the Chengguan Commune Lock Factory . . . the county government acted only as a facilitator and go-between in getting the enterprise started. The initial entrepreneurial spark came from within the brigade itself[14].

Our analysis of the role of the county government in promoting development in Shulu through the late 1960s and the 1970s concluded with the following (again, in somewhat abbreviated form).

County government in contemporary China has usually been characterised as having the capacity either to carry out or to obstruct policies decided by superordinate authorities. Our study of Shulu suggests that under certain circumstances the county can also play a significant role in initiating polices of local developmental benefit, and in co-ordinating their administration in concert with other levels of government. The analytical problem that remains is to specify the conditions under which the county can play this role with greater or lesser effectiveness.

Doubtless one important condition is *a sense of collective purpose and problem-solving determination among county leaders and citizens*, allowing the former to make plans behind which the latter can unite. Why this happens more in some counties and less in others has much to do with factors relating to local history, patterns of economic and social differentiation, treatment received from the larger state, and the quality of county government leadership. Shulu County has an illustrious local history, is relatively homogeneous in geographic, ethnic and economic terms, has received a modest share of attention and small rewards from the state, and is blessed with leaders of talent who projected a strong sense of the county as a whole and genuine commitment to its development.

It seems evident, that at least a certain degree of *financial capacity* is a second condition contributing to a county government's ability to plan effectively for local development, and to the likelihood that the people of the county will respond positively to those plans. But financial capacity does not exist in an administrative or political vacuum. Shulu's ability to undertake its important water conservancy project depended not only upon its successes in local industrial development which generated the financial wherewithal to plan for development, but also upon a degree of *administrative autonomy* putting some of the fruits of that development at the disposal of county leaders. This is not to say that, at least in Shulu, the county could undertake such projects on its own, independently of other levels of government, or that its leaders would want to. They might well prefer to share the responsibility and risk with their superiors. Even in the striking example of the water conservation project, the county government was the *administrative impresario* – providing the core funding, obtaining funds from other sources, and organizing itself as well as other government agencies to contribute in various ways to the project – but *not the sole actor* in carrying it off.

This raises the question of the relationship between the county and the higher levels of the state. We have found it analytically useful to regard the county government as the meeting point between vertically linked administrative processes and structures – like the state budget or the ministerial systems (*xitong*) – and *horizontally* oriented ones – like the extra-budgetary fund, the Revolutionary Committee (or its successor, the People's Government) or the Planning Commission. Our first concluding point is that these *characterisations of administrative processes as 'vertical' or 'horizontal' are not absolute*; much ambiguity remained in these processes and relationships. For example, in the 'vertical' state budgetary process, the county authorities negotiated on behalf of the county as a whole for reduced revenue or expanded expenditure allocations. And of course 'horizontal' organisations like the People's Government or the Planning Commission still worked within guidelines set by, and still had to answer to, higher level authorities of the state.

But – and this is our second point – conflicts between vertical and horizontal organisational formations were bound to arise for several reasons. To begin with, there are the normal conflicts in any complex organisation between people in bureaucratic units with responsibilities of a more horizontal or vertical character. There will be conflicting demands and intense competition for economic resources between any level of locality and the wider units of the state and society. But other factors exist which are more specific to the county level in the Chinese case. One has to do with the county's specific location in the Chinese layered structure. It is true that the county is entirely a unit of the state, as opposed to the commune, which has had more of a mixed state-collective character. Nevertheless, officials serving at the county level are low enough in the hierarchy to have direct, face-to-face contact with leading grassroots cadres of local communities . . . at the same time, they also have direct, face-to-face as well as more bureaucratic relationships with higher levels of the state. Tensions and conflicts between local and regional/national interests, between 'state' and 'society', and between horizontal and vertical administrative organisations will therefore be felt acutely and very *personally* at the county level. If these tensions are not effectively mediated or resolved, they could result in serious damage to the economic development and political life of the county and/or the wider territorial units of which it is an important part.

Our third concluding point is, thus, that the case of Shulu helps specify some of the ways in which these problems can be resolved productively. The most prominent example is the 1977–78 water conservancy project, which brought together horizontally oriented financial and organisational resources – capital from the extra-budgetary fund, credit from the rural collective sector (in the form of cash, materials and labour), and co-ordination from the Planning Commission and the county government – with vertically linked ones – monies from the state, released time from obligations to provide labour for state-run projects, technical assistance and so forth.

In this and other instances, Shulu County shows us what a county government, located toward the bottom of the centralised political and bureaucratic hierarchy of a state socialist system, can do to promote its own economic development in the face of serious historical, natural, economic and structural obstacles.[15]

THE DEVELOPMENTAL STATE IN SHULU DURING THE POST-MAOIST PERIOD

The burden of this argument about Shulu in the Maoist period is that it evinced a developmental pattern rather more successful, and much less bureaucratic or top-down statist, than the popular (and to a significant degree ideologically-formed) caricature of the Maoist period would suggest.[16] Rather, the Shulu political economy was statist, but in a way which left room for developmental initiative and co-ordination by local state agencies at the county level. It can be termed 'developmental' statist in the specific sense in which that term was used above.

The popular (and, again, partly ideological) caricature of the post-Maoist period as anti-statist is also confounded by the reality of Shulu. What is most striking about Shulu in the early 1980s was the continuity of the county government's developmental role. It maintained its horizontal, co-ordinative function, its primary commitment to developmental promotion rather than profit-making, its concern with balance in development, and its combination of planning, markets and indirect economic levers to guide development.

The best example is the spectacular Hebei No. 1 Market. In the wake of the post-Maoist reforms in commerce, the town of Xinji became flooded with peddlers. By 1983, the traffic and congestion had become intolerable, and it had become impossible to carry out commercial regulation work such as licensing and taxing retail traders and enforcing price regulations. In the fall of 1984 the Industrial and Commercial Management Bureau of what was now the Xinji Municipal government, which was responsible for commercial regulation, formulated a plan for an enormous set of new, integrated market buildings. The Municipal Government approved it, and helped procure the necessary approval of the Shijiazhuang Prefecture Urban Affairs Bureau, which regulates this type of urban land use.

The plan had several dimensions. It called for one huge, multi-story building nearly a city block in length housing large retail outlets of the major industrial enterprises in the municipality. In front of this building, the street was to be expanded into a divided, landscaped boulevard, while behind and perpendicular to it were to be erected twenty two-story blocks in ten rows with small shops on the ground floor and apartments upstairs.

These were to be sold as condominia to individual households who would live and do business in the new market, or to state and collective-sector enterprises as retail and residential space. Between the ten rows of low blocks, covered, open-air market stalls were to be built and rented out to other small-scale retailers.

The financial scale of the project was prepossessing. Each of the 351 units in the two-story blocks cost ¥4800 to construct (which comes to ¥1,684,800). The large front building and the stalls and paving were additional. The Municipal Government undertook the horizontal and vertical co-ordination needed to bring it off the drawing boards and into reality. It sent out advertisements to Industrial and Commercial Management Bureaux in every county in Hebei Province and to every provincial-level Industrial and Commercial Management office in the rest of the country. Prospective buyers had to arrange their own financing, which the Municipal Government aggregated to fund the construction costs of the multi-story front building and the two-story blocks. It got the Industrial and Commercial Management Bureau to advance ¥200,000 to pay for the open-air stalls, and provided ¥400,000 from the Municipal Government's state budget to pay for the roads, driveways and sidewalks. By 1986, government officials estimated that ¥1,800,000 in trade volume was being done monthly.

What is perhaps most significant about this project from a developmental state point of view is that the Municipal Government undertook it on a non-profit basis. Hebei No. 1 Market was built by the government in order to resolve serious problems of urban congestion and commercial regulation, not to make money. The government undertook many of the same kinds of vertical and horizontal co-ordination that had been the hallmarks of its developmental role in the late Maoist period. Plan and market came together in a particularly pointed way here: Hebei No. 1 Market is literally a planned market. It left profit-making to the enterprises and shop keepers to whom it sold parts of its real-estate development.

Yet it did not abandon them to the vagaries of the market. The Xinji Industrial and Commercial Management Bureau, in almost classic 'developmental state' fashion, promoted local products and market development in a number of ways. It was planning to introduce electronic scales and other modern equipment retail equipment. It published a daily newsletter listing up-to-date prices of key products and alerting local merchants to lucrative opportunities. It was attempting to resuscitate a traditional method for preparing donkey meat, which had been a local speciality. The products of early efforts to retrieve this lost delicacy were already on sale at the Hebei No. 1 Market, and were quite delicious!

Another example of developmental state activity by the Xinji Municipal Government was its comprehensive programme of urban planning. In the very first year of Dengism, which in so many analyses is associated with the retreat of the state from the economy, Xinji established for the first time an Urban Construction and Environmental Protection Bureau, precisely the sort of agency which capitalist real estate developers and industrialists associate with overweening state power in the economy. The Bureau formulated a comprehensive plan for the town of Xinji, involving relocation of entire factories to an industrial center downwind of the residential area (to be financed partly by state subsidies), the construction of green belts between these sectors, new roadway and parking-lot development and the development and enforcement of environmental protection policies.

Major roadway construction was another developmental initiative undertaken by the municipality. Continuing the Maoist period commitment of the county government to balanced development, systematic efforts have been made both before and since 1978 to build and maintain a network of paved roads to every township (formerly the communes) in the municipality, including both near and far, rich and poor. In one key example, in 1984 the road to Wangkou in extreme southern Xinji was finally paved. This removed the last remaining obstacle to resuscitation of the town's traditional firecracker manufacturing business, which by 1986 was earning ¥5,000,000 from exports to seventeen countries. Wangkou, which had been among the very poorest communes in Shulu in 1978, was now the very richest (as measured by per-capita income). But the importance of road-building by the Municipal Government was far greater than its developmental effects on one locality. For good transportation is absolutely essential to the development of market-based commerce more generally. In agriculture, the success of the 1977–78 water conservancy project placed Shulu agriculture on a solid footing of balanced growth. It was now possible to obtain stable, respectable yields in basic foodgrain and cash crops throughout the county.[17] Xinji's Mayor, Liu Baolu, had in 1979 been the senior agricultural official in the county; at that time he spoke of the central problem in Shulu agriculture as the productive imbalance between different regions of the county due to salinity problems. It was Liu who had been largely responsible for developing the 1977–78 water conservancy project, the success of which may have been a major factor in his elevation to Mayor by 1986. Now that that problem was resolved, he spoke of the key problem in agriculture in terms of fine-tuning cropping. Base areas were to be build around cultivation of grain, cotton, fruit, peanuts and vegetables. This would require the municipal government to undertake detailed land surveys as well as serious training efforts both of and then by agricultural extension staff. The government would invest in agriculture by subsidising seeds and chemical fertiliser.

Water Conservancy Bureau officials also admitted that the responsibility systems in agriculture had led to neglect of irrigation and drainage work, which required a flurry of administrative and political activity by the municipal government. But it was also beginning to subsidise and co-ordinate more elaborate and expensive infrastructure developments such as an underground drip irrigation system imported from Israel(!). The system had an initial cost of ¥2,250 per hectare (including the wells), and the municipal government had plans to put it under 4,000 ha. of orchard land by 1990, at a cost of ¥9,000,000 (almost twice the cost of the huge 1977–78 water conservancy project). The municipal government, through the water conservancy bureau, planned to subsidise 90 per cent of the interest on bank loans that were to be taken out by peasants who put in the system (as well as absorbing the cost of research and development, planning, training, etc.).

THE DEVELOPMENTAL STATE IN SHULU/XINJI: CONCLUSION

Four conclusions emerge from this discussion. First, nearly a decade after the onset of the post-Maoist reforms, local government in Shulu/Xinji was still very active in many of the same sorts of developmental activities in which it had engaged in the late Maoist years. Reform was in evidence in many respects, such as the triumph of the agricultural responsibility system and the extraordinary proliferation of private petty commerce, but so was an active role for the developmental state.

Second, in some major respects this developmental state activity was vital to the continued developmental successes being achieved in Shulu/Xinji. Certainly market-based reform could never have eventuated in the construction of a roadway system which was a prerequisite for the resuscitation and industrialisation of some of the poorest parts of the country. With Alec Nove, we assert that infrastructure is rarely cost-effective in itself, which is why markets won't produce it; but it is cost-effective (and downright essential) from a larger developmental perspective which only government can have.[18] The same could definitely be said of urban planning, and probably also of major projects like the Hebei no. 1 Market or the drip irrigation system.

Third, the developmental activities of the local state in Shulu/Xinji produced a pattern of growth which was planned, rational and balanced in important respects. The Hebei No. 1 Market brought together large factory outlets and individual peddlers. The roadway system benefited the poorest of Shulu towns. Agricultural planning was going forward based on systematic investigation of the capacities of the land and the farmers.

Fourth, this was all being done by a local government which itself stayed out of actual production and profit-making, and contented itself with the more familiar governmental role of creating the conditions for enterprises to produce and profit. It was a developmental but not an entrepreneurial state. The meaning and implications of this distinction will be clarified best by looking at aspects of political economy in Guanghan County, where the local state played rather different roles in the economy, with rather different consequences for local enterprises, entrepreneurship and development.

THE ENTREPRENEURIAL STATE IN GUANGHAN COUNTY

Guanghan County lies northeast of Chengdu, Sichuan Province, its county seat situated thirty kilometres out along the major trunk road and railway leading toward Xi'an. During then Provincial Secretary Zhao Ziyang's tenure in Sichuan during the earliest days of post-Maoist reform, it was selected as a keypoint for experimentation in institutional restructuring – in particular for the separation of Party leadership from government administration. Located in the fertile Chengdu Plain, it is well endowed for agriculture. With 8.7 per cent of its population classified as non-rural householders, in 1985 it was slightly more urbanised than Xinji. But it is much more densely populated, with 925 people per km.^{2} and fifteen people per cultivated hectare. Thus it has given great emphasis to industry, which in 1985 accounted for two-thirds of gross output value. Only with these levels of industrialisation could per-capita rural incomes remain at the relatively high level of ¥602.

What follows makes no pretense to a comprehensive account of development in Guanghan. That will have to await a forthcoming analysis of the quantitative data and interviews conducted in Guanghan. Rather, the present discussion deals with the most interesting aspects of the Guanghan political economy, all of which differ from the pattern observed in Shulu/Xinji.

The first concerns the activities of the Guanghan County Federation of Rural Supply and Marketing Cooperatives in building a ten-story convention center in the county seat. Since their establishment in the early 1950s of course, the rural supply and marketing cooperatives had served the commercial needs of the rural area, replacing private shops and peddlers. As the post-Maoist reforms got under way, however, many of these came under criticism for having lost their collective character and having become in effect arms (or, in more picturesque language, tentacles) of state power over the countryside. Yet in Guanghan, a locality chosen to be at the leading edge of reform, the supply and marketing cooperatives seem to have come gradually under increased state control. In 1983, a 'partnership' between the cooperatives and the Federation was formed. (This contrasts sharply with Shulu/Xinji, where the cooperatives had come under the control of the State Bureau in 1977 but were then returned to collective ownership in 1983). By 1986, the Guanghan Federation – which, according to its director Zhang Zhiguo, was an administrative not an economic agency (i.e., not an enterprise) – was nevertheless acting very much like an enterprise. Having observed that the reforms were creating a wave of commercial and industrial convention business nationally and regionally, and that Guanghan's location near the hub city of Chengdu as well as its ready access to transport facilities (on a major road and railway, and even with its own small airport!), the Federation decided to build an urban skyscraper containing a trade convention center, hotel and restaurants. When I jokingly asked Mr. Zhang if I could invest in the project, he said that he had obtained all the financing he needed (thank you very much!), but that he would welcome my bringing in convention business! This was entrepreneurship, not development administration.

The way in which the project was financed was also a model of entrepreneurial acumen. Total cost was projected to be ¥3,000,000. It was raised by the Federation from rural investors. This came through syndicated loans from peasant investors, whose participation in the project was solicited through the Rural Supply and Marketing Cooperative network. These loans were to be repaid at 12 per cent interest, though, in an arrangement whose details were less than clear, if the project proved financially successful, this could rise to a maximum of 15.7 per cent. Second, ¥1,200,000 was borrowed from the bank; in all likelihood this was the Agricultural Bank (since this urban skyscraper was being built by the agency in charge of rural commerce!). If so, this would be significant because it would avoid the Construction Bank which was established to finance, but also to oversee and tightly regulate, capital construction.[19] This probably also required the establishment of a (dummy) corporation or enterprise, since, according to the Director of the Agricultural Bank, administrative agencies are not permitted to borrow from the bank.

Third, the remaining ¥1,000,000 came from the Federation's own finances. This in turn had two sources. Some came from loans from the rural supply and marketing cooperatives themselves, who received an interest rate of 17.9 per cent . To reduce the level of borrowing at this high interest rate, and because of the general scarcity of funding for capital construction outside the state plan, the rest came from loans from banks in poor minority areas in northern and western Sichuan, including the Aba and Ganzi Autonomous Regions (which happen also to be Tibetan nationality areas). The interest rate for such loans was set through 'negotiation' – i.e., at some sort of market-like rate – and so was variable. In 1985 it was 11.35 per cent, which made it a real bargain for the Guanghan Federation. Indeed, this interest rate was lower than that paid by the Federation to the local peasant investors (who no doubt were much wealthier than the Aba and Ganzi depositors). The Director of the Guanghan Agricultural Bank confirmed that Guanghan banks did very little lending but a good deal of borrowing on the inter-bank financial market. (By contrast, Xinji bankers were not involved in any such financial market.) He argued that in poor areas like Aba and Ganzi there is excess liquidity in the banks because of the shortage of investment possibilities. As a result, banks there were unable to meet their profit targets. Thus, starting in 1984 they were permitted to loan funds to other banks in richer areas where demand for credit was greater. In a classic free-marketeer fashion, he said, 'So you see, everyone benefits.' Obviously, though, there are serious implications here for issues of balanced development and equality between rich and poor areas.

Clearly, banking itself had become an entrepreneurial activity in Guanghan. Banks there had profit targets, which they had little trouble reaching because the generally high level of entrepreneurial activity in the county created a strong demand for credit. (By contrast, Xinji banks had no profit targets, though the possibility was being discussed in late 1986.) The Guanghan Agricultural Bank was permitted to retain 9 per cent of its in-target and over-target profits. It was establishing trust companies to enable credit to flow among enterprises, and taking a share of such transactions for its trouble. (By contrast, Xinji banks had not established trust companies.) This orientation of banking to profit-making and entrepreneurship could create difficulties for county government planners. Though in several cases the banks had worked closely with the county government in establishing new enterprises, the Director of the Agricultural Bank said that the government had no power to force the bank to loan money for its projects. Indeed, he said, 'we can prefer to loan to a project not run by the county government over one run by it if the former is a superior [i.e., more financially attractive – MB] project'. The Director of the Construction Bank also confirmed this for his institution.

Like any proper entrepreneurial activity, banking was also beginning to generate competition between state agencies. The Guanghan Federation of Rural Supply and Marketing Cooperatives was competing with the Agricultural Bank for the private liquidity in the countryside by selling shares at interest rates (of 12–14 per cent) in excess of those being paid by the Bank on deposits, by removing upper limits for share investment, and by opening share sales to urban dwellers, cadres, and even people who lived outside the county. (By contrast, shares in the Xinji Rural Supply and Marketing Cooperatives were paying 10 per cent interest, which would encourage the peasants there to establish their own enterprises, thereby shifting the locus of entrepreneurship away from the state.) The Federation Director admitted that the largest share purchasers tended to come from outside Guanghan, because that way these investors could more easily keep their financial affairs private. He also volunteered that many of these people were former members of exploiting classes or people who were dubbed 'speculators' and 'capitalist tails' during the Maoist years. Here, then, we have a glimpse of some of the social bases and implications of the entrepreneurial state.

Another example of entrepreneurship by a state agency was the establishment in Guanghan City of a new nylon conveyor belt factory by the Guanghan Second Light Industry Bureau. To help raise the capital in the very tight and expensive Guanghan credit market, the bureau formed a joint venture with its sibling bureau in Liuchuan County of – one might have guessed! – Aba Autonomous Region. Each bureau borrowed the funds from its own local banks, notwithstanding the prohibition on banks loaning to state agencies for projects outside the state plan. Besides sending 'a factory vice-director and a few workers,' it is not clear that the Liuchuan bureau contributed anything to the project but financing, presumably at relatively low rates. So even though the Liuchuan bureau invested ¥550,000 in the project to the Guanghan Bureau's ¥450,000, it remained the junior partner. Here again the shrewd entrepreneurial state served as a magnet attracting scarce developmental funds from a poor area to a rich one.

WHY THE DEVELOPMENTAL STATE IN XINJI? WHY THE ENTREPRENEURIAL STATE IN GUANGHAN?

In Shulu/Xinji, the developmental state in the post-Maoist period is partly a product of the developmental state of the Maoist period. County-wide planning was an important activity during the 1960s and 1970s, and leadership, institutions and values committed to planning had become hegemonic at that time. That hegemony carried across what had often been portrayed as the watershed or even epistemic break that is supposed to have occurred at the Third Plenum of the Eleventh Party Central Committee in December 1978.[20] In the Xinji of 1986, there was important continuity of leadership with the Shulu of the 1970s: Liu Baolu, a local man who had worked his way up to be the county official in charge of agriculture in a decade whose agricultural policies have now been roundly condemned and abolished, was the new mayor. At the institutional level, the municipal government of the 1980s was making comprehensive economic plans in the same way that it had in the late 1970s when it was a county government. There were definite resemblances between the conception, scope and developmental implications of infrastructural projects of the 1970s (like the water conservancy project) and the 1980s (like the Hebei No. 1 Market or the ongoing commitment to road building). More intangibly, the same sorts of commitment to values of balanced, comprehensive development of the county/municipality as a whole, and of local pride, which Shulu leaders evinced in 1979 (when, for example, they used urban industrial profits to pay for a major project to solve a hard-core rural problem) were still evident in 1986 (when, for example, they looked with undisguised delight at the hub-bub of local townspeople and peasants buying from and selling to each other at the crowded Hebei No. 1 Market).

Xinji's relatively remote location may also be a factor in first producing and then reproducing its developmental state pathway. In the Maoist period, each of its various vertically-linked bureaux were just one among many subordinate units of prefectural and provincial systems. There was little in Shulu's location or its natural endowments to attract much developmental attention from the state ministries. Moreover, in those days there was little in the way of significant market-based forces operating in Shulu of which individual bureaux could take entrepreneurial advantage. Shulu's very remoteness and, from the point of view of the higher levels of the vertically-oriented state, its very ordinariness meant that its economic development required the initiative of its horizontally-oriented county government.

Finally, if Shulu's conditions provided a poor context for entrepreneurship, they also seem to have demanded a comprehensive approach to development. With few links of entrepreneurship or dependency to the larger economy, Shulu growth would, its leaders realised, have to be somewhat auto-centric. Local demand would have to drive development.[21] Insofar as this was deeply constrained by the weak and uneven rural base, the countryside would have to be the object of development early on. And given the nature of the rural problems of Shulu – specifically, the

Heilongang – this would require massive investment and coordination which only the county government as a whole could tackle.

Since Guanghan was not the subject of our detailed research in earlier years, discussion of the historical reasons for its affinities to entrepreneurial statism must be more tentative. To the extent that its county government was immobilised during the Cultural Revolution decade, it would have been difficult for Guanghan to assert the roles of planning and horizontal coordination that we have found in Shulu/Xinji at that time. Moreover, Guanghan was singled out for local and then national attention early in the reform period, when state planning and coordination were being attacked; indeed, Guanghan was an explicit model of and, therefore, weapon in that attack. This did not create auspicious conditions for active county government leadership over development.

Why, then, would it eventuate in the active economic role for individual bureaux suggested by the entrepreneurial state model? The answer has to do with a basic but overlooked feature of state socialist reform: when emphasis is put on enterprise development, the bureaux are extremely well situated – perhaps better than any other institution or group – to develop enterprises. They face little competition from the private sector, which has been weakened by the centralised state socialism that preceded reform. Horizontally-oriented organs such as county governments may lack the flexibility to jump into the fast-moving entrepreneurial game as quickly and effectively as the smaller, leaner bureaux. For this same reason, the bureaux may also be better able to conceal their economic control of enterprises than local governments or planning agencies, whose horizontality may bring their activities to the attention of a wider range of potential critics and competitors.

Guanghan's location near a huge city and on major transport routes may also have played into the logic of entrepreneurial statism, simply by providing a plethora of entrepreneurial opportunities. Inasmuch as many of these would be oriented to increasingly segmented markets beyond the county, they would be better suited to direct contact between enterprises or agencies in Guanghan – rather than the more integrated and eclectic local government – and those beyond. And as noted above, the fast-moving Chengdu economy would also require rapid and flexible responses from Guanghan, and these could be better provided by bureaux (especially under increasing decentralisation of vertical control) than by bulkier governments. Finally, Guanghan's relatively stronger and more balanced economic base may have reduced the need for the kinds of major developmental projects to which the government as a whole is best suited (as in Shulu/Xinji).

CONCLUSIONS

This paper has advanced several arguments. First, the existing paradigms of centralisation/decentralisation are inadequate for understanding the political economy of Chinese development as it is occurring at the levels where actual production is being planned, administered and carried out. The appropriate question is not centralisation or decentralisation, but the relationships among central state and enterprise as intermediated at the level of the local state. This is why the county or municipality is an important subject of study. For this same reason, the appropriate question is also not decentralisation I (to the enterprise) or II (to the local state), but rather their relationship.

Second, while the developmental state paradigm is a great improvement that avoids the manichean defects of previous paradigms, it too requires further specification and elaboration. In particular, the major lacuna of entrepreneurship needs to be factored into the analysis of development under state socialism of both the centralised and the reformist type. When this is done, the question of the nature, locus, obstacles to and effects of entrepreneurship can be raised, and, consequently, a variety of models of the developmental role of the state can be formulated. Here two have been advanced, in the manner of inductive model-building based on two cases of local government political economy. It is entirely possible that other developmental models could also be advanced. Indeed, doing so could only promote our understanding.

Third, these two cases deeply challenge, each in their own way, the prevailing wisdoms about the reform project and its relationship to the Maoist project that preceded it. Specifically, the 'developmental state' of Shulu/Xinji resonates to the key principles of socialist reform. The county/municipality government works to create the conditions for market-based development, but lets state run, collective and even private enterprises engage in the actual entrepreneurship that results in productive activity. The developmental state in Shulu/Xinji is true to the Dengist demand that the state stay out of actual production and that it respect the law of value and allow it to operate through markets. (Thus, Chen Lanzhang, Deputy Director of the Municipal Government Office, said that the county government had built no large new factories in the early 1980s, though this was a period of economic boom.) It has strong resonances to 'market socialism' or 'planned commodity economy', where the state stays above the competitive fray but works to keep that fray vibrant. Yet its activities also strongly resemble, and even seem to have originated in, the kinds of planning and resource mobilisation it undertook in the

Maoist period (and which Gordon White has dubbed, in an insightful term which China studies has all too conveniently forgotten, 'developmental Maoism.'[22])

By contrast, the entrepreneurial state of Guanghan – which, it bears reiteration at this point, was an early model of reform – is much more involved in actual productive activity than is the Shulu/Xinji developmental state with its developmental Maoist undertones. County government bureaux are directly and feverishly involved in starting new enterprises, procuring finance, scrambling for inputs and competing for output markets. Far from getting out of the economy, as the reform programme demands, the reform model of Guanghan is intensely enmeshed in its day-to-day production investment purchasing and marketing. County level organs in Guanghan like the Federation of Rural Supply and Marketing Cooperatives had the character of state capitalists, seeking profits wherever they could find them, even in areas well beyond their administrative purview (as in the Federation building a convention center.) The economic role of the government as a whole can perhaps be compared to a diversified holding company whose component parts have great autonomy and may even occasionally compete with each other.

Fourth, our analysis suggests that the developmental state leaves open the possibility of a much more balanced market than does the entrepreneurial state. In Shulu/Xinji some of the 1986 success stories were the formerly poorest areas. Every township was now connected into the national network of paved roads (and to easy access to the railway system through the Xinji state). Peasant peddlers and small collective enterprises brushed elbows with huge state factories at the Hebei No. 1 Market. The Director of the huge Xinji Fur and Leather Tanning Factory complained about stiff competition from small village-based collective workshops. His factory's retail outlet at the Hebei No. 1 Market was sleepier than the small retailers in stalls right outside its door. This was a market which was well planned both physically and in terms of the evenness of market power of its participants.

In Guanghan the market too was booming. But it appeared to be a market with much less equal participants. Large state bureaux were competing breathlessly for capital and inputs, which undoubtedly put a squeeze on smaller operators in the collective or private sectors. It also limited the development possibilities of other poor localities whose liquidity flowed into the cauldron of Guanghan economic growth, facilitated in their journey by state agencies such as the banks, the Second Light Industry Bureau, and the Federation of Rural Supply and Marketing Cooperatives.

Fifth, the developmental state model may tend to produce a more rational, publicly – or popular-oriented, and even perhaps egalitarian developmental outcome than does the entrepreneurial state model. In Xinji in 1986 market forces were booming, but they were a product of state activity and in turn they reinforced in palpable ways the ability of the state to serve genuine public needs, by providing a new park, workers' cultural palace and theatre and planning a more orderly and pleasant urban environment. Meanwhile the government was not feathering its own nest. In 1986, for example, the Xinji guest house was located in the same sturdy, purely functional block structure it had occupied seven years earlier, despite the intervening boom. Its motor pool was full of the same old Shanghai sedans. County Party Secretary Bai Runzhang complained that the county government only owned two cars.

In Guanghan, with the state preoccupied with entrepreneurship, little energy or resources seemed left for the construction of public goods like the new park, workers' palace and theatre in Xinji. By contrast, urban construction in Guanghan took the form of investment in neon lights and snappy new storefronts that had the decided look of a little Hong Kong. Urban planning also seemed to go by the boards: street markets remained crowded and noisy. Yet the bureaux clearly had at their disposal resources which they spent on themselves. The Guanghan Guest House was brand new, and sported automated doors, a mirrored, gold-lit lobby, carpet, modern furniture, and a television and refrigerator in each room. And its motor pool full of Japanese cars would make Xinji Secretary, Bai Runzhang, envious.

In short, then, Dengism (or, at least until 1989, Zhaoism) may not always be what it claims to be. Statism is alive and well, and taking some heteroclite forms with rather varied implications and effects. Real events challenge us to depart from all the old saws about China and socialist reform and reconceptualise the whole reform project. Local development can be truest to 'market socialist' reform when it grows most surely out of Maoism (at least developmental Maoism) and when it maintains its resonances to that now scorned way of doing things. Meanwhile, overt models of socialist reform may in fact involve a much heavier state foot on the market scale.

NOTES

Part of the research reflected in this paper was conducted in Shulu County, Hebei, in 1979, jointly with Phyllis Andors, Stephen Andors, Mitch Meisner and Vivienne Shue. The paper draws on the analysis and, where cited, even some of the text of a forthcoming volume to which all of us have contributed. It also is based upon field research done by Vivienne Shue and me in Xinji Municipality (formerly Shulu) and in Guanghan County, Sichuan, in 1986. Aside from those sections of the paper drawn from the forthcoming volume, the rest of the paper is my responsibility, though it has benefited greatly from everything I have learned from my collaborators. I also wish to thank the Ford Foundation, the National Endowment for the Humanities, and Oberlin College for their financial support of the field research. My deepest gratitude goes to the people and the leadership of Shulu/Xinji and of Guanghan for their exemplary cooperation in arranging and tolerating hours upon hours of briefings, and to the Chinese People's Association for Friendship with Foreign Countries and the Chinese Academy of Social Sciences for sponsoring the 1979 trip. Finally, and luckily for us, the whole field research project rested on the able shoulders of Su Guang and Pu Ning (in 1979) and Wang Shaoguang (in 1986).

1. The most prominent example of the simplistic resuscitation of a totalitarian approach was Simon Leys, *Chinese Shadows* (Harmondsworth, Middlesex: Penguin, 1978). A more sophisticated and measured approach is Tang Tsou, 'Back from the Brink of Revolutionary "Feudal" Totalitarianism,' in *State and Society in Contemporary China*, ed. Victor Nee and David Mozingo (Ithaca: Cornell University Press, 1983), pp. 53–88.

2. This argument has appeared in a number of forms. Gordon White has applied it specifically to the political realm in 'The Post-Revolutionary Chinese State,' in *State and Society in Contemporary China*, ed. Victor Nee and David Mozingo (Ithaca: Cornell University Press, 1983), pp. 27–52. For analyses covering the more general realm of political economy, see Dorothy Solinger (ed.), *Three Visions of Chinese Socialism* (Boulder: Westview Press, 1984); Peter Van Ness and Satish Raichur, 'Dilemmas of Socialist Development: An Analysis of Strategic Lines in China, 1949–81,' in *China from Mao to Deng*, ed. Bulletin of Concerned Asian Scholars (Armonk, NY: M.E. Sharpe, 1983), pp. 77–89; and Gordon White, 'Revolutionary Socialist Development in the Third World: An Overview' and 'Chinese Development Strategy After Mao,' in *Revolutionary Socialist Development in the Third World*, Gordon White, Robin Murray and Christine White (eds) (Lexington: University Press of Kentucky, 1983), pp. 1–34 and 155–92.

3. Franz Schurmann, *Ideology and Organisation in Communist China* (Berkeley: University of California Press, 1968), pp. 175–8, 196–200 and passim. For just two examples of the early return to Schurmann's analysis of decentralisation(s), see Mitch Meisner

and Marc Blecher, 'Administrative Level and Agrarian Structure, 1975–1980: The County (W)as Focal Point in Chinese Rural Development Policy', in *China's New Development Strategy*, Jack Gray and Gordon White (eds) (London: Academic Press, 1982), p. 58; and Gordon White, 'Chinese Development Strategy After Mao', p. 157.

4. Robert Wade and Gordon White (eds), *Developmental States in East Asia: Capitalist and Socialist* (Brighton: Institute of Development Studies Bulletin XV, 2, April 1984); Wade and White (eds), *Developmental States in East Asia, A Research Report to the Gatsby Charitable Foundation* (Brighton: Institute of Development Studies Research Report #16, November 1985); and Gordon White (ed.), *Developmental States in East Asia* (London, Macmillan, 1988).

5. Wade and White, 'Introduction', in *Developmental States in East Asia, A Research Report*, p. 11.

6. It might reduce the level of administrative or bureaucratic coordination for the individual enterprise, though. That is, in the entrepreneurial state, the bureaux could use their power and organisational resources to help their own enterprises obtain needed credit, permits, licenses, inputs and sales opportunities; while under the developmental state model the enterprises, because somewhat more autonomous, would have to fend more for themselves in these areas of bureaucratic and commercial activity. Thus it is possible that individual enterprises might be less flexible and perhaps even less efficient under the developmental state model. The tradeoff would be that the degree of coordination among the enterprises might be higher.

7. An example discussed below is the water conservancy project built in Xinji Municipality (when it was still known as Shulu County).

8. Examples discussed below include the Hebei No. 1 Market and the program of roadway construction, both undertaken by Xinji Municipality.

9. Gordon White, 'The Role of the State in China's Socialist Industrialisation,' in *Developmental States in East Asia: A Research Report*, pp. 227–8.

10. Vivienne Shue, 'Beyond the Budget: Finance Organization and Reform in a Chinese County,' *Modern China* x, 2 (April 1984), pp. 147–86.

11. Marc Blecher *et al.*, *The Tethered Deer: The Political Economy of Shulu County*, forthcoming.

12. Refer to Lowi's use of the term. See Theodore Lowi, 'Four Systems of Policy, Politics and Choice,' *Public Administration Review* 32 (July-August 1972), pp. 298–309.

13. Blecher *et al.*, *The Tethered Deer*, chapter 6.

14. Both these examples are drawn from Blecher *et al.*, *The Tethered Deer*, chs. 7 & 8 respectively.

15. Blecher, *et al.*, *The Tethered Deer*, ch. 6.

16. It also did not correspond to the opposite caricature of the Maoist period economy as anarchy (though of the non-market!).

17. Average 1985 grain yields in the county were 7.36 tons/ha., and cotton yields were 1.2 tons/ha.

18. Alec Nove, *The Economics of Feasible Socialism* (London: George Allen and Unwin, 1983), p. 201.

19. The Director of the Guanghan Agricultural Bank said that in rich and rapidly developing places like Guanghan, in fact the four state banks – the Agricultural Bank, the Industrial and Commercial Bank, the Construction Bank and the People's Bank – all worked very closely together. It seemed clear that this would have the effect not of extending the regulatory power of the banks over investment, but rather of opening up financial flows in ways that undermined close regulation.

20. This argument has been made most forcefully by Tang Tsou, 'Back From the Brink'.

21. As Jack and Maisie Gray have pointed out, this is the essence of the Maoist rural development strategy. See their 'China's New Agricultural Revolution,' in *The Chinese Economic Reforms* (ed.) Stephan Feuchtwang and Athar Hussain (Beckenham, Kent: Croom Helm, 19830, pp. 151–84.

22. Gordon White, 'Chinese Development Strategy After Mao,' pp. 155–92.

Part 4
State and
Society

12 The State and the Single-Child Policy
Elisabeth J. Croll

To refer to the single-child policy of China is to imply a well-structured programme of unambiguous meanings and mutually exclusive regulations. Its implementation also assumes a singular and authoritative political agent, the state, and by implication willing objects of policy, couples of child-bearing age, who will co-operate by abrogating their fertility decisions to designated others. What a study of the single-child policy and its implementation since its inception in 1979 suggests, however, is that the policy itself constitutes an unstable configuration of meanings constructed and reconstructed over time and space, generating variation and even confusion in the message that is officially formulated and the message that is received by couples or households. Both messages lack specificity and uniformity of sanction. The constituents of the official message are dependent on the formal role of the state and its local representatives and are also mediated by the fluid roles of informal others, be they either peer or volunteer. Moreover, the variety in fertility behaviour responsive to the official message is determined or influenced by the immediate household and family location of the reproductive couple, which have themselves been reconstituted in the same ten years. Indeed what gives the single-child family policy particular interest and significance are the simultaneous changes in representations of the state, coinciding with a decline in state power, and the reconstruction of the household and family as central economic, social and political institutions in post-reform China.[1]

In the past decade there have not only been changes in the state and in household and family institutions, but there has also evolved a new and complex set of relationships between family and state. These are based on an intricate new interlacing of state intervention and withdrawal which together have redefined the public and private or domestic domains and the relations between them that had characterised pre-reform China. The state has, after a period of neglect and disinterest, increasingly intervened in family affairs. Simultaneously that state has increasingly withdrawn from family affairs and, directly and indirectly, assigned a new degree of agency – political, social and economic – to the family. The reforms of recent years have redefined the spheres of family and state responsibility; they have also redefined the relations between family and state, primarily by creating a space between the two where both meet, interact and interject. After the example of Donzelot, this expanding space, a hybrid of public and private or domestic, can be designated as the social.[2] In post-reform China, the social has increasingly become an arena for conflict between the family and state for autonomy, authority, rewards and control of resources. One of the primary arenas of conflict between peasant family and state has been control over family planning and family size. The study of the single-child policy and its implementation in the countryside is indicative of both the newly evolving relations between family and the state and the changes in constitution of each in rural villages.

THE ONE CHILD POLICY

One of the most momentous of the new and radical policies introduced into China since 1978 is the single-child family policy which was distinguished by the degree of state intervention in domestic or household family affairs which it represented. The introduction of this policy could be said to mark a third phase in the relations between family and state with regard to birth control.[3] Initially, in the 1950s and 1960s, the state made available the means and techniques to limit family size, but left birth control decisions to the family itself. Throughout the 1970s there were some flexible negotiations between state and family over local birth quotas determining family birth plans. In the late 1970s, with the introduction of the one-child policy family, plans were no longer to be subject to negotiation. The state demanded that, except in certain circumstances, families should limit themselves to one child only. Because of the sum total of China's population and the projected population growth rates, reproductive decisions were thought to be too important to be left to the individuals, households or families.

It is now almost ten years since fertility decisions were taken out of the domestic and private domain with the purpose of incorporating them wholly into the public and political arena. The implementation of the single-child family programme can be divided into five phases of roughly two years each. In each phase there were changes in the message itself, the means by which that message was communicated and the family response to that message.

(a) 1979–80: Experimentation

In late 1979 the Chinese government suddenly and surprisingly introduced a one-child family policy. It had two particularly distinctive features: first, its novel and universal injunction – one child per couple; second, the number of economic incentives and penalties attached to the policy. The inclusion of quite punitive economic sanctions against those not adhering to official rules marked a departure from past practice. What emerged during the first months, in both the campaign to persuade Chinese peasants to limit their family size to one child and in the practical implementation of the policy, was the degree of confusion and variability inherent in the policy itself. The first published sets of rules and regulations on family size uniformly advocated the birth of one child and categorically in both urban and rural areas 'banned' the birth of a third child under any circumstances.[4] What was not so clear or so uniform at this time, however, was the policy position on the birth of a second child. Yet it was precisely the acceptability or otherwise of a second child which would be the key determinant in the meanings attached to the single-child family policy. Official policies included programmes to 'control' and 'regulate' second births in order to 'reduce' their number. The slogans ranged from 'no second child' to 'no more than two' and there was a range of circumstances, by no means uniform throughout China, under which a second child was permitted. Indeed the regulations enacting the single-child family policy were contained in local, provincial and municipal regulations, for there was no national family planning law applicable throughout the entire country. It seems that a family planning law was drafted which was originally intended to be presented to the Fifth National People's Congress when it met in late 1980. That it did not appear was apparently due to the 'lack of consensus' surrounding certain of its provisions.[5] It is a fair guess that much of the dissent centred around the conditions under which a second child was to be permitted and the severity of the penalties to be attached to the birth of a second child.

Official regulations on the single-child family policy published by various local, municipal and provincial authorities included lists of incentives and penalties, all of which aimed to ensure wealth and privilege for the single-child family and to penalise households not limiting family size to one child.[6] In the first two years of the policy a number of incentives were introduced, including the issue of cash and grain subsidies and benefits to do with health, housing and education. The penalties levied on the birth of a second or subsequent child were the reverse of the incentives; cash fines were to be exacted and sanctions operated in the distribution of grain, health care, education and housing. An important question in the analysis of any incentive scheme is the degree to which it is practically operative – in particular, the source and extent of its funding and the circumstances in which the penalties are exerted. What distinguishes the lists of incentives and disincentives in 1979–80 is the discrepancies in their contents, the wide variation in their funding and the lack of uniformity in their implementation. Thus parents signing the single-child family pledge might receive a cash sum of between Y60 and Y200, or a thermos flask, a face flannel or simply a certificate of merit. Similarly in some cases parents were penalised on the birth of a third or subsequent child by a cash fine of Y3000, in other cases not at all.[7] There have been no cases reported in which the birth of a second child was so penalised. Rather local responses seemed to have ranged from the most stringent, those where a second pregnancy was not permitted to proceed to term, to those where the local authorities not only permitted the birth but also exacted no penalties. In general during these initial years, the campaign to implement the policy was largely educational and designed to popularise the idea of the one-child family.

This emphasis on ideological means of implementation and on education and establishing new norms of behaviour reflected the official belief in China that ideology and organisation can introduce and maintain the momentum of social change. The government believed that if the population could be persuaded to accept the new norms in the long-term national interest, then change would be possible even if it ran directly counter to family interest in the short-term. The main aim of the first single-child campaigns was to identify and explain the dimensions of the population problem and advocate the one-child solution.[8] However, any attempt by the government to implement this new policy was countered by gossip, rumour and incredulity. In 1979–80 it seemed that the twists and turns in official policies over the previous twenty-five years had generated a credibility problem for the government, a cynicism about whether it could hold any policy constant over time. But a substantive change in the formulation, implementation and reception of the policy took place in September 1980 with the publication of an Open Letter on the Question of Controlling Chinese Population which officially confirmed that the new policy was not temporary and tentative but permanent and was about to be consolidated.[9]

(b) 1981–82: Consolidation

Although there was still no family planning law during this second phase of consolidation, the rules and regulations governing the one-child family policy were increasingly standardised, especially in designating the specific circumstances in which a second child was permitted.[10] In the urban areas the exceptions to the one-child rule were few and were mainly to do with health defects in the first born and with cases of sterility and re-marriage. In the rural areas the exceptions embraced a wider number of circumstances including a number of concessions to kinship and the continuation of the family line. Hence a second child was to be permitted where one son had been born for three consecutive generations, where both spouses were only children and where the groom had moved into the bride's household and the wife was the only child, and where a household had only one son capable of begetting heirs. Additionally households in mountainous regions which had economic difficulties were permitted to give birth to a second child. Although there was some attempt to standardise rewards and penalties attached to the policy, these were still largely dependent on the wealth of individual units in which the couples were employed or resided. In the absence of a national policy or nationally allocated funds there was a wide range in the value of rewards for single-child families and penalties for higher parity births.[11]

During this second phase the government embarked on a massive educational campaign to publicise and popularise the one-child policy, and all aspects of the media were marshalled in its support.[12] The government made considerable efforts to explain the population problem to the nation and to establish a direct link between family size and population totals. The main aim of the educational campaign has been to convince the present generation of parents that it is China's 'objective' conditions rather than the Communist Party or the present leadership that do not permit the birth of two or more children. It has also emphasised the costs of educating and employing the younger generation and of providing basic needs for an ever-expanding population which reduce the resources available for accumulation, modernisation and increasing standards of urban and rural livelihood. To communicate and popularise the objectives of the new policy, the Department of Family Planning took specific responsibility for the nation-wide administration and implementation of the single-child family programme. It already had a national network providing comprehensive services throughout China which could be activated in support of the new policy. To persuade families to accept new norms and take practical steps to implement the policy, each family was visited individually by members of the family planning committees of the urban neighbourhood, factory enterprise or rural production team. Their task was to ascertain the couple's attitudes towards the new policy, their contraceptive practices and birth plans and to provide contraceptive services.[13] By the end of this period of consolidation, the single-child policy had been propagated in most regions of China – except for minority nationality areas – and by mid-1981 it was reckoned that some 12.5 million or so couples had taken out single-child family certificates. The majority of these one-child couples resided in the cities.[14]

In the largest cities a high proportion of couples accepted a one-child certificate in 1981–82. In the municipalities of Beijing, Shanghai and Tianjin the rate of certification might be as high as 90 per cent and in other cities upwards of 60 per cent.[15] The reasons for acceptance were several. First, there was already a large number of political controls in the cities where resources from housing to theatre tickets were allocated by the state. In these cities overcrowding and the shortage of housing and other resources lent credence to the official account of the problem. Interestingly the unprecedented rise in the standard of living and availability of consumer goods in the cities alongside the introduction of radical family planning policies had the effect of suggesting an immediate and direct correlation between the two. It is evident from interviews that the single-child policy could not have been pushed to the degree it was if it had not been for this coincidence. In the cities too the sex of the first born was less important given the common establishment of separate households on marriage and the widespread availability of pensions and services for the elderly. However, despite these mediating factors, family planning personnel still found it difficult to implement the policy fully in urban areas and they maintained that even in the cities constant vigilance was required since couples would take advantage of any hint of relaxation in the policy. Meanwhile, during this period of consolidation, the one-child policy was also extended for the first time into the rural areas.

Although the birth rate in the rural areas was estimated to have declined significantly, from 2.3 per cent in 1971 to 1.2 per cent in 1979,[16] neither the decline in the birth rate nor the number of single-child families was as great as in the towns and cities. Estimates of the proportion of couples with one child who were certificated as single-child families in villages for which there are figures ranged from between 20 and 50 per cent.[17] From 1981 onwards, however, reports suggested that the birth rate was again rising and that there were increasing difficulties in implementing the single child policy in rural areas, the result of a fundamental conflict between national policies towards production and reproduction. Each of these made different, even contradictory, demands on the peasant household which was at one and the same time the reproductive unit and increasingly the productive unit.[18] On the other hand the state demanded one child; on the other it demanded that peasant households take responsibility for production, diversify their economies and expand their income-generating activities. Thus the income and welfare of a peasant household were increasingly dependent on the organisation and distribution of its family labour resources.

In any society where labour forms the major part of the total means of production, where control over labour is a major source of socio-economic differentiation and where the private hiring of labour is prohibited, the reproduction of family labour becomes the major means of expanding the resources of a household and increasing its production. If the reproduction of labour power had replaced landed property as an important source of wealth and the chief source of differentials within the previous rural commune system, then rural policies introduced into the countryside from 1978 exacerbated this trend by intensifying the demands on family labour resources and increasing their value to the household. In 1982 published surveys and reports demonstrated the correlation between size of family and income by suggesting that most of the 'ten thousand *jin* households' and 'ten thousand *yuan* households' which had emerged during the previous two years were large families.

This conflict in the state's demands on the peasant household had probably never been greater with the result that the operation of incentives and disincentives was unable to mediate this contradiction. As in the cities, there was a wide variation in the value of rewards and penalties and the degree to which they were implemented. But even if economic sanctions were fully implemented in the countryside, they constituted less of a deterrent to peasant households which had access to many resources not available to urban households: for instance, food supplies could be produced on their land allocations, housing was privately owned and health and educational facilities were not as well developed as in urban areas. The increasing autonomy of the peasant household as a result of the rural economic reforms meant that local government institutions no longer had unified control of food, income and resource distribution and were therefore not in the same position to reward and penalise their member households.

By 1982 in the face of increasing problems in the implementation of the one-child policy, it seemed that the Chinese government had three alternative strategies at its disposal. The first was to continue to promote the single-child family policy despite all the problems associated with its implementation and its major conflict with current economic policies. Alternatively the government could modify the new economic policies or the single-child family policy to lessen the conflict between the two. In 1982 it seemed unlikely that the government would want to do so. However it did ponder the problem of labour supply and granted permission to peasant households to hire labour as an alternative to reproducing its own labour supply. This marked a major departure from past policies and perhaps more than any other factor confirmed the commitment of the government to implementing the single-child family policy. At the same time there were also signs that some sections of the leadership thought that one-child policy would never succeed in rural areas and it would therefore be better to lower the targets and allow say 1.5 or 2 children per couple or aim for an 80 per cent acceptance rate in establishing one-child families in rural areas.[19] By 1983 however it was increasingly evident that the government perceived the population problem and the rising birth rate in the countryside to be too serious to allow any relaxation of the single-child policy.

(c) 1983–84: Coercion

The years 1983–84 were marked not so much by a change of policy as a change in the means to achieve its goals. New penalties were introduced to increase peer and cadre pressure on parents contemplating an out-of-plan birth. In work or residential units, for example, fellow workers were fined if one of their number proceeded with the birth, and family planning cadres were themselves fined sometimes by as much as Y100 if out-of-plan births occurred within the unit for which they were responsible.[20] Instances of enforced IUD insertions for women with one child, sterilisations for women with two children and abortions for unapproved pregnancies were increasingly reported in the media. In particular the number of sterilisations performed within an administrative area became a criterion of its success in family planning. During 1983 several provincial administrations outlined the main task of their family planning programmes as 'improving and furthering ligation and vasectomy work'.[21] Administrative areas at all levels had quotas for the number of sterilisation operations to be performed within their boundaries and nationally the number of sterilisations showed a sharp rise. In February 1983, a month of peak campaigning, an estimated 8.86 million sterilisation operations took place in China.[22] For Hebei province it was reported that 1.77 million ligations and vasectomies or 85.9 per cent of its annual quota had been performed by the end of May.[23]

During this dramatic increase, family planning regulations included several references to 'compulsory sterilisation'. Most of the reports of compulsory sterilisation came from Guangdong province in the south of China where the birth rate at the end of 1982, 24.99 per 1000, continued to be the highest of all provinces and municipalities. The large number of two to three child families in Guangdong was attributed to the neglect of birth control technology and in particular to the low level of sterilisation by tubal ligation among women who already had two children.[24] This led to several family planning campaigns in 1983–84, the focus of which was 'compulsory sterilisation for either party, husband or wife, of those couples who already had two children', and later reports from the province subsequently referred to increases in the number of sterilisations performed.

Internationally, the Chinese government showed itself sensitive to the charge of condoning compulsory sterilisations by continuing to emphasise the educational nature of its family planning programmes. In August 1983 a spokesman for the Family Planning Commission stressed that it was China's consistent policy to encourage couples to practise birth control voluntarily, but admitted that forced abortions and sterilisations did occur in some regions.[25] The emerging question was whether there could be an alternative to coercion if persuasion failed and the Chinese government was determined to implement a policy which it believed to be in the national good. This is probably what lay behind the admission made by some provincial leaders, that because the population issue was so important, they must take forceful measures if education failed. However, although forceful measures might solve one set of problems, they generated others.

The reason why education had not yet succeeded in persuading couples to adopt the one-child policy was the continued preference for sons and one of the most publicised repercussions of the new coercion was the increase in female infanticide. This phenomenon was a direct response of peasant households to the stricter implementation of the one-child policy although it is difficult to ascertain the scale of its occurrence.[26] The increases seemed generally more evident in the poorer regions of China which had a history of infanticide and where the practice was still scarcely regarded as a criminal offence. Female infanticide was also more likely to occur in families where the birth of a daughter signified the end of the family line. The rise in prejudice against infant daughters reflected traditional attitudes but also the continuing and very considerable economic value of sons in a peasant household where daughters married out and current economic and social welfare policies primarily rested on the labour of sons. In some of the poorer regions the sex ratios for the newborn showed a high proportion of males, 111–113, to 100 females.[27] These figures, well above the national average of 108.5 to 100, suggested a degree of female infanticide and neglect or under-registration of female infants. Whatever the precise cause of the imbalance, the trend certainly suggested a range of older forms of prejudice and new forms of discrimination against female infants and their mothers. Certainly at the time the reports on infanticide contributed to the growing unpopularity of the one-child policy. It was generally recognised that it was the most unpopular of government policies within China, and outside China it attracted much criticism including the threat of withdrawal of international financial support for China's family planning programmes. It was these combined pressures which contributed to the modification of the one-child policy in 1985.

(d)   1985–86: Moderation

Although the single-child policy remained the official family planning rule, there were changes both in its presentation and implementation. In field investigations, for example, the contracepting rate rather than the single-child rate became the measure for achievement and cause for celebration. Instead of stressing the uniformity and urgency of the single child regulations, the authorities began to promote 'controlled relaxation' and the evolution of appropriate family planning rules to suit specific conditions and regions.[28] Most provincial governments took steps to investigate responses to the single-child family policy and subsequently issued supplementary regulations modifying its implementation.[29] Most of the supplementary regulations permitted more second-parity births and very carefully specified the conditions under which a second child was to be permitted. Couples who came from Hong Kong and Taiwan to settle in China or who were members of minority nationalities continued to be excluded from the one-child regulations. Although it had looked for a time as if the special regulations applicable to these categories might be tightened, they were now to be permitted two or three children depending on nationality. A major change during this period was that a second child was to be permitted in the countryside if either of the parents was an only child and in the cities where both parents were only children. The new rationale behind this change was the assumption that the one-child rule should prevail for a single generation only. A second child was also newly permitted in the countryside where an only son gave birth to a daughter, where the continuation of the family line was threatened by the birth of a single daughter or where the husband had moved into his wife's household on marriage and the first child was a daughter. Previously a second child had been permitted in cases where all these circumstances pertained. Altogether these modifications made major new concessions to the strength of kinship ties and son preference in the countryside.

A second major modification of the policy was the broader authorisation of a second child where peasant couples found themselves in 'practical or financial' difficulties. This was perhaps the most loosely-defined category which lent itself to a wide range of interpretation. These difficulties were defined not so much according to the circumstances of the individual couple as according to location, or to the natural endowments and economic and cultural development of any region. In Sichuan province for example, something of a pace setter in family planning, the province was divided into five physical regions – urban, rural suburbs and plains, hilly, mountainous and high mountainous – each of which was to have regulations appropriate to its conditions; in urban areas, one child only would be permitted; in plains and hilly areas 50 per cent of all couples would be permitted to have two children; and in mountainous and high mountainous regions all couples would be permitted to have a second child.[30] The regulations for other provinces were similar, and it seemed that while there was virtually to be no alteration in implementation in the cities, in the rural areas, despite the specificity of the modified concessions with official emphasis on 'controlled relaxation', there was some verbal slippage. Informally throughout this period in interviews and conversations there was general acknowledgement that there was no *de facto* two-child policy in operation in the countryside – an acknowledgement which in 1987–88 placed the government in checkmate.

(e) 1987–88: Checkmate

A sharp rise in China's birth rate in 1987 led to official demands for the stricter implementation of the one-child family rule on the grounds that failure to keep birth rates in check would jeopardise the country's long-term development. Official fears that the population growth rate would 'get out of control' were based on the rise in birth rate to 21.2 per 1000 in 1987, a rise of 0.4 over the previous year.[31] This rise had marked the sharpest increase for any one year within the previous five years. The total sum of China's population numbered 1.072 billion, around 12 million more than at the end of 1986. If this trend was to continue, the Chinese government feared that the population would exceed by some 50–80 million the general target of 1.2 billion by the year 2000. It was such projected trends which caused the Chinese government increasingly to warn of an impending 'population crisis'. The crisis was said to be exacerbated by both the defiance of millions of couples ignoring the one-child rule and the negligence of family planning cadres in implementing the one-child rule.[32] To avoid such a crisis, the government called for the stricter implementation of the one-child policy by reducing the exceptions to the policy and further penalising offending parents and cadres including the levying of on-the-spot fines. What became increasingly apparent was that, however much the government might wish to tighten the policy, it had also to acknowledge its inability to do so.

The government's first official acknowledgement that it might have severe problems in implementing the one-child policy date from 1984 when policy documents began to accept that its unpopularity was such that there must 'be an enquiry into the views of the people', in order that the policy 'be reasonable', 'well received by the people' and 'practical for cadres to enforce'.[33] Since that time increase in official modification of the policy to permit two children in the countryside confirm that the government had no choice but to acknowledge formally its inability to impose the policy on unwilling parents in the countryside. This trend was largely the result of the marked alteration in the balance of power between family and state in rural China.

THE STATE

The rural economic reforms have brought about a change in local political and economic structures and forms of local political control and authority in the villages. For the first time for many decades there is now a plurality of messages, competitive information channels, multiple sources of status and authority and proliferating formal and informal arenas of economic and socio-political action. On the eve of the reforms and at the time of the formulation of the single-child family policy, it could be argued that the state continued to be the single most important political and socio-economic agent in China with a singular vertical channel of communication and control. In the village the local cadres were the singular representatives of the state and the dominant if not exclusive source of privileged outside knowledge, authority and status. Moreover if the village was somewhat isolated at the base of the vertical command structure, the present household itself was almost entirely encapsulated by a bounded collective productive unit combining political and economic authority.

The village had been incorporated into the commune within which the precepts of collectivisation had demanded that peasant households place a high value on the mobilisation of collective resources, upon co-operation in unprecedented levels of exchange and on the village-wide ownership of the means of production, organised labour and distributed rewards. Outside this unit there were few alternative resources, inputs and rewards. There was little movement of persons and, in the absence of local markets, little mobility in and out of the village of even the most temporary kind so that the primary groups of kin, neighbours and friends overlapped to form a singular village reference group the norms, pressures and sanctions of which were difficult to defy.[34] Peasant households had few ties beyond those of ritual significance outside of the productive unit, and they thus, almost entirely bounded, had very little individual or bargaining power either within or outside of the village. In contrast one of the most important components of the recent economic reforms in China has been the separation at the local level of political and economic authority and the emergence of new political and economic institutions and policies the messages of which might not be mutually supportive or even contradictory in goal or achievement.

Since the introduction of the new Constitution in late 1982, the government has reformed local political structures by substituting new townships and village institutions for the commune, production brigade and team and redefined the scope of their authority and controls.[35] The government has also expected peasant households to join new economic organisations and 'associations' designed to expand production, develop the commodity economy and service the economic enterprises managed by peasant households either individually or jointly.[36] These new economic networks based on common interests rather than location are not spatially bounded and potentially compete with and challenge the authority and control of new local political structures. Although there is still a well-defined vertical line of authority from the capital to the commune, it is not so singular or so exclusive as in the pre-reform years. There are alternative lines of authority, resources and information with alternative messages ruling the village and alternative sources of authority and status within the local community. No longer is the basic-level cadre the sole authority figure in the local community or government information so singularly privileged and directed. Villagers as well as cadres now have access to outside knowledge via multiple channels of communication so that new knowledge is more widely accessible and ignorance less singularly negotiable. Now that collectives no longer distribute income, food and resources, state representatives have fewer sanctions at their disposal. Local-level cadres in a more personal capacity have frequently moved into powerful positions as patrons brokering raw materials, information and other resources and, as part-time brokers and entrepreneurs responsible for their own income-generating activities, they frequently had their minds as much on their own profits and losses as implementing government policies let alone negotiating the new sectional interests in the village.

The local political arena is newly characterised by divisions arising out of a greater competition for village and outside resources and the exacerbation of both quantitative and qualitative differentials between neighbouring peasant households, which makes it increasingly difficult for local state cadres or their basic-level representatives to impose their authority and exercise sanctions within the village.[37] Moreover villagers now have the option of migration or other means of temporary or permanent escape to avoid the vagaries of unwelcome cadre control or intervention. One of the most important repercussions of the rural economic reforms has been the incorporation of the local village populations into broader political and economic institutions and networks so that ties outside the village beyond cadre control have become increasingly important to the individual peasant household. Those that have access to resources, markets and connexions outside of the village are likely to be in the most favoured position to take advantage of the new economic opportunities generated by the reforms. The household thus no longer finds it so necessary or so advantageous to depend on the leadership or inter-relationships within the village which in turn no longer possesses the means to meet its major needs. In the pre-reform era it was the very stability of overlapping economic and political structures and primary groups which not only contributed to the cohesion and boundedness of local communities but also contributed to the ability of the state to intervene in village affairs. The message for the central state is that, as it became less strong and privileged, it has become increasingly ineffectual. If the sum of the reforms was to both frequent and disperse the local community and weaken the authority and control of the state in the village, there has been a corresponding appropriation of control and authority by the peasant household, thereby affecting local-level relations between family and state.

THE FAMILY

Many of the factors affecting the fertility-related expectations and behaviour of couples take their relevance from the locality or from the context of fertility decisions which for most couples of reproductive age are the household or the family which is their primary reference group whether or not they are co-resident. Another of the most important dimensions of the rural economic reforms has been the new focus on the peasant household or family as an economic, social and political unit in the countryside. In analytical terms this paper follows the common practice whereby the term household refers to those members who are co-resident with a common budget, while the term family denotes the larger number of closely-kin related members of different households. The shift in analytical focus from the peasant household to the peasant family in the last few years is largely the result of two simultaneous repercussions of the reforms: the direct reconstitution of the peasant household and the indirect reconstitution of the peasant family, which have affected both perceptions of and values attached to fertility.

In rural China the peasant household is now the most important unit of production based on lands allocated for its long term-use and a new complex range of occupations and responsibilities. It is now demanded of the peasant household that it take primary responsibility for agricultural production,[38] the diversification of its operations and the expansion of its commodity economy,[39] and the consumption and welfare of its members. These new responsibilities have required peasant households to acquire new skills and techniques, take charge of all field management from sowing to harvesting, meet the expenses of production including the hire and exchange of labour, animal labour and small machines, and disposal of agricultural products. Peasant households have been encouraged to diversify their economic activities to include both agricultural and non-agricultural occupations as part of new diversification programmes aimed at developing animal husbandry, cash cropping, industries and commercial activities within the rural economy. To encourage the peasant household to expand its income-generating activities, the government has increased producer prices, provided local incentives and re-established rural fairs and markets where goods may be exchanged at prices set according to local supply and demand.[40]

The individual peasant household is still the chief unit of consumption and welfare in the countryside, but it is now no longer aided and subsidised by collective structures as formerly. As before, the reorganised rural economy continues to demand that the peasant household should provide housing, non-staple foods, clothes and other basic necessities for all its members, but it is also responsible for processing its own staple food supply now that the distribution of grain by the production team to its member households no longer takes place. Additionally, the peasant household is expected to take greater responsibility for the economic support and welfare of its dependants, including its young, unemployed, elderly and disabled or otherwise handicapped members who are not able-bodied enough to be in full-time employment. Previously the production team absorbed all village residents into the labour force in some capacity or another so they all earned work points whose value was calculated simply by dividing the income of the production teams by the total number of work points. Now those without full labour power must be either incorporated into the income generating activities of the peasant household or supported by the peasant household out of its own income.

All these new responsibilities have required that the peasant household have access to a new array of resources including raw materials, means of production, new agricultural techniques, transport facilities and markets which were all previously the responsibility of the collective production unit. Then few demands were made on the initiative and management qualities of the individual peasant household or its special skills, resources and facilities. Indeed the degree to which a peasant household has been able to take advantage of the new economic policies to expand, diversify or specialise is very much dependent on the household's acquiring new and sufficient material and labour resources.[41] In the search for new capital resources, the basis of any household strategy to expand and develop its economy is the generation of income to invest singly or jointly in fixed assets, tools for production and processing, as well as modes of transport. In the absence of inherited capital and accumulated individual material resources, the major means by which a peasant household in present-day China could generate capital was through developing its allocated land resources or accumulating savings from the sideline incomes and wages of its members. In the first instance the expansion, diversification and specialisation of the peasant household economy primarily relied on the accumulation and distribution of its labour resources.

To meet the new and rapidly increasing demands on its labour resources, the peasant household had a number of short and longer term strategies at its disposal. For instance, it might immediately augment its labour resources by hiring labour, although hiring required surplus labour and sufficient cash resources to pay wages. For the majority of peasant households, therefore, it was the intensification of existing family labour resources and the reproduction and recruitment of family labour that underlay household strategies. Although all family members, including children, have been increasingly pressed into some form of income-generating activity whether on or off the farm, there are limits beyond which the intensification of existing family labour resources cannot be pushed. Peasant households have thus sought to expand household size though the reproduction and recruitment of family labour. The reproduction of family labour is a time-honoured means of augmenting the labour force of any household even if it is not immediate in its effects. However, given that family planning policies are likely to severely curtail the expansion of household size by this means in the foreseeable future, the household is more likely to adopt a number of alternative strategies such as the early recruitment of daughters-in-law and the incorporation of more than one nuclear unit within a larger more complex household.

Traditionally it had been a mark of mobility for peasant households to expand their size and elaborate the family structure once there was sufficient wealth.[42] The Chinese sociologist, C. K. Yang, likened the Chinese household to a balloon which was ever ready to inflate should the expansion of its economy allow this.[43] For a brief period in the 1950s, a number of novel demographic and economic factors had occasioned the expansion of the traditionally small nuclear peasant household into a joint household. This period offered a new and unique opportunity for the peasant household, even within the collective, to make use of its expanded labour resources to diversify the economy and accumulate resources.[44] From past experience then, it might be expected that the recent income-generating opportunities would encourage a peasant household to delay household division indefinitely, or at least for a longer period, now that one of the traditional constraints on the expansion of a household – the size of the family estate – had been removed. More than any other period this century, the majority of China's peasant households have extended their estate to include lands (*de facto* ownership), residences, enterprises, tools of production, livestock and household effects that would provide a basis for supporting larger numbers than hitherto. Thus it might be expected given the example of the 1950s, that both the expansion of the family estate and the exacerbated demands on labour could lead to the elaboration of greater numbers of peasant households into complex and joint forms. However there is no evidence of any expansion; if anything there seems to have been a reverse trend with evidence of declining household size, with a number of recent surveys showing there to be a marked rise in the number of smaller, nuclear households of one and two generations, and a corresponding drop in the number of large multi-generational stem and joint households.[45] At the same time it was increasingly clear that the single and nuclear peasant household or average size was unable to meet the new demands made upon it by the economic reforms. It is likely therefore that one of the main factors contributing to the decrease in household size was the emergence of a new family form that both acquired the resources of, yet escaped the disadvantages of, the large joint family household. A less direct expression of the economic reforms has thus been the reconstruction of the family based not on co-residence so much as an *aggregation* of households.

The new and emerging family form is made up of a number of peasant households related by close kinship ties that have developed new or more intensified forms of association and co-operation based on economic, social and political alliances and exchanges. The new family form might be termed the 'aggregate' family because, although families are fragmented into separate households, it is the relationships between them of co-operation and association which are of major importance to the analyst rather than concern with their internal divisions and fragmentation. The bases for this co-operation and association between households within the aggregate family are, first of all, kinship ties usually made up of brothers, fathers' brothers and fathers' brothers' sons, that is of those males descended from a common male antecedent and extending to some three generations.[46] They are also based on residential proximity, and the mobilisation of resources to meet the new economic, social and political demands on the household that guarantee mutual obligations or claims for assistance. These small-clustered kin-related units which had remained the focus of various ritual forms of co-operation prior to 1978 have now been re-invested with new economic and political significance.

The economic significance of the aggregate family may be based on the common establishment and development of a specialised venture or it may have evolved from a division of labour whereby one household undertook to cultivate the lands, another household promoted some kind of commodity production or service and yet another provided transport, technical or commercial marketing expertise.[47] In this way the member households became to a large degree inter-dependent and self-sustaining although they were less likely to be spatially defined or their activities bounded by the village. The aggregate family may thus incorporate kin-related households from outside the village and particularly kin located in small towns and urban centres in order to aid in production and marketing processes. If because of the restrictions on migration in the past, aggregate families have no existing extensive ties beyond the village and across urban and rural divides, they have commonly set out to establish them through marriage, marketing and migration.[48] Analysing the marketing networks and chains of migration has already proved significant and suggest that the study of intra-familial urban and rural relations may come to resemble the dispersed family characteristic of both Republican China before 1949 and Taiwan.[49]

It can be argued that the elaboration of these household networks into economic interest groups which divide the village have altered the power relations between peasant family and state and placed the larger aggregate family in a position increasingly to challenge the authority and controls of the local state political and economic structures. There is some evidence to suggest that their peasant members have themselves perceived the balance of power, both in production and reproduction, to have altered in their favour, increasing their individual and combined bargaining power vis-a-vis the state. In one village, for example, where residents had been reprimanded after they had bared the fields of top soil to make bricks for house construction, they remonstrated that 'now the land had been contracted out for their own use anyone else can mind their own business.'[50] Very early in the decade there were reports of peasants contesting the single child family policy by arguing that they 'now cultivated the land, ate their own grain and brought up their children on their own' or now that 'they had taken responsibility for the land so there was no need for the state to bother about their child birth'.[51] Such bargaining begins to explain the 'defiance' of peasant households against the single-child family policy and the differences in perceptions and practices of the policy between family and state.

In the complex interlacing of state intervention and withdrawal which has marked the reforms, the implementation of the single-child policy marked the most extreme form of intervention in the affairs of the family and community; at the same time the distribution of land and the establishment of the market marked the withdrawal of the state from the economy, leaving the political arena characterised by less predictability or security, competition and fragmentation. It seems that the result has been the dispersion of formal economic and political authority and the emergence of alternative and informal sources of power and status within plural and uncertain systems of authority and control. In the interval between the decline in direct agencies of control and the possible rise of indirect agencies there seems to have been something of a political vacuum within villages and townships, in which peasant households and aggregate families have acquired new bargaining powers. This paper argues that their bargaining power in relation to the state directly affected the implementation of the single-child family programme in the countryside, the phases of which directly reflect the balance of power between family and state. In the future it may be that it is the alterations in this balance of power which may be designated one of the most significant changes occurring in the People's Republic of China during this first decade of reform.

NOTES

1. The subjects of this paper were researched while the author was in receipt of a Leverhulme grant in the Department of Anthropology, School of Oriental and African Studies, University of London.

2. For a definition and explanation of the Social, see Donzelot, Jacques *The Policing of Families* (Hutchinson & Co, London 1979).

3. See Pi Chao-chen, *Population Growth and Policy*, Occasional Monograph Series, no. 9, Interdisciplinary Communication Programme (Smithsonian Institute, Washington 1976); Orleans, L. (ed) *Chinese Approaches to Family Planning*, (M.E. Sharpe, New York 1980).

4. For example see the Sichuan Regulations in Family Planning, B.B.C., *Summary of World Broadcasts: Far East* (hereafter swb) 16 March 1979.

5. *Xinhua*, [New China News Agency] 13 September 1980.

6. See Sichuan Regulations in Family Planning, swb 16 March 1979; Aswani Saith, 'Economic Incentives for the one-child family in rural China', *China Quarterly*, September 1981.

7. 'Problems in Family Planning'. *Renmin Ribao* [People's Daily] 11 April 1980.

8. See Gui Shixin; 'Population Control and Economic Policy', *Zhexue Shehui Kexue Ben* [Philosophy and Social Science], Shanghai Teaching College, 25 April 1980; Chen Muhua, 'Population Control', *Renmin Ribao*, 11 August 1979; 'Population Situation: Theory Studies from an Economic Angle', *Jingji Yanjiu* [Economic Research] 20 May 1979; 'Population Control and Economic Planning', *Renmin Ribao*, 2 June 1980; Li Shiyi, 'Development Trends in Chinese Population Growth', *Beijing Review*, 11 January 1982.

9. See Croll, E. 'The Single-child Family in Beijing: A First Hand Report', in Croll, Elisabeth, Davin, Delia and Kane, Penny, *China's One Child Family Policy* (Macmillan, London 1985).

10. Shanghai Planned Parenthood Regulations, *Jiefang Ribao*, [Liberation Daily] 10 August 1981 in swb August 1981; 'Central Committee and State Council Urge Better Family Planning', *New China News Analysis* 13 March 1982; 'Shanxi Planned Parenthood Regulations', *Shanxi Ribao*, [Shanxi Daily] 17 November 1982 in swb 16 December 1982.

11. See for example 'A Survey of Single-Child Families in Hefei, Anhui Province', by the Population Research Office, Anhui University, 1980, 'One-Child Family Becoming Norm in Beijing West District', *Renkou Yanjiu* [Population Research], 1 January 1981.

12. For full discussion of arguments in support of the policy, see Gui Shixin, *op. cit.*

13. For example, see 'Family Planning in Tianjin', *Tianjin Ribao* [Tianjin Daily] 22 July 1979; 'Family Planning in Shanghai', *Wenhui Bao*, Shanghai, 18 January 1980.

14. Beijing Centre for Communications and Family Planning, *Renkou Lilun Xuanzhang* [Essays in Population Theory], 40.

15. Elisabeth Croll, 'The Chinese Household and its Economy; Urban and Rural Survey Data', Queen Elizabeth House Contemporary China Centre Mimeographed Resource Paper 1982. See also 'A Survey of Single-child Families in Hefei' *op. cit.*

16. Xu Xuehan, 'Resolutely Implement the Policy on Rural Population', *Renmin Ribao*, 5 February 1982.

17. Ibid. Sichuan Provincial Radio Service, Chengdu, 2 January 1981, SWB 22 May 1981; Editorial *Renmin Ribao*, 29 September 1981.

18. For full discussion on this theme, see Elisabeth Croll, 'Production versus Reproduction'. A Threat to China's Development Strategy', *World Development*, vol. 11 no. 6, pp. 67, 481, 1983.

19. Xu Xuehan, *op. cit.*

20. Data from interviews in Beijing, June 1983.

21. *Hebei Ribao*, [Hebei Daily] 19 January 1983, Hunan provincial Service, SWB 10 September 1983.

22. See interviews, Beijing, 1985.

23. Ibid.

24. Guangdong Provincial Radio, 22 April 1983, 8 July 1983. 'Family Planning achievements in Shandong province', SWB 2 November 1983, *Liaoning Ribao*, [Liaoning Daily] 21 May 1983.

25. Reuter's report, *Guardian* 16 June 1983.

26. 'Analysis of Reproduction of the Rural Population, *Jingji Yanjiu* [Economic Research] 20 June 1982; Editor's Note, *Gongren Ribao* [Worker's Daily] 4 August 1982; Yangfan 'Save our Baby Girls', *Zhongguo Qingnian* [China Youth], 9 November 1982; 'Problems Caused by Boy-Girl Imbalance', *Renmin Ribao*, 7 April 1983.

27. *Xinhua News Agency Report*, Beijing, 17 April 1983.

28. National Conference on Population Planning, Xinhua, 11 Oct. 1986; 'Encouragement but no Compulsion for One-child Families', 8 June 1985, eg. Guangxi Province Regulations, SWB 19 April 1985.

29. Shaanxi Provincial Regulations, ibid 2 August 1986.

30. Interview, Sichuan Family Planning Association, November 1984.

31. Reuter's report, Beijing, 14 January 1988.

32. Ibid; Reuter's report 21 January 1988; 'Family Planning in Hunan Province', 19 May 1987; 'Shandong Family Planning Policy' *Renmin Ribao* 2 August 1988.

33. Central Document no. 7, April 1984; for themes see SWB 24 July 1984.

34. For an elaboration of this thesis, see Elisabeth Croll, *The Politics of Marriage in Contemporary China*, Cambridge, Cambridge University Press, 1981.

35. 'More Township Governments and Village Committees Established', *Beijing Review*, 12 March 1984. 'People's Communes No Longer Govern', ibid, 7 Jan. 1985; 'Reform of the Rural Grassroots Political Power Structure', *Renmin Ribao*, 14 November 1986.

36. 'Peasants' Economic Co-ordination Societies', *Renmin Ribao*, 11 July 1985; 'Beefing Up the Rural Co-operative System', *Beijing Review*, 23 June 1986.

37. For an elaboration of this argument see Elisabeth Croll, 'Reform, Local Political Institutions and the Village Economy in China', *Journal of*

Communist Studies, vol. 3, no. 4, December 1987.

38. For articles on the rural responsibility system, see 'Quota Fixing at Household Level', swb, 28 Dec. 1979; 'Discussion on the Systems of Responsibility for Output Quotas by Production Team in Rural People's Communes', *Jingji Yanjiu*, 20 Oct. 1980; 'Fixing Output Quotas for Individual Households', ibid., 20 Jan. 1981; 'Communist Party Central Committee Discusses Agriculture', ncna [New China News Agency], 19 May 1981; 'Prospects for Development of the Double-Contract System', *Renmin Ribao* 9 March 1982.

39. For discussion of domestic sidelines, see Elisabeth Croll, 'The Promotion of Domestic Sideline in Rural China, 1978' in Jack Gray and Gordon White (eds), *China's New Development Strategy* (London; Academic Press, 1982), pp. 235–54; 'Defence of Domestic Sideline Production', swb, 27 April 1978; 'The Encouragement of Domestic Sideline Production', *Jingji Yanjiu*, 20 Aug. 1979.

40. ncna, 14 June 1980; ibid., 30 Aug. 1980.

41. See Croll, Elisabeth, 'New Peasant Family Forms in Rural China'. *The Journal of Peasant Studies*, vol. 14, no. 4, July 1987.

42. C.K. Yang, *Communist Society: The Family and The Village* (Cambridge, MA; MIT Press, 1959); I.B. Taeuber, 'The Families of Chinese Farmers' in M. Freedman (ed.), *Family and Kinship in Chinese Society* (Stanford, CA; Stanford University Press, 1970), pp. 63–86; Croll, *The Politics of Marriage*.

    For discussion of household division prior to 1949, see M. Cohen, *House United, House Divided: The Chinese Family in Taiwan* (New York Columbia University Press, 1976), p. 59; Fei Hsiaotung, 'Peasantry and Gentry', *American Journal of Sociology*, vol. LII (1946), pp. 1–17; M. Freedman, 'The Chinese Domestic Family: Models', *Ve Congres International des Sciences anthropologiques et ethnologiques*, vol. 2, Part I (Paris, 1963), pp. 97–100; Croll, *The Politics of Marriage*.

43. *Communist Society: The Family and the Village* (Cambridge Massachussetts, MIT Press 1959), p. 9.

44. See Croll, *Politics of Marriage*.

45. 'Chinese Families Getting Smaller', swb, 6 April 1984; 'Nuclear Families Dominate Countryside', *Beijing Review*, 7 Jan. 1985.

46. Elisabeth Croll, 'Chiang Village; A Household Survey', *China Quarterly*, Dec. 1977, pp. 786–814; N. Gonzalez, 'Household and Family in Kaixiangong; A Re-Examination', *China Quarterly*, March 1983, pp. 76–89.

47. 'Shanxi Calls for Support for Specialised Households'. swb, 15 Feb 1984; *Renmin Ribao*, 23 Jan. 1984; 'CCP Document no. 1 in the Countryside'. swb, 16 May 1984.

48. 'Marriage Law and Socialist Morality', swb, 4 Feb. 1982; ibid., 14 Dec. 1984; 'Arranged Marriages' *Xinhua*, 8 March 1985. Interviews in China, 1984. Ibid.

49. Lin Yueh Hwa, *The Golden Wing* (London; Routledge, 1948); Cohen, op. cit.
50. John Gittings, 'From Blossoms to Bricks', *China Now*, Summer 1984 pp3–6.
51. 'Rural Population Policy', SWB, 18 Feb. 1982; 'Population and Education in Family Planning Work', *Renmin Ribao*, editorial 29 September 1981; SWB, 24 July 1984.

13 Privatisation and Politics in Rural China

Daniel Kelliher

At the end of the 1970s Deng Xiaoping put together a coalition of economists and officials who shared a painful realisation: state control over the rural economy had grown so pervasive and intrusive that it was stifling development. These reformers decided that the ministries, planning commissions, county officials, procurement agents, and local cadres of the far-flung state apparatus had made Chinese agriculture stagnate. Farmers left to their own devices, they believed, could do better. In fits and starts, the reform coalition began granting significant economic powers to private rural citizens. Perhaps unconsciously, the reformers gradually improvised a programme that relied on the classic prescriptions of privatisation. They cut the powers of unwieldy administrative organs (the communes). They put primary resources (the land) into private hands (family farms). They leased or sold off public enterprises (commune and brigade operations) to private investors. They turned management over to the immediate producers (peasant entrepreneurs and farmers), and expanded the market's scope for allocating goods, labour and income.

In adopting such policies, China's government began to follow a 'logic of privatisation'. This logic has two sides to it. First of all, in a state-dominated economy, when one aspect of economic life is turned over to private hands, gains in productivity and efficiency are often limited unless other aspects of economic life are also privatised. Thus when reformers in a country like China are bent on maximising production, privatisation begets more privatisation, creating more radical changes than the reformers initially envisioned. Secondly, as the state withdraws from direct administration of the economy, it comes to rely on key non-state groups to lead rural development in the direction it desires. The state becomes particularly attentive to groups promoting commercialisation and economic revival, and less sympathetic toward peasants pursuing a traditional farm life which reformers regard as a dead end.

318

The main body of this article looks back to the critical period of Chinese rural reform in the early 1980s and traces out this logic of privatisation in the state's response to controversial changes within the peasantry.

The concluding section of the article turns to the political implications of privatisation in rural China. These implications are tied to the state's changed style for pressing rural policy. Besides privatising the rural economy, Deng Xiaoping's reform coalition adopted a leadership style aimed at cooling the overheated political life of the countryside. Deng's ultra-leftist predecessors had made the grand stage of social experimentation. The left's programme had required an enormous political effort, usually in the form of campaigns playing up class conflicts in rural society. In contrast, the reform leaders have tried to find a new way to enforce state policies without aggravating political tensions. They have been groping toward a rural society that would be stable without ceaseless political campaigns – something roughly akin to the self-regulating farm economy they have tried to create. Accordingly, the reform coalition scrapped the left's grand social agenda and with it the supposed class solidarity with poor and lower-middle peasants. Instead of courting the poor, the reformers have targeted a new group for recruitment to official positions in the countryside: a more talented and successful group whose private economic interests coincide with the reform programme.

This desire to find a new village leadership that will operate without heavy state intervention reinforces the logic of privatisation. This is because the skills that the government and the Chinese Communist Party now seek in prospective rural office-holders are the same skills that lead to success in a privatised economy. In other words, the new target for political recruitment overlaps extensively with the peasant group having the most entrepreneurial talents. With the state encouraging the path-breakers in the rural economy to take the lead in local politics as well, rural China is developing a coherent local leadership enjoying both a concentration of power and backing from the state. In the emerging post-reform countryside, then, the state is cultivating a younger, well-educated rural elite to promote its modernising aims.

1 PRIVATISATION AND THE STATE'S RESPONSE TO A CHANGING PEASANTRY

The reforms brought the Chinese state face to face with a more complex and differentiated rural populace. Although peasants in Mao's China held different job assignments, nearly all had the same relationship to the means of production. Except for minor sidelines and small private plots, commune members collectively owned the means of production. In practice these ownership rights may have been meaningless, but peasants were all in the same boat; they were simply members of the collective.

The contrast after the reforms is striking. In today's more complex market economy, the variety of roles peasants may play is much more diverse. Although Western analysts have debated the effect of the reforms on income stratification,[1] the new, more refined cleavages between peasants amount to more than gaps in wealth. Peasants now have quite different relationships to the means of production. Some are the virtual owners of private farmland; others rent land, and a growing number have left the land altogether. Those who have left farming might lease erstwhile collective enterprises, buy shares in enterprises, or own enterprises outright. And some peasants, owning nothing productive whatever, must sell their labour to a luckier soul who does control some productive asset.

All these more differentiated roles in the economy also create new relationships between peasants: as competitors, as business partners, as landlord and tenant, as boss and employee. The question that this raises concerns the response of the state. Facing a more complex peasantry, the state has had to make repeated choices about which groups in the peasantry to support, which interests to encourage, and which trends to oppose. Considering the Communist Party's traditional opposition to rural capitalism, land markets, and exploitation of hired labourers, some of the choices the state has made in the 1980s have been simply startling. Why has the state backed the new entrepreneurs so adamantly and so publicly? Why has its response to family farmers been so mixed – granting them ever more control over production decisions but little insurance against the perils of a private land tenure system? And why has the state permitted the Communist Party's traditional *bête noire* – land rent – to develop along with a vulnerable group of hired labourers?

To answer to these questions, I would like to look at the state's actions on three controversial issues of the reform period: entrepreneurship, land tenure, and private hiring of labour. Using evidence gathered largely in Hubei at the height of the reforms in that province (i.e. 1983 and 1984), I will argue that the logic of privatisation has governed the state's response to these changes in rural life, and that this logic explains some of the most radical and surprising departures from the traditional rural policies of the Communist Party.

Support for Entrepreneurship

One of the most startling reverses brought by reform has been the state's unrestrained enthusiasm for rural entrepreneurs. These new entrepreneurs are people who have taken advantage of the commercial thrust of the reforms to set up specialised businesses instead of tilling the land for a living. Most of these entrepreneurs are 'specialised households' (*zhuanye hu*), who return their contracted farmland to the collective or rent it out to other families in order to pursue family-sized businesses. Entrepreneurship on a larger scale takes the form of 'economic associations' (*jingji lianhe*), which pool capital from several or many households, and pay out dividends and profits according to investment shares.[2] These businesses engage in every conceivable type of production and service. Some are built from the ground up. Others contract for the use of collective resources, such as a pond, a mill, an orchard, or a factory. If they grow large enough, the new businesses privately hire outside labour.

The new entrepreneurs have been controversial from the outset. Ironically, their greatest troubles grew out of their very success. After the government embraced the slogan, 'Let some peasants get rich first', the new entrepreneurs did just that. As a vice-secretary of the Hubei Party Committee pointed out, 'The majority of the peasant households who have gotten rich first are specialised households'.[3] The trouble was that the entrepreneurs' sudden wealth inspired resentment among neighbours and local officials alike.

Local cadres were the first to express their antagonism. Unsure what to make of the new businesses when they first appeared – and recognising a vague threat to their authority – cadres felt compelled to interfere.[4] When the businesses continued to proliferate, cadres began harassing them and 'extending a hand,' i.e. demanding a cut.[5] This sort of bullying diminished, however, when state support for entrepreneurship became unequivocal, leaving recalcitrant cadres unsure of their ground. After Central Document No. 1 for 1983 came down with its sweeping endorsement of commercial activities,[6] Hubei cadres froze up when faced with decisions about specialised households: 'They don't nod their head yes, they don't shake their heads no; and if anything goes wrong they make themselves scarce'.[7] Such irresolution among cadre opponents of reform gave way to defections into the ranks of the entrepreneurs once cadres realised how profitable commercialisation could be for them. A widely publicised Shanxi survey found that ex-commune cadres comprised a huge proportion (43 per cent) of specialised households.[8] Some Chinese discounted this survey (which Vice Premier Wan Li highlighted in a

1984 speech), saying it was only an attempt to mollify cadres hurt by the reforms, and to encourage them to 'get rich first' as well.[9] But in fact there are good reasons for believing that ex-cadres stood to gain from entrepreneurship, whatever their failings in managing the collective economy. After all, cadres knew best where to find local resources; they had the most personal contacts and management skills; they knew how to use telephones and they had the best access to market information. Their skills as brokers and middlemen, built up over years of experience under the commune system, made China's rural cadres natural aspirants to success under privatisation.

If cadre antagonism proved fleeting, entrepreneurs had to remain on guard against more intransigent resentment from ordinary peasants. 'Households doing conspicuously well,' said one Hubei report, ' . . . are afraid that once they are rich they will attract too much attention and invite trouble.'[10] Trouble sometimes came anonymously, through theft, sabotage, or poisoning of animals.[11] In other cases threats were more direct. A Shaanxi peasant specialising in duck raising became a '10,000–*yuan* household' (a fortune in rural China) in 1982, and was warned by his neighbours: 'You'd better stop before you go too far. Watch out or you might become an example.'[12] Successful entrepreneurs were also victim of extortion perpetrated by fellow villagers. Reports from Anhui said peasants commonly asked members of specialised households for 'loans' they had no intention of repaying – a form of extortion that 'makes the hearts of the specialised household throb with terror.'[13] Peasants have even been known to commit violence against members of the community prospering from private business. In one Jiangsu county, for example, the public security forces were called out 'to protect the haves from the have-nots.'[14]

What was puzzling to many about this conflict was that the state seemed to be taking the side of the best-off, the people least in need of help. Indeed, local officials were instructed to favour private businesses with tax holidays and preferential lines of credit, and to lease out collective assets on terms very profitable to investors.[15] The press gave the impression that the recipients of these favours were reaping magnificent profits. Entrepreneurs with some titles were rich by definition. In many counties across the country, for example, to be designated a specialised household, a family was required to make a gross income well above the county average.[16] Furthermore, entrepreneurs seemed to be favoured with advantages that other peasants could not match. Surveys from Zhejiang and Shanxi showed that specialised households had more educated family members, more ex-cadres and ex-servicemen with special skills, more trained craftsmen, and more labour power.[17] Considering the state's traditional claim of solidarity with the poor and lower-middle peasants, why was it trying so hard to help such a rich and privileged group?

The answer is that a rural development strategy of privatisation made the new entrepreneurs the logical group for the state to pin its hopes on. The goal of state policy was no longer to distribute wealth evenly (a goal that was never fulfilled under the left anyway), but to put resources together in more powerful and productive combinations. This goal gave central reformers little reason to object to the rise of a privileged group within the peasantry. They believed that resources, investment and encouragement should be concentrated where they would have the greatest effect. One central document expressed the idea with this admonition: 'Don't spread things all around the same way you sprinkle pepper!'[18] Instead, according to a Secretariat report, policy should benefit a minority, the 'groups of able people with the "entrepreneurial spirit" (who) will spring up all over the countryside.'[19] This report emphasised that

> not every peasant household has the technical level, the eye for management, or the ability to organise production that are necessary to branch out and develop commodity production. Therefore we must use all the existing resources to the maximum, so that those who have money use their money, those who have strength use their strength, and those with ability use their ability.[20]

The idea driving privatisation was that a group with 'money, strength and ability' – given free rein – could use these assets better than public officials tangled in procedures and hierarchies. And in fact the entrepreneurs acted just as their champions in the reform coalition might have hoped. The entrepreneurs broke across administrative barriers, combining factors of production that used to fall under separate jurisdictions. This ability to cross boundaries and bridge gaps between formerly discrete collectives was one of the main reasons for the success of the new businesses. Tapping resources that had never been joined together before, they advanced the production possibility curve in salients where the collectives had been too rigid to venture.

Besides fulfilling such clear goals of privatisation, the entrepreneurs even helped solve unanticipated difficulties that accompanied privatisation. For example, privatisation of land revealed latent problems of idle resources in farm areas. The higher income and more efficient work associated with family farms created large surpluses of labour and capital. State leaders worried that the accumulating capital might be dissipated in non-productive investment. A Secretariat research unit warned:

Without other outlets, rural surplus labour and capital are bound to be thrown into activities like the 'house-building fever' and short-term investments in which 'a profit is a profit, no matter how you get it.' Idle people, gambling, and superstition will increase day by day. Therefore, as long as the state's financial power is insufficient, we must take the countryside's own surplus labour, idle capital and rich natural resources and put them in motion to form enormous productive power.[21]

The new businesses proved ideal for this purpose. In Hubei, for example, at one commune in Yingcheng County 340 new businesses attracted investments totalling 214,000 yuan from some 1,900 households where the funds had been idle. In Yangxin County (also in Hubei), new entrepreneurial ventures absorbed 70 per cent of the surplus labour, employing nearly one out of four able-bodied peasants in the entire county.[22]

All in all, the entrepreneurs fulfilled so many of the reformers' aims that they were practically the unconscious, unofficial agents of state policy. As the reform coalition saw it, they put the countryside's resources to work, discovering unappreciated productive assets, buying up surplus labour, investing countless bits of idle capital and doing all of this more creatively and efficiently than the old cadres. Privatisation made the entrepreneurs the state's natural partners in the countryside.

If the logic of privatisation helps explain the state's affection for the rural *nouveaux riches*, it also makes sense of China's curious drift into a private system of land tenure.

Attending the Birth of Private Land Tenure and Rent

The vast majority of China's rural people are not peasant entrepreneurs, of course, but farmers whose primary living comes from tilling the land. Like their neighbours who opted for entrepreneurship, these land-tilling peasants saw their lives altered drastically by the changes after Mao's death. The reforms took them out of collective cultivation and set them up on independent family farms.

The basic structure shaping farm life since the reforms is a quasi-commercialised system of land tenure. The core of this new system is the contract, which gives a peasant household control over a parcel of collective land in return for meeting a quota of sales to the state. Within this basic structure (known in China as the 'responsibility system'), the extent of the farmers' claim on the land grew rapidly during the reform period. By the mid-1980s peasants possessed virtually permanent claims on their land, with the right to bequeath the family farm to their children.

As this new system evolved, it came to mimic the features of private land tenure, including the once-reviled practice of land rent. At first the rules governing land contracts strictly limited peasants' prerogatives over the land: 'Commune members only have the right to cultivate their contracted land; they have no ownership rights over it, they are not permitted to rent it out, buy it or sell it, transfer it, abandon it, or hire other people to cultivate it.'[23] Yet practically from the start peasants did all of these things with their contracted land. In other words, they treated it as private, commercial property: something that can be leased, rented, transferred for a fee, or worked by hired labour. Within a few years, central leaders – either explicitly or tacitly – condoned this quick evolution toward a more commercialised system of land tenure. How did the state come to approve of such a system?

This evolution toward a commercial land tenure system began with disturbing observations about the level of investment peasants put into their new family farms. The first land contracts of 1979 and 1980 were awarded for one-year terms, with the expectation that the land would then be reapportioned. However, as the first contract year drew to a close, officials feared that if peasants anticipated a re-shuffling of their plots, then they might neglect the fall planting (of green manure, winter wheat, etc.).[24] Therefore most places renewed each household's contract for the same land, this time for three year terms. Once peasants had three-year contracts in hand, officials began to notice a rash of house-building. 'Encroaching on the land to build houses has become a universal phenomenon,' said one report, ' . . .(as) peasants mistake their rights over contracted land for ownership rights, and build houses on their responsibility fields.'[25] From the peasants' point of view, building a private house on a contracted field was an aggressive act of possession, an assertion of individual control over the land. On the other hand, pouring earnings into a house also expressed peasants' fears that they might lose the land after all. They guessed that if policy changed and the collective repossessed their land, they would probably be allowed to keep their new houses, since dwellings had been private even under the commune system. Thus instead of investing in the land, peasants chose the more prudent course of investing in an asset they thought they could keep their hands on.

This wave of non-productive housing investment worried officials far more than the symbolic issue of encroachment on collective land. One of the principal motives for creating family farms in the first place was to give peasants a private stake in building up a piece of land (with fertilizers, improved irrigation, and so on). If they didn't put these investments into the land, then the whole strategy was ruined. Consequently, when the first three-year contracts were coming to a close in 1983, a debate broke out over giving peasants semi-permanent control over their land. The leaders reasoned that peasants will only invest in land when they know they will reap the rewards, that is, when they expect the land will still be theirs in ten or fifteen years. Otherwise peasants will not invest. That is why (according to this argument) places that eschewed three-year contracts and reapportioned the land annually from 1980 to 1983 suffered declines in output.[26] The press (probably correctly) claimed that most peasants backed longer contracts, and attributed speeches like this one to peasant spokesmen:

> If the contracts don't change for one year, we'll apply chemical fertilizer. If they don't change for two years, we'll plant green manure. If they're good for three years, we'll spread pig and cow manure. Under four-year contracts we'll haul pond sludge to the fields. If it's five years we'll repair the waterworks. And if the contracts don't change for ten years, then we could transform sand dunes into good fields.[27]

People concerned with fairness and equity argued against granting farmers such long-term possession of the land. Birth, death, marriage, or occupational change among family members would inevitably change people-to-land ratios. While these changes could work to ease the pressure on the land for some families, others would be plunged into hardship. Only by re-apportioning land between households from time to time could such inequities be limited.

Although the Chinese press faithfully printed the details of this debate,[28] the reports were tinged with an inexorable sense that higher productivity was tied to settling families permanently on plots of land. In the political climate of the reform period, any issue that pitted fairness against productivity had a foregone conclusion. So it was with this debate on land tenure. Central Document No. 1 for 1984 settled the question with the announcement that peasants would get land contracts of fifteen years or longer.[29] Some peasants hailed this as the 'Second Land Reform.'[30] Farmers with good land rejoiced; those assigned poor land worried; and in some places both sides fought out a complete re-division of the land.[31] Thus the 'responsibility system' of the early reform years evolved into a new system of land tenure based on semi-permanent family farms.

Once China's vast agricultural population was settled on individual farms, the reappearance of land rent was inevitable. With virtually permanent landholdings, peasants needed some mechanism for transferring land between households. Without such a mechanism, the new land tenure system would have been rigid and inefficient, incapable of responding to new commercial developments or population changes. In the mid-1980s state officials tacitly chose the simplest solution: to let individual peasants arrange transfers of land between themselves, lubricating the transaction with some form of payment. In this way a market in land rental sprang up. At first the amount of land involved was quite small. A very rough national survey conducted in April 1983 said only about 1 per cent of the cultivated land had been privately transferred between households at that time. But later surveys showed higher rates of land rental, with as much as 10 per cent of the land changing hands in some counties.[32]

Since land rent was one of the great forms of exploitation attacked in the revolution, many Chinese publications discussing the alienation of land today avoid the word 'rent' in preference for the more neutral term 'transfer' (*zhuanrang*; or sometimes *zhuanbao* 'transfer of contract'). In some cases the word 'transfer' is more accurate, especially when a household wants to pursue a specialised business and returns its contracted land to the collective for re-assignment to someone else. However, this preferred Chinese technology only disguises what is really happening when one household privately 'transfers' its land to another for payment. Some Chinese sources delicately omit any reference to such remuneration, even though there is an overwhelming likelihood that a payment is changing hands either openly or under the table. In fact, the 1983 national survey cited above found that 85 per cent of all land transfers involve payments of rent.[33] Not all Chinese sources are so squeamish about these matters, and speak openly about rent paid in money (*zujin*) or in grain (*zugu*).

Since China has only about one-tenth of a hectare of cultivated land for every member of the rural population, it is easy to understand why farmers would like to rent more land to till.[34] Not every family has the skill, education, capital, or wits to start up a non-farm business, so renting in land is often the only way for a land-tilling family to raise its income. But the motives for renting land out are more complicated, and they are connected to the rise of private entrepreneurship.

The Chinese press cites a variety of minor reasons for people renting land to their fellow villagers: some land is too dispersed or inconvenient to get to; and some families are too short of labour, too old, or too sick to cultivate it.[35] But by all accounts the most common reason why peasants rent out land is that they have some alternative calling – that is an independent enterprise from which they can make more money. Despite recent reports of peasants actually selling land to run a business, peasants generally consider it prudent to maintain rights over contracted land by renting it out rather than selling it. Entrepreneurs prefer this arrangement, for they regard land as insurance against both policy change and business failure.[36] The rental market serves the specialised households particularly well. They can rent out their contracted fields – unloading the headache of the procurement duty on the land and getting a rent payment to boot – and then devote their full time to some pursuit that is more lucrative than farming was in the first place.[37]

This added benefit for specialised households gave the reform leadership yet another reason for acquiescing in the revival of land rent, though it put the reformers in a quandary. To defend their programme against ideological attack, the reformers had always claimed that the basic collectivist structure of rural life had not changed. Thus they insisted that peasants had no ownership rights over their farms: only the collective could own land. But this fiction was hard to maintain if specialised households could turn their contracted fields over to other families and pocket the rent as if *they* owned the land. Yet the reformers condoned this practice of collecting rent for transferred fields. They were committed to private entrepreneurship and wanted to give specialised households every encouragement to plunge full-time into new businesses.

Critics suggested that there was only one way for the reformers to be consistent: when a family took in land relinquished by a specialised household, policy might require a rent payment to the collective (i.e., the legal owner), but surely not to the specialised household. The reform leadership rejected this line of reasoning, and for all practical purposes abandoned the pretense that land is not privately held. Publicly it was claimed that specialised households who rent out their land

> are the vigorous, energetic masters of today's rural cooperative economy. . . . Even if the people who use the (rented) land were to pay the collective, the collective should still turn the payment over to the household that originally contracted for the land. This is only reasonable: for in reality, payment for the transfer of contracted land has the positive effect of encouraging the growth of specialised, socialised production.[38]

This stance on rent was consistent with the leadership's view of specialised households as the progenitors of a modern rural economy. In the leaders' eyes, rent was a legitimate reward to people advancing state policy. And as a practical matter, rent paid to specialised households had the added benefit of concentrating investment funds among the people most aggressively developing the economy.

Opponents objected that renting out land breaks traditional communist structures against profiting from the plight of land-short families.[39] They also worried that land rent might be the first step toward a full-blown land market. Critics feared that peasants' energies might be squandered in efforts to amass land wealth:

> In the process of transferring contracted land, some peasants accept a contract fee. Sometimes this fee is reasonable and sometimes it is similar to rent, or is simply disguised rent, exploitative in nature. If things continue in this way, then land in the peasants' hands will inevitably turn into a means of production with a price on it, and everybody will be out to get land.[40]

At the time that this quoted passage was written (1983), the idea of a land market seemed outlandish. And at the outset of the reforms, in the late 1970s, it was simply unthinkable. Yet in a few short years land became what a private tenure system makes it, i.e., a commodity: a transferable asset, something that can be rented or even sold. It is very doubtful that the reform leaders initially envisaged anything approaching private land tenure. But there is a certain imperative in privatisation. Peasants were given land in hopes that they would work harder and nurture it with investments of savings and labour. To promote productive investment (as opposed to housebuilding) the leaders lengthened the contract period from one year to three years and on to fifteen years and more, ever deepening the peasants' private stake in their land. Peasants naturally came to think of the land as their own, and transfers between families became private transactions. Though the reform leaders may never have intended to create such a system of land tenure, the logic of privatisation carried them ahead. Along the way, obtaining the fruits of one step of privatisation meant acquiescing in the next step.

Hired Labour and the Precariousness of Family Farms

Just as the move toward private land tenure proceeded step by step, China's passage to private hiring of labour grew naturally out of other features of privatisation. With hired labour, the logic of privatisation was straightforward. Once farms and other rural businesses began to operate privately and independently, a private labour market became a necessity. To maintain their flexibility, independence, and productivity, private enterprises need a ready pool of labour. The rapid growth that many of China's rural entrepreneurs achieved in the early 1980s came partly because they were willing to break the longstanding strictures against privately hiring labour. Once it became clear that further growth spurred by entrepreneurship would require an unfettered labour market, the government struck down the restrictions. The need for such a move was simple and clear. What is less obvious is that the expansion of hired labour is tightly connected to the inviability of China's new family farms.

The main source of rural hired labour is farm households. Households that cannot make ends meet on their contracted land are forced to hire out some or all of the family members as labourers to get by. For some, particularly grain farmers, sowing the fields may not be profitable enough for a living. Others simply have too little land. Either the village didn't have enough land to go around in the first place, or the family has outgrown its original share. Other peasants are stuck with deficient land, which is poorly irrigated, infertile, or subject to waterlogging.

Peasants who must turn to wage labour seek it from old collective enterprises still in operation, or else from the independent entrepreneurs, i.e., the specialised households and larger private enterprises. Hiring by land-tilling peasants is less common. Individual landholdings are too small and profit margins too slim for farmers to hire much labour. When they do, it is for seasonal or short-term work, such as irrigation improvements or 'double rush' (*shuang qiang*), when one rice crop must be harvested and another transplanted within a few days. As a general rule, crop-growing families are afraid to hire labour because the weather makes it too risky, for in a bad year the fixed cost of a hired labourer can put a farm into the red.

Hired labourer's prospects depend mainly on what local resources are available to support businesses. Certain coastal provinces with plentiful resources and access to rich markets have developed extraordinarily successful industrial enterprises. In Jiangsu, Zhejiang, Fujian, and Guangdong, these enterprises offer wages that give rural workers much more prosperity than they enjoyed as farmers. But in areas without such resources, hired labourers face harder times. Because crop cultivation employs few labourers, peasants forced onto the labour market from heavily agricultural districts often have to migrate to find work. Itinerant labourers are usually young males (twenty or younger), though middle-aged people too must sometimes take to the road. The places where they are liable to end up are areas with good transport and a variety of resources that can support different enterprises.

One such destination is Yangxin County, on the southern bank of the Yangtze River in Hubei, which has relatively light population in an area rich in resources for aquatic production, various industries, and small coal operations. These enterprises are predominantly private and hire labour from counties north of the river. The counties supplying the labourers (Xishui, Huangqu, Qichun, and Guangji) are almost exclusively agricultural, but suffer from a desperate shortage of cultivated land – less than 0.01 hectare per person, leaving many peasants little choice but to leave home for a temporary job in Yangxin County.[41] Laborers in this situation are usually unskilled, with low educational levels, and mainly do simple manual labour.[42] Working outside their own villages, they lack the connections and the clout (i.e., the connections, *guanxi*) necessary to improve their lot. With the exception of a few skilled master workers (*shifu*), they work for subsistence wages.[43] At that rate the specialised households and private companies who do the hiring can make very large profits.[44]

The income gap between labourers and employers inspires endless debate in Chinese intellectual circles over whether hiring labour amounts to exploitation.[45] But regardless of what intellectuals may think, the reform leaders must regard hired labour as a permanent institution. For one thing, the cohesion and efficiency of the more privatised economy they have created demands it. And more important, the reformers' benign attitude toward hired labour masks a latent hostility against the centrepiece creation of the reforms: the family farm.

The private labour supply is both a consequence of the family farm's efficiency and a token of its failure to meet China's development needs. On the positive side, individual farms generate surplus labour because they use labour too efficiently to absorb all the family's work. On the other hand, this apparent efficiency is also an artifact of small farm size. Many of China's family farms are miniscule – too small to support the whole family – too small, in other words, to be viable. And if the market forces people to abandon the farm for the vagaries of wage labour, that prospect is not so alien to the reformers' hopes for China. In the first place, the reformers are unequivocally eager to get the vast rural populace out of farming and into diversified lines of production. Hired labour is a necessary part of that hope. In the second place, even though the reform leaders put peasants back onto private landholdings, they have no love for traditional family farms. Agriculture in China still has the earmarks of peasant farming, in which the family has only a small amount of land for the main crop and pursues half a dozen sidelines to make ends meet. In contrast to modern farming, this kind of production is unspecialised, providing a high degree of self-sufficiency for the farming family. The farm is 'small but complete', as the Chinese put it.[46] And as far as the reform leaders are concerned, this small but complete farm is a disaster. It is pitiful in size, utterly unsuited for large-scale modern farming.

The reformers are blunt about the fate of traditional peasant agriculture: 'This small peasant economy is an economy without a future'.[47] Peasant farms may be private, but the reform coalition does not value privatisation for its own sake; rather, privatisation is a strategy for development that they have stumbled into perhaps half-knowingly. Modern private farms look nothing like the so-called 'natural' peasant household, producing its own needs and engaging only minimally in the broader economy. What the reformers desire is not self-sufficient cells of stagnation, but economic units engaged in rich and complex transactions with the whole economy.

To create that more complex interaction, the reformers have moved to replace the family farm in two ways. One way, still in the stage of early planning, is (ironically) to re-collectivise agriculture. No one contemplates a return to the communes, but the reformers do envisage some sort of cooperatives: units large enough for mechanised farming, and efficient enough to operate as businesses. In one such model, Doudian village (Fangshan County, Beijing), which was promoted at the Thirteenth Party Congress in 1987, villagers collectively work with modern machinery on land consolidated into farms of roughly twenty-five hectares.[48] The other way the reformers hope to phase out the peasant farm is by further encouraging specialised households. With specialised households the reformers get peasants out of farming and into pursuits that enrich the network of internal connections in the economy. It is their very lack of self-sufficiency that makes specialised households a more attractive form of privatisation than peasant farms. Unlike peasant farmers, specialised households must be engaged in the wider economy: they rely on the market both to sell their output and to buy their consumption goods. The leaders consider them a model that is not only attainable given China's poverty, but the perfect vehicle for 'speeding up the disintegration of the rural natural economy'.[49]

That disintegration is what the reform leaders seek. The life of small farmers desperately short of land is bound to be precarious. If the insecurity of smallholding and the growth of private enterprise combine to produce a private labour market, then the reform coalition is not going to stand in the way. Free hiring of rural workers releases officials from the intricate and monumental problems of labour allocation, just as private enterprise and private land tenure permit the economy to function with less state intervention. Life may be hard for the hired hands, but in a more privatised economy people must fend for themselves.

2 POLITICAL IMPLICATIONS OF PRIVATISATION

China's shift toward privatisation leaves much of the former relationship between state and countryside intact. In spite of the impression given in the Western popular press, the government has not abandoned its powers to a burgeoning rural capitalism. Township (*xiang*) governments have taken over the communes' authority in civil government, public security, judicature, and taxation. Villagers' committees (*cunmin weiyuanhui*) enforce state policies on family planning, health, and education. Local cadres continue to act as brokers, just as they did before the reforms, often placing personal gain before the interests of the village.[50] And although the collectives are much weaker than before, some Western scholars have argued that this only makes villages more vulnerable to a raw form of state power unmediated by the collective bureaucracy.[51]

Yet a change has occurred in the way the state exercises its power in the countryside. With privatisation, China's government pinned its hopes on a radically different set of policies, which are now only barely in place. In the process, the state turned over authority for a great array of decisions to individuals and enterprises. As a result, many of the habitual channels of state coercion over peasants are not available. The state does possess some new tools for influencing peasants' decisions (in the form of more refined price, tax, and monetary policies), but for the most part the reformers seem to be relying on peasant innovators to lead their neighbours by example of material success.

This approach is in keeping with the spirit of privatisation, especially its basic assumption that heavy state intervention in rural life is counterproductive. Instead of mobilising peasants for divisive political struggles, the reformers' new style encourages independent acts that might develop the rural economy. As Deng Xiaoping put it, 'We should let every family and every household think up its own methods for doing things, and let them find more ways to raise production and increase income'.[52] Although such forbearance does not come naturally to Chinese state officials, Deng's followers have been surprisingly faithful to the idea of government restraint.

But this more restrained style of leadership raises a critical question about the enforcement of state policy. The state cannot enjoy confidence that peasants will 'naturally' follow the policies in the reform package. After all, the reformers have openly declared their distrust of the 'natural peasant economy' and its tendencies. So who can the state rely on in the villages to further its policies? Among the village populace the state needs a constituency committed to consolidating the reforms. And among local

officials it needs people with the expertise to recognise promising productive innovations and the zeal to protect fledgling successes – often against
the egalitarian norms of village society. The Hubei Peasant Association put
the question this way:

> Under the new historical conditions, who in the villages should the
> Party ultimately rely on to rally the broad mass of peasants to carry
> out socialist modernised construction?[53]

This search for a constituency and a target for recruitment within the
peasantry is a perennial theme in Chinese Communist Party history.
The Party's traditional solution has been an alliance with the 'poor
and lower-middle peasants'. At times this proclaimed alliance had real
meaning (during the Land Reform, for example), but by the 1960s and
1970s it was a sham long out of touch with social reality. The Party
finally abandoned this pretense of solidarity with the village poor during
the massive, three-and-a-half-year Party rectification that began in 1983.
While the so-called 'third echelon' of younger leaders with better education
and technical know-how was being promoted at the higher ranks, the Party
sought peasants with analogous qualifications in the villages.

Reliable data on Party recruitment in the villages is hard for outsiders
to obtain. But some inferences can be drawn from the Party's stated
intentions, for the Party has been quite vocal and public about what kind
of people it claims to be looking for. In 1982, Deng Liqun (then Party
propaganda chief) identified the rural constituency and recruitment target
that the Party would be concentrating on:

> With the great changes that have occurred in the countryside, it is no
> longer appropriate to continue the class line of 'relying on the poor
> and lower-middle peasants'. What should our work line be, then?
> Some comrades have suggested that we rally and organise the advanced
> element [*xianjin fenzi*] in the villages and rely on them . . . I think that
> until we have a better method we should try this.[54]

Lower-level spokesmen following Deng Liqun's lead were more specific
about who was to be included in this so-called 'advanced element'. The
Hebei Provincial Party Committee targeted peasants who launch more
enterprises, contract for bigger sales to the state, produce more, and
adapt more modern technology for rural use.[55] And Hubei Province
sought out

the village's skilled people, the skilled craftsmen, the middle school graduates, the young people returning to the village after getting an education, the demobilised soldiers, and so on, [who] all have some scientific, technical, or intellectual knowledge.[56]

The close identification between this target for recruitment and the people who have prospered under the reforms is hard to miss. The new entrepreneurs, the specialised households, and the more successful farmers have all the skills and characteristics that the Party says it is seeking. Both groups have better education, technical backgrounds, higher incomes, and experience with more creative forms of management. Targeting this group offers many advantages to the reform leaders. First of all, the entrepreneurs and bigger farmers are perfect models: other peasants can be expected to envy their wealth and emulate their success. The state can also assume that these richer households are politically dependable. They have an overwhelming personal stake in consolidating the reforms. Indeed, as this article has shown, the entrepreneurs in particular have acted as the unconscious champions of reform policy throughout the process of privatisation. Finally, these technically skilled, better educated people represent an alternative to the older cohort of rural cadres. In the old commune system, at the all-important brigade level (where rural industry is concentrated), only half the party members in Hubei had even finished primary school. The provincial Party journal allowed that these old-style peasant Party members may have been indispensable in the revolution, 'but under the new situation, because of their low educational level, they are not fully suited to the needs of building the Four Modernisations'.[57] Privatisation, on the other hand, has brought to the fore a group with the education, skills, management ability, and technical expertise that *do* suit them for that task.

But if privatisation nurtured a new type of person for the Party to cultivate, it also left the traditional pool of recruits feeling abandoned. As this article has shown, in the course of privatisation the leadership became disenchanted with the small peasant farm, as well as the typically illiterate recruit that such farms have traditionally produced for the Party. Some farmers feel keenly that the Party is no longer interested in them. Peasants of ordinary means have complained that the Party regularly 'contacts the rich but not the poor, the families strong in labour power but not those weak in labour power, and those who are doing well but not those who are having trouble'.[58] Grain farmers – who have gained less from reform than any other peasant group[59] – have felt particularly left out, observing that officials devote their most assiduous attention to successful entrepreneurs:

The great majority of cadres want to maintain close links with the keypoint households and specialised households who run industrial and sideline enterprises or grow economic crops. But they aren't willing to be in contact with grain-growing households. The reason is that the economic benefits of grain production are low – you can't draw attention to yourself or get rich growing grain. There is no prestige in it.[60]

Some farmers also resent the official honours bestowed upon rich and specialised households:

We used to think the idea was to take work in the fields as the fundamental thing. But as soon as we saw the attitude of the people at the top, our hearts sank. . . . When they hold model worker meetings they invite the 10,000–yuan households over and over again. It's only the people who grow grain who are always left out in the cold.[61]

Leaving aside such hurt feelings, what difference does it make if the reform coalition sees a more promising constituency among entrepreneurs and richer farmers? The answer depends on what kind of relationship finally crystallises between the rural economic elite and local administration (both Party and government).[62] One possibility is that it doesn't really matter what element of the peasantry the state recruits from. After all, despite decades of wild policy swings, certain state interests have remained immutable: squeezing agriculture to feed industry and supply exports, rigging prices against the countryside, limiting rural-urban migration, and maintaining political control over the vast rural populace. These interests may be so entrenched as to subvert or overpower the particular desires of the people who happen to occupy positions in the local state apparatus. The post-Land Reform alliance with the peasantry is instructive here. Throughout the 1960s and 1970s the state trumpeted its close partnership with the poor and lower-middle peasants, and even recruited most of its local officials from families with that class label. But the poor were hardly empowered. Real power in the countryside stayed in state hands, and it would be difficult to argue that it was exercised primarily to the benefit of the village poor. State interests always came first. Similarly, even if the state today does come to recruit more from the entrepreneurs and other winners in rural reform, that may do little for the targeted group as a whole. Regardless of who holds office, state power is exercised for the state.

A second possibility is that the logic of privatisation may carry the reform coalition to the point where its interests coincide with those of the rural economic elite. As long as state leaders place economic growth before all other values – and as long entrepreneurship and private farms can deliver higher production – then this coincidence of interests grows. One can imagine an educated, successful peasant group occupying local office and consolidating the reform policies with one hand, while pursuing its own economic interests with the other – all under the protection of the state. Opposition to such combined power of state and rural elite would be likely to be weak. Early on a research group working for the Secretariat predicted that even if a minority of peasants did enrich themselves through private investments and use of hired labour, then 'it won't cause any social unrest'.[63] And in fact the countryside has been politically quiescent. The great majority of peasants – the farmers – may not enjoy the same advantages as successful entrepreneurs, but they are far better off than before the reforms. Meanwhile, the people whose interests lie farthest from those of the new elite are the weakest of all: labourers scattered in unfamiliar villages; families with miniature farms and too many mouths to feed; and people without the physical strength to farm. This group is bereft even of an ideology, for the twenty years of blunders starting with the Great Leap Forward corrupted the ideal of egalitarianism that might have rallied the losers and the dispossessed.

One might speculate that if this second possibility were to come to pass – i.e., a growing coincidence of interests between state and rural elite – then it could provide a stable basis for local politics. Considering the government's bitter hostility toward private enterprise barely a decade ago, such an outcome might seem startling. But given the logic of privatisation that has been at work in China, it is not so unthinkable. Indeed, when the same logic operates in other third world countries, the results are commonplace. After all, it is hardly out of the ordinary to see a modernising state in the third world promoting an entrepreneurial elite to develop agriculture and keep the countryside politically quiet. And though some China experts detest the notion that 'their' country bears much resemblance to other third world nations, the potential for growing similarities in China's post-reform rural polity is striking.

NOTES

1. For example, Martin King Whyte, 'Social Trends in China: The Triumph of Inequality?' in A. Doak Barnett and Ralph N. Clough (eds) *Modernizing China: Post-Mao Reform and Development* (Baltimore,

Westview Press, 1986), pp. 103–23.

2. For more information on economic associations, see Wang Guichen, 'Several points to be understood about new economic associations', *Nongye jingji wenti*, [Problems in Agricultural Economy] 1982: 4, pp. 17–19; and Huang Yuehui, 'How should we look at the peasants' new economic associations?' *Xinhua wenzhai* [New China Digest] 1982: 1, pp. 69–70.

3. From a speech reported in *Hubei Ribao* [Hubei Daily], 16 January 1984, p. 1, by Provincial Vice Secretary, Shen Yinluo.

4. This was largely because cadres could not tell what was allowed in the policy confusion of the early reform period. For an example, see Hubei Provincial Agricultural Committee, 'Greatly strengthen and improve rural ideological and political work', *Shehui kexue dongtai* [Social Science Trends] (hereafter SKD) Hubei, 1983: 2 (10 January 1983), p. 20.

5. Yan Nong, 'The development of the 'two households and one alliance' in rural Hebei', SKD 1983: 16 (1 June 1983), p. 13; Xu Chongzheng and Chen Daokui, 'Investigation into the growth of specialized households in Chuxian district', *Lilun zhanxian* [Theoretical Front], 1983: 181 (15 May 1983), p. 8.

6. Specifically, the document gave entrepreneurs approval for private hiring of labour, private purchase of large-scale producer goods (e.g., processing equipment, tractors, trucks), and for pooling of capital in private investment. The document was entitled 'Several problems in current rural economic policy (Central Document no. 1 for 1983)', and extensive excerpts from it were published in *Renmin Ribao* [People's Daily] (hereafter RMRB), 10 April 1983, pp. 1–2. In particular, see Sections 4 and 6.

7. Yan Nong, p. 11.

8. The survey was from Ying County, Shanxi. See 'Get-rich-quick given approval', *South China Morning Post*, 30 January 1984, p. 6; and RMRB, 18 January 1984.

9. I repeatedly encountered this attitude in informal talks with economists, officials, and academics around Wuhan, Hubei, where I was living at the time. On Wan Li's speech, see 'Get-rich-quick given approval', p. 6; and RMRB, 18 January 1984.

10. Yan Nong, p. 11.

11. Ibid., p. 13.

12. Yu Guoyao, 'Trends and problems in the development of rural specialized households', *Jingji yanjiu cankao ziliao*, [Economic Research Reference Materials] (hereafter JYCZ) 1983: 176 (15 November 1983), p. 22.

13. Xu Chongzheng and Chen Daokui, p. 8.

14. The county in question is Suqian; 'Get-rich-quick', p. 6.

15. On tax policy, see Yan Nong, p. 13. On credit for entrepreneurs, see Yangxin County Agricultural Bank, 'Bring the functions of banks fully

into play and actively support the "two households and one alliance"', SKD, 1983: 16, (1 June 1983), pp. 14–18. For examples of leasing of collective enterprises, see Lu Wen, 'Inquiry into the question of private hiring of labour in the countryside', *Nongye jingji congkan* [Collection on Agricultural Economy] (hereafter NJC), 1983: 3, p. 25.

16. Fu Yuxiang, 'On the question of standards for the "two households"', NJC 1984: 1, p. 61. See also Chen Zhiqiang, 'It would be best to abolish the term "keypoint household"', NJC, 1984: 1, p. 45.

17. On the Zhejiang survey, see 'Raising a few new questions about current rural economic development', *Zhejiang Ribao* [Zhejiang Daily], July 21, 1983, p. 3. On the Shanxi survey see 'Get-rich-quick given approval', *South China Morning Post*, 30 January 1984, p. 6.

18. 'Resolution of the Central Committee of the Chinese Communist Party on certain problems in the acceleration of agricultural development (draft)', reprinted by *Chung-kung yen-chiu* [Research on Chinese Communism], 13: 5 (May 1979, #149), p. 160.

19. Research Group on Problems of Chinese Rural Development, *Yi nongcun wei tupo kou shixing fenqu liti kaifa de gaige zhanlue* [Use agriculture as the breakthrough point and open up a differentiated, multi-dimensional reform strategy], dated August 1982, p. 5.

20. Ibid., p. 5. This discussion paper had a heavy influence on Central Document no. 1 for 1983.

21. Ibid., p. 4.

22. Both examples are from Yan Nong, p. 9. For examples of private enterprises employing idle capital and labour in Anhui, see Xu Chongzheng and Chen Daokui, pp. 1–10.

23. 'Conscientiously solve new problems that arise after contracting work to households', *Nongcun gongzuo tongxun* [Rural Work Bulletin] (hereafter NGT), 1981: 11, p. 2.

24. Investigative Group of the Hubei Provincial Agricultural Committee, 'How to practice a responsibility system with output linked to reward in wet rice cultivation', NGT, 1981: 1, p. 11.

25. *Hubei Ribao* [Hubei Daily], 25 October 1981, p. 1.

26. This argument, with examples of such a decline in a Henan commune, appears in Lan Baoqing, 'The problem of stabilizing land in production contracting', NJC, 1983: 4, p. 55.

27. 'When the time limit on land contracts is too short, it is bad for production', NJC, 1983: 6, p. 53

28. A succinct summary of this debate over the length of land contracts is presented in 'When the time limit . . .' pp. 53–6.

29. *Hubei Ribao* [Hubei Daily], 3 March 1983, p. 1.

30. 'When the time limit . . .' p. 55.

31. *Hubei Ribao*, 3 March 1984, p. 1.

32. 'Compilation of materials on agricultural economics (eight): statistics on the circumstances of land transfers in several districts', NJC 1984: 1, pp. 63–5. This compilation presents very rough data from some

fifty-five local surveys on rent and land transfers. It also includes the April 1983 national survey, which covered forty counties in twenty-one provinces.

33. Ibid., p. 63.
34. 'Reference materials on national conditions of China', SKD 1981: 24 (20 August 1981), p. 29.
35. 'Compilation of materials . . . ' p. 63; also Zhong Luoran, pp. 38–9.
36. Adi Ignatius, 'Bitter Harvest', *Wall Street Journal*, 19 January 1988, p. 16.
37. In some cases this means that land changes hands faster where there are more opportunities for setting up specialties besides cultivation. For example, in the Lishui District of Zhejiang, where duck-raising is a big independent enterprise, more than 10 per cent of the land had already been transferred between households by 1983. See Zhou Qiren *et al.*, 'An investigation and preliminary analysis, of the transfer of contracted land', NJC, 1983: 5, p. 26. However, because other factors affect tenancy rates – factors such as the people-to-land ratio, the size of the procurement burden, etc – there is no dependable correlation between the tenancy rate and the number of alternative opportunities for commercial ventures in a given district.
38. Zhou Qiren *et al.*, p. 30.
39. Zhu Nailiang *et al.*, 'Transfer of contracted land in Jiaxing Prefecture, Zhejiang', NJC, 1983:5, p. 32.
40. 'Appropriate adjustments in contracted fields are necessary for perfecting the production responsibility system', *Jihua jingji yanjiu*, (Planned Economy Research) 1983: 33 (30 November 1983), p. 39.
41. Chen Wenke *et al.*, 'A survey of rural operations that privately hire labour in five districts and seven counties of contemporary Hubei', SKD 1983: 28 (1 October 1983), pp. 3–4.
42. Ibid., p. 4.
43. In the early 1980s such wages were 1 to 2 yuan per day. Lu Wen, p. 25. Cf. Chen Wenke, *et al.*
44. For examples, see Lu Wen, p. 25 and Chen Wenke *et al.*
45. A summary of this debate appears in Xu Yongging, 'Several different points of view on the current question of hiring labour in the country-side', NJC, 1983:1, pp. 19–23, 14.
46. Gui Jianping, 'A simple analysis of the problem of the division of labour in our nation's agriculture', JYCD, 1983:175 (14 November 1983), p. 37.
47. Yu Guoyao, 'Family management and the family economy in our nation's agriculture', JYCZ, 1983:100 (30 June 1983), p. 11.
48. Ignatius, p. 16.
49. Xu Chongzheng and Chen Daokui, p. 4.
50. See Jean C. Oi, 'Commercializing China's Rural Cadres', *Problems of Communism*, 35:5 (September-October 1986), pp. 1–14.
51. See Vivienne Shue, *The Reach of the State* (Stanford: Stanford University Press, 1988).

52. Deng, quoted in EMRB, 20 May 1981, p. 4.

53. Investigative Group of the Hubei Provincial Peasant Association and the Hubei Provincial Academy of Social Sciences, 'An appraisal of the peasant ranks in the present stage', NJC, 1983:2, p. 36.

54. In all likelihood Deng Liqun himself, never a strong reformist, had misgivings about offering Party support to this part of the peasantry, and his reluctance shows in his speech. The quotation is from the speech he gave, on 1 November 1982, at the National Conference on Rural Ideological and Political Work. Deng Liqun, 'Some opinions on strengthening and improving rural ideological and political work', JYCZ, 1983:1 (1 January 1983), p. 16.

55. Research Office of the Hebei Provincial Party Committee, 'Investigation of the state of the peasant ranks', NJC, 1983:2, p. 40.

56. Fan Zuogang, 'The rise and basic characteristics of the contemporary advanced stratum of the peasantry', SKD, 1983:2 (10 January 1983), p. 15.

57. Tu Zhaojing, 'The Party Committee of Henggou Commune in Xianning County pays attention to recruiting educated peasants into the Party', *Dangyuan shenghuo* [Party Members' Life] (Hubei, 1981) 2, p. 30.

58. Tingsiqiao Commune Party Committee, Xianning County, 'Study the new situation, solve new problems', *Dangyuan shenghuo* [Party Members' Life] [Hubei], 1983:7, p. 22.

59. For an analysis of why grain farmers fared so poorly compared to growers of economic crops, see State Price Bureau, Agricultural Product Price Section, 'Preliminary analysis of nationwide costs and profits for major agricultural products in 1981', *Jingji yanjiu ziliao* [Economic Research Materials], 1983:3, pp. 22–31.

60. Xu Jinbiao *et al.*, 'Why aren't the peasants willing to till the land?', NJC, 1984:1, p. 58.

61. Zhou Yegao, 'Pay attention to solving the problems that specialized grain households and keypoint grain households run into in the course of development', NJC, 1983:5, p. 61.

62. For future scenarios different from the possibilities I present here, see Gordon White, 'The Impact of Economic Reforms in the Chinese Countryside: Towards the Politics of Social Capitalism?' *Modern China*, 13:4 (October 1987), especially pp. 435–7.

63. This estimate of the effect of the new policies was made in August 1982, when the formulation of Central Document no. 1 for 1983 was still under discussion. It appears in a discussion paper put together for the use of the Secretariat Research Group on Problems of Chinese Development, p. 5.

Index